student

peter 355

Java™ Distributed Computing

lp -diats_ebw 3 द5fg

lp_i -diats_ebw3 द5fg

THE JAVA™ SERIES

Exploring Java™

Java™ Threads

Java™ Network Programming

Java™ Virtual Machine

Java™ AWT Reference

Java™ Language Reference

Java™ Fundamental Classes Reference

Database Programming with JDBC™ and Java™

Java™ Distributed Computing

Developing Java Beans™

Also from O'Reilly

Java™ in a Nutshell

Java™ in a Nutshell, Deluxe Edition

Java™ Examples in a Nutshell

Netscape IFC in a Nutshell

Java™ Distributed Computing

Jim Farley

O'REILLY™

Cambridge • Köln • Paris • Sebastopol • Tokyo

Java™ Distributed Computing
by Jim Farley

Copyright © 1998 O'Reilly & Associates, Inc. All rights reserved.
Printed in the United States of America.

Cover photo Copyright © 1997 O'Reilly & Associates, Inc. All rights reserved.

Published by O'Reilly & Associates, Inc., 101 Morris Street, Sebastopol, CA 95472.

Editor: Mike Loukides

Production Editor: Madeleine Newell

Printing History:

        January 1998:   First Edition

This book is printed on acid-free paper with 85% recycled content, 15% post-consumer waste. O'Reilly & Associates is committed to using paper with the highest recycled content available consistent with high quality.

ISBN: 1-56592-206-9

Table of Contents

Preface

In a sense, distributed computing has been with us since the beginning of computer technology. A conventional computer can be thought of as "internally distributed," in the sense that separate, distinct devices within the computer are responsible for certain well-defined tasks (arithmetic/logic operations, operator stack storage, short/long-term data storage). These "distributed" devices are interconnected by communication pathways that carry information (register values, data) and messages (assembler instructions, microcode instructions). The sources and destinations of these various pathways are literally hardwired, and the "protocols" that they use to carry information and messages are rigidly defined and highly specific. Reorganizing the distribution scheme of these devices involves chip fabrication, soldering, and the recoding of microprograms, or the construction of a completely new computer. This level of inflexibility offers benefits, however, in terms of processing speed and information-transfer latencies. The functions expected of a computing device at this level are very well defined and bounded (perform arithmetic and logic operations on data, and store the results); therefore, the architecture of the device can and should be highly optimized for these tasks.

The history of truly distributed computing begins with the first day that someone tapped a mainframe operator on the shoulder and asked, "Hey, is there any way we can both use that?" Display terminals, with no computing capabilities themselves, were developed to be attached to monolithic central computing devices, and to communicate with them in very rigid and limited protocols. This allowed multiple users to access and submit jobs to the mainframe. Other I/O devices also needed to be attached to the mainframe, generally to store and retrieve data to/from other non-volatile forms (printed storage such as paper tape and punch cards, and later magnetic storage devices). For the most part, the physical links and communications protocols used to hook in these devices were custom designed for each case, and not reusable for other devices.

Meanwhile, people began to desire personal, dedicated computing resources that were available on demand, not when the mainframe schedule said so. The personal computer fit the bill, and its popularity has been growing ever since. Personal computers and workstations, despite the larger numbers of units, followed a similar evolutionary path to mainframes with respect to peripheral devices. Many and varied hardware and communications protocols were born to allow printers, disk drives, pointing devices, and the like to be connected to people's desktop computers. At first, peripheral vendors saw these custom-fit solutions as a potential for competitive advantage in the market; i.e., make your hardware or software faster or more laden with features than the next product, to become the preferred vendor of whatever it is you make. Gradually, both users and makers of personal computers became weary of this game. Users became frustrated with the lack of consistency in the installation, use, and maintenance of these devices, and computer makers were faced with an array of hardware and software interfaces, from which they had to choose the most advantageous ones to support directly in their hardware and operating systems. This became one of the major attractions for buyers of Apple's computer line, second only to their user-friendly operating system. Apple defined and strictly controlled the hardware and software interfaces to their systems, thereby guaranteeing that any third-party devices or software that followed their specifications and standards would operate correctly with their computers.

The concept of standards for hardware and software interfaces caught on at many levels. Standards for every level of distributed computing, from hardware interfaces, network cabling, and physical-level communications protocols, all the way up to application-level protocols, were developed, refined, and promoted in the marketplace. Some standards achieved a critical usage mass, for various reasons, and persist today, such as Ethernet, TCP/IP, and RPC. Others were less popular, and faded with time.

Today, both computing devices and network bandwidth have begun to achieve commodity status. A set of standard protocols, some of which make up the World Wide Web, are beginning to evolve into a worldwide network operating system. Specifics about the type of hardware, operating system, and network being used are becoming more and more irrelevant, making information and tools to process information more and more easily deployable and available. Security protocols have been defined to help owners of information and services restrict access to them. Researchers and developers are looking forward to the next evolutionary steps in information technology, such as autonomous agents and enterprise-wide distributed object systems. In the midst of this revolutionary period, Java™ can be viewed as both a product and a catalyst of all of these trends. Java offers an environment in which the network is truly the computer, and specifics such as operating system features and transport protocols become even more blurred and less important, though not yet completely irrelevant. The Java language and environment promise to play a prominent part in the next generation of distributed computing.

What Does This Book Cover?

This book is an overview of the tools and techniques that are at your disposal for building distributed computing systems in Java. In most cases, these tools are provided inherently in the Java API itself, such as the Java Remote Method Invocation (RMI) API, the Java Security API, and the Java™ Database Connectivity (JDBC) package. Other tools are standards and protocols that exist independently of Java and its environment, but are supported within Java, either through its core APIs or by add-on APIs offered by third-party vendors. Some examples include the Common Object Request Broker Adapter (CORBA) standards, the multicast IP protocol, and the Secure Socket Layer (SSL) standard.

I intend this book to serve as both explanatory and reference material for you, the professional developer. Most of the book is made up of detailed explanations of concepts, tools, and techniques that come into play in most distributed computing situations. At the same time, for readers who are more familiar with the subject matter, the text and code examples are broken up into subject areas that should make it fairly easy to reference important bits.

Organization

The first four chapters of the book (after the Introduction) cover some fundamental tools that come into play in most distributed applications: basic networking tools, distributed objects, multithreading, and security measures. The last five chapters go into detail about some common types of distributed applications: message-passing systems, multitier systems involving databases, bandwidth-limited systems, and systems that allow multiple distributed users or user agents to collaborate dynamically over a network; and discuss the special issues that arise in each.

The figure on the next page shows the dependence of the various chapters on each other, to give you a sense of the order (random or otherwise) that you can choose as you journey through the book. Since the Introduction covers some concepts and terminology that will persist throughout the book, I'd suggest reading it before any of the others. The next four chapters can be read in just about any order, depending on your level of experience with each topic. Since the later chapters use concepts from all of the chapters in the first part of the book, you should have a basic understanding of their topics, either from personal experience or from reading the earlier chapters, before delving into the second part of the book.

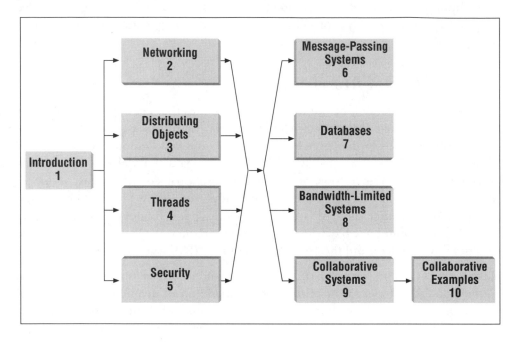

Who Should Read This Book?

This book covers writing distributed applications in Java. A good foundation in the Java language itself, i.e., its syntax and structure, is assumed throughout the book. Thorough knowledge of the Java API is less important, since many of the core Java APIs are discussed in the early chapters, from the standpoint of their support for distributed applications.

Since Java is an object-oriented language, it's only natural that some of the discussion in the book will involve concepts like classes, interfaces, instances, inheritance, and methods; therefore, a decent understanding of these will help. At times we also touch on some object-oriented design concepts, like using abstract interfaces to provide implementation-independent APIs, but these discussions are pretty limited and the concepts are laid out fairly well. I've tried to keep these such that you don't need to be deeply entrenched in object-oriented jargon to follow the discussion.

Throughout the book I assume that you are motivated to build or expand on your understanding of distributed application development in Java. Whether you're a Java developer looking to branch out into distributed systems, or a distributed systems developer looking to apply your experience in a Java environment, you should find this book a practical, and hopefully enjoyable, guide during your explorations, and a useful reference while you're in the thick of developing remote computing applications.

About the Source Code

The source code for all of the examples in this book is available online. On the World Wide Web, go to *http://www.ora.com/catalog/javadc/*. You can also retrieve the files via FTP (either with your web browser or another FTP client) at *ftp://ftp.ora.com/published/oreilly/java/javadc/*. I've tried to segregate the code into two groups of packages: utilities and examples. The *dcj.utils* packages include Java classes from the book that have potential for use in real applications. The *dcj.examples* packages include the code that's primarily explanatory in nature, but probably not of direct practical use in most situations.

Several of the examples will compile and run under either Java™ Developer's Kit (JDK) 1.0 or 1.1; many of them, especially those based on RMI, require features from JDK 1.1. With a few exceptions, all that's required to run the examples is the standard JDK 1.1 API. The exceptions are the CORBA examples in Chapter 3, *Distributing Objects*, which require JavaIDL or another CORBA environment for Java, and a few of the encryption examples in Chapter 5, *Security*, which require the classes in the Java™ Cryptography Extension (JCE) from Sun.

Conventions Used in This Book

This book uses the following typographic conventions:

A `constant width` font is used for:

- Anything that might appear in a Java program, including keywords, operators, datatypes, method names, variable names, class names, and interface names

- Command lines and options that should be typed verbatim on the screen (bold is used in Appendix D to highlight reference items).

- Tags that might appear in an HTML document

An *italic* font is used for:

- New terms where they are defined

- Pathnames, filenames, and program names (however, if the program name is also the name of a Java class, it is given in constant width, like other class names)

- Internet addresses, such as domain names and URLs

Acknowledgments

I'm indebted to numerous people who have contributed to making this book a reality. My wife, Sandra Mallalieu, endured being a part-time widow during most of the writing of the book, taking solace in the company of our semi-orphaned pets. My comrades and former teammates at GE Corporate Research and Development were in large part the catalysts for the genesis of this book. I'm especially grateful to Rick Arthur, Andy Deitsch, Bill Smith, Jon Stillman, and the rest of the Information Technology Lab staff for being compatriots and intellectual sparring partners during my time in their company. As always, I owe enormous thanks to Andrea Schmitz for being inspirational, supportive, and an all-around Good Person. My thanks also go to Bill Lorensen, for getting me hooked on objects oh-so-many years ago, and to John Bloomer, for getting me in touch with O'Reilly to kick off this whole thing. I'd also like to thank my current team in the Information Technology group at the Harvard Business School, whose exploits have helped me to focus on some of the more practical facets of the subject matter.

Of course, the book itself wouldn't be what it is without my editor at O'Reilly, Mike Loukides, who helped guide the direction of the book at many levels. The technical reviewers: Andy Deitsch, Jonathan Knudsen, Tom McGinn, and Don Bolinger, provided invaluable comments that prompted some significant additions to the content.

The efforts of the design and production team at O'Reilly brought the whole thing to its final fruition. Madeleine Newell was the production editor; John Files copyedited the manuscript; David Futato and Sheryl Avruch provided quality control; Mike Sierra took care of conversion and gave technical support; Seth Maislin produced the index; Robert Romano produced the figures; Edie Freedman designed the cover, and Nancy Priest created the inside layout.

Introduction

For the past decade, "distributed computing" has been one of the biggest buzz phrases in the computer industry. At this point in the information age, we know how to build networks; we use thousands of engineering workstations and personal computers to do our work, instead of huge behemoths in glass-walled rooms. Surely we ought to be able to use our networks of smaller computers to work together on larger tasks. And we do—an act as simple as reading a web page requires the cooperation of two computers (a client and a server) plus other computers that make sure the data gets from one location to the other. However, simple browsing (i.e., a largely one-way data exchange) isn't what we usually mean when we talk about distributed computing. We usually mean something where there's more interaction between the systems involved.

You can think about distributed computing in terms of breaking down an application into individual computing *agents* that can be distributed on a network of computers, yet still work together to do cooperative tasks. The motivations for distributing an application this way are many. Here are a few of the more common ones:

- Computing things in parallel by breaking a problem into smaller pieces enables you to solve larger problems without resorting to larger computers. Instead, you can use smaller, cheaper, easier-to-find computers.

- Large data sets are typically difficult to relocate, or easier to control and administer located where they are, so users have to rely on remote data servers to provide needed information.

- Redundant processing agents on multiple networked computers can be used by systems that need fault tolerance. If a machine or agent process goes down, the job can still carry on.

There are many other motivations, and plenty of subtle variations on the ones listed here.

Assorted tools and standards for assembling distributed computing applications have been developed over the years. These started as low-level data transmission APIs and protocols, such as RPC and DCE, and have recently begun to evolve into object-based distribution schemes, such as CORBA, RMI, and OpenDoc. These programming tools essentially provide a protocol for transmitting structured data (and, in some cases, actual runnable code) over a network connection. Java offers a language and an environment that encompass various levels of distributed computing development, from low-level network communication to distributed objects and agents, while also having built-in support for secure applications, multiple threads of control, and integration with other Internet-based protocols and services.

This chapter gives an introduction to distributed application development, and how Java can be used as a tool towards this end. In the following chapters, we'll start by reviewing some essential background material on network programming, threads, and security. Then we'll move into a series of chapters that explore different distributed problems in detail. Where appropriate, we'll use RMI, CORBA, or a homegrown protocol to implement examples. If you are developing distributed applications, you need to be familiar with all possible solutions and where they're appropriate; so where we choose a particular tool, we'll try to discuss how things would be better or worse if you chose a different set of tools in building something similar.

Anatomy of a Distributed Application

A distributed application is built upon several layers. At the lowest level, a network connects a group of host computers together so that they can talk to each other. Network protocols like TCP/IP let the computers send data to each other over the network by providing the ability to package and address data for delivery to another machine. Higher-level services can be defined on top of the network protocol, such as directory services and security protocols. Finally, the distributed application itself runs on top of these layers, using the mid-level services and network protocols as well as the computer operating systems to perform coordinated tasks across the network.

At the application level, a distributed application can be broken down into the following parts:

Processes

A typical computer operating system on a computer host can run several processes at once. A process is created by describing a sequence of steps in a programming language, compiling the program into an executable form, and running the executable in the operating system. While it's running, a process has access to the resources of the computer (such as CPU time and I/O devices) through the operating system. A process can be completely devoted to a particular application, or several applications can use a single process to perform tasks.

Threads

Every process has at least one thread of control. Some operating systems support the creation of multiple threads of control within a single process. Each thread in a process can run independently from the other threads, although there is usually some synchronization between them. One thread might monitor input from a socket connection, for example, while another might listen for user events (keystrokes, mouse movements, etc.) and provide feedback to the user through output devices (monitor, speakers, etc.). At some point, input from the input stream may require feedback from the user. At this point, the two threads will need to coordinate the transfer of input data to the user's attention.

Objects

Programs written in object-oriented languages are made up of cooperating objects. One simple definition of an object is a group of related data, with methods available for querying or altering the data (`getName()`, `set-Name()`), or for taking some action based on the data (`sendName(OutputStream o)`). A process can be made up of one or more objects, and these objects can be accessed by one or more threads within the process. And with the introduction of distributed object technology like RMI and CORBA, an object can also be logically spread across multiple processes, on multiple computers.

Agents

For the sake of this book, we will use the term "agent" as a general way to refer to significant functional elements of a distributed application.* While a process, a thread, and an object are pretty well-defined entities, an agent (at least the definition we'll use for the sake of this book) is a higher-level system component, defined around a particular function, or utility, or role in the overall system. A remote banking application, for example, might be broken down into a customer agent, a transaction agent and an information

---

* The term "agent" is overused in the technology community. In the more formal sense of the word, an agent is a computing entity that is a bit more intelligent and autonomous than an object. An agent is supposed to be capable of having goals that it needs to accomplish, such as retrieving information of a certain type from a large database or remote data sources. Some agents can monitor their progress towards achieving their goals at a higher level than just successful execution of methods, like an object. The definition of agent that we're using here is a lot less formal than this, and a bit more general.

brokerage agent. Agents can be distributed across multiple processes, and can be made up of multiple objects and threads in these processes. Our customer agent might be made up of an object in a process running on a client desktop that's listening for data and updating the local display, along with an object in a process running on the bank server, issuing queries and sending the data back to the client. There are two objects running in distinct processes on separate machines, but together we can consider them to make up one customer agent, with client-side elements and server-side elements.

So a distributed application can be thought of as a coordinated group of agents working to accomplish some goal. Each of these agents can be distributed across multiple processes on remote hosts, and can consist of multiple objects or threads of control. Agents can also belong to more than one application at once. You may be developing an automated teller machine application, for example, which consists of an account database server, with customer request agents distributed across the network submitting requests. The account server agent and the customer request agents are agents within the ATM application, but they might also serve agents residing at the financial institution's headquarters, as part of an administrative application.

Requirements for Developing Distributed Applications

Now that we've defined some terms that can be used to discuss distributed applications, we can start to look at what goes into developing these applications. In this section we'll discuss some of the issues that you face when developing distributed systems, and what kinds of tools and capabilities you'll need in order to address these issues. The next section will describe how Java provides these tools and capabilities.

Partitioning and Distributing Data and Functions

If you think of the computer hosts and network connections available for a distributed application to use as a "virtual machine," then one of the primary tasks you have is to engineer an optimal mapping of processes, objects, threads and agents to the various parts of this virtual machine. In some cases, a straightforward client/server partitioning based on data requirements can be used. Computational tasks can be distributed based on the data needs of the application: maximize local data needed for processing, and minimize data transfers over the network. In other, more compute-intensive applications, you can partition the system based upon the functional requirements of the system, with data mapped to the most logical compute host. This method of partitioning is especially useful when the overhead associated with data transfers is negligible compared to the computing time spent at the various hosts.

In the best of all possible worlds, you could develop modules based upon either data- or functionally driven partitioning. You could then distribute these modules as needed throughout a virtual machine comprised of computers and communication links, and easily connect the modules to establish the data flow required by the application. These module interconnections should be as flexible and transparent as possible, since they may need to be adjusted at any point during development or deployment of the distributed system.

Flexible, Extendible Communication Protocols

The type and format of the information that's sent between agents in a distributed system is subject to many varied and changing requirements. Some of them are a result of the data/function partitioning issues discussed in the previous section. The allocation of tasks and data to agents in the distributed system has a direct influence on what type of data will need to be communicated between agents, how much data will be transferred, and how complicated the communication protocol between agents needs to be. If most of our data is sitting on the host where it's needed, then communications will be mostly short, simple messages to report status, instruct other agents to start processing, etc. If central data servers are providing lots of data to remote agents, then the communication protocol will be more complex and connections between nodes in the system will stay open longer. You need to be able to implement various styles of communication, and adapt them to evolving requirements.

The communication protocols a given agent will need to understand might also be dictated by legacy systems that need to be incorporated into the system. These legacy systems might control data or functionality that's critical to enabling a given system, but are not easily transferable to a new system. Support for these protocols should be available, or easily attainable, in your distributed application development environment. In the worst case, when support for a required protocol is unavailable due to its obscurity or the expense associated with the available support, you should have the option to develop the required protocol support yourself, and have a reasonable way of incorporating the extended communications abilities into the existing infrastructure.

Multithreading Requirements

Agents often have to execute several threads of control at once, either to service requests from multiple remote agents, or block on I/O while processing data, or for any number of other reasons. Multithreading is often an effective way to optimize the use of various resources, such as CPU time, local storage devices, or network bandwidth. The ability to create and control multiple threads of control is especially important in developing distributed applications, since distributed agents are typically more asynchronous than agents within a single process on a single host. The environments in which agents are running can be very heterogeneous, too, and we don't want every agent in a distributed application to be a slave to the slowest, most heavily loaded agent in the system. We don't want our multiprocessor compute server, for example, to be sitting idle while it waits for a slow client desktop to read and render the results of an analysis. We would want a single thread on the compute server to be servicing the slow client, and while the client is crawling along trying to read data and draw graphs on its display, other threads on the compute server can be doing useful work, like analyzing the data from other clients.

Security Issues

The information transactions that occur between computing agents often need to be secure from outside observation, when information of a sensitive nature needs to be shared between agents. In situations where an outside agent not under the host's direct control is allowed to interact with local agents, it is also wise to have reasonable security measures available to authenticate the source of the agent, and to prevent the agent from wreaking havoc once it gains access to local processing resources. So at a minimum a secure distributed application needs a way to *authenticate* the identity of agents, define resource *access* levels for agents, and *encrypt* data for transmission between agents.

What Does Java Provide?

The original design motivations behind Java and its predecessor, Oak, were concerned mainly with reliability, simplicity, and architecture neutrality. Subsequently, as the potential for Java as an "Internet programming language" was seen by its developers at Sun Microsystems, support for networking, security, and multithreaded operations was incorporated or improved. All of these features of the Java language and environment also make for a very powerful distributed application development environment. This is, of course, no accident. The requirements for developing an Internet-based application overlap to a great extent with those of distributed application development.

In this section, we review some of the features of Java that are of particular interest in distributed applications, and how they help to address some of the issues described in the previous section.

Object-Oriented Environment

Java is a "pure" object-oriented language, in the sense that the smallest programmatic building block is a class. A data structure or function cannot exist or be accessed at runtime except as an element of a class definition. This results in a well-defined, structured programming environment in which all domain concepts and operations are mapped into class representations and transactions between them. This is advantageous for systems development in general, but also has benefits specifically for you as the distributed system developer. An object, as an instance of a class, can be thought of as a computing agent. Its level of sophistication as an autonomous agent is determined by the complexity of its methods and data representations, as well as its role within the object model of the system, and the runtime object community defining the distributed system. Distributing a system implemented in Java, therefore, can be thought of as simply distributing its objects in a reasonable way, and establishing networked communication links between them using Java's built-in network support. If you have the luxury of designing a distributed system from the ground up, then your object model and class hierarchy can be specified with distribution issues incorporated.

Abstract Interfaces

Java's support for abstract object interfaces is another valuable tool for developing distributed systems. An interface describes the operations, messages, and queries a class of objects is capable of servicing, without providing any information about how these abilities are implemented. If a class is declared as implementing a specified interface, then the class has to implement the methods specified in the interface. The advantage of implementation-neutral interfaces is that other agents in the system can be implemented to talk to the specified interface without knowing how the interface is actually implemented in a class. By insulating the class implementation from those using the interface, we can change the implementation as needed. If a class needs to be moved to a remote host, then the local implementation of the interface can act as a surrogate or stub, forwarding calls to the interface over the network to the remote class.

Abstract interfaces are a powerful part of the Java language and are used to implement critical elements of the Java API. The platform independence of the Abstract Windowing Toolkit (AWT) is accomplished using abstract component interfaces that are implemented on each platform using the native windowing system (the X Window System, Macintosh, Windows, etc.). Certain key packages in the core Java API, such as the `java.security` package, also make use of interfaces to allow for specialized implementations by third-party vendors. The Java Remote Method Invocation (RMI) package uses abstract interfaces to define local stubs for remote objects. The concept of abstract interfaces is also common in other distributed object systems such as CORBA, in which interfaces defined in Interface Definition Language (IDL) define the object model of a CORBA system.* The Inter-Language Unification system (ILU), developed at Xerox PARC, also depends upon an implementation-neutral interface language called Interface Specification Language (ISL).†

Platform Independence

Code written in Java can be compiled into platform-independent bytecodes using Sun's Java compiler, or any of the many third-party Java compilers now on the market. These bytecodes run on the Java Virtual Machine, a virtual hardware architecture which is implemented in software running on a "real" machine and its operating system. Java bytecodes can be run on any platform with a Java Virtual Machine. At the time of this writing, a Java VM is available for most major Unix variants, OS/2, Windows95 and NT, MacOS, and a variety of other operating systems.

This is a major boon for you, since it allows virtually any available PC or workstation to be home to an agent in a distributed system. Once the elements of the system have been specified using Java classes and compiled into Java bytecodes, they can migrate without recompilation to any of the hosts available. This makes for easy data- and load-balancing across the network. There is even support in the Java API for downloading a class definition (its bytecodes) through a network connection, creating an instance of the class, and incorporating the new object into the running process. This is possible because Java bytecodes are runnable on the Java Virtual Machine, which is guaranteed to be underneath any Java application or applet.

Fault Tolerance Through Exception Handling

Java supports throwing and catching errors and exceptions, both system-defined and application-defined. Any method can throw an exception; it is the calling method's responsibility to handle the exception, or propagate the exception up the calling chain. Handling an exception is a matter of wrapping any potential exception-causing code with a `try/catch/finally` statement, where each `catch` clause handles a particular type of exception. If a method chooses to ignore particular exceptions, then it must declare that it throws the exceptions it is ignoring. When a called method generates an exception, it will be propagated up the calling chain to be handled by a `catch` clause in a calling method, or, if

---

* More information about CORBA and IDL can be obtained from the Object Management Group at *http://www.omg.org/.*

† See the ILU home page at *ftp://ftp.parc.xerox.com/pub/ilu/ilu.html.*

not, to result in a stack dump and exit from the Java process. After all is said and done, whether the `try` block runs to completion without a problem, or an exception gets thrown, the code in the `finally` block is always called. So you can use the `finally` block to clean up any resources you created in the `try` block, for example, and be sure that the cleanup will take place whether an exception is thrown or not.

An agent can be written to handle the exceptions that can be thrown by each method it calls. Additionally, since any subclass of `java.io.Throwable` can be declared in a method's `throws` clause, an application can define its own types of exceptions to indicate specific abnormalities. Since an exception is represented as an object in the Java environment, these application-specific exceptions can carry with them data and methods that can be used to characterize, diagnose, and potentially recover from them.

Network Support

The Java API includes multilevel support for network communications. Low-level sockets can be established between agents, and data communication protocols can be layered on top of the socket connection. The `java.io` package contains several stream classes intended for filtering and preprocessing input and output data streams. APIs built on top of the basic networking support in Java provide higher-level networking capabilities, such as distributed objects, remote connections to database servers, directory services, etc.

While the majority of this book will be concerned with the use of distributed object schemes like RMI, along with other higher-level networking APIs, it's also important to get a feeling for the basic networking capabilities included in the core Java API. Figure 1-1 shows a simple network application involving a client and a server; the client sends commands to the server, the server executes the commands and sends responses back to the client. To demonstrate the network support in Java and how it can be exploited for distributed applications, Examples 1-1 through 1-4 show an implementation of this simple client-server system using sockets and input/output streams. The implementation includes the following elements:

- A set of command objects that represent our command protocol between the client and the server

- A subclass of `java.io.DataInputStream` that understands our protocol

- A client that can send commands in the right format to the server, and a server that can accept client connections, read commands using our specialized stream, and send responses back

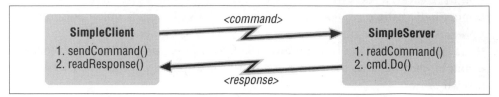

Figure 1-1. A simple client/server system

The client connects to the server over a socket, then sends commands to the server over the socket. The server uses the specialized `DataInputStream` to read the commands from the socket. The input stream automatically creates the right command object based on the type of message from the client (e.g., a "GET" message will be converted into a `GetCmd` object). The server then executes the command and sends the result to the client over the socket.

Example 1-1 shows a set of classes that represent the commands a client can send to our server. The `SimpleCmd` class simply holds a single `String` argument and has an abstract `Do()` method that subclasses will implement to do the right thing for the particular command they represent. Our protocol consists of three basic commands: "GET," "HEAD," and "POST,"* along with a command to close the connection, "DONE." The `GetCmd`, `HeadCmd`, `PostCmd`, and `DoneCmd` classes derived from `SimpleCmd` represent these commands.

Example 1-1. Commands for the Client-Server System

```
package dcj.examples;

import java.lang.*;

abstract class SimpleCmd
{
  protected String arg;

  public SimpleCmd(String inArg) {
    arg = inArg;
  }

  public abstract String Do();
}

class GetCmd extends SimpleCmd
{
```

---

* Sound familiar? These commands are the heart of the HTTP protocol, which in turn is the heart of the World Wide Web.

Example 1-1. Commands for the Client-Server System (continued)

```
  public GetCmd(String s) { super(s); }

  public String Do() {
    String result = arg + " Gotten\n";
    return result;
  }
}


public class HeadCmd extends SimpleCmd
{
  public HeadCmd(String s) { super(s); }
  public String Do() {
    String result = "Head \"" + arg + "\" processed.\n";
    return result;
  }
}


class PostCmd extends SimpleCmd
{
  public PostCmd(String s) { super(s); }

  public String Do() {
    String result = arg + " Posted\n";
    return result;
  }
}


class DoneCmd extends SimpleCmd
{
  public DoneCmd() { super(""); };

  public String Do() {
    String result = "All done.\n";
    return result;
  }
}
```

The classes in Example 1-1 represent the communication protocol for our client-server application, and the `SimpleCmdInputStream` class in Example 1-2 acts as the communication link that understands this protocol. The `SimpleCmdInputStream` is a subclass of `java.io.DataInputStream` that adds a `readCommand()` method to its interface. This method parses the data coming in over the stream, determines which command is being sent, and constructs the corresponding command class from Example 1-1.

Example 1-2. A Specialized DataInputStream

```java
package dcj.examples;

import java.lang.*;
import java.io.*;
import java.net.*;

public class SimpleCmdInputStream extends DataInputStream
{
  public SimpleCmdInputStream(InputStream in) {
    super(in);
  }

  public String readString() throws IOException {
    StringBuffer strBuf = new StringBuffer();
    boolean hitSpace = false;
    while (!hitSpace) {
      char c = readChar();
      hitSpace = Character.isSpace(c);
      if (!hitSpace)
        strBuf.append(c);
    }

    String str = new String(strBuf);
    return str;
  }

  public SimpleCmd readCommand() throws IOException {
    SimpleCmd cmd;
    String commStr = readString();
    if (commStr.compareTo("HEAD") == 0)
      cmd = new HeadCmd(readString());
    else if (commStr.compareTo("GET") == 0)
      cmd = new GetCmd(readString());
    else if (commStr.compareTo("POST") == 0)
      cmd = new PostCmd(readString());
    else if (commStr.compareTo("DONE") == 0)
      cmd = new DoneCmd();
    else
      throw new IOException("Unknown command.");

    return cmd;
  }
}
```

Finally, the SimpleClient in Example 1-3 and SimpleServer in Example 1-4 serve as the client and server agents in our distributed system. Our Simple-Client is very simple indeed. In its constructor, it opens a socket to a server on a given host and port number. Its main() method makes a SimpleClient object using command-line arguments that specify the host and port to connect to, then calls the sendCommands() method on the client. This method just sends a few commands in the right format to the server over the OutputStream from the socket connection.

Notice that the client's socket is closed in its finalize() method. This method will only get called after all references to the client are gone, and the system garbage-collector runs to mark the object as finalizable. If it's important that the socket be closed immediately after the client is done with it, you may want to close the socket explicitly at the end of the sendCommands() method.

Example 1-3. A Simple Client

```
package dcj.examples;

import java.lang.*;
import java.net.*;
import java.io.*;

public class SimpleClient
{
  // Our socket connection to the server
  protected Socket serverConn;

  // The input command stream from the server
  protected SimpleCmdInputStream inStream;

  public SimpleClient(String host, int port)
      throws IllegalArgumentException {
    try {
      System.out.println("Trying to connect to " + host + " " + port);
      serverConn = new Socket(host, port);
    }
    catch (UnknownHostException e) {
      throw new IllegalArgumentException("Bad host name given.");
    }
    catch (IOException e) {
      System.out.println("SimpleClient: " + e);
      System.exit(1);
    }

    System.out.println("Made server connection.");
  }

  public static void main(String argv[]) {
    if (argv.length < 2) {
      System.out.println("Usage: java SimpleClient [host] [port]");
```

Example 1-3. A Simple Client (continued)

```
      System.exit(1);
   }

   String host = argv[0];
   int port = 3000;
   try {
     port = Integer.parseInt(argv[1]);
   }
   catch (NumberFormatException e) {}

   SimpleClient client = new SimpleClient(host, port);
   client.sendCommands();
 }

public void sendCommands() {
   try {
     OutputStreamWriter wout =
       new OutputStreamWriter(serverConn.getOutputStream());
     BufferedReader rin = new BufferedReader(
       new InputStreamReader(serverConn.getInputStream()));

     // Send a GET command...
     wout.write("GET goodies ");
     // ...and receive the results
     String result = rin.readLine();
     System.out.println("Server says: \"" + result + "\"");

     // Now try a POST command
     wout.write("POST goodies ");
     // ...and receive the results
     result = rin.readLine();
     System.out.println("Server says: \"" + result + "\"");

     // All done, tell the server so
     wout.writeChars("DONE ");
     result = rin.readLine();
     System.out.println("Server says: \"" + result + "\"");
   }
   catch (IOException e) {
     System.out.println("SimpleClient: " + e);
     System.exit(1);
   }
 }

public synchronized void finalize() {
   System.out.println("Closing down SimpleClient...");
   try { serverConn.close(); }
   catch (IOException e) {
```

Example 1-3. A Simple Client (continued)

```
        System.out.println("SimpleClient: " + e);
        System.exit(1);
      }
    }
}
```

The `SimpleServer` class has a constructor that binds itself to a given port, and a `listen()` method that continually checks that port for client connections. Its `main()` method creates a `SimpleServer` for a port specified with command-line arguments, then calls the server's `listen()` method. The `listen()` method loops continuously, waiting for a client to connect to its port. When a client connects, the server creates a `Socket` to the client, then calls its `service-Client()` method to parse the client's commands and act on them. The `serviceClient()` takes the `InputStream` from the client socket, and wraps our `SimpleCmdInputStream` around it. Then the method loops, calling the `readCommand()` method on the stream to get the client's commands. If the client sends a DONE command, then the loop stops and the method returns. Until then, each command is read from the stream, and the `Do()` method is called on each. The string returned from the `Do()` call is returned to the client over the `OutputStream` from the client socket.

Example 1-4. A Simple Server

```
package dcj.examples;

import java.net.*;
import java.io.*;
import java.lang.*;

// A generic server that listens on a port and connects to any clients it
// finds. Made to extend Thread, so that an application can have multiple
// server threads servicing several ports, if necessary.

public class SimpleServer
{
  protected int portNo = 3000; // Port to listen to for clients
  protected ServerSocket clientConnect;

  public SimpleServer(int port) throws IllegalArgumentException {
    if (port <= 0)
      throw new IllegalArgumentException(
                  "Bad port number given to SimpleServer constructor.");

      // Try making a ServerSocket to the given port
      System.out.println("Connecting server socket to port...");
      try { clientConnect = new ServerSocket(port); }
```

Example 1-4. A Simple Server (continued)

```java
    catch (IOException e) {
      System.out.println("Failed to connect to port " + port);
      System.exit(1);
    }

    // Made the connection, so set the local port number
    this.portNo = port;
  }

  public static void main(String argv[]) {
    int port = 3000;
    if (argv.length > 0) {
      int tmp = port;
      try {
        tmp = Integer.parseInt(argv[0]);
      }
      catch (NumberFormatException e) {}

      port = tmp;
    }

    SimpleServer server = new SimpleServer(port);
    System.out.println("SimpleServer running on port " + port + "...");
    server.listen();
  }

  public void listen() {
    // Listen to port for client connection requests.
    try {
      System.out.println("Waiting for clients...");
      while (true) {
        Socket clientReq = clientConnect.accept();
        System.out.println("Got a client...");
        serviceClient(clientReq);
      }
    }
    catch (IOException e) {
      System.out.println("IO exception while listening for clients.");
      System.exit(1);
    }
  }

  public void serviceClient(Socket clientConn) {
    SimpleCmdInputStream inStream = null;
    DataOutputStream outStream = null;
    try {
      inStream = new SimpleCmdInputStream(clientConn.getInputStream());
      outStream = new DataOutputStream(clientConn.getOutputStream());
```

Example 1-4. A Simple Server (continued)

```
  }
catch (IOException e) {
  System.out.println("SimpleServer: Error getting I/O streams.");
}

SimpleCmd cmd = null;
System.out.println("Attempting to read commands...");
while (cmd == null ||
       !(cmd instanceOf DomeCmd)) {
  try { cmd = inStream.readCommand(); }
  catch (IOException e) {
    System.out.println("SimpleServer: " + e);
    System.exit(1);
  }

  if (cmd != null) {
    String result = cmd.Do();
    try { outStream.writeBytes(result); }
    catch (IOException e) {
      System.out.println("SimpleServer: " + e);
      System.exit(1);
    }
  }
}

public synchronized void finalize() {
  System.out.println("Shutting down SimpleServer running on port "
                     + portNo);
}
}
```

(handwritten annotation) cmd.getClass().getName().compareTo ('dcj.example.DomeCmd').(...)

We could easily adapt this simple communication scheme to other applications with different protocols. We would just need to define new subclasses of SimpleCmd, and update our SimpleCmdInputStream to parse them correctly. If we wanted to get exotic, we could expand our communication scheme to implement a "meta-protocol" between agents in the system. The first piece of information passed between two agents when they establish a socket connection would be the protocol they want to use to communicate with each other. Using the class download capabilities mentioned in the previous section, we could actually load a subclass of java.io.InputStream over the newly created socket, create an instance of the class, and attach it to the socket itself. We won't indulge ourselves in this exotic exercise in this chapter, however.

What all of this demonstrates is that Java's network support provides a quick way to develop the communication elements of a basic distributed system. Java's other core features, such as platform-independent bytecodes, facilitate the development of more complex network transactions, such as agents dynamically building a protocol for talking to each other by exchanging class definitions. The core Java API also includes built-in support for sharing Java objects between remote agents, with its RMI package. Objects that implement the `java.io.Serializable` interface can be converted to byte streams and transmitted over a network connection to a remote Java process, where they can be "reconstituted" into copies of the original objects. Other packages are available for using CORBA to distribute objects within a Java distributed application. We'll discuss both methods for distributed Java objects in later chapters.

Security

Java provides two dimensions of security for distributed systems: a secure local runtime environment, and the ability to engage in secure remote transactions.

Runtime environment

At the same time that Java facilitates the distribution of system elements across the network, it makes it easy for the recipient of these system elements to verify that they can't compromise the security of the local environment. If Java code is run in the context of an applet, then the Java Virtual Machine places rather severe restrictions on its operation and capabilities. It's allowed virtually no access to the local file system, very restricted network access (e.g., it can only open a network connection back to the server it was loaded from), no access to local code or libraries outside of the Java environment, and restricted thread manipulation capabilities, among other things. In addition, any class definitions loaded over the network, whether from a Java applet or a Java application, are subjected to a stringent byte-code verification process, in which the syntax and operations of the bytecodes are checked for incorrect or potentially malicious behavior.

Secure remote transactions

In the section "Network Support," we demonstrated how Java simplifies the creation, manipulation, and extension of network communications sockets. This capability of the environment makes it easy to add user authentication and data encryption to establish secure network links, assuming that the basic encryption and authentication algorithms already exist. Suppose, for example, that we wanted to use public key encryption to establish secure, authenticated connections to named agents on remote machines. We can extend the `BufferedInputStream` and `BufferedOutputStream` classes in `java.net` to authenticate and decrypt incoming data, and to sign and encrypt outgoing data. Example 1-5 displays the encrypted input stream.

Example 1-5. Encrypted Input Stream

```
import java.io.*;

public abstract class EncryptedInputStream extends BufferedInputStream
{
    public EncryptedInputStream(InputStream in);
        // Assumes the key ID and signature will be embedded
        // in the incoming data
    public EncryptedInputStream(InputStream in, String id);
        // Will only allow communication once identified
        // entity is authenticated with a public key

    // Protected methods
    public int decrypt(int) throws SecurityException;
    public int decrypt(byte[] b) throws SecurityException;
    public int decrypt(byte[] b, int off, int len)
        throws SecurityException;

    // Public methods
    public int read() throws IOException, SecurityException
    {
        return decrypt(super.read());
    }

    public int read(byte[] b) throws IOException, SecurityException
    {
        super.read(b);
        return decrypt(b);
    }

    public int read(byte[] b, int off, int len)
        throws IOException, SecurityException
    {
        super.read(b, off, len);
        return decrypt(b, off, len);
    }
}
```

Of course, the example is greatly simplified by the fact that we haven't actually implemented the `EncryptedInputStream.decrypt()` methods, which are at the heart of the matter, since they actually detect key IDs and signatures, look up public keys on some key list in memory or on disk, and decrypt the incoming data stream once the agent at the other end has been authenticated. We've also avoided the issues of data expansion or compression caused by encryption. When an `EncryptedInputStream` is asked to read *n* bytes of data, the intention is typically to read *n* decrypted bytes. Any change in data size would have to be made opaque by the `decrypt()` methods.

Once we establish an encrypted communications stream with the remote agent, we can layer any kind of data protocol we like on top of it. For example, our simple GET/HEAD/POST messaging scheme from an earlier example could be carried out securely by simply putting an encrypted input/output stream pair underneath:

```
public SecureClientServer
{
    public SecureClientServer(String host, int port)
        throws SecurityException
    {
        Socket comm = new Socket(host, port);
        InputStream rawIn = comm.getInputStream();
        EncryptedInputStream secureIn =
            new EncryptedInputStream(rawIn);
        SimpleMessageInputStream msgIn =
            new SimpleMessageInputStream(secureIn);

        // Start reading and processing commands from the
        // (now encrypted) input stream
        while (true)
        {
            try {
                SimpleCmd cmd = msgIn.readCommand();
                cmd.Do();
            }
            catch (IOException e) {}
    // Remainder of class implementation omitted
        ...
}
```

Of course, this assumes that the agent at the other end of the socket has been suitably augmented to encrypt and decrypt streams.

These examples have simply alluded to how the basic network capabilities of Java could be extended to support secure network communications. The `java.security` package provides a framework for implementing the authentication and encryption algorithms needed to complete our secure input stream example. The authentication process could be implemented using the `KeyPair` and `Signature` classes, for example. We'll discuss the `java.security` API in more detail in a later chapter.

Multithreading Support

The ability to generate multithreaded agents is a fundamental feature of Java. Any class that you create can extend the `java.lang.Thread` class by providing its own implementation of a `run()` method. When the thread is started, this `run()`

method will be called and your class can do its work within a separate thread of control. This is one way to delegate tasks to threads in a given agent; another is to have your workhorse classes derive from `java.lang.Runnable`, and allocate them as needed to threads or thread groups. Any class implementing the `Runnable` interface (which essentially means providing a `run()` method that represents the body of work to be done in the thread) can be wrapped with a thread by simply creating a new `Thread` with the `Runnable` object as the argument.

Java also lets you tweak the performance of a given agent through control and manipulation of its threads. Threads are assigned priorities that are publicly pollable and settable, giving you (or even some intelligent agent) the ability to suggest how processing time is allocated to threads by the Virtual Machine. Threads can also be made to yield to other threads, to sleep for some period of time, to suspend indefinitely, or to go away altogether. These kinds of operations become important, for example, in asynchronous systems, in which a thread is tasked with client polling and spawns new threads to service client requests.

2

In this chapter:
- *Sockets and Streams*
- *URLs,
  URLConnections,
  and ContentHandlers*
- *The ClassLoader*

Networking in Java

We saw in Chapter 1 how the socket and stream classes in the `java.net` and `java.io` packages could be used to do basic networking between agents. In this chapter we take a more detailed look at the networking support in Java, as the foundation for distributed systems. The topics we'll cover include:

- Sockets for low-level network connections

- Streams for formatted data and messaging protocols

- URL, URLConnection, and ContentHandler classes

- The ClassLoader as an object distribution scheme

We'll look at these topics in increasing pecking order from the networking perspective. Sockets first, since they are the most primitive communication object in the Java API; then streams, which let you impose some order on the data flowing over these sockets; next, the classes associated with the HTTP protocol, namely, the URL, URLConnection, and ContentHandler classes; finally, the ClassLoader, which, when coupled with the others, offers the ability to transmit actual Java classes over the wire.

Sockets and Streams

The `java.net` package provides an object-oriented framework for the creation and use of Internet Protocol (IP)* sockets. In this section, we'll take a look at these classes and what they offer.

---

* The Internet Protocol is the predominant networking protocol today, being the protocol in use on the Internet and on most corporate WANs and LANs.

IP Addressing

Before communicating with another party, you must first know how to address your messages so they can be delivered correctly. Notice that I didn't say that you need to know where the other party is located—once a scheme for encoding a location is established, I simply need to know my party's encoded address to communicate. On IP networks, the addressing scheme in use is based on hosts and port numbers.

A given host computer on an IP network has a hostname and a numeric address. Either of these, in their fully qualified forms, is a unique identifier for a host on the network. The JavaSoft home page, for example, resides on a host named *www.javasoft.com*, which currently has the IP address *204.160.241.98*. Either of these addresses can be used to locate the machine on an IP network. The textual name for the machine is called its Domain Name Services (DNS) name, which can be thought of as a kind of alias for the numeric IP address.

In the Java API, the `InetAddress` class represents an IP address. You can query an `InetAddress` for the name of the host using its `getHostName()` method, and for its numeric address using `getAddress()`. Notice that, even though we can uniquely specify a host with its IP address, we do not necessarily know its physical location. I look at the web pages on *www.javasoft.com* regularly, but I don't know where the machine is (though I could guess that it's in California somewhere). Conversely, even if I knew where the machine was physically, it wouldn't do me a bit of good if I didn't know its IP address (unless someone was kind enough to label the machine with it, or left a terminal window open on the server's console for me to get its IP address directly).

Now, you typically don't want to communicate with a given host, but rather with one or many agent processes running on the host. To engage in network communications, each process must associate itself with a port on the host, identified by a number. HTTP servers, for example, typically attach themselves to port 80 on their host machine. When you ask to connect to *http://www.javasoft.com/* from your web browser, the browser automatically assumes the default port and attempts to connect to the process running on *www.javasoft.com* listening to port 80. If this process is an HTTP server process that understands the commands that the browser is sending, the browser and the server will commence communications.

This host/port scheme is the basis of the IP addressing protocol, and is supported directly in the Java API. All network connections are specified using an `Inet-Address` and a port number. The Java environment does the hard work of initiating the IP protocol communications and creating Java objects that represent these network connections.

Your Basic Socket

At the core of Java's networking support are the Socket and DatagramSocket classes in `java.net`. These classes define channels for communication between processes over an IP network. A new socket is created by specifying a host, either by name or with an `InetAddress` object, and a port number on the host. There are two basic flavors of network sockets on IP networks: those that use the Transport Control Protocol (TCP) and those that use the Unreliable Datagram Protocol (UDP). TCP is a reliable protocol in which data packets are guaranteed to be delivered, and delivered in order. If a packet expected at the receiving end of a TCP socket doesn't arrive in a set period of time, then it is assumed lost, and the packet is requested from the sender again. The receiver doesn't move on to the next packet until the first is received. UDP, on the other hand, makes no guarantees about delivery of packets, or the order in which packets are delivered. The sender transmits a UDP packet, and it either makes it to the receiver or it doesn't. TCP sockets are used in the large majority of IP applications. UDP sockets are typically used in bandwidth-limited applications, where the overhead associated with resending packets is not tolerable. A good example of this is real-time network audio applications. If you are delivering packets of audio information over the network to be played in real-time, then there is no point in resending a late packet. By the time it gets delivered it will be useless, since the audio track must play continuously and sequentially, without backtracking.

The Socket class is used for creating TCP connections over an IP network. A Socket is typically created using an `InetAddress` to specify the remote host, and a port number to which the host can connect. A process on the remote host must be listening on that port number for incoming connection requests. In Java, this can be done using a `ServerSocket`:

```
// Listen to port 5000 on the local host for socket connection requests
ServerSocket s = new ServerSocket(5000);
while (true) {
    // Wait for a connection request from a client
    Socket clientConn = s.accept();
    InputStream in = clientConn.getInputStream();
    OutputStream out = clientConn.getOutputStream();
    // Now we have input and output streams connected to our client, do
    // something with them...
```

On client side, the code simply creates a socket to the remote host on the specified port (5000, in this case):

```
// Create the socket
InetAddress addr = InetAddress.getByName("our.remote.host");
Socket s = new Socket(addr, 5000);
InputStream in = s.getInputStream();
```

```
OutputStream out = s.getOutputStream();
// We've got input/output streams to the remote process,
// now do something with them...
```

UDP socket connections are created and used through the `DatagramSocket` and `DatagramPacket` classes. A `DatagramSocket` sends and receives data using UDP packets, represented as `DatagramPacket` objects. Before two agents can talk to each other over a UDP connection, they both have to have a `DatagramSocket` connected to a port on their local machines. This is done by simply creating a `DatagramSocket` object:

```
DatagramSocket udpSocket = new DatagramSocket(5000);
```

In this example we are connecting a UDP socket to a specific port (5000) on the local host. If we don't particularly care which port is used, then we can construct the `DatagramSocket` without specifying the port. An unused port on the local host will be used, and we can find out which one by asking the new socket for its port number:

```
DatagramSocket udpSocket = new DatagramSocket();
int portNo = udpSocket.getLocalPort();
```

In order for two agents to send data to each other over a UDP socket, they must know the host name and port number of each other's socket connection. So they will either have preordained ports for each other and will create `Datagram-Sockets` using these port numbers, or they will create a socket on a random local port and transmit their port numbers to each other over another connection.

Data is sent over a `DatagramSocket` using `DatagramPacket` objects. Each `DatagramPacket` contains a data buffer, the address of the remote host to send the data to, and the port number the remote agent is listening to. So to send a buffer of data to a process listening to port 5000 on host *my.host.com*, we would do something like this:

```
byte[] dataBuf = {'h', 'i', ' ', 't', 'h', 'e', 'r', 'e'};
InetAddress addr = InetAddress.getByName("my.host.com");
DatagramPacket p =
    new DatagramPacket(dataBuf, dataBuf.length, addr, 5000);
udpSocket.send(p);
```

The remote process can receive the data in the form of a `DatagramPacket` by calling the `receive()` method on its `DatagramSocket`. The received `Data-gramPacket` will have the host address and port of the sender filled in as a side-effect of the call.

Note that in all of the examples, we would have to catch the appropriate exceptions and handle them. Sending a `DatagramPacket`, for example, can generate an `IOException` if the network transmission fails for some reason. A robust networked program will catch this exception and behave appropriately, perhaps by resending the packet if the application warrants, or perhaps by simply noting the lost packet and continuing.

Multicast Sockets

There is a subset of the IP protocol that supports *multicasting*. Multicasting can be thought of as broadcasting data over a network connection to many connected agents, as opposed to unicasting packets between two agents on a normal connection. Multicasting is done using UDP packets that are broadcast out on a multicast IP address. Any agent "listening in" to that IP address will receive the data packets that are broadcast. The analogy to radio and television broadcasting is no accident—the very first practical uses of multicast IP were for broadcasting audio and video over the Internet from special events.[*]

Java supports multicast IP through the `java.net.MulticastSocket` class, which is an extension of the `DatagramSocket` class. Joining a multicast group is done almost the same way that you would establish a UDP connection between two agents. Each agent that wants to listen on the multicast address creates a `MulticastSocket` and then joins the multicast session by calling the `join-Group()` method on the `MulticastSocket`:

```
MulticastSocket ms = new MulticastSocket();
InetAddress sessAddr = InetAddress.getByName("224.2.76.24");
ms.joinGroup(sessAddr);
```

Once the connection to the multicast session is established, the agent can read data being broadcast on the multicast "channel":

```
byte[] audioBuf = new byte[1024];
DatagramPacket dp = new DatagramPacket(audioBuf, 1024);
ms.receive(dp);
// Play the data on a fictitious audio device
myAudioDevice.play(dp.getData());
```

Data can also be sent out on the multicast channel to all the other listening agents using the `send()` method on the `MulticastSocket`.

Once the broadcast is over, or we simply want to stop listening, we can disconnect from the session using the `leaveGroup()` method:

```
ms.leaveGroup(sessAddr);
```

Multicasting is useful when we want to connect many agents together on a common communication channel. Shared audio and video channels are the most

---

[*] For more information on the history of the multicast backbone (MBONE) and its current state, visit *http://www.mbone.com/*.

obvious uses, but multicasting can also be applied in collaborative tools like shared whiteboards, or between application servers performing synchronization tasks, like load balancing. However, since multicast IP is based on UDP, you have to be willing to accept the possibility of losing some data along the way, and dealing with it gracefully. Also, since clients can join a multicast session asynchronously, they have to be ready to synchronize themselves with the current state of the multicast session when they join.

Streams, Readers, and Writers for Input and Output

Once we make a connection between two processes over the network, we need a simple, easy way to send and receive data in different formats over the connection. Java provides this through the stream classes in the `java.io` package. Included in the `java.io` package are the `InputStream` and `OutputStream` classes and their subclasses for byte-based I/O, and the `Reader` and `Writer` classes and their subclasses for character-based I/O. The `InputStream` and `OutputStream` classes handle data as bytes, with basic methods for reading and writing bytes and byte arrays. Their subclasses can connect to various sources and destinations (files, string buffers), and provide methods for directly sending and receiving basic Java data types, like floating-point values. The `Reader` and `Writer` classes transmit data in the form of 16-bit Unicode characters, which provides a platform-independent way to send and receive textual data. Like the `InputStream` and `OutputStream` subclasses, the subclasses of `Reader` and `Writer` specialize in terms of their source and destination types.

A `Socket`, once it's created, can be queried for its input/output streams using `getInputStream()` and `getOutputStream()`. These methods return instances of `InputStream` and `OutputStream`, respectively. If you need to exchange mostly character-based data between two agents in your distributed system, then you can wrap the `InputStream` with an `InputStreamReader` (a subclass of `Reader`), or the `OutputStream` with an `OutputStreamWriter` (a subclass of `Writer`).

Another way to create an interprocess communication link is to use the `java.lang.Runtime` interface to execute a process, then obtain the input and output streams from the returned `Process` object, as shown in Example 2-1. You would do this if you had a local subtask that needed to run in a separate process, but with which you still needed to exchange messages.

Example 2-1. Interprocess I/O Using Runtime-Executed Processes

```
Runtime r = Runtime.getRuntime();
Process p = r.exec("/bin/ls /tmp");
InputStream in = p.getInputStream();
OutputStream out = p.getOutputStream();
```

From the abstract I/O classes, the `java.io` package offers several specializations which vary the format of the data transmitted over the stream, as well as the type of data source/receiver at the ends of the stream. The `InputStream`, `Output-Stream`, `Reader`, and `Writer` classes provide basic interfaces for data I/O (`read()` and `write()` methods that just transfer bytes, byte arrays, characters and character arrays). To define data types and communication protocols on top of these base classes, Java offers the `FilterInputStream` and `FilterOutput-Stream` classes for byte-oriented I/O, and the `FilterReader` and `FilterWriter` for character-based I/O. Subclasses of these offer a higher level of control and structure to the data transfers. A `BufferedInputStream` or `BufferedReader` uses a memory buffer for efficient reading of data. The over-head associated with data read requests is minimized by performing large data reads into a buffer, and offering data to the caller from the local buffer until it's been exhausted. This feature can be used to minimize the latency associated with slow source devices and communication media. The `BufferedOutputStream` or `BufferedWriter` performs the same service on outgoing data. A `Pushback-InputStream` or `PushbackReader` provides a buffer for pushing back data onto the incoming data stream. This is useful in parsing applications, where the next branch in the parse tree is determined by peeking at the next few bytes or characters in the stream, and then letting the subparser operate on the data. The other interesting subclasses of `FilterInputStream` and `FilterOutput-Stream` are the `DataInputStream` and `DataOutputStream` classes. These classes read and write Java data primitives in a portable binary format. There aren't similar subclasses of `FilterReader` and `FilterWriter`, since `Readers` and `Writers` only transfer character data, and the serialized form of Java data types are represented in bytes.

Besides being useful in their own right for manipulating and formatting input/output data streams, the subclasses of `FilterInputStream`, `Filter-OutputStream`, `FilterReader`, and `FilterWriter` are also well suited for further specialization to define application-specific data stream protocols. Each of the stream classes offers a constructor method, which accepts an `InputStream` or `OutputStream` as an argument. Likewise, the `FilterReader` class has a constructor that accepts a `Reader`, and `FilterWriter` has a constructor that accepts a `Writer` object. In each case, the constructor argument is taken as the source or sink of the stream that is to be filtered, which enables the construction of stream filter "pipelines." So defining a special-purpose data protocol is simply a matter of subclassing from an appropriate I/O class, and wrapping an existing data source or sink with the new filter.

For example, if we wanted to read an XDR-formatted* data stream, we could write a subclass of `FilterInputStream` that would offer the same methods to read Java primitive data types as `DataInputStream`, but would be implemented to parse the XDR format, rather than the portable binary format of the `DataInput-Stream`. Example 2-2 shows a skeleton for the input version of this kind of stream; Example 2-3 shows a sample application using the stream. The application first connects to a host and port, where presumably another process is waiting to accept this connection. The remote process uses XDR-formatted data to communicate, so we wrap the input stream from the socket connection with our `XDRInputStream` and begin reading data.

Example 2-2. An InputStream Subclass for Reading XDR-Formatted Data

```
package dcj.examples;

import java.io.*;
import java.net.*;

class XDRInputStream extends FilterInputStream {
  public XDRInputStream(InputStream in) {
    super(in);
  }

  // Overridden methods from FilterInputStream, implemented
  // to read XDR-formatted data

  public boolean readBoolean() throws IOException;
  public byte    readByte() throws IOException;
  public int     readUnsignedByte() thows IOException;
  public float   readFloat() thows IOException;
  // Other readXXX() methods omitted in this example...

  // We'll assume this stream doesn't support mark/reset operations

  public boolean markSupported() { return false; }
}
```

Example 2-3. Example XDRInputStream Client

```
import dcj.examples.XDRInputStream;
import java.io.*;

class XDRInputExample
{
  public static void main(String argv[])
    {
```

---

* XDR is the binary format underlying Remote Procedure Call (RPC) data connections.

Example 2-3. Example XDRInputStream Client (continued)

```
    String host = argv[0];

    // Default port is 5001
    int port = 5001;

    try
      {
        port = Integer.parseInt(argv[1]);
      }
    catch (NumberFormatException e)
      {
        System.out.println("Bad port number given, using default "
                           + port);
      }

    // Try connecting to specified host and port
    Socket serverConn = null;
    try { serverConn = new Socket(host, port); }
    catch (UnknownHostException e)
      {
        System.out.println("Bad host name given.");
        System.exit(1);
      }

    // Wrap an XDR stream around the input stream
    XDRInputStream xin = new XDRInputStream(serverConn.getInputStream());

    // Start reading expected data from XDR-formatted stream
    int numVals = xin.readInt();
    float val1 = xin.readFloat();
    ...
  }
}
```

The classes in the `java.io` package also offer the ability to specialize the sources and destinations of data. Table 2-1 summarizes the various stream, writer, and reader classes in `java.io`, and the types of sources and destinations that they can access. The purpose and use of the file, byte-array, and string classes are fairly obvious, and we won't spend any time going into detail about them here, since we'll see them being used in some of the examples later in the book. The stream classes that allow communication between threads deserve some explanation, though.

The `PipedInputStream` and `PipedOutputStream` classes access data from each other. That is, a `PipedInputStream` reads data from a `PipedOutput-Stream`, and a `PipedOutputStream` writes data to a `PipedInputStream`.

Table 2-1. Source and Destination Types Supported by java.io

Source/Destination Type	Input/OutputStream Class	Reader/Writer Class

Remote or local process	`InputStream`
	`OutputStream`
	(created from `Socket` or from `Process`)
		`InputStreamReader`
		`OutputStreamWriter`
		(wrappers around `InputStream` or `OutputStream` objects)

Disk files	`FileInputStream` `FileOutputStream`	`FileReader` `FileWriter`
In-memory data buffers	`ByteArrayInputStream` `ByteArrayOutputStream`	`CharArrayReader` `CharArrayWriter`
In-memory string buffers	`StringBufferInputStream` (input only) (deprecated in JDK 1.1, use `StringReader` instead)	`StringReader` `StringWriter`
Threads within same process	`PipedInputStream` `PipedOutputStream`	`PipedReader` `PipedWriter`

This class design allows the developer to establish data pipes between threads in the same process. Example 2-4 and Example 2-5 show client and server classes that use piped streams to transfer information, and Example 2-6 shows an application of these classes.

Example 2-4. A Piped Client

```
package dcj.examples;

import java.lang.*;
import java.net.*;
import java.io.*;
import java.util.*;

public class PipedClient extends Thread
{
  PipedInputStream pin;
  PipedOutputStream pout;

  public PipedClient(PipedInputStream in, PipedOutputStream out)
  {
    pin = in;
    pout = out;
  }

  public void run()
  {
    // Wrap a data stream around the input and output streams
    DataInputStream din = new DataInputStream(pin);
```

Example 2-4. A Piped Client (continued)

```
DataOutputStream dout = new DataOutputStream(pout);

// Say hello to the server...
try
  {
    System.out.println("PipedClient: Writing greeting to server...");
    dout.writeChars("hello from PipedClient\n");
  }
catch (IOException e)
  {
    System.out.println("PipedClient: Couldn't get response.");
    System.exit(1);
  }

// See if it says hello back...
try
  {
    System.out.println("PipedClient: Reading response from server...");
    String response = din.readLine();
    System.out.println("PipedClient: Server said: \""
                           + response + "\"");
  }
catch (IOException e)
  {
    System.out.println("PipedClient: Failed to connect to peer.");
  }

stop();
  }
}
```

The example shows two threads, a client and a server, talking to each other over
piped streams. The `PipedClient` class accepts a `PipedInputStream` and
`PipedOutputStream` as constructor arguments; the `PipedServer` class does
the same. Both are extensions of the `Thread` class. The client attempts to send a
"hello" message to the server over its output stream, then listens for a response on
its input stream. The server listens for the "hello" from the client on its input
stream, then sends a response back on its output stream. The `PipedStreamEx-
ample` class sets up the stream connections for the threads by creating two pairs
of piped streams. It then creates a `PipedClient` and a `PipedServer`, sends
each the input stream from one pair and the output stream from the other, and
tells each of them to start their threads. The important feature of this example is
that the piped streams are connected to each other within the same process, and
are not connected to any remote hosts.

Example 2-5. A Piped Server

```
package dcj.examples;

import java.lang.*;
import java.net.*;
import java.io.*;

public class PipedServer extends Thread
{
  PipedInputStream pin;
  PipedOutputStream pout;

  public PipedServer(PipedInputStream in, PipedOutputStream out)
  {
    pin = in;
    pout = out;
  }

  public void run()
  {
    // Wrap a data stream around the input and output streams
    DataInputStream din = new DataInputStream(pin);
    DataOutputStream dout = new DataOutputStream(pout);

    // Wait for the client to say hello...
    try
      {
        System.out.println("PipedServer: Reading from client...");
        String clientHello = din.readLine();
        System.out.println("PipedServer: Client said: \""
                           + clientHello + "\"");
      }
    catch (IOException e)
      {
        System.out.println("PipedServer: Couldn't get hello from client.");
        stop();
      }

    // ...and say hello back.
    try
      {
        System.out.println("PipedServer: Writing response to client...");
        dout.writeChars("hello I am the server.\n");
      }
    catch (IOException e)
      {
        System.out.println("PipedServer: Failed to connect to client.");
      }
    stop();
```

Example 2-5. A Piped Server (continued)

```
  }
}
```

Example 2-6. Piped Stream Application

```
package dcj.examples;

import java.net.*;
import java.io.*;
import java.lang.*;

import dcj.examples.PipedClient;
import dcj.examples.PipedServer;

class PipedStreamExample {
  public static void main(String argv[]) {
    // Make two pairs of connected piped streams
    PipedInputStream pinc = null;
    PipedInputStream pins = null;
    PipedOutputStream poutc = null;
    PipedOutputStream pouts = null;

    try {
      pinc = new PipedInputStream();
      pins = new PipedInputStream();
      poutc = new PipedOutputStream(pins);
      pouts = new PipedOutputStream(pinc);
    }
    catch (IOException e) {
      System.out.println(
        "PipedStreamExample: Failed to build piped streams.");
      System.exit(1);
    }

    // Make the client and server threads, connected by the streams
    PipedClient pc = new PipedClient(pinc, poutc);
    PipedServer ps = new PipedServer(pins, pouts);

    // Start the threads
    System.out.println("Starting server...");
    ps.start();
    System.out.println("Starting client...");
    pc.start();

    // Wait for threads to end
    try {
      ps.join();
      pc.join();
```

Example 2-6. Piped Stream Application (continued)

```
    }
    catch (InterruptedException e) {}

    System.exit(0);
  }
}
```

Note that a similar scenario could be set up using the `PipedReader` and `PipedWriter` classes, if you knew the two threads were going to exchange character arrays.

URLs, URLConnections, and ContentHandlers

The `java.net` package, in addition to object-oriented representations of IP sockets, also provides objects that support the HTTP protocol for accessing data in the form of addressable documents. HTTP is really an extension of the underlying IP protocol we discussed earlier, designed specifically to provide a way to address different kinds of documents, or pieces of data, distributed on the network. In the rest of this book, we'll see numerous examples of distributed applications whose agents use customized or standard communications protocols to talk to each other. If there is an HTTP server "agent" available on one of the hosts in our distributed application, then we can use the classes discussed in this section to ask it for data documents using the standard HTTP protocol.

To address a specific document or data object, we use a Uniform Resource Locator (URL), which includes four address elements: the protocol, host, port, and document. The Java representation for a URL is the URL class, which is constructed with a given protocol, host, port, and document filename. Once the URL object is constructed, it allows the user to make the necessary requests to connect to the HTTP server of the data object, query for information about the object, and download the object. The content of the object can be accessed using the `getContent()`, `openConnection()`, or `openStream()` methods on the URL object. Of these three methods, `openStream()` is simplest. The `openStream()` method returns an `InputStream` that can be used to read the data contents directly.

When you call `openConnection()` on a URL object, you get a `URLConnection` in return. You can use the `URLConnection` to query the data connection's header information for the data object's length, the type of data it contains, the data encoding, etc. You can also control aspects of the data connection that determine when the data object can be pulled from a local cache, whether input or output is to be done over the data connection, and when unmodified data should be read from the server.

The `getContent()` method downloads the data object and returns an `Object` containing the data. Using this method relies upon having a content handler that supports the object's data format and is capable of converting it into a Java object. The `java.net` package allows you to extend the available content handlers using the `ContentHandler` and `ContentHandlerFactory` classes. A `ContentHandler` accepts a `URLConnection`, reads the data from the associated data object, and constructs an appropriate `Object` instance to represent the data object in the Java environment. It is the job of the system-wide `ContentHandlerFactory` to associate the proper `ContentHandler` with each data object referenced by a URL. When `getContent()` is called on a URL or `URLConnection` object, the `ContentHandlerFactory` is queried for a `ContentHandler` that can read the format of the data at the other end of the connection. The `ContentHandlerFactory` checks the MIME type and encoding of the data object, and returns a `ContentHandler` for that MIME type. The `ContentHandler` that's returned is then asked for an `Object` representing the data by calling its `getContent()` method with the `URLConnection`. Typically, the `ContentHandler` reads the raw data from the `URLConnection`'s `InputStream`, formats the data into an appropriate object representation, and returns the object to the caller.

Suppose we want to connect to an HTTP server containing computational fluid dynamics (CFD) data files stored in a proprietary format. Suppose these data files have a ".cfd" suffix, and we decide to reserve the MIME type "application/cfd" for these data files. Now, assuming that the HTTP server has been properly configured to export this MIME type in the content headers its transmits, we can use Java's HTTP support to access these data files from our application by creating our own `ContentHandler` subclass that is capable of reading the data stream and converting it to an appropriate Java object. Example 2-7 shows a CFDContentHandler that does just this. Its `getContent()` method creates a `CFDDataSet` object from the data read from the input stream of the `URLConnection` argument. It assumes that the incoming data is of the expected type and format for the `CFDDataSet`; a more robust implementation would check the MIME type of the `URLConnection` and warn the user if the type doesn't match.

Example 2-7. A ContentHandler for CFD File

```
import java.net.*;
import dcj.examples.Networking.CFDDataSet;

public class CFDContentHandler extends ContentHandler {
```

Example 2-7. A ContentHandler for CFD File (continued)

```
  public Object getContent(URLConnection u) {
    CFDDataSet d = new CFDDataSet();
    try {
      InputStream in = u.getInputStream();
      byte[] buffer = new byte[1024];
      while (in.read(buffer) > 0) {
        d.addData(buffer);
      }
    }
    catch (Exception e) {
      e.printStackTrace();
    }

    return d;
  }
}
```

To use our `CFDContentHandler` to read CFD files, we still need to register a new `ContentHandlerFactory` that knows about the `CFDContentHandler`. The `CFDContentHandlerFactory` in Example 2-8 creates `CFDContent-Handlers` for the `application/cfd` MIME type. It ignores any other MIME types, but we could also implement it with a reference to a default `ContentHandlerFactory` that can handle other MIME types.

Example 2-8. A Specialized ContentHandlerFactory for CFD Data Files

```
package dcj.examples.Networking;

import java.net.*;

public class CFDContentHandlerFactory
    implements ContentHandlerFactory {
  public ContentHandler createContentHandler(String mimetype) {
    if (mimetype.compareTo("application/cfd") == 0) {
      return new CFDContentHandler();
    }
    else
      return null;
  }
}
```

Finally, our application can read CFD data files from an HTTP server by first registering the specialized `ContentHandlerFactory`, and then requesting a CFD file from the HTTP server on which it lives:

```
URLConnection.setContentHandlerFactory(new CFDContentHandlerFactory());
URL cfdURL = new URL("http://my.data.server/datasets/bigset.cfd");
CFDDataSet data = (CFDDataSet)cfdURL.getContent();
```

When and Where Are URLs Practical?

As we've seen in earlier sections of this chapter, we can transmit data around a distributed system using sockets and streams. This method has the advantage of being efficient, since we are using basic IP sockets with minimal protocol overhead getting between us and our data. The downside is that it is our responsibility to know the type and format of the data we're transmitting and receiving. The communication protocol must be mutually agreed upon by all participating computing agents, or we have to establish our own means for communicating metadata about the kind of information with which we are dealing.

Java's HTTP support classes, on the other hand, provide a standard means for serving and accessing data objects, and for easily identifying the type and format of these objects. To make a piece of data available from a URL, we need to install it in the content section of an HTTP server, and configure the server to transmit the appropriate MIME type when the data is accessed. On the receiving end, we simply need to use the data object's URL to access the document, ask the corresponding `URLConnection` for the type and encoding of the data, and respond accordingly. The downside is that HTTP imposes plenty of protocol overhead on the data stream, which reduces our net data bandwidth between computing agents. Our data is now sharing space in network packets with IP protocol *and* HTTP protocol. Another downside is the relatively basic and simplistic resource naming facility that HTTP provides, compared to formal directory naming services like NIS and LDAP. The simple conclusion is that, for distributed applications that are severely bandwidth-limited, or that need to support complicated resource hierarchies, using the HTTP protocol to access data is probably not the appropriate method. On the other hand, if you have the luxury of some extra communications bandwidth, and the CPU time to use it, and your resource groupings are relatively simple, then using URLs to access data is a possibility you should consider.

The ClassLoader

The Java runtime environment is based upon a virtual machine that interprets, verifies, and executes classes in the form of platform-independent bytecodes. In addition, the Java API includes a mechanism for you to load class definitions in their bytecode form, and integrate them into the runtime environment so that instances of the classes can be constructed and used. When your Java files are compiled, a similar mechanism is invoked whenever an `import` statement is encountered. The referenced class or package of classes is loaded from files in bytecode format, using the CLASSPATH environment variable to locate them on the local file system.

In addition to this default policy for loading classes, the `java.lang.Class-Loader` class allows the user to define custom policies and mechanisms for locating and loading classes into the runtime environment. The `ClassLoader` is an abstract class. Subclasses must define an implementation for the `load-Class()` method, which is responsible for locating the class based upon the given string name, loading the bytecodes comprising the class definition, and (optionally) resolving the class. A class has to be resolved before it can be constructed or before any of its methods can be called. Resolving a class includes finding all of the other classes that it depends on, and loading them into the runtime as well.

The `ClassLoader` is an important element of the network support in the Java API. It's used as the basis for supporting Java applets in most Java-enabled web browsers, for example. When an HTML page includes an `APPLET` tag that references a Java class on the HTTP server, a `ClassLoader` instance within the browser's Java runtime is used to load the bytecodes of the class into the virtual machine, create an instance of the class, and then execute methods on the new object. Note that this is different from the concept of distributing *objects* using RMI or CORBA. Rather than creating an object on one host and allowing a process on a remote host to call methods on that object, the `ClassLoader` lets an agent read the bytecodes making up a class definition, and then create an object within its own process. In the rest of this section we'll look at how we can directly use the `ClassLoader` interface to distribute *classes* in a network environment.

Loading Classes from the Network

Now, in looking at the overall object model defined by the Java API, we can think of the `java.lang.ClassLoader` class as an abstract interface for the loading of classes into the runtime environment, and the `java.io.InputStream` class as the basis for loading data into the runtime environment from different sources and in different formats. An obvious next step would seem to be to put them together, and form the basis for loading classes from all of the sources accessible from subclasses of `InputStream`. So that's just what we've done, and the result is the `StreamClassLoader` shown in Example 2-9.

Example 2-9. A Network ClassLoader

```
package dcj.util;

import java.lang.*;
import java.net.*;
import java.io.*;
import java.util.Hashtable;
```

Example 2-9. A Network ClassLoader (continued)

```
public abstract class StreamClassLoader extends ClassLoader
{
  // Instance variables and default initializations
  Hashtable classCache = new Hashtable();
  InputStream source = null;

  // Constructor
  public StreamClassLoader()
  { }

  // Parse a class name from a class locator (URL, filename, etc.)
  protected abstract String parseClassName(String classLoc)
    throws ClassNotFoundException;

  // Initialize the input stream from a class locator
  protected abstract void    initStream(String classLoc)
    throws IOException;

  // Read a class from the input stream
  protected abstract Class    readClass(String classLoc, String className)
    throws IOException, ClassNotFoundException;

  // Implement the ClassLoader loadClass() method.
  // First argument is now interpreted as a class locator, rather than
  // simply a class name.
  public Class loadClass(String classLoc, boolean resolve)
    throws ClassNotFoundException
    {
      String className = parseClassName(classLoc);
      Class c = (Class)classCache.get(className);

      // If class is not in cache...
      if (c == null)
        {
          // ...try initializing our stream to its location
          try { initStream(classLoc); }
          catch (IOException e)
            {
              throw new ClassNotFoundException(
                      "Failed opening stream to URL.");
            }

          // Read the class from the input stream
          try { c = readClass(classLoc, className); }
          catch (IOException e)
            {
              throw new ClassNotFoundException(
```

Example 2-9. A Network ClassLoader (continued)

```
                        "Failed reading class from stream: " + e);
        }
    }

    // Add the new class to the cache for the next reference.
    // Note that we cache based on the class name, not locator.
    classCache.put(className, c);

    // Resolve the class, if requested.
    if (resolve)
      resolveClass(c);

    return c;
    }
}
```

The abstract `StreamClassLoader` class provides a generic interface for implementing and using stream-based class loaders. It accomplishes this in part by changing the semantics of the string argument to the `loadClass()` method on `ClassLoader`. Whereas `ClassLoader` defines this argument as the name of the class being sought, the `StreamClassLoader` broadens the definition to include class "locators" in general. A class locator may be a URL, a host/port/file-name combination, or some other means for addressing a class located on the network, or anywhere else accessible via an input stream. Subclasses of `Stream-ClassLoader` must define the class locator format they expect, by implementing the `parseClassName()` method.

The other element of the `StreamClassLoader` framework is an implementation of `loadClass()` which allows subclasses to initialize and read their input streams to bring the requested class into the local environment. If the class locator string is successfully parsed by `parseClassName()`, then the `Stream-ClassLoader` calls `initStream()`, passing the class locator. This method should attempt to initialize the stream to the class specified by the locator. If successful, the `StreamClassLoader` next calls its `readClass()` method, passing the class locator and class name. This returns the newly constructed `Class` object, which is then optionally resolved and returned to the caller.

To demonstrate a practical extension of the `StreamClassLoader`, Example 2-10 shows a `URLClassLoader`, which loads classes that are located at URLs on HTTP servers. In this case, a class locator is expected to be in the form of a valid URL. The `URLClassLoader` utilizes the `URL` and `URLConnection` classes to implement the `parseClassName()`, `initStream()`, and `read-Class()` methods, as you might expect.

Example 2-10. A URL-based ClassLoader

```java
package dcj.util;

import java.lang.*;
import java.net.*;
import java.io.*;
import java.util.Hashtable;

public class URLClassLoader extends StreamClassLoader
{
  URL classURL = null;
  InputStream classStream = null;

  protected String parseClassName(String classLoc)
     throws ClassNotFoundException
  {
    String className = null;

    // Try constructing a URL around the class locator
    try { classURL = new URL(classLoc); }
    catch (MalformedURLException e)
      {
        throw new ClassNotFoundException("Bad URL \"" + classLoc +
                                     "\" given: " + e);
      }

    System.out.println("File = " + classURL.getFile());
    System.out.println("Host = " + classURL.getHost());

    // Get the file name from the URL
    String filename = classURL.getFile();

    // Make sure we're referencing a class file, then parse the class name
    if (! filename.endsWith(".class"))
      throw new ClassNotFoundException("Non-class URL given.");
    else
      className = filename.substring(0, filename.lastIndexOf(".class"));

    System.out.println("Classname = " + className);

    return className;
  }

  protected void initStream(String classLoc) throws IOException
  {
    // Ask the URL to open a stream to the class object
    classStream = classURL.openStream();
  }
```

Example 2-10. A URL-based ClassLoader (continued)

```
protected Class readClass(String classLoc, String className)
    throws IOException, ClassNotFoundException
{
  // See how large the class file is...
  URLConnection conn = classURL.openConnection();
  int classSize = conn.getContentLength();
  System.out.println("Class file is " + classSize + " bytes.");

  // Read the class bytecodes from the stream
  DataInputStream dataIn = new DataInputStream(classStream);
  int avail = dataIn.available();
  System.out.println("Available = " + avail);
  System.out.println("URLClassLoader: Reading class from stream...");
  byte[] classData = new byte[classSize];
  dataIn.readFully(classData);

  // Parse the class definition from the bytecodes
  Class c = null;
  System.out.println("URLClassLoader: Defining class...");
  try { c = defineClass(classData, 0, classData.length); }
  catch (ClassFormatError e)
    {
      throw new ClassNotFoundException(
        "Format error found in class data.");
    }

  return c;
}
}
```

The parseClassName() implementation attempts to construct a URL object from the class locator. If an exception is raised, then an invalid URL has been passed in, and a ClassNotFoundException is thrown by the method. If the URL is successfully constructed, it is queried for the file name portion of the URL. The file suffix is checked to ensure that a ".class" file is being referenced, then the base of the file name is returned as the class name. The initStream() implementation simply calls openStream() on the URL object constructed from the class locator. If an IOException results, it is allowed to propagate up the call stack to loadClass(), which assumes that the class file addressed by the URL is inaccessible, and throws a ClassNotFoundException. Finally, the read-Class() method reads the class bytecodes into a buffer by calling readFully() on the InputStream from the URL. An IOException will be allowed to propagate up to loadClass(), which throws a ClassNotFound-Exception. After successfully reading the bytecodes, readClass() next calls defineClass() to parse the class definition into a Class object, which is returned to the caller. If `defineClass()` generates a `ClassFormatError`, then a `ClassNotFoundException` is thrown, which `loadClass()` allows to propagate to the caller. Although catching an error, as opposed to an exception, goes against Java design doctrine, in this particular situation it may be a useful thing to do. Notice, however, that we've chosen to "convert" the error into a `ClassNotFoundException`. By doing this, we're saying that a format error in the loaded class should be considered as a missing class in the next level up the call stack.

We could implement other subclasses of the `StreamClassLoader` that use other network protocols to import Java bytecodes into the local runtime. This, however, is left as an exercise for the reader.* We should note here that a Java-enabled browser uses something like our `URLClassLoader` to load classes for applets referenced in Web pages. A relative or absolute URL referring to a main applet class is passed to a network class loader, which does something along the lines of what happens in our `readClass()` method.

---

* :)

3

Distributing Objects

Distributed objects are a potentially powerful tool that has only become broadly available for developers at large in the past few years. The power of distributing objects is not in the fact that a bunch of objects are scattered across the network. The power lies in that any agent in your system can directly interact with an object that "lives" on a remote host. Distributed objects, if they're done right, really give you a tool for opening up your distributed system's resources across the board. And with a good distributed object scheme you can do this as precisely or as broadly as you'd like.

The first three sections of this chapter go over the motivations for distributing objects, what makes distributed object systems so useful, and what makes up a "good" distributed object system. Readers who are already familiar with basic distributed object issues can skip these sections and go on to the following sections, where we discuss two major distributed object protocols that are available in the Java environment: CORBA and RMI.

Although this chapter will cover the use of both RMI and CORBA for distributing objects, the rest of the book primarily uses examples that are based on RMI, where distributed objects are needed. We chose to do this because RMI is a simpler API and lets us write relatively simple examples that still demonstrate useful concepts, without getting bogged down in CORBA API specifics. Some of the examples, if converted to be used in production environments, might be better off implemented in CORBA.

Why Distribute Objects?

In Chapter 1, we discussed some of the optimal data/function partitioning capabilities that you'd like to have available when developing distributed applications. These included being able to distribute data/function "modules" freely and transparently, and have these modules be defined based on application structure rather than network distribution influences. Distributed object systems try to address these issues by letting developers take their programming objects and have them "run" on a remote host rather than the local host. The goal of most distributed object systems is to let any object reside anywhere on the network, and allow an application to interact with these objects exactly the same way as they do with a local object. Additional features found in some distributed object schemes are the ability to construct an object on one host and transmit it to another host, and the ability for an agent on one host to create a new object on another host.

The value of distributed objects is more obvious in larger, more complicated applications than in smaller, simpler ones. That's because much of the trade-off between distributed objects and other techniques, like message passing, is between simplicity and robustness. In a smaller application with just a few object types and critical operations, it's not difficult to put together a catalog of simple messages that would let remote agents perform all of their critical operation through on-line transactions. With a larger application, this catalog of messages gets complicated and difficult to maintain. It's also more difficult to extend a large message-passing system if new objects and operations are added. So being able to distribute the objects in our system directly saves us a lot of design overhead, and makes a large distributed system easier to maintain in the long run.

What's So Tough About Distributing Objects?

OK, so we think distributing objects is a good idea, but why do distributed object systems like CORBA and, to a lesser degree, Java RMI, seem so big and complicated? In Chapter 2 we saw how the core Java API, especially the `java.net` and `java.io` packages, gives us easy access to the network and key network protocols. They also let us layer application-specific operations on top of the network pretty easily. It seems like all that we'd need to do is extend these packages to allow objects to invoke each other's methods over the network, and we'd have a basic distributed object system. To get a feeling for the complexity of distributed object systems, let's look at what it would take to put together one of our own using just the core Java API, without utilizing the RMI package or the object input/output streams in the `java.io` package.

Creating Remote Objects

The essential requirements in a distributed object system are the ability to create or invoke objects on a remote host or process, and interact with them as if they were objects within our own process. It seems logical that we would need some kind of message protocol for sending requests to remote agents to create new objects, to invoke methods on these objects, and to delete the objects when we're done with them. As we saw in Chapter 2, the networking support in the Java API makes it very easy to implement a message protocol. But what kinds of things does a message protocol have to do if it's supporting a distributed object system?

To create a remote object, we need to reference a class, provide constructor arguments for the class, and receive a reference to the created object in return. This object reference will be used to invoke methods on the object, and eventually to ask the remote agent to destroy the object when we are done with it. So the data we will need to send over the network include *class references*, *object references*, *method references*, and *method arguments*.

The first item is easy—we already saw in Chapter 2 how the `ClassLoader` can be used to send class definitions over the network. If we want to create a new remote object from a given class, we can send the class definition to the remote host, and tell it to build one using a default constructor. Object references require some thought, though. These are not the same as local Java object references. We need to have an object reference that we can package up and send over the network, i.e., one that's *serializable*. This object reference, once we receive it, will still need to refer back to the original object on the remote host, so that when we call methods on it the method invocations are deferred to the "source" object on the remote host. One simple way to implement remote object references is to build an object lookup table into the remote agent. When a client requests a new object, the remote agent builds the requested object, puts the object into the table, and sends the table index of the object to the client. If we use sockets and streams to send requests and object references back and forth between remote agents, a client might request a remote object with something like this:

```
Class myClass = Class.forName("Myclass");
Socket objConn = new Socket("object.server.net", 1234);
OutputStreamWriter out =
    new ObjectStreamWriter(objConn.getOutputStream());
DataInputStream in = new DataInputStream(objConn.getInputStream());

out.write("new " + myClass.getName());
int objRef = in.readInt();
```

The integer `objRef` returned by the remote server can be used to reference the new remote object. On the other end of the socket, the agent receiving the request for the remote object may handle the request like this:

```
Hashtable objTable = new Hashtable();
ServerSocket server = ...;
Socket conn;
// Accept the connection from the client
if ((conn = server.accept()) != null) {
    DataOutputStream out =
        new DataObjectStream(conn.getOutputStream());
    BufferedReader in = new BufferedReader(
        new InputStreamReader(conn.getInputStream()));
    String cmd = in.readLine();
    // Parse the command type from the command string
    if (parseCmd(cmd).compareTo("new") == 0) {
        // The client wants a new object created,
        // so parse the class name from the command string
        String classname = parseClass(cmd);
        // Create the Class object and make an instance
        Class reqClass = Class.forName(classname);
        Object obj = reqClass.newInstance();
        // Register the object and return the integer
        // identifier/reference to the client
        Integer objID = nextID();
        objTable.put(objID, obj);
        out.writeInt(objID.intValue());
    }
}
```

The object server reads the class name sent by the requestor, looks up the class using the static `Class.forName()` method, and creates a new instance of the class by calling the `newInstance()` method on the `Class` object. Once the object has been created, the server generates a unique identifier for the object and sends it back to the requestor. Note that we've already limited our remote object scheme, by forcing the use of default constructors, e.g., those with no arguments. The remote host creates the requested object by calling `newInstance()` on its class, which is equivalent to creating the object by calling the class constructor with no arguments. Since we don't (yet) have a way to specify methods on classes over the network, or a way to send arguments to these methods, we have to live with this limitation for now.

Remote Method Calls

Now that the requestor has a reference to an object on the remote host, it needs a way to invoke methods on the object. Since Java, as of JDK 1.1, allows us to query a class or object for its declared methods and data members, the local agent can get a direct reference to the method that it wants to invoke on the remote object, in the form of a `Method` object:

```
Class reqClass = Class.forName("Myclass");
Method reqMethod = reqClass.getDeclaredMethod("getName", null);
```

In this example, the local agent has retrieved a reference to a `getName()` method, with no arguments, on the class `Myclass`. It could now use this method reference to call the method on a local `Myclass` instance:

```
Myclass obj = new Myclass();
reqMethod.invoke(obj, null);
```

This may seem like a roundabout way to accomplish the same thing as calling `obj.getName()` on the `Myclass` object, and it is. But in order to call a method on our remote object, we need to send a reference to the method over the network to the remote host. One way to do this is to assign identifiers to all of the methods on the class, just like we did for remote objects. Since both the object requestor and the object server can get a list of the class's methods by calling the `getDeclaredMethods()` method on the class, we could simply use the index of the method in the returned list as its identifier. Then the object requestor can call a method on a remote object by simply sending the remote host the object's identifier, and the identifier for the method to call. Assuming that our local agent has the same object reference from the earlier example, the remote method call would look something like this:

```
Method reqMethod = reqClass.getDeclaredMethod("getName", null);
Method[] methodList = reqClass.getDeclaredMethods();
int methodIdx = 0;
for (int i = 0; i < methodList.length; i++) {
    if (reqMethod == methodList[i]) {
        methodIdx = i;
        break;
    }
}
String cmd = "call " + methodIdx + " on " + objRef;
out.writeUTF(cmd);
```

This approach to handling remote method invocation is a general one; it will work for any class that we want to distribute. So far so good. But what about the arguments to the remote methods? And what about the return value from the remote method? Our example used a `getName()` method with no arguments, but if the method does take arguments, we'll need to send these to the remote host as well. We can also assume that a method called "getName" will probably return some kind of `String` value, which we'll need to get back from the remote host. This same problem exists in the creation of the remote object. With our method reference scheme we can now specify which constructor to use when the remote host creates our object, but we still need a way to send the constructor arguments to the remote host.

By now this exercise is beginning to look a lot more serious than we might have expected. In distributed object systems, the task of packaging up method arguments for delivery to the remote object, and the task of gathering up method return values for the client, are referred to as *data marshaling*. One approach we can take to data marshaling is to turn every object argument in a remote method call into a remote object just like we did previously, by generating an object reference and sending that to the remote agent as the method argument. If the method returns an object value, then the remote host can generate a new object reference and send that back to the local host. So now the remote host and the local host are acting as both object servers and object requestors. We started out with the remote host creating objects for the local host to invoke methods on, but now the local host is "serving" objects for method arguments, and the remote host is serving a bunch of new objects for method return values. And if the remote host needs to call any methods on objects that are arguments to other methods, or if the local host needs to call methods on object return values, then we'll need to send method references back and forth for these remote method calls as well.

To further complicate matters, we also have to worry about situations where you don't want a remote object reference sent as the method argument. In some cases, you may want to send objects by copy rather than by reference. In other words, you may just need to send the value of the object from one host to another, and not want changes to an object propagated back to the original source object. How do we serialize and transmit an object's value to a remote agent? One way is to tell the other agent to create a new object of the right type, as we did to create our original remote object, and then indicate the new object as the method argument or return value.

Other Issues

Our hypothetical remote object scheme, using object tables, integer object references based on table location, and integer method references based on the method's index/position in the class definition, is a bit ad-hoc and not very elegant. It will work, but probably not very well. For one thing, it is not very scalable in terms of development complexity and runtime complexity. Each agent on the network is maintaining its own object table and its own set of object identifiers. Each remote method call could potentially generate more entries in the object tables on both ends of the call, for method arguments and for method return values. And since there's no guarantee that two agents won't use the same identifier for two different objects, each agent using remote objects will need to keep its own table of remote object identifiers and the agent they came from. So now each agent has to maintain two object reference tables: one for objects that it is serving to other agents, and another for objects that it is using remotely. A more elegant way to handle this would be to create a naming service for objects, where an agent serving an object could register its objects with the naming service and generate a unique name/address for the object. The naming service would be responsible for mapping named objects to where they actually live. Users of the object could then find the object with one name, rather than a combination of an object ID and the object's host.

Another issue with this remote object scheme is the distribution of workload across the distributed system. In returning an object by value as the result of a method call, for example, the object server instructs the client to create the returned object value. The creation of this object could be a significant effort, depending on the type of object. Under normal, non-distributed conditions the creation of the return value is considered a part of the overhead of calling the method. You would hope that when you invoke this method remotely, all of the overhead, including the creation of the return value, would be off-loaded to the remote host. Instead, we're pushing some of the work to the remote host and keeping some locally. The same issue comes up when an agent invokes a remote method and passes method arguments by value instead of by reference. The calling agent tells the serving agent to create the method argument values on its side, which increases the net overhead on the server side for the remote method call.

Hopefully this extended thought experiment has highlighted some of the serious issues that arise when trying to distribute objects over the network. In the next section, we'll look at the features that a distributed object system needs to have in order to address these issues.

Features of Distributed Object Systems

From our exercise in the previous section, we uncovered some of the features that distributed object systems need. These features, plus some others, are illustrated in Figure 3-1. An object interface specification is used to generate a server *implementation* of a class of objects, an interface between the object implementation and the object manager, sometimes called an object *skeleton*, and a client interface for the class of objects, sometimes called an object *stub*. The skeleton will be used by the server to create new instances of the class of objects and to route remote method calls to the object implementation. The stub will be used by the client to route transactions (method invocations, mostly) to the object on the server. On the server side, the class implementation is passed through a *registration service*, which registers the new class with a *naming service* and an *object manager*, and then stores the class in the server's storage for object skeletons.

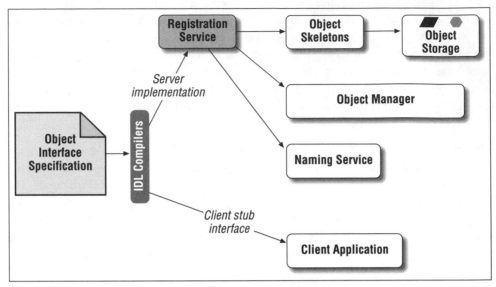

Figure 3-1. General architecture for distributed object systems

With an object fully registered with a server, the client can now request an instance of the class through the naming service. The runtime transactions involved in requesting and using a remote object are shown in Figure 3-2. The naming service routes the client's request to the server's object manager, which creates and initializes the new object using the stored object skeleton. The new object is stored in the server's object storage area, and an object handle is issued back to the client in the form of an object stub interface. This stub is used by the client to interact with the remote object.

While Figure 3-2 illustrates a client-server remote object environment, a remote object scheme can typically be used in a peer-to-peer manner as well. Any agent in the system can act as both a server and a client of remote objects, with each main- taining its own object manager, object skeleton storage, and object instance storage. In some systems the naming service can be shared between distributed agents, while in others each agent maintains its own naming service.

In the following sections we'll look at each element of this general distributed object architecture in more detail.

Object Interface Specification

To provide a truly open system for distributing objects, the distributed object system should allow the client to access objects regardless of their implementation details, like hardware platform and software language. It should also allow the object server to implement an object in whatever way it needs to. Although in this

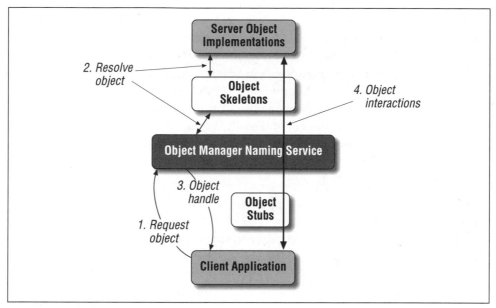

Figure 3-2. Remote object transactions at runtime

book we are talking about implementing systems in Java, you may have valuable services already implemented in C, C++, or Smalltalk, and these services might be expensive to reimplement in Java. In this situation you'd like the option of wrapping your existing services with object interfaces and using them directly via the remote object system.

Some distributed object systems provide a platform-independent means for specifying object interfaces. These object interface descriptions can be converted into server skeletons, which can be compiled and implemented in whatever form the server requires. The same object interfaces can be used to generate client-side stub interfaces. If we're dealing with a Java-based distributed system, then the server skeletons and client stubs will be generated as Java class definitions, which will then be compiled into bytecodes.

In CORBA, object interfaces are described using a platform-independent language called the Interface Definition Language (IDL). Other similar languages are the Interface Specification Language (ISL) in Xerox's Inter-Language Unification (ILU) system, and the Component Object Model language (COM) used in Microsoft's DCOM system.

Object Manager

The object manager is really at the heart of the distributed object system, since it manages the object skeletons and object references on an object server. The object manager plays a role similar to that of an Object Request Broker (ORB) in a CORBA system, or the registry service in RMI, both of which will be discussed in more detail shortly. When a client asks for a new object, the object manager locates the skeleton for the class of object requested, creates a new object based on the skeleton, stores the new object in object storage, and sends a reference to the object back to the client. Remote method calls made by the client are routed through the manager to the proper object on the server, and the manager also routes the results back to the client. Finally, when the client is through with the remote object, it can issue a request to the object manager to destroy the object. The manager removes the object from the server's storage and frees up any resources the object is using.

Some distributed object systems support things like dynamic object activation and deactivation, and persistent objects. The object manager typically handles these functions for the object server. In order to support dynamic object activation and deactivation, the object manager needs to have an activation and deactivation method registered for each object implementation it manages. When a client requests activation of a new instance of an interface, for example, the object manager invokes the activation method for the implementation of the interface, which should generate a new instance. A reference to the new instance is returned to the client. A similar process is used for deactivating objects. If an object is set to be persistent, then the object manager needs a method for storing the object's state when it is deactivated, and for restoring it the next time a client asks for the object.

Depending on the architecture of the distributed object system, the object manager might be located on the host serving the objects, or its functions might be distributed between the client and the server, or it might reside completely on a third host, acting as a liaison between the object client and the object server.

Registration/Naming Service

The registration/naming service acts as an intermediary between the object client and the object manager. Once we have defined an interface to an object, an implementation of the interface needs to be registered with the service so that it can be addressed by clients. In order to create and use an object from a remote host, a client needs a naming service so that it can specify things like the type of object it needs, or the name of a particular object if one already exists on the server. The naming service routes these requests to the proper object server. Once the client has an object reference, the naming service might also be used to route method invocations to their targets.

If the object manager also supports dynamic object activation and persistent objects, then the naming service can also be used to support these functions. If a client asks the service to activate a new instance of a given interface, the naming service can route this request to an object server that has an implementation of that interface. And if an object manager has any persistent objects under its control, the naming service can be notified of this so that requests for the object can be routed correctly.

Object Communication Protocol

In order for the client to interact with the remote object, a general protocol for handling remote object requests is needed. This protocol needs to support, at a minimum, a means for transmitting and receiving object references, method references, and data in the form of objects or basic data types. Ideally we don't want the client application to need to know any details about this protocol. It should simply interact with local object interfaces, letting the object distribution scheme take care of communicating with the remote object behind the scenes. This minimizes the impact on the client application source code, and helps you to be flexible about how clients access remote services.

Development Tools

Of course, we'll need to develop, debug, and maintain the object interfaces, as well as the language-specific implementations of these interfaces, which make up our distributed object system. Object interface editors and project managers, language cross-compilers, and symbolic debuggers are essential tools. The fact that we are developing distributed systems imposes further requirements on these tools, since we need a reasonable method to monitor and diagnose object systems spread across the network. Load simulation and testing tools become very handy here as well, to verify that our server and the network can handle the typical request frequencies and types we expect to see at runtime.

Security

As we have already mentioned, any network interactions carry the potential need for security. In the case of distributed object systems, agents making requests of the object broker may need to be authenticated and authorized to access elements of the object repository, and restricted from other areas and objects. Transactions between agents and the remote objects they are invoking may need to be encrypted to prevent eavesdropping. Ideally, the object distribution scheme will include direct support for these operations. For example, the client may want to "tunnel" the object communication protocol through a secure protocol layer, with public key encryption on either end of the transmission.

Distributed Object Schemes for Java

While there are several distributed object schemes that can be used within the Java environment, we'll only cover two that qualify as serious options for developing your distributed applications: CORBA and RMI. Both of them have their advantages and their limitations, which we'll look at in detail in the following sections.

During this discussion, we'll be using an example involving a generic problem solver, which we'll distribute using both CORBA and RMI. We'll show in each case how instances of this class can be used remotely using these various object distribution schemes. A Java interface for the example class, called `Solver`, is shown in Example 3-1. The `Solver` acts as a generic compute engine that solves numerical problems. Problems are given to the `Solver` in the form of `ProblemSet` objects; the `ProblemSet` interface is shown in Example 3-2. The `ProblemSet` holds all of the information describing a problem to be solved by the `Solver`. The `ProblemSet` also contains fields for the solution to the problem it represents. In our highly simplified example, we're assuming that any problem is described by a single floating-point number, and the solution is also a single floating-point value.

Example 3-1. A Problem Solver Interface

```
package dcj.examples;

import java.io.OutputStream;

//
// Solver:
// An interface to a generic solver that operates on ProblemSets
//

public interface Solver
{
  // Solve the current problem set
  public boolean solve();

  // Solve the given problem set
  public boolean solve(ProblemSet s, int numIters);

  // Get/set the current problem set
  public ProblemSet getProblem();
  public void setProblem(ProblemSet s);

  // Get/set the current iteration setting
  public int getInterations();
  public void setIterations(int numIter);
```

Example 3-1. A Problem Solver Interface (continued)

```
  // Print solution results to the output stream
  public void printResults(OutputStream os);
}
```

Example 3-2. A Problem Set Class

```
package dcj.examples;

public class ProblemSet
{
  protected double value = 0.0;
  protected double solution = 0.0;

  public double getValue() { return value; }
  public double getSolution() { return solution; }
  public void setValue(double v) { value = v; }
  public void setSolution(double s) { solution = s; }
}
```

Our `Solver` interface represents a pretty simple compute engine, but it has some features meant to highlight the attributes of a distributed object scheme. As we said before, the `Solver` accepts problems in the form of `ProblemSet` objects. It also has a single compute parameter, the number of iterations used in solving the problem. Most computational algorithms have parameters that can be used to alter the way a problem is solved: basic iterative methods usually have a maximum number of iterations to run, so we're using that as the only parameter on our simplified `Solver`.

A `Solver` has two `solve()` methods. One has no arguments and causes the `Solver` to solve the default problem using the default settings. The default problem for the `Solver` can be set using the `setProblem()` method, and the default iteration limit can be set using the `setIterations()` method. You can also get these values using the `getProblem()` and `getIterations()` methods on the interface. The other `solve()` method includes arguments that give the problem to be solved, and the iteration limit to use for solving the problem.

This `Solver` interface acts as a sort of litmus test for distributed object schemes. It includes methods that accept `Object` arguments (`ProblemSet`s, specifically), it can maintain its own state (the default problem and default iteration limit), which needs to be kept consistent across method calls from multiple clients, and it includes a method that involves generic I/O. We'll see in the following examples how well both CORBA and RMI support remote implementation of this interface.

CORBA

CORBA, the Common Object Request Broker Adapter, is a distributed object standard developed by members of the Object Management Group (OMG) and their corporate members and sponsors. The first versions of the CORBA standard were developed long before Java was publicized by Sun (the OMG was formed in 1989, the CORBA 1.1 specification was released in 1991, and the first pre-release versions of Java and the HotJava browser were made public in the 1994-1995 timeframe). CORBA is meant to be a generic framework for building systems involving distributed objects. The framework is meant to be platform- and language-independent, in the sense that client stub interfaces to the objects, and the server implementations of these object interfaces, can be specified in any programming language. The stubs and skeletons for the objects must conform to the specifications of the CORBA standard in order for any CORBA client to access your CORBA objects.

The CORBA framework for distributing objects consists of the following elements:

- An Object Request Broker (ORB), which provides clients and servers of distributed objects with the means to make and receive requests of each other. ORBs can also provide object services, such as a Naming Service that lets clients look-up objects by name, or Security Services that provide for secure inter-object communications.

- Methods for specifying the interfaces that objects in the system support. These interfaces specify the operations that can be requested of the object, and any data variables available on the object. CORBA offers two ways to specify object interfaces: an Interface Definition Language (IDL) for static interface definitions, and a Dynamic Invocation Interface (DII), which lets clients access interfaces as first-class objects from an Interface Repository. The DII is analogous in some ways to the Java Reflection API, which was introduced in JDK 1.1.

- A binary protocol for communication between ORBs, called the Internet Inter-ORB Protocol (IIOP).

An earlier version of the CORBA standard did not include a low-level binary specification for the inter-ORB network protocol. Instead, it described the protocol in terms of more generic features that a "compliant" system had to implement. This turned out to be a stumbling block, since vendors were implementing CORBA object servers that couldn't talk to each other, even though they all followed the "standard." The binary protocol for the IIOP was specified in the 2.0 release of the CORBA standard, which closed this hole in the standard.

The Object Request Broker (ORB)

The Object Request Broker is at the core of the CORBA model for distributed objects. It fills the Object Manager role that we described earlier in the generic description of distributed object systems. Both the client and the server of CORBA objects use an ORB to talk to each other, so instead of a single Object Manager (as described in our generic distributed object system), CORBA has an object manager on both the client and server side of a distributed object. This lets any agent in a CORBA system act as both a client and a server of remote objects.

On the client side of an object request, the ORB is responsible for accepting client requests for a remote object, finding the implementation of the object in the distributed system, accepting a client-side reference to the remote object, routing client method calls through the object reference to the remote object implementation, and accepting any results for the client. On the server side, the ORB lets object servers register new objects. When a client requests an object, the server ORB receives the request from the client ORB, and uses the object's skeleton interface to invoke the object's activation method. The server ORB generates an object reference for the new object, and sends this reference back to the client. The client ORB converts the reference into a language-specific form (a Java stub object, in our case), and the client uses this reference to invoke methods on the remote object. When the client invokes a method on a remote object, the server ORB receives the request and calls the method on the object implementation through its skeleton interface. Any return values are marshaled by the server ORB and sent back to the client ORB, where they are unmarshaled and delivered to the client program. So ORBs really provide the backbone of the CORBA distributed object system.

The Interface Definition Language (IDL)

Distributed objects in a CORBA application are described in the Interface Definition Language (IDL). The IDL provides a platform- and implementation-independent way to define what kinds of operations an object is capable of performing. Example 3-3 shows an IDL interface for a simplified bank account server. The IDL specification indicates that the BankServer object will have three methods: one to verify a PIN number against an account, one to get specifics about an account, and one to process a transaction against an account.

Example 3-3. A Basic IDL Interface

```
module Examples {
  interface BankServer {
    boolean verifyPIN(in long acctNo, in long pin);
    void getAcctSpecifics(in long acctNo, in string customerName,
```

Example 3-3. A Basic IDL Interface (continued)

```
                    out double balance, out boolean isChecking);
   boolean processTransaction(in Transaction t, in long acctNo);
  }
}
```

The IDL language shares a lot of the features of C++ in terms of defining classes and their methods. Since we're talking about distributed objects, however, IDL forces you to specify additional information about your object's interface, like which method arguments are input-only, output-only, or two-way data transfers. This is done using additional keywords on method arguments, before their type specifications. These keywords are in, out, and inout. In the BankServer interface, the two arguments to the verifyPIN() method are declared as in parameters, since they are only used as input to the method and don't need to be read back when the method returns. The getAcctSpecifics() method has two in parameters and two out parameters. The two out arguments are read back from the server when the method returns as output values. An inout argument is both fed to the method as an input parameter, and read back when the method returns as an output value. When the IDL interface is compiled into a client stub and a server skeleton, the input/output specifiers on method arguments are used to generate the code to marshal and unmarshal the method arguments correctly.

Server Implementations

Once an IDL interface for a class has been written, it can be translated into a client stub and a server skeleton. IDL translators exist for C, C++, Smalltalk, Ada, Java, and other common languages. The stub and skeleton don't have to be compiled into the same programming language—this is a principle feature of the CORBA architecture. The client could be a Java applet, for example, and use a stub in the form of a Java class definition. The server could implement the same object interface in C++ using an object skeleton defined as a C++ class definition.

The first step in creating a server-side implementation of an object is to compile its IDL interface into both a native-language interface (Java, in our case), and an implementation skeleton. The native interface is simply a mapping of the IDL specification into our implementation language. It acts as the basis for both the server skeleton and the client stub, which will also be specified in the implementation language. The server-side skeleton acts as the base class for implementations of the object interface, and includes CORBA-specific methods that the server ORB can use to map client requests to method calls on the object implementation. You provide an implementation of the object by deriving from the skeleton and writing the implementations for the methods on the object interface. Later we'll see an example of creating a server implementation when we distribute our `Solver` class using CORBA.

Once you've defined an implementation for the object, you need to register the object implementation with the server ORB and, optionally, with a CORBA Naming Service, so that clients can find the object on the network and get references to it. You create an ORB from within your server process by creating an instance of an ORB interface. In Java, this is done by creating an instance of the `org.omg.CORBA.ORB` object. The interface to the Naming Service might also be provided in the form of a Java class that you create by requesting a reference to a Naming Service object from the ORB object. Once you have access to the Naming Service interface, you can create an instance of your object implementation and register it. Clients can then connect to your object through their own ORBs and Naming Services, assuming that they know your host name and the name that you used to register the object.

Client Stubs

The client uses a stub to access the data and methods on the remote instance of the object. A stub is generated using an IDL compiler, the same way that the server implementation skeleton was generated. Like the skeleton, the stub contains CORBA-specific methods that the client ORB can use to marshal method arguments to be sent to the server, and to unmarshal return values and output parameters. When a client requests a remote object reference, it's given the reference in the form of an instance of the stub interface.

A client can get a reference to a remote object by creating an ORB that is connected to the remote server hosting the object, and then asking the ORB to find the object on the remote server. The ORB initialization process will include arguments that let you specify, as a client, which remote host and port to talk to for remote object transactions. Once the ORB has been created, you can use the ORB's Naming Service to ask for a remote object by name. The name would have to match the name used by the server when it registered the object implementation. The client ORB makes a connection to the server ORB and asks for the named object. If it's found, the client ORB creates a reference to the object as an instance of the stub generated from the IDL interface. The client can then call methods on the stub interface, which are routed by the client ORB to the server ORB, where the method calls are executed on the actual server object implementation.

A CORBA Solver

Now let's see how we would both serve and use our `Solver` class in a CORBA environment. For our example we are going to use the JavaIDL package provided by Sun as our CORBA implementation. It provides an IDL-to-Java compiler, a basic ORB implementation, and a basic Naming Service implementation. Since a standard IDL-to-Java mapping has been submitted to the OMG by a group of the most prominent CORBA software vendors, almost all of the details about using CORBA in a Java environment will apply to any other CORBA implementation in Java.

The IDL interface

First, we need an IDL version of the class, which is shown in Example 3-4. This IDL interface represents some, but not all, of the functionality that I originally expressed in terms of the Java interface in Example 3-1. It also includes an IDL specification for the `ProblemSet` interface in Example 3-2.

Example 3-4. IDL Solver Interface

```
module DCJ {
  module examples {

    interface ProblemSet {
      double getValue();
      void setValue(in double v);
      double getSolution();
      void setSolution(in double s);
    };

    interface Solver {
      // Solve the current problem set
      boolean solveCurrent();

      // Solve the given problem set
      boolean solve(inout ProblemSet s, in long numIters);

      // Get/set current problem
      ProblemSet getProblem();
      void setProblem(inout ProblemSet p);

      // Get/set current iteration setting
      unsigned long getIterations();
      void setIterations(in unsigned long i);
    };
  };
};
```

You can see that there are some subtle differences between the IDL and Java interfaces for our classes. All the method arguments in the IDL interface are preceded by in, out, or inout, which indicates whether the argument is write-only, read-only, or read/write, respectively (from the perspective of the client). Since the purpose of IDL is strictly to define an interface to an object, there's no need to specify constructors for the object. Notice that we had to change the name of no-argument solve() method to be solveCurrent() in the IDL interface. IDL doesn't support overloading the names of methods, so we had to give one of our solve() methods a more descriptive name. The rest of the methods declared in the IDL interface directly correspond to methods on the original Java interface.

The client stubs

Now that we have our IDL interface, we can run it through our IDL-to-Java compiler (called, predicatably enough, idltojava) to generate a base Java interface, along with a Java stub for the client and a Java skeleton for the class implementation. Using JavaIDL,[*] the base interface and client stub are created by simply executing this command:

```
myhost% idltojava -fclient Solver.idl
```

Other CORBA implementations will have their own toolset and command-line arguments for compiling the IDL interfaces for your application. The Java base interface for the Solver generated by the IDL-to-Java compiler is shown in Example 3-5. Since we also included an interface for the ProblemSet object in our IDL file, the compiler also generated a base Java interface for it, shown in Example 3-6.

Example 3-5. CORBA-Generated Solver Base Interface

```
/*
 * File: ./DCJ/examples/Solver.java
 * From: Solver.idl
 *   By: idltojava JavaIDL Wed Mar 5 17:02:26 1997
 */

package DCJ.examples;
public interface Solver
    extends org.omg.CORBA.Object {
    boolean solveCurrent();
    boolean solve(DCJ.examples.ProblemSetHolder s, int numIters);
    DCJ.examples.ProblemSet getProblem();
    void setProblem(DCJ.examples.ProblemSetHolder p);
```

---

[*] The CORBA examples shown in this chapter were compiled and tested using the early-access release of JavaIDL.

Example 3-5. CORBA-Generated Solver Base Interface (continued)

```
    int getIterations();
    void setIterations(int i);
}
```

Here are some important things to note about the `Solver` base class in Example 3-5:

- Our module definitions from the IDL file have been converted into a package specification in the base Java interface. In the IDL, we declared that the `ProblemSet` and `Solver` interfaces were contained within the `examples` module, which was further contained within the `DCJ` module. In the generated Java code, the classes are kept in the `DCJ.examples` package.

- Where we've declared `inout` method arguments that are objects, the `idlto-java` compiler has put "holder" types into the Java base class. For each interface defined in IDL, the IDL-to-Java compiler not only generates a Java base class for the interface, it also generates "holder" Java classes for the object. The "holder" class name is just the interface name with an appended "Holder" (e.g., `SolverHolder`, `ProblemSetHolder`). The holder classes act as streamable versions of the main class; the ORB uses these holder classes to transmit instances of the interface as remote method arguments. You can access the actual class by using the `value` attribute on the `Holder` objects. (For example, `SolverHolder.value` is a reference to the actual `Solver` object.)

Example 3-6. CORBA-Generated ProblemSet Base Interface

```
/*
 * File: ./DCJ/examples/ProblemSet.java
 * From: Solver.idl
 *   By: idltojava JavaIDL Wed Mar 5 17:02:26 1997
 */

package DCJ.examples;
public interface ProblemSet
    extends org.omg.CORBA.Object {
    double getValue();
    void setValue(double v);
    double getSolution();
    void setSolution(double s);
}
```

The compiler also generated the client stubs for the interfaces in our IDL file. In each case, the generated client stub implements the Java base interface for the object. The client stubs also extend the `org.omg.CORBA.portable.Object-Impl` class, which provides the interface used by the client ORB to marshal and unmarshal remote method arguments, among other things. The start of the generated client stub for the `Solver` looks like this:

```
public class _SolverStub
    extends org.omg.CORBA.portable.ObjectImpl
    implements dcj.examples.Solver {
        ...
```

We'll leave out the remainder of the client stub definitions, since they primarily include low-level details about the interface between the stub and the ORB that we won't be concerned with here. When you're developing systems using CORBA, you should never have to be concerned with the internal details of the client stub or the server skeleton anyway. The IDL-to-Java compiler does the right thing with your IDL definitions, and all the client needs to know is the base Java interface for the remote object.

The server skeleton and implementation

The same IDL `Solver` interface can be used to generate a skeleton for a server implementation of a class. This is done by invoking the following:

```
myhost% idltojava -fserver Solver.idl
```

This will regenerate the Java base interface, but will also generate a skeleton for our object implementation. Like the client stub, our server skeleton contains mostly code related to the ORB/skeleton interface, details that you won't need to be concerned with most of the time. The only aspect we'll mention is that the server skeleton also implements the base Java interface, as well as the `org.omg.CORBA.portable.ObjectImpl` class. It also implements the interface `org.omg.CORBA.portable.Skeleton`, which the server ORB will be looking for when invoking methods on the object implementation:

```
public abstract class _SolverImplBase
    extends org.omg.CORBA.portable.ObjectImpl
    implements DCJ.examples.Solver, org.omg.CORBA.portable.Skeleton {
```

Note that the `_SolverImplBase` class is declared `abstract` by the compiler, since it doesn't implement any of the methods that we declared in our IDL interface. Again, since the `ProblemSet` interface was defined in the same IDL file, a Java skeleton for the `ProblemSet` was also generated.

The last step in setting up our remote object for business is to extend the `_SolverImplBase` class and the `_ProblemSetImplBase` class, and implement the methods defined in their base interfaces. Our implementation of the `Solver` interface is shown in Example 3-7. The `CORBASolverImpl` provides implementations of all of the methods from the base `Solver` interface in Example 3-5, including the ever-critical `solve()` method. In this case, our `Solver` simply

performs a square-root operation on the problem value. Our implementation of
the `ProblemSet` interface is shown in Example 3-8.

Example 3-7. Java Implementation of the Solver Interface

```java
package DCJ.examples;

import java.lang.*;
import java.io.*;
import org.omg.CORBA.*;
import org.omg.CosNaming.*;

public class CORBASolverImpl extends _SolverImplBase {

  protected int numIterations = 1; // not used for this Solver...
  protected ProblemSetHolder currProblem = null;

  // Constructors
  public CORBASolverImpl() { super(); }
  public CORBASolverImpl(int numIter) {
    super();
    numIterations = numIter;
  }


  public ProblemSet getProblem() {
    return currProblem.value;
  }

  public void setProblem(ProblemSetHolder ph) {
    currProblem = ph;
  }

  public int getIterations() {
    return numIterations;
  }

  public void setIterations(int i) {
    numIterations = i;
  }

  public boolean solveCurrent() {
    System.out.println("Solving current problem...");
    return solve(currProblem, numIterations);
  }

  public boolean solve(ProblemSetHolder sh, int numIters) {
    ProblemSet s = sh.value;
    boolean success = true;
```

Example 3-7. Java Implementation of the Solver Interface (continued)

```java
    if (s == null) {
      System.out.println("No problem to solve.");
      return false;
    }

    System.out.println("Problem value = " + s.getValue());

    // Solve problem here...
    try {
      s.setSolution(Math.sqrt(s.getValue()));
    }
    catch (ArithmeticException e) {
      System.out.println("Badly-formed problem.");
      success = false;
    }

    System.out.println("Problem solution = " + s.getSolution());

    return success;
  }

  public static void main(String argv[]) {

    try {
      // create and initialize the ORB
      System.out.println("Initializing ORB...");
      ORB orb = ORB.init(argv, null);

      // Create a Solver and register it with the ORB
      System.out.println("Connecting solver to ORB...");
      CORBASolverImpl solver = new CORBASolverImpl();
      orb.connect(solver);

      // Get the naming service from the ORB
      System.out.println("Getting reference to Naming Service...");
      org.omg.CORBA.Object ncObj =
        orb.resolve_initial_references("NameService");
      NamingContext ncRef = NamingContextHelper.narrow(ncObj);

      // Bind the Solver object to a name
      System.out.println("Registering Solver with Naming Service...");
      NameComponent comp = new NameComponent("Solver", "");
      NameComponent path[] = {comp};
      ncRef.rebind(path, solver);

      // Wait for client requests
      System.out.println("Waiting for clients...");
      java.lang.Object dummySync = new java.lang.Object();
```

Example 3-7. Java Implementation of the Solver Interface (continued)

```
      synchronized (dummySync) {
        dummySync.wait();
      }
    }
    catch (Exception e) {
      System.err.println(e);
      e.printStackTrace(System.out);
    }
  }
}
```

Example 3-8. Java Implementation of the ProblemSet Interface

```
package DCJ.examples;

public class ProblemSetImpl extends _ProblemSetImplBase {
  protected double value;
  protected double solution;

  public double getValue() { return value; }
  public void setValue(double v) { value = v; }
  public double getSolution() { return solution; }
  public void setSolution(double s) { solution = s; }
}
```

In addition to implementations for the `Solver` interface methods, our `CORBA-SolverImpl` class also includes a `main()` routine that creates a `Solver` instance and registers it with a local ORB. The registration routine first creates a local server ORB:

```
ORB orb = ORB.init(argv, null);
```

The command-line arguments to the main routine are passed into the ORB initialization routine so that it can parse any ORB-specific parameters that the user may provide. Next, the routine creates an instance of our `Solver` implementation, and connects the object to the ORB:

```
CORBASolverImpl solver = new CORBASolverImpl();
orb.connect(solver);
```

The next step is to get a reference to the ORB's naming service and register the object under a name:

```
org.omg.CORBA.Object ncObj =
    orb.resolve_initial_references("NameService");
NamingContext ncRef = NamingContextHelper.narrow(ncObj);
    ...
NameComponent comp = new NameComponent("Solver", "");
NameComponent path[] = {comp};
ncRef.rebind(path, solver);
```

The `NameComponent` that we create is the thing that tells the naming service what the name of the object is supposed to be on this ORB. Finally, we need to keep the server process alive while we wait for clients to invoke methods on our `Solver`. If the `main()` routine exits, then the surrounding process will exit and the ORB object we created will be destroyed. So to keep the `main()` routine from exiting, we enter an infinite wait:

```
java.lang.Object dummySync = new java.lang.Object();
synchronized (dummySync) {
    dummySync.wait();
}
```

The Solver client

OK, we've got our client stubs and server skeletons generated, we've written Java implementations for the interfaces, and our `Solver` implementation includes a `main()` routine that registers a `Solver` object with a server ORB. Now all we need is a client to use the `Solver`. Example 3-9 shows a simple client. All it does is create a client ORB, get a reference to the ORB's naming service, and ask it for a reference to the `Solver` by asking for it by name. The initial reference that we get from the ORB is a generic CORBA `Object`, which needs to be "narrowed" to get a reference to the actual `Solver` object reference using the `Solver-Helper.narrow()` method. We had to do the same thing when getting a reference to the `NamingContext` from the ORB. The `SolverHelper` interface is generated automatically by the `idltojava` compiler from the `Solver`'s IDL interface. Once the client has a `Solver` stub reference, it creates a problem and asks the `Solver` to solve it. If we're successful, the remote `Solver` object will receive our request, solve the problem, and return the results to the client.

Example 3-9. A Client for the Remote Solver

```
package DCJ.examples;

import org.omg.CORBA.*;
import org.omg.CosNaming.*;

public class CORBASolverClient {
  public static void main(String argv[]) {
    try {
      // Create an ORB
      ORB orb = ORB.init(argv, null);

      // Get a reference to the Naming Service
      org.omg.CORBA.Object obj =
        orb.resolve_initial_references("NameService");
      NamingContext nc = NamingContextHelper.narrow(obj);
```

Example 3-9. A Client for the Remote Solver (continued)

```
      // Get a reference to the Solver on the remote host
      NameComponent comp = new NameComponent("Solver", "");
      NameComponent path[] = {comp};
      org.omg.CORBA.Object sobj = nc.resolve(path);
      Solver solver = SolverHelper.narrow(sobj);

      // Make a problem and ask the solver to solve it
      ProblemSet s = new ProblemSetImpl();
      s.setValue(173.39);
      solver.solve(new ProblemSetHolder(s), 1);

      // Print out solution
      System.out.println("Problem = " + s.getValue());
      System.out.println("Solution = " + s.getSolution());
    }
    catch (Exception e) {
      System.out.println(e) ;
      e.printStackTrace(System.out);
    }
  }
}
```

Pulling it all together

At this point, we've got all the Java code for our CORBA Solver and the sample client. To see the system in practice, we have to compile all of the Java code using the javac compiler, and copy the bytecodes to both the server and client hosts. Both hosts will also need to have a Java CORBA implementation available in the form of its class files. On the object implementation server, we need to have a CORBA Naming Service running, which listens to a port for object requests. In the JavaIDL system, we start the Naming Service with a command like the following:

```
objhost% nameserv -ORBInitialPort 1050
```

This starts the Naming Service process listening to port 1050 on the host. Next, we need to run our server implementation process to register one of our Solver objects with an ORB on the server. We can run our server process with this command:

```
objhost% java DCJ.examples.CORBASolverImpl -ORBInitialPort 1050
```

The ORBInitialPort command-line argument is provided for initialization of the server ORB. When the arguments are passed into the ORB's initialization routine, the ORB start-up routine will parse out this argument, and will know that the ORB needs to work with the Naming Service running on port 1050.

Now all we need to do is run our client:

```
client% java DCJ.examples.CORBASolverClient -ORBInitialHost objhost \
    -ORBInitialPort 1050
```

The `ORBInitialHost` and `ORBInitialPort` arguments are passed into the
client's ORB initialization call. The ORB will use these arguments to connect itself
to the specified remote host and port for naming services. When the client asks
the Naming Service for a reference to the object named "Solver," it gets a reference to the `Solver` object being served by the server process. The remote
`Solver` solves our problem and returns the results, which our client prints out
for us:

```
Problem = 173.39
Solution = 13.1678
```

Java RMI

The Java Remote Method Invocation (RMI) package is a Java-centric scheme for
distributed objects that is now a part of the core Java API. RMI offers some of the
critical elements of a distributed object system for Java, plus some other features
that are made possible by the fact that RMI is a Java-only system. RMI has object
communication facilities that are analogous to CORBA's IIOP, and its object serialization system provides a way for you to transfer or request an object instance by
value from one remote process to another.

Remote Object Interfaces

Since RMI is a Java-only distributed object scheme, all object interfaces are written
in Java. Client stubs and server skeletons are generated from this interface, but
using a slightly different process than in CORBA. First, the interface for the
remote object has to be written as extending the `java.rmi.Remote` interface.
The `Remote` interface doesn't introduce any methods to the object's interface; it
just serves to mark remote objects for the RMI system. Also, all methods in the
interface must be declared as throwing the `java.rmi.RemoteException`. The
`RemoteException` is the base class for many of the exceptions that RMI defines
for remote operations, and the RMI engineers decided to expose the exception
model in the interfaces of all RMI remote objects. This is one of the drawbacks of
RMI: it requires you to alter an existing interface in order to apply it to a distributed environment.

Server Implementations

Once the remote object's Java interface is defined, a server implementation of the
interface can be written. In addition to implementing the object's interface, the

server also typically extends the `java.rmi.server.UnicastRemoteObject` class. `UnicastRemoteObject` is an extension of the `RemoteServer` class, which acts as a base class for server implementations of objects in RMI. Subclasses of `RemoteServer` can implement different kinds of object distribution schemes, like replicated objects, multicast objects, or point-to-point communications. The current version of RMI (1.1) only supports remote objects that use point-to-point communication, and `UnicastRemoteObject` is the only subclass of `Remote-Server` provided. RMI doesn't require your server classes to derive from a `RemoteServer` subclass, but doing so lets your server inherit specialized implementations of some methods from `Object` (`hashCode()`, `equals()`, and `toString()`) so that they do the right thing in a remote object scenario. If you decide that you don't want to subclass from a `RemoteServer` subclass for some reason, then you have to either provide your own special implementations for these methods or live with the fact that these methods may not behave consistently on your remote objects. For example, if you have two client stubs that refer to the same remote object, you would probably want their `hashCode()` methods to return the same value, but the standard `Object` implementation will return independent hash codes for the two stubs. The same inconsistency applies to the standard `equals()` and `toString()` methods.

The RMI Registry

In RMI, the registry serves the role of the Object Manager and Naming Service for the distributed object system. The registry runs in its own Java runtime environment on the host that's serving objects. Unlike CORBA, the RMI registry is only required to be running on the server of a remote object. Clients of the object use classes in the RMI package to communicate with the remote registry to look up objects on the server. You start an RMI registry on a host by running the `rmireg-istry` command, which is included in the standard JDK distribution. By default, the registry listens to port 1099 on the local host for connections, but you can specify any port for the registry process by using a command-line option:

```
objhost% rmiregistry 4001
```

Once the registry is running on the server, you can register object implementations by name, using the `java.rmi.Naming` interface. We'll see the details of registering server implementations in the next section. A registered class on a host can then be located by a client by using the `lookup()` method on the `Naming` interface. You address remote objects using a URL-like scheme. For example,

```
MyObject obj1 =
    (MyObject)Naming.lookup("rmi://objhost.myorg.com/Object1");
```

will look up an object registered on the host `objhost.myorg.com` under the name `Object1`. You can have multiple registries running on a server host, and address them independently using their port assignments. For example, if you have two registries running on the `objhost` server, one on port 1099 and another on port 2099, you can locate objects in either registry using URLs that include the port numbers:

```
MyObject obj1 =
    (MyObject)Naming.lookup("rmi://objhost.myorg.com:1099/Object1");
MyObject obj2 =
    (MyObject)Naming.lookup("rmi://objhost.myorg.com:2099/Object2");
```

Client Stubs and Server Skeletons

Once you've defined your object's interface and derived a server implementation for the object, you can create a client stub and server skeleton for your object. First the interface and the server implementation are compiled into bytecodes using the `javac` compiler, just like normal classes. Once we have the bytecodes for the interface and the server implementation, we have to generate the linkage from the client through the RMI registry to the object implementation we just generated. This is done using the RMI stub compiler, `rmic`. Suppose we've defined a remote interface called `MyObject`, and we've written a server implementation called `MyObjectImpl`, and compiled both of these into bytecodes. Assuming that we have the compiled classes in our CLASSPATH, we would generate the RMI stub and skeleton for the class with the `rmic` compiler:

```
myhost% rmic MyObject
```

The `rmic` compiler bootstraps off of the Java bytecodes for the object interface and implementation to generate a client stub and a server skeleton for the class. A client stub is returned to a client when a remote instance of the class is requested through the `Naming` interface. The stub has hooks into the object serialization subsystem in RMI for marshaling method parameters.

The server skeleton acts as an interface between the RMI registry and instances of the object implementation residing on a host. When a client request for a method invocation on an object is received, the skeleton is called on to extract the serialized parameters and pass them to the object implementation.

Registering and Using a Remote Object

Now we have a compiled interface and implementation for our remote object, and we've created the client stub and server skeleton using the `rmic` compiler. The final hurdle is to register an instance of our implementation on a remote server, and then look up the object on a client. Since RMI is a Java-centric API, we can rely on the bytecodes for the interface, the implementation, the rmic-generated stub, and skeleton being loaded automatically over the network into the Java runtimes at the clients. A server process has to register an instance of the implementation with a RMI registry running on the server:

```
MyObjectImpl obj = new MyObjectImpl();
Naming.rebind("Object1", obj);
```

Once this is done, a client can get a reference to the remote object by connecting to the remote registry and asking for the object by name:

```
System.setSecurityManager(new java.rmi.RMISecurityManager());
MyObject objStub = (MyObject)Naming.lookup("rmi://objhost/Object1");
```

Before loading the remote object stub, we installed a special RMI security manager with the System object. The RMI security manager enforces a security policy for remote stubs to prevent them from doing illicit snooping or sabotage when they're loaded into your local Java environment from a network source. If a client doesn't install an RMI security manager, then stub classes can only be loadable from the local file system.

Serializing Objects

Another Java facility that supports RMI is object serialization. The java.io package includes classes that can convert an object into a stream of bytes and reassemble the bytes back into an identical copy of the original object. Using these classes, an object in one process can be serialized and transmitted over a network connection to another process on a remote host. The object (or at least a copy of it) can then be reassembled on the remote host.

An object that you want to serialize has to implement the java.io.Serializable interface. With this done, an object can be written just as easily to a file, a string buffer, or a network socket. For example, assuming that Foo is a class that implements Serializable, the following code writes Foo on an object output stream, which sends it to the underlying I/O stream:

```
Foo myFoo = new Foo();
OutputStream out = ... // Create output stream to object destination
ObjectOutputStream oOut = new ObjectOutputStream(out);
oOut.writeObject(myFoo);
```

The object can be reconstructed just as easily:

```
InputStream in = ... // Create input stream from source of object
ObjectInputStream oIn = new ObjectInputStream(in);
Foo myFoo = (Foo)oIn.readObject();
```

We've simplified things a bit by ignoring any exceptions generated by these code snippets. Note that serializing objects and sending them over a network connection is very different from the functionality provided by the `ClassLoader`, which we saw earlier in this book. The `ClassLoader` loads class definitions into the Java runtime, so that new instances of the class can be created. The object serialization facility allows an actual object to be serialized in its entirety, transmitted to any destination, and then reconstructed as a precise replica of the original.

When you serialize an object, all of the objects that it references as data members will also be serialized, and all of their object references will be serialized, and so on. If you attempt to serialize an object that doesn't implement the `Serializable` interface, or an object that refers to non-serializable objects, then a `NotSerializableException` will be thrown. Method arguments that aren't objects are serialized automatically using their standard byte stream formats.

In RMI, the serialization facility is used to marshal and unmarshal method arguments that are objects, but that are not remote objects. Any object argument to a method on a remote object in RMI must implement the `Serializable` interface, since the argument will be serialized and transmitted to the remote host during the remote method invocation.

An RMI Solver

Now let's go back to our `Solver` example and distribute it using RMI. First, we would have to rewrite the `Solver` interface so that it implements the `java.rmi.Remote` interface. The methods on the interface also have to be specified as throwing `RemoteExceptions`. This modified version of the `Solver` interface, the `RMISolver`, is shown in Example 3-10.

Example 3-10. Interface for a RMI Solver

```
package dcj.examples.rmi;

import java.rmi.*;
import java.io.OutputStream;

public interface RMISolver extends java.rmi.Remote
{
   public boolean solve() throws RemoteException;
   public boolean solve(RMIProblemSet s,
                        int numIters) throws RemoteException;

   public RMIProblemSet getProblem() throws RemoteException;
   public boolean setProblem(RMIProblemSet s) throws RemoteException;
   public int getIterations() throws RemoteException;
   public boolean setIterations(int numIter) throws RemoteException;
}
```

There are two methods in this interface, the `solve()` method with arguments, and the `setProblem()` method, where we have problem set arguments that we want to pass into the remote method invocation. We could achieve this by creating a version of the `ProblemSet` class that implements the `Serializable` interface. If we did that, the problem set would be sent to the remote host by value—the remote object would be operating on a copy of the problem set. But in both of these cases we want to pass the problem set by reference; we want the remote `Solver` to operate on the same problem set object that we have on the client, so that when the solution is stored in the problem set, we will see it automatically on the client. We can do this in RMI by making a remote version of the `ProblemSet` class. With an RMI-enabled `ProblemSet` interface, we can use an instance of an implementation of the interface as an argument to remote methods, and the remote object will receive a stub to the local `ProblemSet`. The RMI version of the `ProblemSet` interface, the `RMIProblemSet`, is shown in Example 3-11.

Example 3-11. Interface for an RMI ProblemSet

```
package dcj.examples.rmi;

import java.rmi.*;

public interface RMIProblemSet extends Remote {
   public double getValue() throws RemoteException;
   public double getSolution() throws RemoteException;
   public void setValue(double v) throws RemoteException;
   public void setSolution(double s) throws RemoteException;
}
```

Now we'll need to write server-side implementations of these interfaces. Our server-side implementation of the `RMISolver` derives from `java.rmi.UnicastRemoteObject`, and is shown in Example 3-12. The implementation of the `RMIProblemSet` interface is shown in Example 3-13. It also extends the `UnicastRemoteObject` class.

Example 3-12. Implementation of the RMISolver

```
package dcj.examples.rmi;

import java.rmi.*;
import java.rmi.server.UnicastRemoteObject;
import java.io.*;

public class RMISolverImpl
    extends UnicastRemoteObject
    implements RMISolver {
```

Example 3-12. Implementation of the RMISolver (continued)

```java
  // Protected implementation variables
  protected int numIterations = 1; // not used for this Solver...
  protected RMIProblemSet currProblem = null;

  // Constructors
  public RMISolverImpl() throws RemoteException { super(); }
  public RMISolverImpl(int numIter) throws RemoteException {
    super();
    numIterations = numIter;
  }

  // Public methods
  public boolean solve() throws RemoteException {
    System.out.println("Solving current problem...");
    return solve(currProblem, numIterations);
  }

  public boolean solve(RMIProblemSet s, int numIters)
      throws RemoteException {
    boolean success = true;

    if (s == null) {
      System.out.println("No problem to solve.");
      return false;
    }

    System.out.println("Problem value = " + s.getValue());

    // Solve problem here...
    try {
      s.setSolution(Math.sqrt(s.getValue()));
    }
    catch (ArithmeticException e) {
      System.out.println("Badly-formed problem.");
      success = false;
    }

    System.out.println("Problem solution = " + s.getSolution());

    return success;
  }

  public RMIProblemSet getProblem() throws RemoteException {
    return currProblem;
  }

  public boolean setProblem(RMIProblemSet s) throws RemoteException {
    currProblem = s;
```

Example 3-12. Implementation of the RMISolver (continued)

```java
      return true;
  }

  public int getIterations() throws RemoteException {
    return numIterations;
  }

  public boolean setIterations(int numIter) throws RemoteException {
    numIterations = numIter;
    return true;
  }

  public static void main(String argv[]) {
    try {
      // Register an instance of RMISolverImpl with the
      // RMI Naming service
      String name = "TheSolver";
      System.out.println("Registering RMISolverImpl as \"" + name + "\"");
      RMISolverImpl solver = new RMISolverImpl();
      Naming.rebind(name, solver);
      System.out.println("Remote Solver ready...");
    }
    catch (Exception e) {
      System.out.println("Caught exception while registering: " + e);
    }
  }
}
```

Example 3-13. Implementation of the RMIProblemSet

```java
package dcj.examples.rmi;

import java.rmi.*;
import java.rmi.server.UnicastRemoteObject;

public class RMIProblemSetImpl
    extends java.rmi.server.UnicastRemoteObject
    implements RMIProblemSet {

  protected double value;
  protected double solution;

  public RMIProblemSetImpl() throws RemoteException {
    value = 0.0;
    solution = 0.0;
  }
```

Example 3-13. Implementation of the RMIProblemSet (continued)

```
public double getValue() throws RemoteException {
  return value;
}

public double getSolution() throws RemoteException {
  return solution;
}

public void setValue(double v) throws RemoteException {
  value = v;
}

public void setSolution(double s) throws RemoteException {
  solution = s;
}
}
```

These implementations of our `Solver` and `ProblemSet` interfaces are very similar to those that we created for the earlier CORBA examples. As in our earlier examples, the `Solver` simply performs a square root on the `ProblemSet` floating-point value. The `RMISolverImpl` has a `main()` method that registers a `RMISolverImpl` object with the local RMI registry.

Now we compile our interfaces and our server implementations into bytecodes, then generate their client stubs and server skeletons using the `rmic` compiler:

```
myhost% rmic dcj.examples.rmi.RMIProblemSetImpl
myhost% rmic dcj.examples.rmi.RMISolverImpl
```

The last required item is a client to use our remote object. The `RMISolver-Client` in Example 3-14 is a simple client for the remote solver. The client has a single `main()` method where it gets a stub for the remote solver and asks it to solve a problem. The first line of the `main()` method installs the `RMISecurity-Manager`. Next, the client looks up the solver registered on the remote server through the `Naming.lookup()` method. Once it has the `RMISolver` stub, it creates a `RMIProblemSetImpl` object (our RMI-enabled `ProblemSet` implementation), and passes it into the solver's `solve()` method. The remote solver receives a stub to the `RMIProblemSetImpl` object on the client host, and solves the problem it represents. The methods that the remote `RMISolver` calls on the `RMIProblemSet` stub are invoked remotely on the `RMIProblemSetImpl` object on the client. Once the `solve()` method returns, our client can get the problem solution from the `RMIProblemSetImpl` object that it passed into the remote method call.

Example 3-14. An RMISolver Client

```
package dcj.examples.rmi;

import java.rmi.*;
import java.rmi.server.*;

public class RMISolverClient {
  public static void main(String argv[]) {
    // Install a security manager that can handle remote stubs
    System.setSecurityManager(new RMISecurityManager());

    // Get a remote reference to the RMISolver class
    String name = "rmi://objhost.myorg.com/TheSolver";
    System.out.println("Looking up " + name + "...");
    RMISolver solver = null;
    try {
      solver = (RMISolver)Naming.lookup(name);
    }
    catch (Exception e) {
      System.out.println("Caught an exception looking up Solver.");
      System.exit(1);
    }

    // Make a problem set for the solver
    RMIProblemSetImpl s = null;

    try {
      s = new RMIProblemSetImpl();
      s.setValue(Double.valueOf(argv[0]).doubleValue());
    }
    catch (Exception e) {
      System.out.println("Caught exception initializing problem.");
      e.printStackTrace();
    }

    // Ask solver to solve
    try {
      if (solver.solve(s, 1)) {
        System.out.println("Solver returned solution: " +
                            s.getSolution());
      }
      else {
        System.out.println(
          "Solver was unable to solve problem with value = " +
          s.getValue());
      }
    }
    catch (RemoteException e) {
      System.out.println("Caught remote exception.");
```

Example 3-14. An RMISolver Client (continued)

```
    System.exit(1);
  }
 }
}
```

Finally, we're ready to try our distributed object system. First, we start a registry on the host that is serving objects through the Naming service:

```
objhost% rmiregistry &
```

Now we can register a `RMISolverImpl` object by running the `main()` method on the `RMISolverImpl` class:

```
objhost% java dcj.examples.rmi.RMISolverImpl
Registering RMISolverImpl as "TheSolver"
Remote Solver ready...
```

Back on our client host, we can run the client class:

```
client% java dcj.examples.rmi.RMISolverClient 47.0
Looking up "rmi://objhost.myorg.com/TheSolver"...
Solver returned solution: 6.855654600401044
```

Our remote solver has solved our problem for us.

It's important to note here that the `ProblemSet` we're sending to the remote `Solver` object through a remote method call isn't being served in the same way as the `Solver` object. The `Solver` server doesn't need to lookup the `ProblemSet` object through the RMI registry. A stub interface to the client-side `RMIProblemSetImpl` object is automatically generated on the server side by the underlying RMI system.

RMI vs. CORBA

In this chapter we've implemented the simple distributed compute engine using both CORBA and RMI, and we've seen many similarities between the two in terms of functionality. There are also some critical differences between the two technologies. In order for you to understand which distributed object scheme is right for whatever system you're facing, it's important to spell out these differences.

The Language Barrier: Advantage or Disadvantage?

As we mentioned before, RMI is a Java-centric distributed object system. The only way currently to integrate code written in other languages into a RMI system is to use the Java native-code interface to link a remote object implementation in Java to C or C++ code. This is a possibility, but definitely not something for the faint of heart. The native-code interface in Java is complicated, and can quickly lead to fragile or difficult-to-maintain code. CORBA, on the other hand, is designed to be language-independent. Object interfaces are specified in a language that is independent of the actual implementation language. This interface description can then be compiled into whatever implementation language suits the job and the environment.

This distinction is really at the heart of the split between the two technologies. RMI, as a Java-centric system, inherits all of the benefits of Java. An RMI system is immediately cross-platform; any subsystem of the distributed system can be relocated to any host that has a Java virtual machine handy. Also, the virtual machine architecture of Java allows us to do some rather interesting things in an RMI system that just aren't possible in CORBA. For example, using RMI and the object serialization in the `java.io` package, we can implement an agent-based system where clients subclass and specialize an `Agent` interface, set the operating parameter values for the agent, and then send the object in its entirety to a remote "sandbox" server, where the object will act in our name to negotiate on some issue (airline ticket prices, stocks and bonds, order-fulfillment schedules, etc.). The remote server only knows that each agent has to implement an agreed-upon interface, but doesn't know anything about how each agent is implemented, even though the agent is running on the server itself. In CORBA, objects can never really leave their implementation hosts; they can only roam the network in the virtual sense, sending stub references to themselves and to clients. We don't have the option of offloading an object from one host to another.

However, CORBA doesn't require a commitment to a single implementation language. We can pick and choose how different elements of a distributed system are implemented based on the issues at hand. Legacy systems may dictate our implementation language in some cases (large COBOL systems like to be spoken to in COBOL, for example). Performance may be an issue in other cases. Heavy computational tasks like computational fluid dynamics and finite-element modeling are best written in languages that can be compiled down to native hardware instructions, like C and C++. The Java virtual machine architecture is a disadvantage here, since an additional interpretation layer is added to the processing of instructions. The Java just-in-time compilers (JIT) are capable of generating native instructions from Java bytecodes, but there is still an additional piece of overhead in running each piece of Java code. If we know that migrating system elements around the network is not necessary, then natively compiled Java code can be permanently installed, but by doing this we're sacrificing the critical "run everywhere" aspect of Java.

If we're using CORBA in these cases, we can take IDL interface definitions for our objects, compile them into COBOL, C, C++, or whatever languages we need at the various nodes in our distributed system. As long as the ORB implementations that we use at each node support a standard inter-ORB protocol like IIOP, the various CORBA objects implemented in various languages can interact with each other just fine.

Other Differences

In addition to this core distinction between CORBA and RMI, there are other differences to keep in mind:

- Relatively speaking, RMI can be easier to master, especially for experienced Java programmers, than CORBA. CORBA is a rich, extensive family of standards and interfaces, and delving into the details of these interfaces is sometimes overkill for the task at hand.

- CORBA is a more mature standard than RMI, and has had time to gain richer implementations. The CORBA standard is a fairly comprehensive one in terms of distributed objects, and there are CORBA implementations out there that provide many more services and distribution options than RMI or Java. The CORBA Services specifications, for example, include comprehensive high-level interfaces for naming, security, and transaction services (see Appendix B).

- Various low-level technical details about the two schemes may be seen as advantages or disadvantages to you as a developer: the fact that RMI imposes additional `throws` clauses in your remote interface is one that we've already mentioned, and CORBA's peer-to-peer ORB communication model as opposed to RMI's server-centric model may be another.

The Bottom Line

So which is better, CORBA or RMI? Basically, it depends. If you're looking at a system that you're building from scratch, with no hooks to legacy systems and fairly mainstream requirements in terms of performance and other language features, then RMI may be the most effective and efficient tool for you to use. On the other hand, if you're linking your distributed system to legacy services implemented in other languages, or if there is the possibility that subsystems of your application will need to migrate to other languages in the future, or if your system depends strongly on services that are available in CORBA and not in RMI, or if critical subsystems have highly-specialized requirements that Java can't meet, then CORBA may be your best bet.

4.

Threads

In this chapter we will take a look at Java's support for multithreaded applications. The ability to create multithreaded applications is critical in distributed computing systems, since in many cases you'll want multiple clients to be able to make requests to agents in your system, and you'd like the agents to be as responsive as possible. Supporting asynchronous transactions introduces some new issues in developing any distributed application, and we'll take a look at how the thread support in Java helps you manage these issues.

Thread and Runnable

The Java API includes two classes that embody the core thread support in the language. These classes are `java.lang.Thread` and `java.lang.Runnable`. They allow you to define threads of control in your application, and to manage threads in terms of runtime resources and running state.

As the name suggests, `java.lang.Thread` represents a thread of control. It offers methods that allow you to set the priority of the thread, to assign a thread to a thread group (more on these in a later section), and to control the running state of the thread (e.g., whether it is running or suspended).

The `java.lang.Runnable` interface represents the body of a thread. Classes that implement the `Runnable` interface provide their own `run()` methods that determine what their thread actually does while running. In fact, `run()` is the only method defined by the `Runnable` interface. If a `Thread` is constructed with a `Runnable` object as its body, the `run()` method on the `Runnable` will be called when the thread is started.

Making a Thread

The choice between extending the `Thread` class or implementing the `Runnable` interface with your application objects is sometimes not an obvious one. It's also usually not very important. Essentially, the difference between the two classes is that a `Thread` is supposed to represent *how* a thread of control runs (its priority level, the name for the thread), and a `Runnable` defines *what* a thread runs. In both cases, defining a subclass usually involves implementing the `run()` method to do whatever work you want done in the separate thread of control.

Most of the time we want to specify what runs in a thread, so in most cases you may want to implement the `Runnable` interface. With a `Runnable` subclass, you can use the same object with different types of `Thread` subclasses, depending on the application. You might use your implementation of `Runnable` inside a standard `Thread` in one case, and in another you might run it in a subclass of `Thread` that sends a notice across the network when it's started.

On the other hand, directly extending `Thread` can make your classes slightly easier to use. You just create one of your `Thread` subclasses and run it, instead of creating a `Runnable` subclass, putting into another `Thread`, and running it. Also, if your application objects are subclasses of `Thread`, then you can access them directly by asking the system for the current thread, or the threads in the current thread group, etc. Then you can cast the object to its subclass and call specialized methods on it, maybe to ask it how far it's gotten on whatever task you gave it.

In the next sections we'll look at how to both implement `Runnable` and extend `Thread` to make an object that executes in an independent thread. We'll return to our `Solver` example, making it usable in a multithreaded agent within a distributed system. The examples in this section will use fairly basic network communications, based on sockets and I/O streams, but the concepts extend pretty easily to distributed object scenarios.

Implementing Runnable

Suppose we wanted to make an implementation of our `Solver` interface (from Example 3-1) that was runnable within a thread. We may want to wrap the solver with a multithreaded server so that multiple clients can submit `ProblemSets`. In this case, there isn't really a compelling reason to extend the `Thread` class with the functionality of our `Solver`, since we don't have any special requirements on how the thread is run. So we would probably choose to implement the `Runnable` interface with the `RunnableSolver` class shown in Example 4-1.

Example 4-1. A Solver Runnable Within a Thread

```
package dcj.examples;

import java.lang.Runnable;
import java.io.*;

//
// RunnableSolver - An implementation of Solver that can be used as the
//                  the body of a Thread.
//

public class RunnableSolver implements Runnable, Solver {
  // Protected implementation variables
  protected ProblemSet currProblem = null;
  protected OutputStream clientOut = null; // Destination for solutions
  protected InputStream clientIn = null;   // Source of problems

  // Constructors
  public RunnableSolver(InputStream cin, OutputStream cout) {
    super();
    clientIn = cin;
    clientOut = cout;
  }

  public boolean Solve() {
    boolean success = true;
    SimpleCmdInputStream sin = new SimpleCmdInputStream(clientIn);
    String inStr = null;
    try {
      System.out.println("Reading from client...");
      inStr = sin.readString();
    }
    catch (IOException e) {
      System.out.println("Error reading data from client.");
      return false;
    }

    if (inStr.compareTo("problem") == 0) {
      try {
        inStr = sin.readString();
      }
      catch (IOException e) {
        System.out.println("Error reading data from client.");
        return false;
      }

      System.out.println("Got \"" + inStr + "\" from client.");
      double problem = Double.valueOf(inStr).doubleValue();
      ProblemSet p = new ProblemSet();
```

Example 4-1. A Solver Runnable Within a Thread (continued)

```
      p.Value(problem);           = P. setValue(problem)
      success = Solve(p);
    }
    else {
      System.out.println("Error reading problem from client.");
      return false;
    }

    return success;
  }

public boolean Solve(ProblemSet s) {
    boolean success = true;

    if (s == null) {
      System.out.println("No problem to solve.");
      return false;
    }

    System.out.println("Problem value = " + s.Value());   S.getValue());

    // Solve problem here...
    try {                SetSolution
      s.Solution(Math.sqrt(s.Value()));
    }
    catch (ArithmeticException e) {
      System.out.println("Badly-formed problem.");
      success = false;
    }

    System.out.println("Problem solution = " + s.Solution());     get
    System.out.println("Sending solution to output...");

    // Write the solution to the designated output destination
    try {
      DataOutputStream dout = new DataOutputStream(clientOut);
      dout.writeChars("solution=" + s.Solution() + "\n");
    }                                        get
    catch (IOException e) {
      System.out.println("Error writing results to output.");
      success = false;
    }

    return success;
  }

public boolean Problem(ProblemSet s) {
    currProblem = s;
```

Example 4-1. A Solver Runnable Within a Thread (continued)

```
    return true;
  }

  public boolean Iterations(int dummy) {
    // Not used on this solver
    return false;
  }

  public void PrintResults(OutputStream os) {
    PrintStream pos = new PrintStream(os);
    pos.println("Problem solution: " + currProblem.Solution());
  }

  public void run() {
    Solve();
  }
}
```

Here are the critical features to note about the RunnableSolver in Example 4-1:

Constructor with input/output stream arguments

> The constructor defined for RunnableSolver takes an InputStream and an OutputStream as arguments. These will be used by the solver to read the problem to be solved and to write out the results of the solver. The input/output streams could be attached to an active agent/client over a socket or pipe, or they might be connected to static data source/destinations like files, databases, etc.

Implementations of Solve() methods from Solver interface

> The RunnableSolver implementation of Solve() first attempts to read the problem to be solved from its input stream. If successful, it calls the overridden Solve() method with the ProblemSet as the argument. The Solve(ProblemSet) implementation solves the problem, then writes the results to the solver's output stream.

Implementation of run() method from Runnable

> The RunnableSolver's run() method simply calls Solve() to solve the current problem.

All together, the RunnableSolver class provides a Solver that can be created with connections to just about any kind of "client," and then wrapped with a Thread and run. The run() method calls Solve(), which reads the problem from the client, solves it, and writes the result to the client.

To demonstrate its use in action, Example 4-2 shows a RunnableSolveServer class that extends our SimpleServer class from Chapter 1. The RunnableSolverServer accepts connections from remote clients, and assigns a RunnableSolver to solve each client's problem. It creates a solver with the input and output streams from the socket connection to the client, then wraps the solver in a thread and starts the thread.

Example 4-2. A Server for the Runnable Solver

```
package dcj.examples;

import java.io.*;
import java.net.*;

class RunnableSolverServer extends SimpleServer {
  public RunnableSolverServer() { super(3000); }
  public RunnableSolverServer(int port) { super(port); }

  public static void main(String argv[]) {
    int port = 3000;
    if (argv.length > 0) {
      try {
        port = Integer.parseInt(argv[0]);
      }
      catch (NumberFormatException e) {
        System.err.println("Bad port number given.");
        System.err.println("   Using default port.");
      }
    }

    RunnableSolverServer server = new RunnableSolverServer(port);
    System.out.println("RunnableSolverServer running on port " + port);
    server.run();
  }

  // Override SimpleServer's serviceClient() method to spawn Solver threads
  // on each client connection.
  public void serviceClient(Socket clientConn) {
    InputStream inStream = null;
    OutputStream outStream = null;

    try {
      inStream = clientConn.getInputStream();
      outStream = clientConn.getOutputStream();
    }
    catch (IOException e) {
      System.out.println(
        "RunnableSolverServer: Error getting I/O streams.");
      System.exit(1);
    }
```

Example 4-2. A Server for the Runnable Solver (continued)

```
    RunnableSolver s = new RunnableSolver(inStream, outStream);
    Thread t = new Thread(s);
    t.start();
  }
}
```

Example 4-3 shows `RunnableSolverClient`, a sample client to the `Runnable-SolverServer`. It simply makes a socket connection to the `RunnableSolverServer`'s host and port, writes the problem to the socket's output stream, and waits for the answer on the input stream.

Example 4-3. A Client for the Runnable Solver

```
package dcj.examples;

import java.lang.*;
import java.net.*;
import java.io.*;

public class RunnableSolverClient extends SimpleClient {
  ProblemSet problem;

  public RunnableSolverClient(String host, int port, double pval) {
    super(host, port);
    problem = new ProblemSet();
    problem.Value(pval);
  }

  public static void main(String argv[]) {
    if (argv.length < 3) {
      System.out.println(
          "Usage: java RunnableSolverClient [host] [port] [problem]");
      System.exit(1);
    }

    String host = argv[0];
    int port = 3000;
    double pval = 0;
    try {
      port = Integer.parseInt(argv[1]);
      pval = Double.valueOf(argv[2]).doubleValue();
    }
    catch (NumberFormatException e) {
      System.err.println("Bad port number or problem value given.");
    }

    RunnableSolverClient client =
      new RunnableSolverClient(host, port, pval);
```

Example 4-3. A Client for the Runnable Solver (continued)

```
    System.out.println("Attaching client to " + host + ":" + port + "...");
    client.run();
  }

  public void run() {
    try {
      OutputStreamWriter wout =
        new OutputStreamWriter(serverConn.getOutputStream());
      BufferedReader rin = new BufferedReader(
        new InputStreamReader(serverConn.getInputStream()));

      // Send a problem...
      wout.write("problem " + problem.Value() + " ");
      // ...and read the solution
      String result = rin.readLine();
    }
    catch (IOException e) {
      System.out.println("RunnableSolverClient: " + e);
      System.exit(1);
    }
  }
}
```

We've reused some classes from Chapter 1 to implement our RunnableSolver-
Server and RunnableSolverClient. The RunnableSolverServer is an
extension of our SimpleServer, which simply overrides the service-
Client() method to attach a RunnableSolver to the client socket. The
RunnableSolverClient is an extension of the SimpleClient. This allows us
to use the constructor of SimpleClient to establish the socket connection to
the server. All we need to do is provide a new implementation of the main()
method that accepts an additional argument (the problem to be solved), and override the run() method from SimpleClient to do the required communication
with the server.

Extending Thread

Making a Solver subclass that extends Thread requires just a few minor
changes to our Runnable version. The same run() method can be used on our
Thread subclass as on the RunnableSolver, but in this case it's overriding the
run() from Thread rather than from Runnable.

To make our multithreaded server work with the Thread-derived Solver, we
only have to change its serviceClient() implementation slightly. Rather than
creating a RunnableSolver and wrapping a thread around it, a Thread-

derived `Solver` acts as both the `Solver` and the thread, so we only need to create one for the incoming client, then `start()` it:

```
ThreadSolver ts = new ThreadSolver(inStream, outStream);
ts.start();
```

Our client will work with the `Thread`-derived `Solver` without changes. It just wants to connect to a `Solver` over a socket—it doesn't care if the Solver is running as a `Thread`, or running inside another `Thread`.

Managing Threads at Runtime

In addition to changing the running state of your application threads, the Java API allows you to do some basic thread management at runtime. The functionality provided includes thread *synchronization*, organization of threads into thread *groups*, and influencing the thread scheduler by setting thread *priorities*. Before we see how all of these can come into play in a distributed application, let's go over them briefly so that we have a feeling for what kinds of capabilities they provide.

Synchronizing Threads

When you have multiple threads in an application, it sometimes becomes necessary to synchronize them with respect to a particular method or block of code. This usually occurs when multiple threads are updating the same data asynchronously. To ensure that these changes are consistent throughout the application, we need to make sure that one thread can't start updating the data before another thread is finished reading or updating the same data. If we let this occur, then the data will be left in an inconsistent state, and one or both threads will not get the correct result.

Java allows you to define critical regions of code using the `synchronized` statement. A method or block of code is synchronized on a class, object, or array, depending on the context of the `synchronized` keyword. If you use the `synchronized` modifier on a static method of a class, for example, then before the method is executed, the Java virtual machine obtains an exclusive "lock" on the class. A thread that attempts to enter this block of code has to get the lock before the code in the synchronized block is executed. If another thread is executing in this critical section at the time, the thread will block until the running thread exits the critical section and the lock on the class is released.

If a non-static method is declared `synchronized`, then the virtual machine obtains a lock on the object on which the method is invoked. If you define a synchronized block of code, then you have to specify the class, object, or array on which to synchronize.

Thread Groups

The Java API also lets you organize threads into groups, represented by the `ThreadGroup` class. A `ThreadGroup` can contain individual threads, or other thread groups, to create a thread hierarchy. The benefit of thread groups is a mixture of security and convenience. Thread groups are secure because threads in a group can't access the parent thread of their group. This allows you to isolate certain threads from other threads and prevent them from monitoring or modifying each other.

Convenience comes from the methods provided on the `ThreadGroup` class for performing "batch" operations on the group of threads. The `start()` method on `ThreadGroup` starts all of the threads in the group, for example. Similar methods exist for suspending, resuming, stopping, and destroying the threads in the group.

Priorities

The Java virtual machine is a process running under the operating system for the platform it's on. The operating system is responsible for allocating CPU time among the processes running on the system. When CPU time is allocated to the Java runtime, the virtual machine is responsible for allocating CPU time to each of the threads in the Java process. How much CPU time is given to a thread, and when, is determined by the virtual machine using a simple scheduling algorithm called fixed-priority scheduling. When a Java process starts, there are one or more threads that are in the runnable state (i.e., not in the stopped state described earlier). These threads all need to use a CPU. The Java runtime chooses the highest priority thread to run first. If all of the threads have the same priority, then a thread is chosen using a round-robin scheme. The currently running thread will continue to run until it yields the CPU, or a higher-priority thread becomes runnable (e.g., is created and its `start()` method is called), or until the CPU time slice allocated to the thread runs out (on systems that support thread time-slicing). When a thread loses the CPU, the next thread to run is chosen using the same algorithm that was used to pick the first thread: highest priority wins, or if there is more than one thread with the highest priority, one is picked in round-robin fashion.

All this means that there is no guarantee that the highest priority thread is running at any given time during the life of a process. Even if you ensure that one thread in your process has a higher priority than all the others, that thread might lose control of the CPU if it's suspended by some external agent, or if it yields the CPU itself, or if the underlying platform implements thread time-slicing and its time slice runs out. So thread priorities should only be used to influence the relative runtime behavior of the threads in your process, and shouldn't be used to implement synchronized interactions between threads. If one thread has to finish before another one can complete its job, then you should implement some kind of completion flag for the second thread to check, or use `wait()` and `notify()` to synchronize the threads, rather than giving the first thread a higher priority than the second. Depending on the number of CPU cycles each thread needs to finish, and whether the Java runtime is running on a time-slicing system or not, the second thread could still finish before the first, even with its lower priority.

Networked Threads

We've seen how to make separate threads of control in a Java applet or application, and we've discussed the various ways that the Java API allows you to manage threads at runtime. Now we'll go over some of the issues that arise with multithreaded distributed applications, and how the Java environment helps you deal with them.

Asynchronous Agents

The threaded implementation of our `Solver` interface in Example 4-1 shows how multithreaded servers can be implemented in Java. This allows our server to respond to clients asynchronously and to service their requests in parallel, which can reduce the amount of time a client has to wait for a response. The alternative is to have a server with only one thread servicing clients on a first-come, first-serve basis. So if client A is the first client to make a request, the server begins processing it right away. If client B makes a request while the server is processing client A's job, then B will have to wait for the server to finish A's job before its job can be started. In fact, client B won't even get an acknowledgment from the server until client A's job is done. With the multithreaded server, an independent thread can listen for client requests and acknowledge them almost immediately (or as soon as the thread scheduler gives it a CPU time slice). And with the jobs being allocated to separate threads for processing, the CPU resources will be spread out between the two jobs, and B's job will potentially finish sooner (though client A's job might finish later, since it is now getting less than 100% of the CPU).

Threads are useful in any distributed system where we want an agent to respond to asynchronous messages. By isolating communications in a separate thread, the other threads in the process can continue to do useful work while the communications thread blocks on a socket waiting for messages. The client process shown in Example 4-3 only has a single thread, since it doesn't really have anything else to do but wait for the server to send a response. But we could easily reuse these classes in a multithreaded client as a single communications thread, or as multiple threads talking to multiple servers.

Distributed ThreadGroups

You can probably imagine situations where it would be useful to define a Thread-Group that includes Threads from several agent processes in a distributed application. A distributed database application, for example, might be designed such that each agent contains a thread responsible for routing SQL calls to one of the databases in the system. If the database suddenly becomes temporarily unavailable, perhaps for some administrative task, then you might like to be able to perform a batch suspend() on all of the threads in the distributed system responsible for that database, to guarantee that the blocked threads don't attempt database connections until the database is fully online. When the database administration is complete and we get confirmation that the database is online, we can send a batch resume() to the distributed thread group to activate the threads again.

Unfortunately, since the ThreadGroup class in the java.lang package is implemented with nearly all of the critical methods defined as final, we can't just extend this class to implement a distributed thread group. However, we can implement a distributed thread group by defining a class that can handle the network communications and use the existing ThreadGroup interface.

Example 4-4 shows the DistThreadGroup class, which represents a group of threads distributed across the network. It basically acts as a local agent for a set of ThreadGroups across the network, which might also include a ThreadGroup on the local host. The DistThreadGroup has two major tasks:

- When a state change is requested locally (e.g., to suspend the thread group), it broadcasts the request to all other threads in the distributed group so that the entire distributed thread group changes state.

- It listens to a port on the local host for messages from other agents to change its state.

Example 4-4. A Distributed Thread Group

```
package dcj.utils.Thread;

import java.lang.*;

/*
 * DistThreadGroup
 *
 *      Local representation of a group of threads distributed across
 * processes on the network. Allows for the definition and control of
```

Example 4-4. A Distributed Thread Group (continued)

```
 * distributed threads.
 *
 */

public class DistThreadGroup extends Thread {
  // Protected instance variables
  protected ThreadGroup  localGroup;
  protected HashTable    remoteGroups;
  protected ServerSocket incoming;
  protected int          localPort;

  // Class variables
  static final int       hostIdx = 0;
  static final int       portIdx = 1;

  // Public constructors
  public DistThreadGroup(ThreadGroup g, int port) {
    localGroup = g;
    localPort = port;
  }

  public DistThreadGroup(int port) {
    localGroup = new ThreadGroup();
    localPort = port;
  }

  public DistThreadGroup(String rHost, int rPort, String gname, int port) {
    localGroup = new ThreadGroup();
    localPort = port
    Add(gname, rHost, rPort);
  }

  // Add a remote thread group to this group
  public void Add(String gname, String host, int port) {
    RmtThreadGroup rg = new RmtThreadGroup(host, port);
    remoteGroups.put(gname, rg);
  }

  // Remove a thread group from this group
  public void Remove(String gname) {
    remoteGroups.remove(gname);
  }

  // Get the local thread group belonging to this distributed group
  public ThreadGroup GetLocalGroup() {
    return localGroup;
  }
```

Example 4-4. A Distributed Thread Group (continued)

```
// Implementation of Thread::run - checks its port on the current machine
// waiting for messages from remote members of this group.
public void run() {
  incoming = new ServerSocket(localPort);
  while (true) {
    Socket peer = incoming.accept();
    DataInputStream is = new DataInputStream(peer.getInputStream());
    String input = is.readUTF();
    if (input.compareTo("suspend") == 0)
      suspend();
    else if (input.compareTo("resume") == 0)
      resume();
    //
    // Check for other messages here ("stop", "start", etc.)
    // ...
    else {
      System.out.println("DistThreadGroup: Received unknown command \""
                         + input + "\"");
    }
  }
}


// Suspend the group of threads. If requested, the suspend
// command is sent to the remote threads first, then the local group
// is suspended.
public synchronized void suspend(boolean bcast) {
  if (bcast)
    broadcastCmd("suspend");

  if (localGroup)
    localGroup.suspend();
}


// Resume the group of threads. If requested, the resume
// command is sent to the remote threads first, then the
// local group is resumed.
public synchronized void resume(boolean bcast) {
  if (bcast)
    broadcastCmd("resume");

  if (localGroup)
    localGroup.resume();
}


//
// Implement other methods corresponding to ThreadGroup methods here
// (e.g. resume(), stop())
// ...
```

Example 4-4. A Distributed Thread Group (continued)

```
// Broadcast the given message to the remote thread groups.
protected void broadcastCmd(String cmd) {
  Enumeration e = remoteGroups.elements();
  while (e.hasMoreElements()) {
    RmtThreadGroup rg = (RmtThreadGroup)e.nextElement();
    try {
      Socket s = new Socket(rg.getHost(), rg.getPort());
      DataOutputStream os = new DataOutputStream(s.getOutputStream());
      os.writeUTF(cmd);
    }
    catch (Exception e) {
      System.out.println("DistThreadGroup: Failed to " + cmd
                         " group at \"" + rg.getHost() + ":"
                         + rg.getPort());
    }
  }
}
}
```

The `DistThreadGroup` represents the distributed thread group using a local `ThreadGroup` and a hashtable of remote thread groups. The remote thread groups are represented by a `RmtThreadGroup` class, which for this example is simply a host/port pair, as shown in Example 4-5. The host and port number pairs indicate how to contact the `DistThreadGroups` running on the remote host, and they are keyed in the hashtable using a name, which is just a way to refer to the remote group locally.

Example 4-5. A Utility Class for Tracking Remote Thread Groups

```
package dcj.utils.Thread;

import java.lang.String;

public class RmtThreadGroup {
  protected String host = "";
  protected int port = 0;

  public RmtThreadGroup() {}

  public RmtThreadGroup(String h, int p) {
    host = h;
    port = p;
  }

  public String getHost() { return host; }
  public int getPort() { return port; }
```

Example 4-5. A Utility Class for Tracking Remote Thread Groups (continued)

```
  public void setHost(String h) { host = h; }
  public void setPort(int p) { port = p; }
}
```

When a state change is made to the `DistThreadGroup` by calling one of its methods, the change is broadcast to the remote thread groups, then the change is made to the local thread group. To broadcast the change, we sequentially open a socket to each remote thread group's host and port number, then send a message to the remote group indicating the change to make. The only methods shown in the example are the `suspend()` and `resume()` methods, but you can imagine how the other `ThreadGroup` methods would be implemented. If its `bcast` argument is `true`, then the `suspend()` and `resume()` methods use the `broadcastCmd()` method to send the same command to each remote thread group. The `broadcastCmd()` method iterates through the contents of the hashtable, and for each host/port pair, it opens up a socket to the host, attaches a `DataOutputStream` to the output stream of the socket, and sends the command string to the remote process. After the command has been broadcast to the remote groups, then the `suspend()` and `resume()` methods call the corresponding method on the local `ThreadGroup`, either suspending or resuming all of its threads.

Each `DistThreadGroup` is also a `Thread`, whose `run()` method listens on a port for messages coming in from remote thread groups, telling it to change its state. When a connection is made on its port, the `DistThreadGroup` checks for a message on the socket's input stream. It then calls the appropriate method as indicated by the message. Note that when receiving state-change messages over the socket, the `DistThreadGroup` calls its own state-change method with the `bcast` argument set to `false`. We assume that the agent originating the message will broadcast it to the other agents in the distributed group, so the receiving agent doesn't need to repeat the broadcast.

One flaw in this design is that the `DistThreadGroup` could be added locally to the `ThreadGroup` that it's managing. If a request to suspend the distributed group is received, then the `DistThreadGroup` will suspend the remote groups, and then suspend the local group—and in the process suspend itself. If we try to call `resume()` on the same `DistThreadGroup` object, the method won't run, because the `DistThreadGroup`'s local thread is still suspended. We won't be able to resume the distributed thread group until the `resume()` method is called directly on either the `DistThreadGroup`, or on its local `ThreadGroup`.

Improving Efficiency with Thread Priorities

As we mentioned previously, thread priorities don't guarantee a particular processing order. They only influence the thread scheduling algorithm. But this influence can be a powerful way to control the *perceived* performance of your application, especially in situations where you have a good idea of how quickly you want the threads to run relative to each other.

As always, things are more complicated in a distributed system, where there are processes located across the network, each containing its own threads and thread priorities. Presumably, these processes are working together to complete some job, so ideally we'd like to have the thread priorities coordinated to match the relationships between the processes and threads in the system. What this means exactly depends on the job you're trying to do and the environment in which you're trying to do it.

Let's assume that you're running your distributed system in an ideal environment: each host has the same operating system, CPU resources, memory, current load, etc. Now suppose that you're running a group of identical agent processes on this cluster of hosts, with the same number of agents on each host. Maybe each agent is solving a piece of a large problem, like a finite-element analysis; or perhaps each agent represents a node in a replicated database system. Under these assumptions, we should be able to come up with optimal thread priorities for the threads in each agent in the system. Since the hosts and the agents are completely homogenous, we can use a single host and agent, figure out the best thread priorities for that agent, and then use those priorities on all of the other agents in the distributed system.

In the distributed solver, for example, each agent is made up of two threads: one responsible for solving its piece of the problem, and another responsible for communicating with other agents in the system (broadcasting status or results, for example). The `RunnableSolverServer` classes are threads that listen for client requests and the `RunnableSolver` classes are threads that are "spun off" by the server to handle each request coming from remote clients. In general, we want to give the communication thread a higher priority than the CPU threads, so that it has a chance of getting some CPU time to check for requests, or to send off a few messages before the computation continues. Unless the computing job we give the `RunnableSolvers` is really trivial, the `RunnableSolver` threads are going to be running full-speed almost continuously, demanding as much CPU time as they can get. If we give them a higher priority than the I/O thread, the I/O thread will probably be blocked for long periods of time waiting for the computing threads either to finish or to `yield()` to other threads running on the same CPU.

If we can't rely on homogeneous agents and hosts, finding the best set of priorities for the threads in each agent isn't so simple. If we have several different kinds of agents composed of various types of threads, and these threads are interacting with each other in various ways, then we need to understand the major trends in these interactions in order to come up with optimal thread priorities for each agent. If we also have different types of hosts in our distributed system, we can't make assumptions about the underlying system that the Java runtime is using (single- or multiple-CPU, time-slicing or not, other applications sharing CPU load, etc.), so we can't foresee exactly how threads will be allocated CPU time and program it into our application.

In some cases the only way to make effective use of thread priorities is to have some way of monitoring the performance of your distributed system, and set thread priorities dynamically at runtime. Monitoring system performance is an issue of its own, and we won't go into detail about it here. Setting thread priorities dynamically is supported by the Java API within a single process on a single Java virtual machine, but we have to come up with a way to set priorities on threads across a distributed system. One way to do this is to extend our `DistThread-Group` class in Example 4-4 to allow us to both get and set priorities on threads in the entire distributed group. We could add `getPriority()` and `setPriority()` methods, for example, that take the remote group name as an argument, as well as the name of a thread in the remote thread group. This message could be passed on to the remote group the same way we pass state-change messages. Another approach would be to make a version of `DistThreadGroup` that is also an RMI remote object. Then remote agents could get a stub for the `DistThreadGroup` and call the `getPriority()` and `setPriority()` methods directly.

Now that I've shown how distributed thread priority manipulation is possible in the Java environment, I have to admit that it's probably not something that will be commonly used. The overhead that you'll need to monitor and reason about the running state of the distributed system in order to calculate optimal thread priorities will usually outweigh the performance improvements that you'll be able to get by trying to influence thread scheduling.

Synchronizing Distributed Threads

The ability to synchronize threads is a necessity in situations where data is accessible and modifiable by multiple threads. This synchronization is easily extendible to distributed situations, where data is accessible to multiple agents on the network. The simplest example is one where some runtime data in a Java process is accessible by multiple agents in a distributed application. If we wanted to allow clients to query our multithreaded solvers for their current problem sets, we could easily synchronize this access by making the `Problem()` methods on the `Solvers` synchronized. Since this method is the only means for accessing a problem set, doing a local synchronization on it ensures that every accessor, whether it's a local thread or an external agent making a request over a socket, will have synchronous access to the data.

Security

Security becomes an issue as soon as you allow your computing resources to come in contact with the rest of the world. With the recent explosion in the use of networks, preserving the security of data and the resources that carry data has become a primary concern. An open communications port on any computing device almost always carries the potential for abuse: a malicious party may steal or damage sensitive information, network bandwidth, or any other resource associated with your site. Security measures can increase the effort needed for an intruder to gain access to these resources.

In this chapter, we'll look at the Java Security API and how you can use it to make the agents in your distributed application safe from network hostility. We'll briefly discuss the kinds of security concerns you should have as a distributed application developer, and what tools are available in the Java environment for addressing these issues. Some of the issues we'll discuss are common across most applications, so the Java language developers have provided integrated features in the runtime environment that attempt to address them. An example of one of these features is the bytecode verifier, which prevents some kinds of malicious code from running on your machine. Other issues are only important in specific domains and applications, and it's your duty to determine how important these issues are to your particular application, what kinds of measures need to be taken, and how much effort needs to be invested in implementing these measures. For example, consider data theft from communications links. Is your data valuable enough to protect with data encryption, and if so, what level of encryption is appropriate, given the value of the data and the level of effort you can expect from those trying to steal it?

The subject of security in networked environments is worthy of several books' worth of material, and you can find many readings on the subject. In this book, we will only have a superficial discussion of the technical aspects of network security and cryptography, with limited excursions into the details only where it is necessary to support a solid understanding of the topic. From this foundation, we can take an educated look at the security options available to you in the Java Security API, and where you might find them useful.

The next section of this chapter discusses general security issues in networked environments. If you're already familiar with this topic, you can jump right to the later sections, which discuss the design and use of cryptographic security measures through the Java Security API.

Security Issues and Concerns

Just about everything making up a site on a computer network is a resource with potential value. The most obvious resource you need to worry about is information—the data being sent over the network and the information residing on your host computers. Other resources that could be targets are the applications on your hosts, the CPU resources of your computers, even the bandwidth available on your communications links. A hostile party may want to steal these resources or do damage to them.

Following are some of the things an attacker may do to steal or destroy your resources:

Eavesdrop on network communications
> The hostile agent may physically tap into network lines, or set up rogue programs on other hosts to watch for interesting traffic. They may be trying to steal information, or gather information that will help them steal or damage other resources.

Set up imposter agents or data sources
> This will let them fool you into sending valuable information or giving access to resources they shouldn't have. Our `Solver` servers could be accessed by intruders acting as legitimate clients, and used to solve their numerical problems; or a hostile party could flood the server with `ProblemSets` to be solved, rendering the server useless to the legitimate users. Clients of the `Solver` are also vulnerable, since a hostile party could set up an imposter `Solver` meant to steal the problem data submitted by clients, or they could purposely generate erroneous results. If the attacker manages to figure out that the clients are trying to solve for stress levels in a finite-element model, for example, then the imposter server could be set up to return results that indicate abnormally high or low stress levels in critical sections of the model.

This could cause someone to design a bridge that will collapse, or that's too expensive to build.

Directly or indirectly intrude on your site

Once attackers have located your site, and maybe even stolen some information about what's on the site, they may try to break in to your host and steal or destroy resources directly. For example, attackers may try to crack passwords so that they can log onto your system. A more sophisticated approach is to take advantage of the class-loading and distributed-object features of Java to inject hostile agents directly into a remote host. For example, a client of the `RMISolver` from Chapter 3 downloads a stub class that it uses for remote method calls to the server. A sophisticated attacker might try to create a "synthetic" remote stub, one whose methods have been modified to steal and transmit valuable information back to the attacker, or to do damage to the remote host from the inside.

This discussion leads us to the following list of general security concerns for the distributed application developer:

Verification of the identity of remote agents

Any time you open a network connection to a remote host, either directly, using the `java.net.Socket` and `ServerSocket` classes, or indirectly, using higher-level operations like connecting to a remote object, you should be concerned about whose agent you are really communicating with, and on which host machine the agent actually resides.

Ensuring that transmitted data is only received and understood by the intended recipient

If you assume that your network transmissions can be tapped into by a hostile party, then you may need to take measures to ensure that only the destination agent is able to interpret and reuse the information you're sending.

Verification of "visiting" agents for correctness and security holes

Internet-based languages such as Java have brought with them the common practice of allowing agents to "visit" your local environment, either as distributed objects or as applets embedded in an HTML page. So you need a means for screening incoming agents for questionable behavior.

Fortification of the local environment against damage

If your other security measures fail and a malicious agent manages to gain access to your local Java runtime environment, you want to minimize or prevent any damage the agent can cause.

Luckily for us, the Java language developers have decided that the last two issues mentioned in the preceding list will be handled inherently by the Java language and runtime. Verification of incoming Java objects is handled by the runtime byte-code verifier. Any classes loaded over the network as applets or distributed objects are checked for correct bytecode syntax and for basic malicious operations. Some of these questionable operations are attempts to manipulate memory addresses directly, or to replace core system classes with network-loaded versions. On top of this, the Java runtime puts restrictions on any loaded code, depending on its source. Applets have minimal access to the local system, for example, and any code has restricted access to classes outside of its own package scope.

If we assume that the Java language developers have done their job in dealing with the last two issues, that leaves the first two for you to worry about as an application developer. Verifying the identity of a remote agent or the source of incoming data requires some kind of *certification and authentication* process. Keeping communications private on a semiprivate or public communications link involves the use of *data encryption*. Again, the Java language developers are looking out for you. The Java Security API, introduced in the 1.1 version of the Java Developers' Kit (JDK™), provides a framework for integrating these security measures into your applications.

The java.security Package

The Java Security API is a framework for implementing and using security measures in the Java environment. The Java Security API is included in the core Java API, in the form of the `java.security` package.

Architectural Overview

The security package really provides two APIs: one for users of security algorithms, and another for the implementors or *providers* of these algorithms.

The User API

The user API is designed to let you use different cryptographic algorithms in your application without having to know how they are implemented by providers. All you need to know is an algorithm's name. As an example, you can create a new key-pair generator using the Digital Signature Algorithm (DSA) with the following call:

```
KeyPairGenerator myGen = KeyPairGenerator.getInstance("DSA");
```

You can take this new object and ask it for key pairs to be used to sign messages, without knowing how the key pairs are being generated. If you wanted to use a different algorithm to implement your key-pair generator, you would just change the algorithm name in the preceding line of code. The rest of your code that uses the object can usually remain unchanged.

In the same way that cryptographic algorithms are specified by name, providers of these algorithms are also specified by name. If you wanted to use an implementation of DSA from a specific provider, then you could ask for it by name when you create an object:

```
KeyPairGenerator myGen =
    KeyPairGenerator.getInstance("DSA", "MY_PROVIDER");
```

Although the Security API lets you hide from the details of cryptographic algorithms if you want to, it also lets you use those details if you need to. Underneath the generic, algorithm-independent interfaces provided by the Security API, like the `KeyPairGenerator` in our example, implementations of these interfaces will use algorithm-specific subclasses. If you need to give details about the algorithm and its specific parameters, then you can access these algorithm-specific interfaces for the objects you create by casting:

```
DSAKeyPairGenerator myDSAGen =
    (DSAKeyPairGenerator)KeyPairGenerator.getInstance("DSA");
DSAParams myParams = new DSAParams(myP, myQ, myG);
myDSAGen.initialize(myParams, new SecureRandom(mySeed));
```

In this case, since we asked for a key-pair generator for the DSA algorithm, we know that the returned object will implement the `DSAKeyPairGenerator` interface. So we can cast the object to this type, and call algorithm-specific methods on the interface.

The Provider API

Companies or individuals that provide implementations of security algorithms can add their own implementations to the `java.security` API using the `Provider` interface. The provider creates implementations of the relevant interfaces in the API (`Signature`, `KeyPairGenerator`, etc.), then creates a subclass of the `Provider` interface. The `Provider` subclass will register the algorithms with the Security API, so that users can ask for their implementation of algorithms by name. So if you had implemented a better, faster version of the MD5 message digest format you would create a subclass of the `java.security.MessageDigest` class that used your implementation, and then create a subclass of `Provider` that would register your MD5 implementation under your chosen provider name ("Jim's Security," for example). Then a user of the Security API would use your MD5 implementation through the Security API by just asking for it by name:

```
MessageDigest digest =
    MessageDigest.getInstance("MD5", "Jim's Security");
```

The Core Security API

The high-level facilities provided by the Security API cover the *identification* of agents and the *encoding* or *decoding* of information passed between agents. These are the same issues we identified as critical security issues in an earlier section, since indentifying agents involves the *certification* and *authentication* of the agents, while data encoding and decoding requires some form of *encryption.*

The initial public release of the Java Security API in the JDK 1.1 included APIs for identifying and verifying agents, and using message digests and digital signatures. At the time of this writing, there is also an extension package, the Java Cryptography Extension (JCE™), that adds encryption interfaces to the Security API. These extensions are separated from the main Security API because the encryption code used in the JCE is not exportable outside the United States. In this chapter we'll discuss both elements of the overall Security API, but be warned that to use the encryption classes, such as `Ciphers`, you'll need to be a U.S. or Canadian citizen and download the JCE package from the Javasoft site.

The overall Java Security API includes interfaces for the following:

Identity management
> These interfaces let you represent the identities of agents and create access control lists (ACLs) for resources that reference these identities. These interfaces include `Principal`, `Identity`, `Signer`, and the `java.security.acl` package.

Digital signatures
> Digital signatures are used to sign messages and data, so that the receiver can verify the identity of the sender. Signatures are often implemented using public/private key pairs—a message is signed using the sender's private key, and the signature can be verified on the other end using the corresponding public key. The interfaces provided for generating and using digital signatures include `Key`, `KeyGenerator`, `KeyPairGenerator`, `Signature`, and `MessageDigest`.

Data encryption
> Encryption algorithms are used to encode and decode data for secure transmission between agents. The key interface here is the `Cipher`, which is a general representation of an encryption algorithm.

In the rest of this chapter, we'll be looking at adding security to distributed applications using the Java Security API. To fuel the discussion, we'll be extending the simple agent shown in Example 5-1 to include user authentication and data encryption. The `SimpleAgent` is a basic network client that opens up a socket to a remote agent at a particular host and port number, and starts exchanging

messages with it. The `SimpleAgent` keeps a queue of outgoing messages in its
`msgQueue` data member: messages are added to the queue with the `addMsg()`
method, and the `nextMsg()` method takes the first message off the queue and
returns it. The `SimpleAgent` constructor takes a host name and port number as
arguments, and opens a socket connection to the process listening to that port on
the remote host. If the connection is made, it retrieves the input and output
streams from the socket. The `SimpleAgent` also extends `Thread`, and its `run()`
method is a loop in which it sends the next message in its queue to the remote
process, reads a response message from the remote process, and handles the
message by calling its `processMsg()` method. In this example, the
`processMsg()` method does nothing, but subclasses of `SimpleAgent` could
implement this method to interpret the message and act on it.

Example 5-1. A Simple Agent Class

```
package dcj.examples.security;

import java.lang.*;
import java.net.*;
import java.io.*;
import java.util.Vector;

public class SimpleAgent extends Thread {
  // Our socket connection to the server
  protected Socket serverConn;

  // The input/output streams from the other agent
  protected InputStream inStream;
  protected OutputStream outStream;

  // Message queue
  Vector msgQueue;

  public SimpleAgent(String host, int port)
      throws IllegalArgumentException {
    try {
      serverConn = new Socket(host, port);
    }
    catch (UnknownHostException e) {
      throw new IllegalArgumentException("Bad host name given.");
    }
    catch (IOException e) {
      System.out.println("SimpleAgent: " + e);
      System.exit(1);
    }

    try {
      inStream = new DataInputStream(serverConn.getInputStream());
```

Example 5-1. A Simple Agent Class (continued)

```
    outStream = new DataOutputStream(serverConn.getOutputStream());
  }
  catch (Exception e) {
    inStream = null;
    outStream = null;
  }
}

public synchronized void addMsg(String msg) {
  msgQueue.addElement(msg);
}

protected synchronized String nextMsg() {
  String msg = null;
  if (msgQueue.size() > 0) {
    msg = (String)msgQueue.elementAt(0);
    msgQueue.removeElementAt(0);
  }
  return msg;
}

// Close the connection to the server when finished.
protected void closeConnection() {
  try {
    serverConn.close();
  }
  catch (Exception e) {}
  inStream = null;
  outStream = null;
}

public void run() {
  // Go into infinite loop, sending messages, receiving responses, and
  // processing them...
  DataInputStream din = (DataInputStream)inStream;
  DataOutputStream dout = (DataOutputStream)outStream;
  while (true) {
    String msg = nextMsg();
    if (msg != null) {
      String inMsg = "", inToken = "";
      try {
        dout.writeChars(msg);
        while (inToken.compareTo("END") != 0) {
          inToken = din.readUTF();
          inMsg = inMsg + " " + inToken;
        }
        processMsg(inMsg);
      }
```

Example 5-1. A Simple Agent Class (continued)

```
        catch (Exception e) {}
      }
    }
  }

  protected void processMsg(String msg) {}
}
```

To use the `SimpleAgent` class, you would create one first, using the host and port number of the remote agent with which you want it to communicate. Then you would call its `run()` method to start the message-passing process:

```
SimpleAgent myAgent = new SimpleAgent("remote.host.org", 1234);
myAgent.run();
```

In the examples in the remainder of this chapter, we'll add identity authentication and data encryption to this simple agent, to make sure that the information passed in its messages is secure. Although we'll be using a credit agent as our example application, we go into any details about the message protocol being used. These details aren't critical in a discussion about security, since our security measures will apply to any message protocol we decide to use.

Identities and Access Control

The `Identity` class represents an agent within the Security API. `Identity` implements the `Principal` interface, which is a generic representation of a person, group, or other named entity. An `Identity` has a name, which it inherits from the `Principal` interface, and other information that verifies the identity of the agent (a public key and assorted certificates, for example). A `Signer` is a subclass of `Identity` that also includes a private key that can be used to sign data. We'll discuss public and private keys and how they are created in more detail later in the chapter.

An `Identity` is created using a name for the agent being represented:

```
Identity fredsID = new Identity("Fred");
```

A public key and any available certificates can be added to Fred's identity to support the validity of his identity:

```
PublicKey fredsKey = ... // Get Fred's key
Certificate fredsCert = ... // Get Fred's certificate
Certificate fredsRSACert = ... // Get another certificate for Fred
fredsID.setPublicKey(fredsKey);
fredsID.addCertificate(fredsCert);
fredsID.addCertificate(fredsRSACert);
```

If we are also able to sign data using Fred's identity, then we'll also have a private key for Fred, and we can create a `Signer` object for him:

```
Signer signingFred = new Signer("Fred");
PrivateKey fredsSigningKey = ... // Get Fred's private key
signingFred.setPrivateKey(fredsSigningKey);
```

Access Control Lists

The `java.security.acl` package includes interfaces that let you define specific access rights for individual agents or groups of agents. In the same style as the rest of the Security API, this package defines an API for access-control lists, with few of the interfaces actually implemented in the package. Sun has provided a default implementation of the ACL package in their `sun.security.acl` package. In this section we'll use classes from Sun's implementation to demonstrate how to use ACLs.

Central to the `java.security.acl` package is the `Acl` interface, which represents an access-control list. An `Acl` has a group of owners associated with it, represented by `Principal` objects. *Principal* is a term often used in security circles to refer to a user or agent acting as a party in a secure transaction. Since both `Identity` and `Signer` are subclasses of `Principal`, you can use instances of either wherever a `Principal` is called for. Only owners of the `Acl` are supposed to be able to modify the `Acl`. Implementations of the `Acl` interface should enforce this by checking the keys and certificates on the `Principals` of the owners, to be sure that the agent creating or modifying the ACL has access to the certified elements of the identity of one of the owners of the ACL.

Each entry in the access-control list is represented as an `AclEntry` object, which associates specific identities with the permissions they have over the resource being controlled. An entry is added to the `Acl` using the `addEntry()` method, which takes the `Principal` for the entity and its `AclEntry` as arguments.

Each `AclEntry` defines a set of permissions given to the `Principal` over the resource being protected. Specific types of permission are represented using the `Permission` interface, which doesn't actually implement any behavior, but acts as a placeholder for subclasses that distinguish permissions in application-specific ways (permission names, binary typecodes, etc.). The `sun.security.acl` package provides an implementation of `Permission` called `PermissionImpl` that uses strings to identify permission types (e.g., "READ", "WRITE").

The `Principal` for an `AclEntry` is set using the `setPrincipal()` method on the entry. Once this is done, permissions for the `Principal` are added to the entry using the `addPermission()` method:

```
// Define a set of permission types
Permission read = new PermissionImpl("READ");
```

```
Permission create = new PermissionImpl("CREATE");
Permission update = new PermissionImpl("UPDATE");
Permission destroy = new PermissionImpl("DESTROY");
// Create some Principals
Principal person1 = new PrincipalImpl("Fred");
Principal person2 = new PrincipalImpl("Sally");
// Make an entry for each principal
AclEntry entry1 = new AclEntryImpl(person1);
AclEntry entry2 = new AclEntryImpl(person2);
// Give each principal their permissions:
// Fred can only read the resource
entry1.addPermission(read);
// Sally can do anything
entry2.addPermission(read);
entry2.addPermission(create);
entry2.addPermission(update);
entry2.addPermission(destroy);
```

Notice that we've used `PrincipalImpl` objects to represent `Principals` in the `Acl`. The `PrincipalImpl` class is a subclass of the `Principal` interface provided in the `sun.security.acl` package. In a real application, we would probably use an `Identity` or `Signer` object to represent a principal in the `Acl`. This would allow us to verify a digital signature from a remote client before we would allow that remote client to access the resource protected by the `Acl`.

Once the `AclEntrys` have been created, they can be added to the `Acl` with the `addEntry()` method. The method takes two arguments: a `Principal` argument that corresponds to the owner of the `Acl` making the entry, and the `AclEntry` itself. For example:

```
Principal myID = ... // Get my identity
Acl myAcl = ... // Create the Acl, setting me as an owner
// Now add the entries created above.
myAcl.addEntry(myID, entry1);
myAcl.addEntry(myID, entry2);
```

With the ACL in place, we can check incoming agents for the necessary permissions to do specific actions. If an agent contacts our agent and asks to update a resource, we can check the ACL of that resource for write permission for that agent using their `Principal`:

```
Principal remoteAgent = ... // Initialize Principal for remote agent
if (myAcl.checkPermission(remoteAgent, update)) {
    // Let the update action go through
}
else {
    // Disallow the action, and tell the agent
    // that it doesn't have the right permissions
}
```

Keys: Public, Private, and Secret

The Java Security API makes heavy use of both secret key and public key cryptography. The basics of creating and managing keys are provided by the Key interface and the KeyPair, KeyGenerator, and KeyPairGenerator classes in the java.security package.

Before we delve into how keys are supported in the Security API, it's important to understand the basics of public key cryptography algorithms, and the differences between them and the more well known secret key algorithms. Most of the features in the Java Security API, and most modern security APIs in general, support both secret key and public key algorithms. Readers that are already familiar with the concept of public key cryptography can skip over the next few sections.

Secret Keys

Early cryptographic systems used secret key methods for encoding private data. Secret key cryptography depends on the use of private keys for authentication and encryption. Two parties have to exchange secret keys with each other over some private, secure communications channel, and these keys are used to encode and decode messages. Each party has to have the other party's secret key in order to decode their messages. If attackers manage to steal or intercept a secret key, then they can listen in on communications or even impersonate one of the parties by sending encrypted messages using the stolen secret key.

Secret key cryptography has the advantage of simplicity. Algorithms for implementing secret key schemes are generally simpler and faster than the more complicated public key schemes. But there are some obvious problems with secret key cryptography. The basis for the security of the system is the secret key itself, but the secret key must be given to any agent that needs to communicate securely with you. This opens up the possibility of keys being stolen in transit, and finding a separate, secure way to transmit secret keys may be inconvenient, expensive, or just impossible.

Public Key Methods

In 1976, Diffie and Hellman published a paper describing a means for two parties to share cryptographic keys over a public communications channel without compromising the security of their private transmissions.* Essentially, the tech-

---

* Diffie & Hellman, "New Directions in Cryptography," IEEE Transactions on Information Theory IT-22, November 1976.

nique involves the use of two keys by each party, a *private* key and a *public* key. A message encrypted with one party's public key can only be decrypted with that party's private key. At the start of a conversation, two parties independently choose random private keys, which they keep to themselves. Then they generate a public key that is based on their private key. This public key can be freely shared with anyone, and can be used to encrypt messages to the party that owns the corresponding private key. Having the public key doesn't do an information thief any good, since it can't be used on its own to decrypt messages—you have to have the corresponding private key to do that. Public key encryption techniques are sometimes called *asymmetric* techniques, since a different process and key are used for encrypting messages than for decrypting messages.

The original form of public key cryptography described by Diffie and Hellman was vulnerable to the host-spoofing attack we described earlier, where a third party impersonates one or both of the communicating parties in order to steal the information being transmitted. Since public keys are transmitted as clear data, if a third party were to insert itself between the two agents on the network, it could intercept the public keys from each agent, and replace them with its own public key or keys. The two parties would then encrypt messages using the hostile party's keys. The hostile party could intercept these messages, decrypt them with its private keys, and re-encrypt them using the original intercepted public keys. This information theft could go on indefinitely, since the two parties wouldn't have any sign that a third party had injected itself into their conversation (except maybe some additional latency). To close this security hole, the concept of *public key certificates* was developed, to allow each party to verify the correspondence of a public key with a particular person or organization. A certificate contains some person's name and public key, and has been encrypted by the private key of a certification authority. The certification authority is an organization responsible for verifying the person's identity; it has made its public key widely available, so it can be used to decrypt the certificates it issues. When starting a network session, each party sends its certificate. When the certificate is received, the certifying authority's public key can be used to check the certificate for authenticity. If it checks out, then we can be assured that the public key for the other party is authentic. So a third party can't impersonate another by issuing a false public key, since they don't have a certificate matching the fake public key to the person they're trying to impersonate.

Public key cryptography, when it's extended to include certificates for authenticating the owner of public keys, is a powerful way to authenticate agents and carry out secure communications with them. And we can carry out secure communications without the need for secondary, private channels for secret key transmissions. The main disadvantage to public key methods is the additional overhead involved in encoding and decoding information. Since it relies on a more complex mathematical algorithm, secure public key I/O involves using more CPU time per kilobyte of data transferred and received.

Keys in the Java Security API

The Key interface represents a cryptographic key. The key could be a public or private key for public key algorithms such as RSA, or it could be a secret key for algorithms based on them, such as some block-cipher algorithms. A Key has an algorithm associated with it, and the name of the algorithm can be gotten using the getAlgorithm() method. Key generation is algorithm-specific, and knowing the algorithm used to generate a key can be important later. There are PublicKey and PrivateKey subclasses of Key that represent the public and private elements of a key pair, and there is also a SecretKey subclass for secret keys. These subclasses don't add any functionality to the Key interface. They just provide a way to distinguish one type of key from another.

The KeyPair class is a holder for a PublicKey and its corresponding PrivateKey. You can get the private and public elements of the KeyPair using the getPrivate() and getPublic() methods.

Key pairs are generated through the KeyPairGenerator class. A KeyPairGenerator instance is created using the static getInstance() method, using an algorithm name to specify what type of keys are needed:

```
KeyPairGenerator keyPairGen = KeyPairGenerator.getInstance("RSA");
```

Every key-pair generator has a strength factor and a random number generator parameter that can be changed using the initialize() methods on KeyPairGenerator before generating any keys:

```
keyPairGen.initialize(1024, new SecureRandom());
```

The SecureRandom class is a pseudo-random number generator provided in the java.security package. The strength and random-number generator parameters are interpreted and used in algorithm-specific ways by the actual implementations of the KeyPairGenerator class. You can also initialize a key-pair generator with algorithm-specific parameters by casting the generated KeyPairGenerator object to its subtype, and calling specialized initialize() methods for the subclass. For example, we created a generator for the RSA algorithm, so we can cast our KeyPairGenerator to an RSAKeyPairGenerator and call its initialize method, which takes a strength parameter, a public exponent for the key generation, and a random-number generator:

```
RSAKeyPairGenerator rsaKeyPairGen = (RSAKeyPairGenerator)keyPairGen;
BigInteger myExp = ... // Create custom exponent
rsaPairKeyGen.initialize(1024, myExp, new SecureRandom());
```

You should only need to do this algorithm-specific initialization if you have specific values for the algorithm parameters that are required by your application. Implementations of the `KeyPairGenerator` class will generally provide default values for all of their algorithm parameters.

Once the `KeyPairGenerator` is created and, if necessary, initialized, then you create a new `KeyPair` using the `generateKeyPair()` method:

```
KeyPair myKeyPair = keyPairGen.generateKeyPair();
```

Secret key algorithms require the use of `SecretKey` objects instead of public/private key-pairs. `SecretKeys` are generated using the `KeyGenerator` class. A `KeyGenerator` is created for a particular algorithm, using the static `getInstance()` method on `KeyGenerator`:

```
KeyGenerator keyGen = KeyGenerator.getInstance("DES");
```

The `KeyGenerator` can be initialized, if necessary, with a random-number generator if the default one is not sufficient:

```
keyGen.initialize(new SecureRandom(mySeed));
```

Finally, a new `SecretKey` can be generated using the `generateKey()` method:

```
SecretKey myKey = keyGen.generateKey();
```

The public, private, and secret keys generated this way can be used to create digital signatures, create message digests, and encrypt data, as described in the coming sections.

Digital Signatures

Certification and authentication are used to protect access to resources in general, by ensuring that only those authorized to have them can get them. An entity (e.g., person, host, software agent) is given some kind of *certification* of their identity or membership in a particular group (e.g., "Fred Smith," "employee of company X," "all computers in department Y"). The entity has to offer this certificate in order to be *authenticated* and given access to the resources being protected.

A typical example of certification in practice is restricting FTP sites to a selected list of hosts on the network. A remote host has to provide its IP address when requesting an FTP connection to the site. The restricted FTP site looks up the IP address in its access table to see if the remote host is certified to access the files on this server. The IP address, then, is acting as an access certificate for this transaction, and the FTP server authenticates the remote host by checking the IP address against its access table. In encrypted data transfers, the encryption key is also acting as a sort of certificate for the receiving party, indicating that they have authority to read the information being sent.

A Motivating Example: A Credit Agent

If you look closely at our SimpleAgent example in Example 5-1, you'll notice that the agent doesn't make any attempt to check who is at the other end of the socket that it opens. In some applications, this might not be a problem. But let's suppose that we're designing a database query agent for a credit-card holding company, servicing requests for credit information about account holders. We decide to implement this query agent with a subclass of SimpleAgent called CreditAgent, shown in Example 5-2. This subclass implements the processMsg() method from SimpleAgent by checking each message from the remote agent for information about the identity of the account being checked. Once the account name has been retrieved from the client's message, the CreditAgent retrieves the information from the database with a getCreditData() method. (In this example, the getCreditData() method isn't fully implemented.) The processMsg() method puts the retrieved account information into a return message, and adds the message to the queue to be sent to the remote agent.

Example 5-2. A Networked Credit Agent

```
package dcj.examples.security;

import java.io.*;

public class CreditAgent extends SimpleAgent {
  public CreditAgent(String host, int port) {
    super(host, port);
  }

  protected void processMsg(String msg) {
    String name = null;
    String cmd = null;
    String retMsg = new String();

    // Parse the command and account name from the input stream.
    StreamTokenizer stok = new StreamTokenizer(new StringReader(msg));
    try {
      stok.nextToken();
      cmd = stok.sval;
      name = stok.sval;
    }
    catch (IOException e) {}

    if (cmd.compareTo("GET") == 0) {
      String cData = getCreditData(name);
      retMsg = name + " " + cData;
    }
```

Example 5-2. A Networked Credit Agent (continued)

```
  else {
    retMsg = "UNKNOWN_CMD";
  }

  // Add return message with results to the message queue.
  addMsg(retMsg);
}

protected String getCreditData(String acctName) {
  // Real method would use account name to
  // initiate a database query...
  return "No info available.";
}
}
```

Can you see where this is leading? This agent will obviously need to authenticate the identity of remote agents requesting this sensitive credit information, to ensure that they're authorized to receive it. In its current form, a client only needs to know the name of an account in order to retrieve credit information about that account. This information is readily available to just about anyone who cares to find it, so it certainly doesn't qualify as the basis for authenticating remote agents.

Public Key Signatures for Authentication

The Java Security API provides the `Signature` class as a way to generate a digital signature, or to verify the identity of a remote agent that is sending you data. The `Signature` class uses public/private key pairs to generate and verify signatures. The party sending a signed message generates a signature by taking a piece of data and encoding it using their private key into a digital signature:

```
PrivateKey myKey = ... // Retrieve my private key
byte[] data = ... // Get the data to be signed
Signature mySig = Signature.getInstance("RSA");
mySig.initSign(myKey);
mySig.update(data);
byte[] signedData = mySig.sign();
```

A `Signature` is created using the static `Signature.getInstance()` method with the name of the algorithm for the signature. The signature is initialized for signing by passing a `PrivateKey` into its `initSign()` method. The private key used to initialize the signature presumably comes from a key pair created earlier, where the private key was stored securely on the local host and the public key was communicated to other agents as needed. The signature is given data to be signed using its `update()` method, and the digital signature for the data is gotten by calling the `sign()` method. After this call is made, the `Signature` data is reset, and another piece of data can be signed by calling `update()` and `sign()` in sequence again. Note that the `update()` method can be called more than once before calling `sign()`, if the data to be signed is stored in separate data items in memory.

Now the original data and the digital signature for the data can be sent to another agent to verify our identity. Assuming that the remote agent already has our public key, the data and the signature can be sent over a simple stream connection:

```
DataOutputStream dout = ... // Get an output stream to the agent
dout.writeInt(data.length);
dout.write(data);
dout.writeInt(signedData.length);
dout.write(signedData);
```

Before each set of bytes is sent, we send the size of each chunk of data, so that the remote host knows how many bytes to expect in each piece of data. On the remote host, the data and signature can be read from the stream connection:

```
DataInputStream din = ... // Get an input stream from the signer
int dataLen = din.readInt();
byte data[] = new byte[dataLen];
din.read(data);
int sigLen = din.readInt();
byte sig = new byte[sigLen];
din.read(sig);
```

To verify the signature, the agent creates a `Signature` object using the signer's public key, initializes it with the raw data from the signer, and then verifies the signature from the signer:

```
Signature theirSig = Signature.getInstance("RSA");
PublicKey theirKey = ... // Get public key for remote agent
theirSig.initVerify(theirKey);
theirSig.update(data);
if (theirSig.verify(sig)) {
    System.out.println("Signature checks out.");
}
else {
    System.out.println("Signature failed. Possible imposter found.");
}
```

The agent receiving the signature also uses a `Signature` object to verify the signature. It creates a `Signature` and initializes it for verification by calling its `initVerify()` method with the signing agent's `PublicKey`. The unsigned data from the remote agent is passed into the `Signature` through its `update()` method. Again, the `update()` method can be called multiple times if the data to be verified is stored in multiple objects. Once all of the unsigned data has been passed into the `Signature`, the signed data can be verified against it by passing it into the `verify()` method, which returns a boolean value.

An Authenticating Credit Agent

To make our credit agent more secure, we've created a subclass of our `Simple-Agent` class called `AuthAgent`, shown in Example 5-3. After the `SimpleAgent` constructor creates a socket connection to the remote agent, the `AuthAgent` constructor attempts to authenticate the remote agent by reading a message from the agent with a digital signature. First it reads an identifier for the agent from the input stream, so that it can look up the agent's public key. Then it reads a set of data and the corresponding signature for the data. The agent ID, original data, and data signature are passed to the `authenticate()` method for verification. The `authenticate()` method first looks up the named agent's `PublicKey` from some kind of local storage, using a `lookupKey()` method whose implementation is not shown here. If the key is found, then a `Signature` is created using the algorithm specified by the `PublicKey`. The `Signature` is initialized for verification using the agent's `PublicKey`. Then the original data is passed into the `Signature`'s `update()` method, and the digital signature from the agent is verified by calling the `verify()` method. If the signature checks out, then we initialize an `Identity` data member with the remote agent's name and `PublicKey`.

Example 5-3. An Authenticating Agent

```
package dcj.examples.security;

import java.lang.*;
import java.net.*;
import java.io.*;
import java.security.*;

public class AuthAgent extends SimpleAgent {

  Identity remoteAgent = null;

  public AuthAgent(String host, int port)
      throws IllegalArgumentException {

    super(host, port);
    DataInputStream din = new DataInputStream(inStream);

    // Try to authenticate the remote agent
    try {
      String agentId = din.readUTF();
```

Example 5-3. An Authenticating Agent (continued)

```java
        int dataLen = din.readInt();
        byte[] data = new byte[dataLen];
        din.read(data);
        int sigLen = din.readInt();
        byte[] sig = new byte[sigLen];
        din.read(sig);

        if (!authenticate(agentId, data, sig)) {
          // Failed to authenticate: write error message, close socket and
          // return
          System.out.println("Failed to authenticate remote agent " +
                             agentId);
          closeConnection();
        }
        else {
          // Remote agent is authenticated, first message is a welcome
          addMsg("HELLO " + agentId);
        }
      }
    catch (Exception e) {
      closeConnection();
    }
  }

  protected boolean authenticate(String id, byte[] data, byte[] sig) {
    boolean success = false;
    PublicKey key = lookupKey(id);
    try {
      // Set up a signature with the agent's public key
      Signature agentSig = Signature.getInstance(key.getAlgorithm());
      agentSig.initVerify(key);
      // Try to verify the signature message from the agent
      agentSig.update(data);
      success = agentSig.verify(sig);

      if (success) {
        // Agent checks out, so initialize an identity for it
        remoteAgent = new Identity(id);
        remoteAgent.setPublicKey(key);
      }
    }
    catch (Exception e) {
      System.err.println("Failed to verify agent signature.");
      success = false;
    }

    return success;
  }
}
```

Using this subclass of `SimpleAgent`, we can make our `CreditAgent` authenticate the agents requesting credit data by checking their authenticated identities against an access list. The updated credit agent is called `AuthCreditAgent`, and is shown in Example 5-4. The `AuthCreditAgent` extends the `AuthAgent` subclass, and adds an `Acl` for the credit data it's serving. The constructor, after calling its parent classes' constructors to initialize and authenticate the connection to the remote agent, initializes an `Acl` object with the access rights given to various agents over the credit data by calling its `initACL()` method. This data might be retrieved from a relational database, or from some kind of directory service. (The details of the implementation of `initACL()` are not shown.)

Example 5-4. An Authenticating Credit Agent

```
package dcj.examples.security;

import java.io.*;
import java.security.*;
import java.security.acl.*;

public class AuthCreditAgent extends AuthAgent {

  protected Acl creditACL;

  public AuthCreditAgent(String host, int port) {
    super(host, port);
    // Initialize our access control lists
    initACL();
  }

  protected void initACL() {
    creditACL = new Acl();
    // Read resources and access permissions
    // from a database, initialize the ACL object
    // ...
  }

  protected void processMsg(String msg) {
    String name = null;
    String cmd = null;
    String retMsg = new String();

    // Parse the command and account name from the input stream.
    StreamTokenizer stok = new StreamTokenizer(new StringReader(msg));
    try {
      stok.nextToken();
      cmd = stok.sval;
      name = stok.sval;
    }
```

Example 5-4. An Authenticating Credit Agent (continued)

```
      catch (IOException e) {}

    if (cmd.compareTo("GET") == 0) {
      if (isAuthorized(remoteAgent, name, "READ")) {
        String cData = getCreditData(name);
        retMsg = name + " " + cData;
      }
      else {
        retMsg = "UNAUTHORIZED";
      }
    }
    else {
      retMsg = "UNKNOWN_CMD";
    }

    // Add return message with results to the message queue.
    addMsg(retMsg);
  }

  protected String getCreditData(String acctName) {
    // Real method would use account name to
    // initiate a database query...
    return "No info available.";
  }

  protected boolean isAuthorized(Identity agent,
                             String acctName, String access) {
    boolean auth;
    Permission p = new PermissionImpl(access);
    auth = creditACL.checkPermission(agent, p);
    return auth;
  }
}
```

With the remote agent authenticated and an access control list initialized, the
AuthCreditAgent processes messages in its processMsg() method much as
it did before. The difference is that, before looking up the credit data for an
account and sending it back to the agent, the agent's access is checked by calling
the isAuthorized() method and passing the agent's Identity, the account
name, and the type of access required ("READ" access, in this case). The isAu-
thorized() method simply calls the checkPermission() method on the
ACL object to verify that the authenticated agent has the required permissions on
the account being accessed. In processMsg(), if the agent is authorized, then
the data is retrieved and returned to the agent in a message. If not, then a curt
"UNAUTHORIZED" message is returned to the agent.

Certification: The Last Identity Link

Our credit agent has come a long way from its initial, rather insecure incarnation. A remote agent now has to provide both an account name and a valid digital signature in order to even make a connection with the `AuthCreditAgent`. And once it has the connection, it has to be on the access control list for the account before the credit agent will release any information about it.

What we haven't answered yet is the question of how the client gets added to the access list. Somehow the credit agent has to get the remote agent's public key, verify their identity, and authorize them with the right access privileges based on their identity.

Distributing Certified Public Keys

A `PublicKey` can be distributed to other agents on the network pretty easily. Since the `Key` interface extends `Serializable`, you can send a key over an `ObjectOutputStream` to a remote agent:

```
OutputStream out = socket.getOutputStream();
ObjectOutputStream objOut = new ObjectOutputStream(out);
PublicKey myKey = ... // Get my public key
// Send my name
objOut.writeObject(new String("Jim"));
// Send my key
objOut.writeObject(myKey);
```

The remote agent can read my key off of its input stream and store the key on a local "key-ring":

```
InputStream in = socket.getInputStream();
ObjectInputStream objIn = new ObjectInputStream(in);
String name = (String)objIn.readObject();
PublicKey key = (PublicKey)objIn.readObject();
storeKey(key, name);
```

But who's to say it was really me that sent the key along with my name? As we mentioned earlier, a sneaky attacker could pretend to be me, send an agent my name with her own public key, and proceed to access resources using my identity. As we mentioned earlier, this problem is solved by *certificates*. A certificate acts as corroborating evidence of an agent's identity. In most certification scenarios, a well-known certification authority (CA) verifies the identity of an agent with whatever means it deems necessary, physical or otherwise. When the authority is certain of the agent's identity, a certificate is issued to the agent verifying its identity. The certificate is typically signed with the CA's own digital signature, which has been communicated to parties that will need to verify agents using certificates issued by the CA. This communication may use secure, offline channels, or even nonelectronic delivery by known individuals. In any event, a CA will typically be known by many other agents on the network, and its identity can be reverified if it's believed that their signature has been forged.

Once an agent has a certificate attesting to its identity, it can broadcast its public key to other parties by sending the key over open channels, then sending a digital signature that includes its certificate. The certificate itself can be used as the data to be signed. The party receiving the signature can verify the agent's public key by verifying the signature against the data message, and then verifying the identity behind the public key by checking the certificate with the certification authority that it came from. If the certificate checks out, then we can be assured that the agent is the agent named in the certificate, and that the agent has a private key corresponding to the public key it sent us. In order to break through these security barriers, a hostile attacker would have to fool a certificate authority into thinking she is someone else, which any respectable CA will not allow to happen, or she would have to create a false certificate for her public key from a CA, which is not possible assuming that the certificate can be verified directly with the CA, and that the cryptographic algorithm used by the CA to generate their signature is not breakable.

Various standard certificate formats, such as X.509 and PKCS, have been defined and are in use in digital commerce, secure email, etc. At the time of this writing, the Java Security API does not include an API for generating or verifying these certificates. Support for standard certificate formats is promised in Java 1.2.

Data Encryption

Now we've seen how you can authenticate a remote agent talking to you over the network, but what about the security of the data you're exchanging? Our Auth-CreditAgent checks the identity of the requesting agent before sending account information to them, but once it does, the data is sent unencoded over the network as a message:

```
String msg = nextMsg();
    ...
dout.writeUTF(msg);
```

So if the data is all an attacker is after, and he couldn't easily bypass our authentication system, he could eavesdrop on the network communications and collect the data that way. To prevent this, you want to encode, or *encrypt*, the data before it's transmitted, in such a way that only the intended recipient can decode the data.

Ciphers for Secure Data Transfers

The Java Cryptography Extension to the Java Security API provides the `java.security.Cipher` class for implementing secure, encrypted data transfers. A `Cipher` can be used on the sending end of a transmission to encrypt data, and on the receiving end to decrypt data. A `Cipher` is created using the `getInstance()` method common to the Java Security API, passing in the name of an algorithm to be used for encryption:

```
Cipher sendCipher = Cipher.getInstance("DES");
```

In this example, we're creating a `Cipher` that uses the DES algorithm to encrypt data. This algorithm is a *symmetric* encryption algorithm, which means that it needs to use the same secret key for both the encryption and decryption of data at either end of the transmission link. Other encryption schemes are considered *asymmetric*, in that they use different keys for encryption and decryption. This term is usually used to refer to encryption algorithms that are based on public key methods. With an asymmetric cipher, a message might be encrypted using an agent's public key, and can only be decrypted using the corresponding private key. The advantage of asymmetric encryption is that we can transmit public keys to other agents in the clear. Symmetric encryption requires that we securely transmit a secret key between two parties. The advantage of symmetric encryption is performance; symmetric algorithms usually take less CPU time to encrypt and decrypt data. Where performance is an issue, you can use a combination of symmetric and asymmetric encryption. A secret key can be transmitted between two parties first, using their public keys and asymmetric encryption on the secret key. Then the rest of the communication can be carried out using symmetric encryption, with the secret key.

For sending data, the `Cipher` that we create needs to be initialized with a key to use to encrypt the data. This is done by passing the `Key` into the `initEncrypt()` method on the `Cipher`:

```
Key encodeKey = ...;    // Get key to be used for encrypting data
sendCipher.initEncrypt(encodeKey);
```

The data to be encrypted is passed into the `Cipher`'s `crypt()` method next:

```
byte[] sensitiveData = ...;
byte[] encodedData = sendCipher.crypt(sensitiveData);
```

The encoded data can now be transmitted safely to another party, where it can be decoded only if the right key and algorithm are used.

The procedure for decrypting the message is similar. A `Cipher` object is created just as in the encryption stage, but it is initialized for decryption using the proper key:

```
Key decodeKey = ...;    // Get the key to be used for decrypting data
receiveCipher.initDecrypt(decodeKey);
```

Once the encoded data is received, either over a `Socket` connection or through some other means, the receiver can decrypt it using the `crypt()` methods on the decrypting `Cipher`:

```
byte[] sensitiveData = receiveCipher.crypt(encodedData);
```

Back to Our Credit Agent

Now we can add data encryption to our credit agent, so that the account information sent back to the remote agent is safe from prying eyes. First, we'll make a new subclass of our `SimpleAgent`, called `SecureAgent`, that includes all of the authentication abilities of the `AuthAgent` from Example 5-3, plus the ability to encrypt and decrypt messages. The `SecureAgent` is shown in Example 5-5. The `SecureAgent` has an extra data member, `cryptKey`, which is a `Key` to be used to encrypt and decrypt messages sent to and from the remote agent. For this example, we'll assume that we're using a symmetric, secret key encryption algorithm to encode messages. The key used for the cipher may have been initialized with a handshaking process involving an asymmetric algorithm, as we described earlier.

Example 5-5. An Agent with Authentication and Encryption

```
package dcj.examples.security;

import java.lang.*;
import java.net.*;
import java.io.*;
import java.security.*;

public class SecureAgent extends SimpleAgent {

  // The Identity of the agent we're connected to
  Identity remoteAgent = null;
  // A secret key used to encode/decode messages
  Key cryptKey = null;

  public SecureAgent(String host, int port)
      throws IllegalArgumentException {

    super(host, port);
    DataInputStream din = new DataInputStream(inStream);
```

Example 5-5. An Agent with Authentication and Encryption (continued)

```
    // Try to authenticate the remote agent
    try {
      String agentId = din.readUTF();
      int dataLen = din.readInt();
      byte[] data = new byte[dataLen];
      din.read(data);
      int sigLen = din.readInt();
      byte[] sig = new byte[sigLen];
      din.read(sig);

      if (!authenticate(agentId, data, sig)) {
        // Failed to authenticate: write error message, close socket and
        // return
        System.out.println("Failed to authenticate remote agent "
                           + agentId);
        closeConnection();
      }
      else {
        // Remote agent is authenticated, first message is a welcome
        addMsg("HELLO " + agentId);
      }
    }
    catch (Exception e) {
      closeConnection();
    }
}

protected boolean authenticate(String id, byte[] data, byte[] sig) {
  boolean success = false;
  PublicKey key = lookupKey(id);
  try {
    // Set up a signature with the agent's public key
    Signature agentSig = Signature.getInstance(key.getAlgorithm());
    agentSig.initVerify(key);
    // Try to verify the signature message from the agent
    agentSig.update(data);
    success = agentSig.verify(sig);

    if (success) {
      // Agent checks out, so initialize an identity for it
      remoteAgent = new Identity(id);
      remoteAgent.setPublicKey(key);
      // Get the agent's secret encryption key, too
      cryptKey = lookupSecretKey(id);
    }
  }
  catch (Exception e) {
    System.err.println("Failed to verify agent signature.");
```

Example 5-5. An Agent with Authentication and Encryption (continued)

```
      success = false;
   }

   return success;
 }

 public void run() {
   // Go into infinite loop, sending messages, receiving responses, and
   // processing them...

   DataInputStream din = (DataInputStream)inStream;
   DataOutputStream dout = (DataOutputStream)outStream;

   // Make an encryption Cipher for sending messages...
   String cryptAlgName = cryptKey.getAlgorithm();
   Cipher sendCipher = Cipher.getInstance(cryptAlgName);
   sendCipher.initEncrypt(cryptKey);
   // ...and a decryption Cipher for receiving them.
   Cipher receiveCipher = Cipher.getInstance(cryptAlgName);
   receiveCipher.initDecrypt(cryptKey);

   while (true) {
     String msg = nextMsg();
     if (msg != null) {
       String inMsg = "", inToken = "";
       try {
         // Send encrypted message to agent
         byte[] eData = sendCipher.crypt(msg.getBytes());
         dout.write(eData);

         // Read and decrypt message from agent
         int dataLen = din.readInt();
         eData = new byte[dataLen];
         din.read(eData);
         byte[] clearData = receiveCipher.crypt(eData);
         inMsg = new String(clearData);

         // Process the incoming message
         processMsg(inMsg);
       }
       catch (Exception e) {}
     }
   }
 }
}
```

The `SecureAgent` constructor is identical to the `AuthAgent`, reading a digital signature from the input stream and passing it to the `authenticate()` method.

The authenticate() method is almost the same: the digital signature is checked, and if it is verified, then the agent's Identity is initialized with their PublicKey. An extra step is added, though, to look up the agent's secret key using the aptly named lookupSecretKey() method. The secret key might be stored in a local database, or on a key-ring in memory. A very simple way to store a key-ring would be to put keys in a Hashtable indexed by the identity name, and then serialize the Hashtable object to a file on disk. In this case, the lookupSecretKey() method on our AuthAgent might look something like this:

```
protected SecretKey lookupSecretKey(String id) {
    SecretKey key = null;

    // Get the key-ring file name from the property list for this agent
    String keyringFile = System.getProperty("keyring", "keyring.dat");

    // Try reading the key-ring and looking up the key for the id
    try {
        // Read the key-ring from disk
        ObjectInputStream in =
            new ObjectInputStream(new FileInputStream(keyringFile));
        Hashtable keyring = in.readObject();
        // Lookup the id's key on the ring
        key = (SecretKey)keyring.get(id);
    }
    catch (Exception e) {
        System.err.println("Failure looking up key on keyring.");
        e.printStackTrace(System.err);
    }

    return key;
}
```

The big difference between the AuthAgent and the SecureAgent is in their run() methods. Before the SecureAgent starts sending and receiving messages in the run() method's while loop, it initializes two Ciphers, one for encrypting outgoing messages and one for decrypting incoming messages. It uses the cryptKey to initialize both Ciphers. In the message-passing loop, the SecureAgent encrypts each outgoing message with the send Cipher, and all incoming messages are read as byte arrays, and decrypted using the receive Cipher.

To make our credit agent use the new encryption abilities offered by the SecureAgent, we can just change the class definition and have the agent extend the SecureAgent rather than the AuthAgent. The processMsg() method will work unchanged since the incoming messages have been decrypted in the SecureAgent.run() method before being passed into the processMsg() method.

Choosing a Cryptographic Algorithm

Throughout this chapter we've shown how objects from the Java Security API, such as `KeyPairGenerators` and `Ciphers`, can be created by specifying a particular cryptographic algorithm for the implementation of the object. We haven't yet discussed the issues involved in picking one algorithm over another.

Features of Cryptographic Algorithms

Cryptography includes a broad range of techniques under its umbrella. Some of the characteristics that distinguish one technique from another follow.

Level of protection

Some encryption techniques provide a virtually unbreakable barrier to information theft; others just require a determined attacker with moderate resources to be broken. One way to compare techniques on this level is to estimate how much CPU time would be required on a machine of a given processing speed to iterate through all the possible keys to the encoded data. For example, "A 128-bit XYZ cryptographic key requires 14.5 months of CPU time on an Acme 24-processor server to be broken." But other issues can affect the level of effort required to break the encrypted data, and make it difficult to objectively compare the security of encryption techniques. For example, if the attacker is not familiar with the format of the data being transmitted, and the data isn't easily interpreted on its own, then it may be tough to tell if an attempt to decode the data has worked or not.

Sophistication and complexity

Encryption techniques are usually based upon the mathematical properties of numbers and digital information. The mathematical theories employed in creating encryption techniques vary in their complexity and sophistication; some require poring over many pages of mathematics and statistics journals to be fully understood, while others can be explained using basic concepts of algebra. The resources required to implement and to break a given encryption technique are usually a direct function of its complexity. All other issues being equal, a more complex encryption scheme is normally more expensive to implement, but is also more expensive to break. As an application developer, you'll typically need to trade off efficiency against security. If high throughput is a requirement for your application, you may be willing to use a less complex, and less secure, cryptographic algorithm if it imposes significantly less overhead on your agents.

One-, two-, and many-way cryptography

Depending on the nature of your distributed application, there may be situations in which many parties need to be individually or mutually authenticated by one agent. A secure chat room or whiteboard system, for example, may require mutual authentication by all participating parties. Most authentication schemes directly support one- or two-way agent authentication. Few, if any, have any concept of multi-way authenticated communications. Instead, the developer must maintain a set of two-way-authenticated channels at each agent site. One way to deal with multi-way authentication is to define a group of individuals as a group identity with a single key pair and set of certificates. Every person in this group needs to prove ownership by providing a digital signature verifying that they have access to the group's private key, and some kind of certification of their keys. The viability of this approach really lies in the policies of the certification authority being used. If they agree to certify groups, and have defined a policy for verifying membership in certain groups, then most cryptographic algorithms will support a key pair or certificate associated with a named group rather than a named individual.

Design issues

As we've already mentioned, modern cryptography involves the use of keys for data signing, encoding, and decoding. Some require the secure distribution of private keys between parties, while others allow the parties to use public keys that can be broadcast openly. In our `SecureAgent` example, we used an encoding scheme that required the use of secret keys.

Other design issues involve the low-level implementation details of the algorithm. If we're building an agent to be used in an applet context, then we'd like the implementation of an cryptographic algorithm to be done completely in Java without any native method calls, so that we don't have to distribute native libraries to every agent that will talk to our agent.

Another issue that may seem obvious is the level of standardization of a cryptographic algorithm. If an algorithm is standardized, or at least widely used, then there is a better chance that we can use our security-enabled agents with other people's agents without modifying them.

Financial and legal issues

An issue of a different sort is the expense of using a cryptographic algorithm. Some of the more sophisticated techniques are patented, and require payment of license fees to be used. Others are simply too involved to be implemented by the average developer, and software implementations can be sold for high prices by those who do have the resources to develop them.*

There are also legal and political restrictions to worry about. The United States, for example, has specific restrictions on the types of encryption that can be implemented for export to foreign countries. Currently, there are two separate versions of the Netscape browser: one for international use, and one for use only within the United States. The latter includes a more sophisticated version of the RSA encryption technology, whose export is restricted by the U.S. federal government.

Available Algorithms

There are numerous cryptographic algorithms for data encryption, and a similar number of certification and authentication techniques. Several umbrella security protocols and standards have been developed that incorporate both encryption and authentication facilities. Among them are Netscape's Secure Socket Layer (at the time of this writing, SSL 3.0 is an IETF Internet Draft), the Pretty Good Privacy (PGP) package developed originally by Phil Zimmermann, and the Public Key Cryptography Standard (PKCS) from RSA Laboratories. S-HTTP is a security protocol designed specifically around the HTTP protocol, which differentiates it from these other, more general protocols. The chief motivation behind the development of these packages is to make encryption and authentication technologies easily accessible to developers, and to provide a common protocol for security-enabled applications to interact freely.

Encryption techniques

We've already discussed some of the differences between public key encryption and secret key techniques. Some commonly used secret key encryption algorithms are the Data Encryption Standard (DES), and the International Data Encryption Algorithm (IDEA).

Some common forms of public key encryption in use today are Diffie-Hellman, derived from the original paper describing public key systems; RSA, licensed by RSA Laboratories; and the Digital Signature Algorithm (DSA), developed by the National Institute of Standards and Technology (NIST). Diffie-Hellman uses an encryption algorithm based on factoring prime numbers, while DSA is based on an algorithm involving discrete logarithms. These two algorithms are believed by many cryptographers to be comparably hard to crack. RSA is based upon a combi-

---

* To give an idea of the kind of price tags being put on high-caliber encryption packages, one set of Java encryption classes was listed at a cost of $25,000 for a limited-use license. Depending on the expected usage of the package, the price tag climbs as high as $100,000.

nation of their own public key encryption scheme with other secret key algorithms, such as DES block ciphers.

Certificates and authentication techniques

As we've already seen, certification and authentication schemes are typically founded on an existing public key encryption technique. The RSA public key cryptography system, for example, can be used in combination with a hashing technique to implement an authentication scheme. One party "signs" a message by running it through a known hashing algorithm, and then encrypts the hashed message with their private key to generate a digital signature. The signature is then sent along with the original message to the other party. The receiving party can then decrypt the signature using the sender's public key, and hash the clear message using the same hashing algorithm used to generate the signature. If the hashed message is equal to the decrypted signature, then the receiving party can assume that the sender is the person that owns the public key. In order to impersonate some other party, we would have to know their private key. Otherwise, we wouldn't be able to generate both a clear message and an encrypted, hashed version of the message that check out against each other.

All authentication systems use certificates, which minimally contain an identifier for a party and the party's public key. The most commonly used standard format for digital certificates is the ITU X.509 standard certificate format. SSL, PKCS, and S-HTTP all offer X.509-compliant certification methods within their protocols. RSA can also be used in conjunction with X.509 certificates. Many cryptographic systems, however, resort to nonstandard certificate formats based on their own binary formatting schemes, where a public key, an identifier, and several other parameters, such as expiration times and serial numbers, are serialized and encrypted before being transmitted.

In most cases, the power of a certificate to authenticate a party rests on the certifying authority (CA) that issues and vouches for the certificate. VeriSign, BBN, and even the United States Postal Service offer CA services. Certificate authorities usually provide several levels of certification and require various types of proof of identity. In some cases an email verification is sufficient; other certificates require verification by a notary public before being issued. A certificate issued from a CA must be installed somehow on your host computer in order to be properly broadcast by your network applications when secure transmissions are attempted. The Netscape browser, for example, will use your personal certificate to establish secure HTTP connections when a remote HTTP server requests it.

General Security Protocols

We've already mentioned some of the more common general security protocols in use today. Support for them in the Java environment is becoming more broadly available, but implementation of the cryptographic algorithms underlying these protocols is a complex task that typically requires the backing of a software development company. If public-domain or shareware versions of these protocols do become available they will undoubtedly be few and far between.

Secure Socket Layer (SSL)

The Secure Socket Layer, originally put forth by Netscape and now an Internet Draft of the IETF, defines a general security protocol for private, authenticated communications. SSL is a protocol that layers on top of a network transport protocol (such as TCP/IP), but below application protocols (such as HTTP) or security APIs (such as the Java Security API). The protocol allows agents to choose from a suite of encryption algorithms and authentication schemes, including DES ciphers and RSA cryptography.

In addition to providing communications security with existing cryptographic techniques, SSL also provides a means to extend the protocol to include new encryption methods that may be developed. SSL also provides a session caching facility, where key pairs associated with a connection to a particular party can be retrieved and used to reinstate secure connections in sessionless application protocols, like HTTP.

Pretty Good Privacy (PGP)

PGP was originally developed by Phil Zimmermann as an effort to get effective privacy and authentication tools into the hands of the general technology community. There has been a shroud of controversy surrounding PGP since its public release by Zimmermann, involving United States export laws concerning cryptographic technology. We won't discuss the sordid details here, except to say that there are essentially two versions of PGP: one for use within the United States and Canada, and another for international use, which does not use certain implementations of RSA encryption algorithms.

In terms of the families of encryption algorithms that we discussed in an earlier section, PGP is a hybrid technique that uses public key methods to distribute private keys between agents. The reason for this is efficiency: public key methods are computationally very expensive, and can significantly reduce your data throughput if all data is transmitted with public key encryption. PGP tries to circumvent this by using RSA public key encryption to transmit a pair of random private keys between the two parties securely. Once the agents have each other's private keys, they can proceed to encrypt their messages using faster, private key encryption. Messages are encrypted using a block cipher called IDEA. Note that, while SSL allows us to specify what kind of encryption we would like to use, the encryption scheme used by PGP is fixed.

Authentication in PGP can be implemented with digital signatures, using a method similar to that used by RSA for authentication. An MD5 hashing function and RSA encryption is used to generate the signature.

6

Message-Passing Systems

In this chapter we examine applications that use message-passing schemes to distribute information between agents in a distributed system. The first thing we'll do is define what we mean by "message passing," then we'll look at some ways that messages can be handled by a Java agent. We'll build two versions of a message-passing system. The first is based on a homegrown message-handling system, with `Message` objects being transmitted over I/O streams between `MessageHandlers`. Most of our discussion about message passing will be based on these classes. Near the end of the chapter, we'll look at a message-passing system based on the delegation event model built into the JDK and used by the AWT package. In this case, we'll be using `EventObjects` as our messages, and leveraging the model of event sources and listeners from the JDK to build a message-handling framework.

Messages Defined

Before we start discussing message-passing systems, we need to define what we mean by a *message*. Essentially, a message is a structured piece of information sent from one agent to another over a communication channel. Some messages are requests made to one agent by another, other messages deliver data or notification to another agent. In most applications that we'll discuss, a message consists of a message identifier and, if needed, a set of message arguments. The message identifier tells the receiver the purpose or type of the message. The arguments to the message contain additional information that is interpreted based on the type of message. They may contain the object of an action (e.g., the message "*x y*" means, "Do *x* to *y* and return the result"), or they may contain information used to carry out a request (e.g., "*x a b c*" means, "Do *x*, and use *a*, *b*, and *c* to do it").

Message identifiers are usually simple, unique tokens that differentiate one type of message from another. They may even be simple integer values, where the agents on either end use a look-up table of some sort to match the value with its meaning. Message arguments, on the other hand, can be of many types. Some simple message protocols get away with using only basic data types, like integers, strings, and floating-point values, for message arguments. These arguments can be read and written directly using the `DataInputStream` and `DataOutput-Stream` classes. Other protocols need to use more complicated data types and objects as message arguments. These complex data types can be sent as an ordered sequence of simple data types over a `DataOutputStream`. They can also be transmitted as objects using the Java RMI object serialization support, as discussed in Chapter 3, *Distributing Objects*.

In some very well defined and controlled application environments, a message protocol may not need message identifiers at all. The interactions between agents may be so strictly defined that there's no need to specify the type of message being sent because the receiver is already expecting it. Suppose, for example, that we have two chess-playing agents talking to each other. Assuming that they both always make valid moves and that they both continue to play until checkmate results, the only kind of message they need to exchange is one that contains the next move that they want to make, with an optional argument that indicates if the move results in a "check" or a "checkmate." In this case, there's no need for message identifiers—the messages can just contain the chess players' moves.

In a sense, every network standard and protocol we've discussed so far can be boiled down to some form of message passing. HTTP, SSL, even low-level network protocols like TCP/IP are protocols built around some form of message passing. When we speak of message passing in this chapter, however, we are talking about message passing that is done explicitly by the application programmer. While these other protocols are built around some kind of message-passing protocol, that level of the protocol is hidden from the developer by an API of some kind. For example, SSL is utilized by an application programmer through a class library, where method calls on SSL-related objects are automatically broken down into SSL-compliant messages. Likewise, incoming SSL "messages" are processed and mapped into new data objects and method calls on SSL objects. This is what makes these complicated but powerful protocols so useful: the application programmer doesn't need to know the details of the protocol at the lower level. When we speak of message passing in this chapter, we're referring to situations where the message protocol—the generation and the processing of messages—is defined and performed directly at the application level.

Why Do We Need Messages?

This is a perfectly valid question. If we have object-based communication schemes like CORBA and RMI available in the Java environment, why would we have to resort to passing messages, a simple but restrictive communication method, to transmit information between agents?

While message passing isn't as sophisticated and robust as distributed objects, it's relatively simple to implement using the `java.io` package. The goals of the two approaches are very different. Distributing objects extends an application across the network by making its objects appear to be spread across the hosts in our virtual machine. Message passing serves a much simpler role, defining a simple communication protocol for sending data. Passing messages over I/O streams also avoids the communication overhead involved in using most distributed object schemes, and doesn't require any special network protocols. So message passing is a useful and sometimes necessary tool, particularly in the following situations:

- Communication needs are relatively simple in nature

- Transaction throughput is critical

- The scope of the your system is limited, so that rapid implementation takes precedence over sophistication and flexibility of design

- Special network protocols need to be avoided (e.g., parts of the system need to operate behind a firewall)

- Remote object protocols (e.g., an applet in a browser that doesn't support RMI or CORBA) simply aren't available

Message Processing

When you're developing an agent that will be exchanging messages, it's important to think about how message processing will integrate with the rest of the objects making up the agent. Ideally, you'd like to:

Isolate communications details from application details
> This leaves you free to design the bulk of the classes making up the application around application issues, not issues related to the communication scheme you happen to be using. Likewise, the communications subsystem can be designed and updated independently, based on the communication needs of the overall system.

Provide a structured way to link messages to method calls on application objects
> You need a well-defined way for incoming messages to trigger method calls on application objects, and for object methods to generate messages to remote agents to service requests.

These may seem like conflicting requirements, but we'll see that they can both be satisfied to one degree or another by a single message-processing method.

Asychronous vs. Synchronous Message Handling

A crucial question in designing a message-processing system is whether it needs to be asynchronous or not. In our chess example, the player agents can process messages synchronously, since they'll be handshaking throughout the entire game. That is, one player sends a move (in a message) to the other player; the second player applies the move to its copy of the "playing board," weighs its options, and sends its countermove to the first player. In this simple example, there isn't anything else a player needs to do while choosing its move or waiting for the other player to send its move, so there's no need for the ability to receive and process messages asynchronously.

This isn't usually the case, though. Messages usually trigger some significant processing by an agent, which can be carried on while waiting for any further messages. Agents in an application will usually be better off if they can send and receive messages asynchronously from any other work they may need to do. This "other work" may be in response to these messages, or may be independent of the message passing that's going on. If we were implementing a more sophisticated network game than our simple chess system, each player agent might have plenty of work to do in addition to sending and receiving messages. There may be user input to deal with, multiple remote players to synchronize with, graphical displays to update, and complicated internal models to keep straight. To keep everything in the agent running smoothly, asynchronous message I/O will probably be necessary, so your message-passing scheme should support it.

A Basic Message Processor

Based on our earlier definition of a message, the `BasicMessage` class shown in Example 6-1 is an implementation of a generic message object. It has a message identifier and a list of arguments, all represented as strings. The `BasicMessage` has public methods for querying its identifier (`messageId()`) and its arguments (`argList()`). It also has an abstract `Do()` method, which will be implemented in subclasses of `BasicMessage` to perform whatever is required by the given message. It's in the `Do()` method implementations that we'll both define our message protocol, and link our message-passing scheme to the application objects in the system. For each type of message in our protocol, a subclass of `BasicMessage` can be defined to interpret the message arguments and do whatever is required for that type of message.

Example 6-1. A Basic Message Class

```
package dcj.examples.messageV1;

import java.util.Vector;
```

Example 6-1. A Basic Message Class (continued)

```java
public abstract class BasicMessage
{
  protected String id;
  protected Vector argList;

  public BasicMessage() {
    argList = new Vector();
  }

  public BasicMessage(String mid) {
    id = mid;
    argList = new Vector();
  }

  protected void setId(String mid) {
    id = mid;
  }

  public void addArg(String arg) {
    argList.addElement(arg);
  }

  public String messageID() {
    return id;
  }

  public Vector argList() {
    Vector listCopy = (Vector)argList.clone();
    return listCopy;
  }

  public abstract boolean Do();
}
```

To send and receive messages over a connection to a remote agent, we have the
`BasicMsgHandler`, shown in Example 6-2. This class handles messages in terms
of string *tokens*—a message is simply a series of tokens followed by an "end-of-
message" indicator. The first token is the message identifier, and the rest are arguments to the message. The `readMsg()` method on `BasicMsgHandler` reads
the message identifier of the incoming message first, then calls `buildMes-
sage()` to construct the message object corresponding to the message type. The
`buildMessage()` method is abstract in `BasicMsgHandler`, and is implemented by subclasses to match the message protocol being used.

To support asynchronous message processing, the `BasicMsgHandler` also implements the `Runnable` interface. The `run()` method is a loop that reads a

message, calls the message's `Do()` method, then reads the next message. The `BasicMsgHandler`'s `run()` method does not send messages directly. If a message needs to be sent to the remote agent, it will have to be done inside the `Do()` method of one of the incoming messages, or outside of the `BasicMsg-Handler`'s thread altogether. A static message handler object is associated with the `BasicMsgHandler` class for this purpose. It's initialized by the `BasicMsg-Handler` constructors—when a `BasicMsgHandler` is created, it sets the static handler object to point to itself. In many message-passing applications there is one central message handler for each agent, and it's sometimes convenient to have this message handler globally accessible. For example, the `Do()` method on a `BasicMessage` subclass may need to send a message to the remote agent in response to the message it has just processed. Note that the static message handler object is declared `public`, so an application can change the global handler when necessary.

Example 6-2. A Basic Message Handler

```
package dcj.examples.messageV1;

import java.util.Vector;
import java.lang.*;
import java.io.*;

public abstract class BasicMsgHandler implements Runnable
{
  // Static message handler for applications where only one message
  // handler is used and needs to be globally accessible.
  public static BasicMsgHandler current = null;

  InputStream msgIn;
  OutputStream msgOut;
  StreamTokenizer tokenizer;
  String msgEndToken = "END";

  public BasicMsgHandler(InputStream in, OutputStream out) {
    setStreams(in, out);
    current = this;
  }

  public BasicMsgHandler(InputStream in, OutputStream out,
                         String endToken) {
    msgEndToken = endToken;
    setStreams(in, out);
    current = this;
  }

  protected void setStreams(InputStream in, OutputStream out) {
```

Example 6-2. A Basic Message Handler (continued)

```
    msgIn = in;
    msgOut = out;
  }

  public BasicMessage readMsg() throws IOException {
    BasicMessage msg;
    String token;
    DataInputStream din = new DataInputStream(msgIn);

    token = din.readUTF();
    msg = buildMessage(token);

    if (msg != null) {
      boolean msgEnd = false;
      while (!msgEnd) {
        token = din.readUTF();
        if (token.compareTo(msgEndToken) == 0)
          msgEnd = true;
        else {
          msg.addArg(token);
        }
      }
    }
    return msg;
  }

  public void sendMsg(BasicMessage msg) throws IOException {
    boolean success = true;
    DataOutputStream dout = new DataOutputStream(msgOut);

    dout.writeUTF(msg.messageID());

    Vector args = msg.argList();
    int acnt = args.size();
    for (int i = 0; i < acnt; i++) {
      dout.writeUTF((String)args.elementAt(i));
    }

    dout.writeUTF(msgEndToken);
  }

  public void run() {
    try {
      while (true) {
        BasicMessage msg = readMsg();
        if (msg != null)
          msg.Do();
      }
```

Example 6-2. A Basic Message Handler (continued)

```
    }
    // Treat an IOException as a termination of the message
    // exchange, and let this message-processing thread die.
    catch (IOException e) {}
  }

  protected abstract BasicMessage buildMessage(String msgId);
}
```

These two classes define a framework for simple message-passing protocols. In the next section, we'll see how to use these classes in practice, and how this structure needs to be expanded to support more complex message-passing situations.

Fixed Protocols

If we recall our definition of a message as an identifier followed by a set of arguments, we can break down the possible message protocols into *fixed* and *adaptable* types. In this section we'll discuss fixed protocols, where the set of possible identifiers and the arguments for each type of message are known beforehand and don't change during a communication session. Adaptable protocols have variable argument lists on messages, or variable sets of message types, or both.

Let's return to the chess-player agents that we mentioned earlier and define a fixed protocol that they could use to engage in a game of chess. We'll define a protocol that will let them pass moves back and forth, confirm each other's moves, and concede a game. Then we'll implement this message protocol using our BasicMessage and BasicMsgHandler classes.

Figure 6-1 shows the architecture of the chess-playing system we'll be building in the following sections. On each player's host computer, a ChessPlayer object keeps track of the current board layout and comes up with the player's next move. A ChessServer object handles all of the communication with the remote opponent; it packages up moves from the local player into messages, and ships them off to the opponent's ChessServer. (It also takes messages from the remote opponent and calls the required methods on the local ChessPlayer.)

Before we define the protocol that the distributed chess system will use, let's put together the application-level classes that act as our chess players. The Chess-Player class in Example 6-3 demonstrates the interface to our chess player agents. The ChessPlayer maintains the state of the chess board internally. (We don't show the details of the data structures here, since they're not directly relevant to the topic at hand.) The methods defined on the ChessPlayer interface

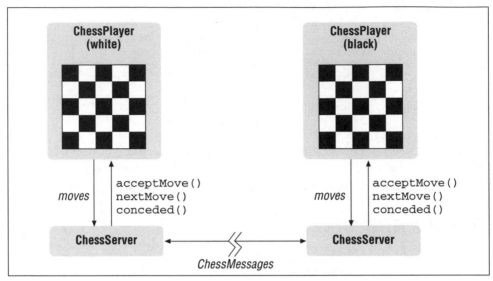

Figure 6-1. Chess system architecture

provide the means for telling the chess player the opposing player's moves, and asking the chess player for its moves.

The `acceptMove()` method is called on a `ChessPlayer` when a move from the opposing player has been received. The requested move is given to the chess player to be confirmed as valid against the current state of the board. Game moves are represented as a "from" position, a "to" position, and a flag indicating whether the move results in a "check," a "checkmate," or neither. The "from" and "to" positions are represented as strings, such as "K3" for "King's 3," "R4" for "Rook's 4," etc. The `nextMove()` method asks the chess player for its next move based on the current board position. The move is returned as the value of the reference arguments. The generated move will not be applied to the game board until the `moveAccepted()` method is called. This indicates that the opposing player has accepted the move and applied it to its copy of the game board. These three methods are used by the two players to submit and confirm each other's moves during a game. Calling a player's `concede()` method tells it that the opponent has conceded the game.

We've designed this application object independently of the fact that we're planning on using message passing. We could be using any communication scheme at all to pass moves between two `ChessPlayers`. We could even create two `Chess-Player` objects within one process and engage in a game by calling methods on each of them in turn.

Example 6-3. A Chess Player Agent

```
package dcj.examples.messageV1;

public class ChessPlayer {
  // Data structures for maintaining chess board state
  // ...

  public static final int CHECK = 0;
  public static final int CHECKMATE = 1;
  public static final int NO_CHECK = 2;

  public ChessPlayer() {
    // Initialize chess board
  }

  public boolean acceptMove(String from, String to,
                            int checkOrMate) {
    // Check validity of requested move.
    // If valid, apply to chess board and return true.
    // If invalid, return false.
    // ...
    return true;
  }

  public boolean nextMove(String from, String to,
                          int checkOrMate) {
    // Generate our next move based on the current
    // state of the game board...
    // ...
    return true;
  }

  public void moveAccepted(String from, String to,
                           int checkOrMate) {
    // Our move was accepted as valid, apply it to the
    // game board...
    // ...
  }

  public void conceded() {
    // We've won!
  }
}
```

Now that we've defined the agents that will be playing the chess game, we can define the message protocol they'll use. First, they'll need a message to pass moves back and forth:

1. `move from to checkOrMate`

   The message identifier is "move," and it contains three arguments. The first is the "from" position (a string), the second is the "to" position (a string), and the third is the integer flag indicating check, checkmate, or neither.

Next, they will need messages to confirm or reject each other's moves:

2. `confirm from to checkFlag`

   The arguments indicate the particular move that was accepted by the opponent.

3. `reject`

   The last move was rejected as invalid by the opponent.

Finally, they need a message to use when a game is being conceded:

4. `concede`

   The opposing player is conceding the game.

The next step is to define the link from these messages to our chess player agents and their corresponding methods. Using our `BasicMessage` and `BasicMsgHandler` classes, we first need to define subclasses of `BasicMessage` corresponding to each of the message types in our protocol. Then we need to extend the `BasicMsgHandler` class to implement a chess server, which will convert incoming messages into corresponding `BasicMessage` subclasses and call their `Do()` methods.

Example 6-4 shows the subclasses of `BasicMessage` corresponding to the message types in our chess-playing protocol. Each of the message objects will need access to the local chess player object in order to translate an incoming message into the appropriate method call on the chess player agent. The `ChessMessage` class acts as a base class for our message objects, providing a reference to a `ChessPlayer`. Now we derive a class for each type of message in our chess protocol. Each of the message objects shown in Example 6-4 can be used for both processing an incoming message of a given type and generating an outgoing message of the same type. Each has a pair of constructors: one accepts a `Chess-Player` object and a list of arguments for the message, and one just accepts a list of the message's arguments. The former is used when an incoming message is being processed, and a call to a method on the `ChessPlayer` will be required. The latter is used for generating outgoing messages, where the local `Chess-Player` object is not necessary.

Example 6-4. Messages in a Chess Protocol

```
package dcj.examples.messageV1;

import java.io.*;

abstract class ChessMessage extends BasicMessage {
  protected ChessPlayer player;

  public ChessMessage(ChessPlayer p) { player = p; }
  public ChessMessage()              { player = null; }
}

class MoveMessage extends ChessMessage {
  public MoveMessage(ChessPlayer p) {
    super(p);
    setId("move");
  }

  public MoveMessage(String from, String to, int checkFlag) {
    setId("move");
    addArg(from);
    addArg(to);
    addArg(Integer.toString(checkFlag));
  }

  public boolean Do() {
    boolean success = true;
    BasicMsgHandler handler = BasicMsgHandler.current;

    String from = (String)argList.elementAt(0);
    String to = (String)argList.elementAt(1);
    String checkStr = (String)argList.elementAt(2);
    int checkFlag = Integer.valueOf(checkStr).intValue();

    try {
      if (!player.acceptMove(from, to, checkFlag)) {
        handler.sendMsg(new RejectMoveMessage());
      }
      else {
        ConfirmMoveMessage cmmsg =
          new ConfirmMoveMessage(from, to, checkFlag);
        handler.sendMsg(cmmsg);

        // We accepted the opponent's move, now send them
        // our countermove, unless they just mated us...
        if (checkFlag == ChessPlayer.CHECKMATE) {
          ConcedeMessage cmsg = new ConcedeMessage();
          handler.sendMsg(cmsg);
        }
```

Example 6-4. Messages in a Chess Protocol (continued)

```
        else {
          player.nextMove(from, to, checkFlag);
          MoveMessage mmsg = new MoveMessage(from, to, checkFlag);
          handler.sendMsg(mmsg);
        }
      }
    }
    catch (IOException e) {
      success = false;
    }
    return success;
  }
}

class ConfirmMoveMessage extends ChessMessage {
  public ConfirmMoveMessage(String from, String to, int checkFlag) {
    setId("confirm");
    addArg(from);
    addArg(to);
    addArg(Integer.toString(checkFlag));
  }

  public ConfirmMoveMessage(ChessPlayer p) {
    super(p);
    setId("confirm");
  }

  public boolean Do() {
    boolean success = true;

    // Opponent accepted our last move, so record it on our
    // copy of the game board.
    String from = (String)argList.elementAt(0);
    String to = (String)argList.elementAt(1);
    String cmateStr = (String)argList.elementAt(2);
    int checkOrMate = Integer.valueOf(cmateStr).intValue();
    player.moveAccepted(from, to, checkOrMate);
    return success;
  }
}

class RejectMoveMessage extends ChessMessage {
  public RejectMoveMessage() {
    setId("reject");
  }

  public RejectMoveMessage(ChessPlayer p) {
    super(p);
```

Example 6-4. Messages in a Chess Protocol (continued)

```
      setId("reject");
  }

  public boolean Do() {
    boolean success = true;
    String newFrom = "";
    String newTo = "";
    int newCheckFlag = ChessPlayer.NO_CHECK;
    BasicMsgHandler handler = BasicMsgHandler.current;

    try {
      if (player.nextMove(newFrom, newTo, newCheckFlag)) {
        MoveMessage mmsg =
          new MoveMessage(newFrom, newTo, newCheckFlag);
        handler.sendMsg(mmsg);
      }
      else {
        // Our player didn't come up with another move, so
        // concede the game
        handler.sendMsg(new ConcedeMessage());
      }
    }
    catch (IOException e) {
      success = false;
    }

    return success;
  }
}

class ConcedeMessage extends ChessMessage {
  public ConcedeMessage() {
    setId("concede");
  }

  public ConcedeMessage(ChessPlayer p) {
    super(p);
    setId("concede");
  }

  public boolean Do() {
    player.conceded();
    return true;
  }
}
```

These message classes are used by the `ChessServer` class in Example 6-5 to convert incoming messages into method calls on the local `ChessPlayer`, and to generate outgoing messages for the remote chess player. A `ChessServer` is

constructed with an input and output stream connecting it to the remote opponent. The ChessServer makes a new ChessPlayer in its constructor to act as
the local player. The ChessServer's buildMessage() method checks each
incoming message identifier and constructs the appropriate message object for
each, passing the local ChessPlayer reference into each constructor. When the
message's Do() method is called in the implementation of run() inherited from
BasicMsgHandler, the message arguments, if any, will be parsed, and the appropriate method will be called on the local ChessPlayer.

Example 6-5. A Chess Server

```java
package dcj.examples.messageV1;

import java.io.*;

public class ChessServer extends BasicMsgHandler
{
  ChessPlayer player;

  public ChessServer(InputStream in, OutputStream out) {
    super(in, out);
    player = new ChessPlayer();
  }

  public ChessPlayer getPlayer() {
    return player;
  }

  protected BasicMessage buildMessage(String msgId) {
    BasicMessage msg = null;

    System.out.println("Got message type \"" + msgId + "\"");

    if (msgId.compareTo("move") == 0) {
      msg = new MoveMessage(player);
    }
    else if (msgId.compareTo("confirm") == 0) {
      msg = new ConfirmMoveMessage(player);
    }
    else if (msgId.compareTo("reject") == 0) {
      msg = new RejectMoveMessage(player);
    }
    else if (msgId.compareTo("concede") == 0) {
      msg = new ConcedeMessage(player);
    }

    return msg;
  }
}
```

To see the chess message protocol in action, let's walk through a hypothetical game played between two players on the network. First, the two processes containing the player objects need to establish a socket connection with corresponding input/output streams. (We won't show the details of this, since we've already seen some examples of creating socket connections, and there's nothing new or exciting about this one.) Once the socket connection is made, each player process passes the input and output streams from the socket to the constructor for a `ChessServer`. The `ChessServer` constructor passes the input and output streams to the `BasicMsgHandler` constructor, then creates a local `Chess-Player` object. One of the player processes (let's call it the "white" player) starts the game by requesting a move from the `ChessPlayer`, wraps the move into a `MoveMessage` object, and tells the `ChessServer` to send the message by calling its `sendMsg()` method with the message object. A section of code like the following is used:

```
// Create the server and get the local player object
ChessServer server = new ChessServer(ins, outs);
ChessPlayer player = server.getPlayer();

// Get the player's first move, and generate a move message
String from, to;
int checkFlag;
player.nextMove(from, to, checkFlag);
MoveMessage mmsg = new MoveMessage(from, to, checkFlag);

// Send the move message to the opponent
server.sendMsg(mmsg);
```

The opponent player process (the "black" player) can start off by wrapping its `ChessServer` in a `Thread` and calling its `run()` method, causing it to enter its message-reading loop. The black player receives the move message from the white player, converts the message into a `MoveMessage` object, then calls the `Do()` method on the message object. The `Do()` method on `MoveMessage` takes the move from the white player and passes it to the black `ChessPlayer` through its `acceptMove()` method. If the black `ChessPlayer` accepts the move, then a `ConfirmMoveMessage` is constructed and returned to the white player to signal that the move has been accepted. The white player's `ChessServer` will receive the confirmation message, and the `Do()` method on the `ConfirmMoveMessage` object will tell the white player that its last move was accepted. If the white player's move was a checkmate, then a `ConcedeMessage` is also constructed and sent to the white player. If not, then the black player is asked for its countermove, and it's sent as a `MoveMessage` to the white player. The black player's `ChessServer` then waits for a confirmation or rejection of the move from the white player.

If the white player's first move was not accepted by the black player, then a `RejectMoveMessage` is constructed and sent to the white player. The white player's `ChessServer` receives the rejection message, converts it into a local `RejectMoveMessage` object, and the message's `Do()` method asks the white player for another move. If a new move is given, it is wrapped in a `MoveMessage` object and sent back to the black player. If not, this is taken as a concession of the game, and a `ConcedeMessage` object is constructed to send a concede message to the black player.

This message passing continues until one of the players receives and accepts a checkmate move and concedes the game, or until one of the players fails to generate a countermove, which acts as a forfeit of the game.

Heterogeneous Argument Lists

This message-passing example was kept simple by avoiding some of the common issues that arise even with fixed message protocols. The messages in the chess protocol consist only of string tokens, delimited by a set of special characters. This allowed us to define a single `readMsg()` method on our `BasicMsgHandler` class that we could reuse in our chess game example. It also allowed us to represent all message arguments using a list of strings in our `BasicMessage` class. If we know that every message is a sequence of strings ending with a special "end-of-message" string, then we can read and store each message from the input stream in the same way, without knowing what type of message was being read. This is just what the `readMsg()` method does—after checking the message identifier in the `buildMessage()` method to see which message object to create, `readMsg()` reads each message from the input stream the same way:

```
while (!msgEnd) {
    token = din.readUTF();
    if (token.compareTo(msgEndToken) == 0)
        msgEnd = true;
    else {
        msg.addArg(token);
    }
}
```

Typically, we can't be this simplistic, since messages may need to contain data of various types. Actually, we didn't completely escape this issue; notice that the "move" message has an argument (the "checkFlag" argument) that is supposed to be an integer, not a string. We got around the limitation of our message-passing facility by converting the integer to a string on sending the message, and then converting back to an integer on the receiving end.

In order to add the ability to send and receive heterogeneous argument lists on messages, we would need to update our message-passing facility so that each message class reads and converts its own arguments from the input stream. Another option would be to have `BasicMsgHandler` convert the arguments to their proper types in its `readMsg()` method. This could be done by having the `readMsg()` method know the format of all of the message types the `BasicMsg-Handler` supports. This would put the entire protocol definition in the `Basic-MsgHandler` class, which makes updating the message protocol more difficult. Overall, having the message objects parse their own arguments leaves our message-passing facility more flexible for future changes.

Example 6-6 shows a new version of the `BasicMessage` class that handles heterogeneous argument lists. The argument list is still implemented using a `Vector`, but the `Vector` now contains references to `Objects` rather than `Strings`. Message arguments are offered and accepted by the new `BasicMessage` class as `Objects` as well.

Example 6-6. Updated Basic Message Class

```java
package dcj.examples.messageV2;

import java.util.Vector;
import java.io.*;

abstract class BasicMessage
{
  protected String id;
  protected Vector argList;
  String endToken = "END";

  public BasicMessage() {
    argList = new Vector();
  }

  public BasicMessage(String mid) {
    id = mid;
    argList = new Vector();
  }

  protected void setId(String mid) {
    id = mid;
  }

  public void addArg(Object arg) {
    argList.addElement(arg);
  }

  public String messageID() {
```

Example 6-6. Updated Basic Message Class (continued)

```java
      return id;
  }

  public Vector argList() {
    Vector listCopy = (Vector)argList.clone();
    return listCopy;
  }

  public boolean readArgs(InputStream ins) {
    boolean success = true;
    DataInputStream din = new DataInputStream(ins);

    // Read tokens until the "end-of-message" token is seen.
    try {
      String token = din.readUTF();
      while (token.compareTo(endToken) != 0) {
        addArg(token);
        token = din.readUTF();
      }
    }
    catch (IOException e) {
      // Failed to read complete argument list.
      success = false;
    }
    return success;
  }

  public boolean writeArgs(OutputStream outs) {
    int len = argList.size();
    boolean success = true;
    DataOutputStream dout = new DataOutputStream(outs);

    // Write each argument in order
    try {
      for (int i = 0; i < len; i++) {
        String arg = (String)argList.elementAt(i);
        dout.writeUTF(arg);
      }

      // Finish with the end-of-message token
      dout.writeUTF(endToken);
    }
    catch (IOException e) {
      success = false;
    }
    return success;
  }
```

Example 6-6. Updated Basic Message Class (continued)

```
  public abstract String Do();
}
```

To allow message objects to parse their own arguments, `BasicMessage` has two additional methods: `readArgs()` and `writeArgs()`. The `readArgs()` method takes an `InputStream` as its only argument, and is meant to read the arguments for the message from the `InputStream`. The default implementation of `readArgs()` provided on the `BasicMessage` class is stolen from the `readMsg()` method from the original `BasicMsgHandler` class; it treats the incoming message as a sequence of string tokens ending with a known "end-of-message" token. The `writeArgs()` method takes an `OutputStream` as an argument, and writes the message arguments to the output stream. The default implementation is copied from the `sendMsg()` method from the original `BasicMsgHandler`; it converts each argument to a `String` and writes it to the output stream. The "end-of-message" token is sent after the message arguments to mark the end of the message.

The message classes for our chess protocol need to be updated to match the new `BasicMessage` class. The most significant changes are to the `MoveMessage` and `ConfirmMoveMessage` classes, since they now need to provide their own implementations of the `readArgs()` and `writeArgs()` methods. Example 6-7 shows the updated `MoveMessage` class. Its `readArgs()` method reads the arguments defining the chess move (*from* and *to* strings, and a *check/checkmate* flag) from the `InputStream`, and its `writeArgs()` method writes the same arguments to the `OutputStream`.

Example 6-7. Updated MoveMessage Class

```
class MoveMessage extends ChessMessage {
  public MoveMessage(ChessPlayer p) {
    super(p);
    setId("move");
  }

  public MoveMessage(String from, String to, int checkFlag) {
    setId("move");
    addArg(from);
    addArg(to);
    addArg(new Integer(checkFlag));
  }

  public boolean Do() {
    boolean success = true;
    BasicMsgHandler handler = BasicMsgHandler.current;
```

Example 6-7. Updated MoveMessage Class (continued)

```
    String from = (String)argList.elementAt(0);
    String to = (String)argList.elementAt(1);
    Integer checkInt = (Integer)argList.elementAt(2);
    int checkFlag = checkInt.intValue();

    try {
      if (!player.acceptMove(from, to, checkFlag)) {
        handler.sendMsg(new RejectMoveMessage());
      }
      else {
        ConfirmMoveMessage ccmsg =
          new ConfirmMoveMessage(from, to, checkFlag);
        handler.sendMsg(ccmsg);

        // We accepted the opponent's move, now send them
        // our countermove, unless they just mated us...
        if (checkFlag == ChessPlayer.CHECKMATE) {
          ConcedeMessage cmsg = new ConcedeMessage();
          handler.sendMsg(cmsg);
        }
        else {
          player.nextMove(from, to, checkFlag);
          MoveMessage mmsg = new MoveMessage(from, to, checkFlag);
          handler.sendMsg(mmsg);
        }
      }
    }
    catch (IOException e) {
      success = false;
    }
    return success;
  }

  public boolean readArgs(InputStream ins) {
    boolean success = true;

    DataInputStream din = new DataInputStream(ins);

    try {
      String from = din.readUTF();
      addArg(from);
      String to = din.readUTF();
      addArg(to);
      int checkFlag = din.readInt();
      addArg(new Integer(checkFlag));

      // Got all of our arguments, now watch for the
      // end-of-message token
```

Example 6-7. Updated MoveMessage Class (continued)

```
      String temp = din.readUTF();
      while (temp.compareTo(endToken) != 0) {
        temp = din.readUTF();
      }
    }
    catch (Exception e) {
      success = false;
    }

    return success;
  }

  public boolean writeArgs(OutputStream outs) {
    boolean success = true;
    DataOutputStream dout = new DataOutputStream(outs);

    String from = (String) argList.elementAt(0);
    String to = (String)argList.elementAt(1);
    Integer tmpInt = (Integer)argList.elementAt(2);
    int checkFlag = tmpInt.intValue();

    try {
      dout.writeUTF(from);
      dout.writeUTF(to);
      dout.writeInt(checkFlag);
      dout.writeUTF(endToken);
    }
    catch (IOException e) {
      success = false;
    }
    return success;
  }
}
```

The only change required to the `BasicMsgHandler` class is to update its `readMsg()` and `sendMsg()` methods to delegate the reading and writing of arguments to the message objects they create:

```
    public BasicMessage readMsg() throws IOException {
        BasicMessage msg;
        String token;
        DataInputStream din = new DataInputStream(msgIn);

        // Get message ID and build corresponding BasicMessage
        token = din.readUTF();
        msg = buildMessage(token);

        // Tell message to read its args
        if (msg != null && msg.readArgs(msgIn))
```

```
        return msg;
    else
        return null;
}
public void sendMsg(BasicMessage msg) throws IOException {
    boolean success = true;
    DataOutputStream dout = new DataOutputStream(msgOut);
    // Send message ID
    dout.writeUTF(msg.messageID());
    // Tell message to send its arguments
    msg.writeArgs(msgOut);
}
```

Objects as Message Arguments

With this new version of our message-passing facility, we can define message types that have arguments of any data type that can be transmitted over an I/O stream. We can even use the object serialization facility built into the Java I/O package to use objects as message arguments.

Suppose we define an object to represent a chess move in our chess protocol example. Example 6-8 shows a ChessMove class that encapsulates in a single object the *from*, *to*, and *checkFlag* arguments corresponding to a chess move. We can easily alter our MoveMessage and ConfirmMoveMessage classes to use a ChessMove object as its single message argument. The updated MoveMessage class is shown in Example 6-9. The readArgs() and writeArgs() methods now use ObjectInputStreams and ObjectOutputStreams to read and write the ChessMove argument over the network.

Example 6-8. A ChessMove Class

```
package dcj.examples.messageV2;

class ChessMove {
  String fromPos;
  String toPos;
  int checkFlag;

  public ChessMove(String from, String to, int ckFlag) {
    fromPos = from;
    toPos = to;
    checkFlag = ckFlag;
  }

  public String from() {
    return fromPos;
  }
```

Example 6-8. A ChessMove Class (continued)

```
  public String to() {
    return toPos;
  }

  public int checkFlag() {
    return checkFlag;
  }
}
```

Example 6-9. A MoveMessage Class with Object Argument

```
class MoveMessage extends ChessMessage {
  public MoveMessage(ChessPlayer p) {
    super(p);
    setId("move");
  }

  public MoveMessage(String from, String to, int checkFlag) {
    setId("move");
    ChessMove move = new ChessMove(from, to, checkFlag);
    addArg(move);
  }

  public String Do() {
    BasicMsgHandler handler = BasicMsgHandler.current;
    ChessMove move = (ChessMove)argList.elementAt(0);

    if (!player.acceptMove(move.from(), move.to(), move.checkFlag())) {
      handler.sendMsg(new RejectMoveMessage());
    }
    else {
      ConfirmMoveMessage ccmsg =
        new ConfirmMoveMessage(move.from(), move.to(), move.checkFlag());
      handler.sendMsg(ccmsg);

      // We accepted the opponent's move, now send them
      // our countermove, unless they just mated us...
      if (checkFlag == ChessPlayer.CHECKMATE) {
        ConcedeMessage cmsg = new ConcedeMessage();
        handler.sendMsg(cmsg);
      }
      else {
        String from, to;
        int checkFlag;
        player.nextMove(from, to, checkFlag);
        MoveMessage mmsg = new MoveMessage(from, to, checkFlag);
        handler.sendMsg(mmsg);
      }
```

Example 6-9. A MoveMessage Class with Object Argument (continued)

```
    }
  }

  public boolean readArgs(InputStream ins) {
    boolean success = true;

    DataInputStream din = new DataInputStream(ins);
    ObjectInputStream oin = new ObjectInputStream(ins);

    try {
      ChessMove move = (ChessMove)oin.readObject();
      addArg(move);

      // Got all of our arguments, now watch for the
      // end-of-message token
      String temp = din.readUTF();
      while (temp.compareTo(endToken) != 0) {
        temp = din.readUTF();
      }
    }
    catch (Exception e) {
      success = false;
    }

    return success;
  }


  public boolean writeArgs(OutputStream outs) {
    boolean success = true;
    DataOutputStream dout = new DataOutputStream(outs);
    ObjectOutputStream oout = new ObjectOutputStream(outs);
    ChessMove move = (ChessMove)argList.elementAt(0);

    try {
      oout.writeObject(move);
      dout.writeUTF(endToken);
    }
    catch (IOException e) {
      success = false;
    }
    return success;
  }
}
```

Adaptable Protocols

There are situations where an application's message protocol may change while the application is running. First we'll examine the ways in which a message protocol can vary during runtime, then we'll see how our message-passing facility would need to be modified to support these adaptable message protocols.

Variable Number of Arguments

The most common situation encountered in message passing is a message whose argument list varies in length. Some arguments are actually lists of values, whose size is not known by the receiver beforehand. A multiuser server may provide a way to ask for its current list of users, for example. Optional arguments are another cause for variable-length argument lists. Continuing with the multiuser server example, a request for its list of current users may be a message with some optional arguments that control how much data is returned. A "verbose" argument may indicate that the caller wants all available information on the current users. When this argument is not present, a more condensed set of data is returned.

These possibilities imply that the recipient of a message may require information on the number of arguments to expect. In our previous examples, the message objects handling incoming messages were hardwired to expect a given number of messages, with each argument always having the same meaning. The `readArgs()` method on `MoveMessage` in Example 6-7 reads in the expected argument list, then waits for the end-of-message string. If any additional arguments were included with the message, they would be skipped over in the `while` loop that searches for the end of the message. If an argument were left off of the message, then the end-of-message token would be read in (erroneously) as the last message argument, and `readArgs()` would wait for another end-of-message token. If the remote agent sends another message, its contents would be skipped and the end-of-message token would trigger an exit from the `readArgs()` method. If the remote agent is waiting for a response before sending another message, then communications would be deadlocked at this point—the receiver would be waiting for an end-of-message token that it had already read, and the sender would be waiting for the receiver to process the message and send a response.

Variable Message Argument Types

Occasionally the data types of a message's arguments can vary as well. A message meant to request information about a bank account, for example, may identify the account using a numeric account number, or may be allowed to specify the account by name (e.g., "JSmith-savings-1"). The receiver would need to know which form of the argument is being used so that an integer value isn't read as a string, or vice versa. In our chess game example, suppose that, after updating our protocol to use `ChessMove` objects as arguments, we still wanted to support earlier versions of the message protocol that used three separate arguments to represent a chess move. The same message identifier could now be followed by either a single serialized object, or two strings followed by an integer. The `Move-Message` class would need to have some indication of which data types to expect in order to decode the data on the input stream.

Adaptable Message Types

There are times when the message types in the protocol may change at runtime. Perhaps the agents need to negotiate a suitable protocol that both can support before engaging in a conversation. These protocol negotiations are fairly common in complex multimedia protocols, or in some network services protocols. A server or a client may not support the entire protocol, or may require different protocol dialects for backwards compatibility.

Another application for adaptable message protocols is in distributed services that need to be highly reliable and cannot be shut down for any significant period of time. If an update to the message protocol for such a service is required, it would ideally be added to the system while it is online.

An Adaptable Message Handler

One way to deal with variable-length argument lists and variable-type arguments is to tag each message argument in a message with information about its type. We could define a set of argument type identifiers, one for each data type that we are going to support in our message protocol, and precede each argument with its type identifier when we send it. We could include basic data types (e.g., integer, floating-point, character, string), as well as more complex data types (e.g., lists of basic data types). This would help to both identify and verify the type of incoming arguments. Having lists of basic data types helps us deal with variable-length argument lists. If we also include a message argument count, sent over the network before the actual arguments, we can deal with optional arguments and many of the other situations leading to variable argument lists.

These measures would help us implement more robust message protocols, but they come with a price. Tagging each argument with a type identifier complicates the process of updating a message protocol. If we decide in the future to change an argument to be of a type not previously used in our protocol, then we not only have to update the corresponding message classes on all of our networked agents, we also have to update the table of type identifiers to include the new data type. Also, this type identification information, as well as the argument count information, add overhead. The overhead is generally insignificant, but in bandwidth-restricted situations, it may be enough to be a problem.

Dealing with a message protocol with varying message *types* requires a bit more sophistication. Strange as it may seem, the easiest case to handle is one where the entire message protocol changes during an application's lifetime. In situations like this, we simply need to disable one `BasicMsgHandler`, and create another using the same input and output streams. Of course, we would need to know precisely when messages belonging to the new protocol would start coming in. If we are running the `BasicMsgHandler` within its own thread, we just need to call the thread's `stop()` method, wrap the new `BasicMsgHandler` with a new thread, and `start()` the thread.

The same approach can be used if a modified version of the current protocol is expected to take over in midstream. If we have two separate subclasses of `Basic-MsgHandler` implemented for the two protocol variants, then we just have to follow the process sketched out above to switch from one to the other.

A tougher situation occurs when we periodically want to add message types to the current protocol. We may not know beforehand which message types will be needed while the application is running, which would mean that we couldn't create a message-handler subclass to support all possible message types. A particular message protocol may need to be augmented with additional message types after two agents finish negotiating the details of the protocol they will use. Or we may want to provide a more generic message management facility, where multiple sub-systems can add their own message types to the protocol. A manufacturing data management system, for example, may use a message protocol that includes messages for a machine diagnostic system, a machine scheduling algorithm, and an automatic material ordering system. Each subset of the message protocol may need to be refined and updated as the system (and the factory) evolves and grows, and while the system remains continuously operational.

To support situations like these, our message-processing facility needs to be expanded to allow adding individual message types and groups of message types at runtime. Example 6-10 shows the final version of our `BasicMsgHandler`, renamed `MessageHandler`, which has been updated to support these requirements. The `MessageHandler` now has a vector of `Message` objects that act as prototype messages in the message protocol. New message types can be added to the handler by calling the `MessageHandler`'s `addMessageType()` method with a prototype `Message` object of the new type.

Example 6-10. The Message Handler Class

```
package dcj.util.message;

import java.util.Vector;
import java.io.*;

public class MessageHandler implements Runnable
{
  // A global MessageHandler, for applications where one central
  // handler is used.
  public static MessageHandler current = null;

  InputStream msgIn;
  OutputStream msgOut;
  Vector msgPrototypes;

  public MessageHandler() {}
  public MessageHandler(InputStream in, OutputStream out) {
    setStreams(in, out);
  }

  public void setStreams(InputStream in, OutputStream out) {
    msgIn = in;
    msgOut = out;
  }

  public void addMessageType(Message prototype) {
    msgPrototypes.addElement(prototype);
  }

  public Message readMsg() throws IOException {
    Message msg = null;
    DataInputStream din = new DataInputStream(msgIn);

    String msgId = din.readUTF();
    msg = buildMessage(msgId);
    if (msg != null && msg.readArgs(msgIn)) {
      return msg;
    }
    else {
      return null;
    }
  }

  public void sendMsg(Message msg) throws IOException {
    boolean success = true;
    DataOutputStream dout = new DataOutputStream(msgOut);

    dout.writeUTF(msg.messageID());
```

Example 6-10. The Message Handler Class (continued)

```
      msg.writeArgs(msgOut);
  }

  public void run() {
    try {
      while (true) {
        Message msg = readMsg();
        if (msg != null) {
          msg.Do();
        }
      }
    }
    // Treat an IOException as a termination of the message
    // exchange, and let this message-processing thread die.
    catch (IOException e) {}
  }

  protected Message buildMessage(String msgId) {
    Message msg = null;
    int numMTypes = msgPrototypes.size();
    for (int i = 0; i < numMTypes; i++) {
      Message m = (Message)msgPrototypes.elementAt(i);
      if (m.handles(msgId)) {
        msg = m.newCopy();
        break;
      }
    }
    return msg;
  }
}
```

The `Message` class referenced in the `MessageHandler` interface is a slightly modified version of our `BasicMessage` class, and is shown in Example 6-11. This new version of the message class includes a `handles()` method and a `newCopy()` method. After the `MessageHandler` reads a message identifier in its `readMsg()` method, it calls its `buildMessage()` method to construct the message object corresponding to the identifier. The `buildMessage()` method sequentially calls the `handles()` method on each `Message` object in the prototype list to see whether the `Message` recognizes the message identifier. If `handles()` returns `true`, a copy of the prototype message is made to handle the incoming message. The `newCopy()` method on `Message` returns a new `Message` object of the same type as the `Message` on which it is called. The new `Message` object is returned to `MessageHandler`'s `readMsg()` method, where it is told to read its arguments from the input stream as before.

Example 6-11. The Message Class

```
package dcj.util.message;

import java.io.*;
import java.util.Vector;

public abstract class Message
{
  protected String id;
  protected Vector argList;
  protected String endToken = "END";

  public Message() {
    argList = new Vector();
  }

  public Message(String mid) {
    id = mid;
    argList = new Vector();
  }

  protected void addArg(Object arg) {
    argList.addElement(arg);
  }

  public String messageID() {
    return id;
  }

  public void setId(String mid) {
    id = mid;
  }

  public Vector argList() {
    Vector listCopy = (Vector)argList.clone();
    return listCopy;
  }

  public boolean readArgs(InputStream ins) {
    boolean success = true;
    DataInputStream din = new DataInputStream(ins);

    // Read tokens until the "end-of-message" token is seen.
    try {
      String token = din.readUTF();
      while (token.compareTo(endToken) != 0) {
        addArg(token);
        token = din.readUTF();
      }
```

Example 6-11. The Message Class (continued)

```
    }
    catch (IOException e) {
      // Failed to read complete argument list.
      success = false;
    }
    return success;
  }

  public boolean writeArgs(OutputStream outs) {
    int len = argList.size();
    boolean success = true;
    DataOutputStream dout = new DataOutputStream(outs);

    // Write each argument in order
    try {
      for (int i = 0; i < len; i++) {
        String arg = (String)argList.elementAt(i);
        dout.writeUTF(arg);
      }

      // Finish with the end-of-message token
      dout.writeUTF(endToken);
    }
    catch (IOException e) {
      success = false;
    }
    return success;
  }

  public abstract boolean Do();
  public abstract boolean handles(String msgId);
  public abstract Message newCopy();
}
```

With this final version of our message-passing and message-processing facility, we're able to define types of messages by creating subclasses of the `Message` class that can read the message with its arguments and perform the proper task based on the contents of the message. We can define complete message protocols in several ways using the `MessageHandler` class. A subclass of `MessageHandler` can be defined that recognizes the various message identifiers in the protocol directly in its `buildMessage()` method. A `MessageHandler` subclass could also be written that automatically adds the needed `Message` prototypes to its internal list, and then uses the default `buildMessage()` implementation to ask each `Message` object if it recognizes an incoming message's type. A third option, made possible by the fact that `MessageHandler` now has no abstract methods, is for a distributed application to construct a generic `MessageHandler` object, then add the necessary `Message` prototypes to the generic `MessageHandler` using its `addMessageType()` method. The `buildMessage()` method would then be able to create `Message` objects corresponding to the incoming messages.

The techniques we discussed earlier for handling variable argument lists and argument types can also be applied within our new message-handling system. A new implementation of the `MoveMessage` class from our chess examples demonstrates this in Example 6-12. The class has been modified to allow it to support two versions of the message argument list: one uses the `from`, `to`, and `checkFlag` arguments, and another uses a serialized `ChessMove` object. The message includes an optional new string argument that indicates whether the chess move is being sent as a `ChessMove` object. The `readArgs()` method reads the first argument as a string, then checks the string's value. If the string's value is equal to "MOBJ," then the chess move argument is being sent as a `ChessMove` object, and an `ObjectInputStream` is used to read it. If not, then the chess move is being sent in the older format of two strings and an integer, and the `DataInputStream` is used to read the remaining arguments. The `writeArgs()` method sends out the new argument, then transmits its chess move as a serialized `ChessMove` object.

Example 6-12. Backwards Compatible MoveMessage Class

```
class MoveMessage extends ChessMessage {
  public MoveMessage(ChessPlayer p) {
    super(p);
    setId("move");
  }

  public MoveMessage(String from, String to, int checkFlag) {
    setId("move");
    ChessMove move = new ChessMove(from, to, checkFlag);
    addArg(move);
  }

  public boolean Do() {
    boolean success = true;
    ChessMove move = (ChessMove)argList.elementAt(1);
    String to = move.to();
    String from = move.from();
    int checkFlag = move.checkFlag();

    try {
      if (!player.acceptMove(from, to, checkFlag)) {
        MessageHandler.current.sendMsg(new RejectMoveMessage());
      }
      else {
        ConfirmMoveMessage ccmsg =
```

Example 6-12. Backwards Compatible MoveMessage Class (continued)

```
            new ConfirmMoveMessage(move);
        MessageHandler.current.sendMsg(ccmsg);

        // We accepted the opponent's move, now send them
        // our countermove, unless they just mated us...
        if (checkFlag == ChessPlayer.CHECKMATE) {
          ConcedeMessage cmsg = new ConcedeMessage();
          MessageHandler.current.sendMsg(cmsg);
        }
        else {
          player.nextMove(from, to, checkFlag);
          MoveMessage mmsg = new MoveMessage(from, to, checkFlag);
          MessageHandler.current.sendMsg(mmsg);
        }
      }
    }
  }
  catch (IOException e) {
    success = false;
  }

  return success;
}

public boolean readArgs(InputStream ins) {
  boolean success = true;

  DataInputStream din = new DataInputStream(ins);

  try {
    String temp = din.readUTF();
    if (temp.compareTo("MOBJ") == 0) {
      ObjectInputStream oin = new ObjectInputStream(ins);
      ChessMove move = (ChessMove)oin.readObject();
      addArg(move);
    }
    else {
      String to = din.readUTF();
      int checkFlag = din.readInt();
      ChessMove move = new ChessMove(temp, to, checkFlag);
      addArg(move);
    }

    // Got all of our arguments, now watch for the
    // end-of-message token
    temp = din.readUTF();
    while (temp.compareTo(endToken) != 0) {
      temp = din.readUTF();
    }
```

Example 6-12. Backwards Compatible MoveMessage Class (continued)

```
    }
    catch (Exception e) {
      success = false;
    }

    return success;
  }

  public boolean writeArgs(OutputStream outs) {
    boolean success = true;
    DataOutputStream dout = new DataOutputStream(outs);
    ObjectOutputStream oout = new ObjectOutputStream(outs);
    ChessMove move = (ChessMove)argList.elementAt(0);

    try {
      dout.writeUTF("MOBJ");
      oout.writeObject(move);
    }
    catch (IOException e) {
      success = false;
    }

    return success;
  }

  public boolean handles(String mid) {
    if (mid.compareTo("move") == 0)
      return true;
    else
      return false;
  }

  public Message newCopy() {
    return(new MoveMessage(player));
  }
}
```

With this version of our `MoveMessage` class, we can talk to `ChessPlayer` agents
using either the new or old versions of the class. We could have handled the variable argument list by adding an argument count to the argument list, but then
our previous version of the `MoveMessage` class would also have to be modified to
send the new argument. This would defeat the purpose, since our original intent
was to provide backwards compatibility with the previous version of our chess
protocol.

Message Passing with Java Events

During the course of this chapter, we've built up our own message-handling frame-work from scratch, relying on basic sockets, I/O streams, and object serialization to implement a protocol for sending, receiving, and handling messages. In this section, we'll look at merging a message-passing framework with the Java event model that's used in the AWT package for handling GUI events. The advantage of using events is the possibility of integrating your distributed system with other systems based on the Java event model, including AWT-based applications or applets.

Event Model Overview

The event model included in the Java API (version 1.1 and later) is generic enough to build event-handling protocols for general applications, not just GUI-related ones. The Java event model is based on `EventObjects` that are created by various event sources and handled by classes that implement an `EventLis-tener` interface.

Different types of events are defined by creating subclasses of the `EventObject` class. The `EventObject` class only contains a source `Object`. Subclasses of `EventObject` can add additional data to represent event specifics. For example, the AWT package defines a `KeyEvent` subclass that represents keyboard events. The `KeyEvent` class contains data fields that specify which key was pressed to generate the event.

The Java event model is called a *delegation* model; events are generated by a source of some kind, and `EventListeners` register themselves with the event source to handle specific types of events. When an event arrives, the event source delegates the handling of the event to the `EventListeners` registered with it. The Java AWT package uses this event model by defining various GUI components that are sources of user events. User events are modeled as subclasses of `EventObject`. Various types of `EventListeners` are registered with the GUI components to receive specific user event types, like mouse events, keyboard events, etc.

Distributed Events

In our case, we want to send and receive events over a network between distrib-uted agents. For each node in our distributed system, we'll need to receive messages in the form of events from one or many remote agents, and we'll need to send messages to other agents. One model to use in building this event-based message-passing system is to follow the lead of our previous message-handler examples, and have event "transceivers" at each node in the system. For the local node, these event transceivers would act as both sources of events and as event handlers or listeners, passing local events to remote agents.

Along these lines, we have the `EventTransceiver` class shown in Example 6-13. This class connects itself to a single remote agent to exchange events with it. This limited form of an event transceiver will be sufficient to implement an event-based version of our chess-playing example. We'll leave it to the reader to extend this class to handle multiple remote agents.

Example 6-13. An Event Transceiver

```
package dcj.util.message;

import java.util.*;
import java.net.*;
import java.io.*;

public class EventTransceiver implements EventHandler extends Thread {
  // A hashtable of handlers for specific events
  private Hashtable handlers = new Hashtable();
  // A list of handlers that want all events
  private Vector globalHandlers = new Vector();

  // Our connection to a remote agent
  InputStream evIn = null;
  OutputStream evOut = null;

  public EventTransceiver(String host, int port) {
    try {
      InetAddress a = InetAddress.getByName(host);
      connect(a, port);
    }
    catch (Exception e) {}
  }

  public EventTransceiver(InetAddress a, int port) {
    connect(a, port);
  }

  void connect(InetAddress a, int port) {
    try {
      Socket s = new Socket(a, port);
      evIn = s.getInputStream();
      evOut = s.getOutputStream();
    }
    catch (Exception e) {
      evIn = null;
      evOut = null;
    }
```

Example 6-13. An Event Transceiver (continued)

```java
  }

  public EventTransceiver(InputStream in, OutputStream out) {
    setStreams(in, out);
  }

  void setStreams(InputStream in, OutputStream out) {
    evIn = in;
    evOut = out;
  }

  public void sendEvent(EventObject ev) throws IOException {
    ObjectOutputStream oout = new ObjectOutputStream(evOut);
    oout.writeObject(ev);
  }

  EventObject receiveEvent() throws IOException {
    ObjectInputStream oin = new ObjectInputStream(evIn);
    EventObject ev = null;
    try {
      ev = (EventObject)oin.readObject();
    }
    catch (ClassCastException e) {
      System.out.println("Non-event object sent to EventTransceiver");
    }
    catch (ClassNotFoundException e2) {
      System.out.println(
        "Unresolvable object type sent to EventTransceiver");
    }

    return ev;
  }

  void distributeEvent(EventObject ev) {
    // Send event to all "global" handlers
    Enumeration e = globalHandlers.elements();
    while (e.hasMoreElements()){
      EventHandler h = (EventHandler)e.nextElement();
      h.handleEvent(ev);
    }

    // Send event to handlers targeting the event's class
    Class evClass = ev.getClass();
    Vector evHandlers = (Vector)handlers.get(evClass);
    e = evHandlers.elements();
    while (e.hasMoreElements()) {
      EventHandler h = (EventHandler)e.nextElement();
      h.handleEvent(ev);
```

Example 6-13. An Event Transceiver (continued)

```java
      }
  }

  // No default behavior for handling events...
  public void handleEvent(EventObject e) {}

  // Register a handler that wants all events.
  public void addHandler(EventHandler eh) {
    if (!globalHandlers.contains(eh)) {
      globalHandlers.addElement(eh);
    }
  }

  // Register a handler for a specific type of event
  public void addHandler(EventHandler eh, EventObject e) {
    Class eClass = e.getClass();
    addHandler(eh, eClass);
  }

  public void addHandler(EventHandler eh, Class ec) {
    Vector evHandlers = (Vector)handlers.get(ec);
    if (evHandlers == null) {
      evHandlers = new Vector();
      handlers.put(ec, evHandlers);
    }
    if (!evHandlers.contains(eh)) {
      evHandlers.addElement(eh);
    }
  }

  // Remove a handler from all lists
  public void removeHandler(EventHandler eh) {
    globalHandlers.removeElement(eh);
    Enumeration ecList = handlers.keys();
    while (ecList.hasMoreElements()) {
      Vector evHandlers =
        (Vector)handlers.get(ecList.nextElement());
      if (evHandlers != null) {
        evHandlers.removeElement(eh);
      }
    }
  }

  // Remove a handler for a specific event type
  public void removeHandler(EventHandler eh, EventObject e) {
    removeHandler(eh, e.getClass());
  }
```

Example 6-13. An Event Transceiver (continued)

```java
  public void removeHandler(EventHandler eh, Class ec) {
    Vector evHandlers = (Vector)handlers.get(ec);
    if (evHandlers != null) {
      evHandlers.removeElement(eh);
    }
  }


  // If run as an independent thread, just loop listening
  // for events from the remote agent, and distribute them
  // to registered handlers
  public void run() {
    try {
      while (true) {
        EventObject e = receiveEvent();
        if (e != null)
          distributeEvent(e);
      }
    }
    // Treat an IOException as termination of the event
    // input stream, and let this handler thread die
    catch (IOException e) {}
  }
}
```

The `EventTransceiver` class extends an `EventHandler` interface, which is an extension of the `java.util.EventListener` interface that adds a `handleEvent()` method (see Example 6-14). The `EventTransceiver` maintains its connection to a remote agent as an I/O stream pair. It has two constructors that take arguments specifying a remote agent to which to connect: one uses a hostname and port number, the other uses an `InetAddress` and port number. These two constructors use the host and port information to open a socket to the remote agent and get the `InputStream` and `OutputStream` from the socket. A third constructor accepts an `InputStream` and `OutputStream` that are preconnected to a source and destination for events, respectively.

Example 6-14. EventHandler Interface

```java
package dcj.util.message;

import java.util.EventListener;
import java.util.EventObject;

public interface EventHandler extends EventListener {
  public void handleEvent(EventObject e);
}
```

The `EventTransceiver` interface includes `addHandler()` methods that let you attach `EventHandlers` to this event source. You can register a handler for any events, or you can register a handler for a specific type of event by providing a second argument that's either an instance of an `EventObject` subclass, or the `Class` object for the subclass itself. The `EventTransceiver` keeps the registered handlers in a hashtable of `Vectors` that hold the `EventHandlers`; the sets of handlers are hashed by the `EventObject` subclass under which they were registered. Handlers can be removed from the transceiver using the corresponding `removeHandler()` methods. The `distributeEvent()` method takes an `EventObject` instance and passes it to the registered handlers. First it calls the `handleEvent()` method on any handlers registered to receive all events. Then it looks up the handlers registered for the specific type of event by getting the `Class` of the `EventObject`, and getting the `Vector` of `EventHandlers` from its table of handlers. It passes the `EventObject` to the `handleEvent()` method of any handlers it finds.

The `EventTransceiver` has a `sendEvent()` method for sending an `Event-Object` directly to its remote agent, and a `receiveEvent()` method that does a blocking read on the `InputStream` (using an `ObjectInputStream` wrapper) for an `EventObject` from the remote agent. The `EventTransceiver` also extends `Thread`, and in its `run()` method it performs an infinite loop, reading events from its `InputStream` using its `receiveEvent()` method and distributing them by calling its own `distributeEvent()` method.

Using the `EventTransceiver` class, implementing our chess-playing server is just a matter of subclassing a `ChessEventServer` class, as shown in Example 6-15. The `ChessEventServer` maintains its own `ChessPlayer` object, and it mediates a game between its player and a remote player, much like the message-passing `ChessServer` in Example 6-5. In its constructors, the `ChessEventServer` registers with itself to receive `ChessMoveEvent` and `ChessConcedeEvent` events.

Example 6-15. An Event-Based Chess Server

```
package dcj.examples.message;

import dcj.util.message.*;
import java.util.*;
import java.net.*;
import java.io.IOException;

public class ChessEventServer extends EventTransceiver {
  ChessPlayer player = new ChessPlayer();

  public ChessEventServer(String host, int port) {
```

Example 6-15. An Event-Based Chess Server (continued)

```java
    super(host, port);
    register();
  }

  public ChessEventServer(InetAddress host, int port) {
    super(host, port);
    register();
  }

  void register() {
    // Add ourselves to this handler's list for
    // chess-related events
    try {
      addHandler(this, Class.forName("ChessMoveEvent"));
      addHandler(this, Class.forName("ChessConcedeEvent"));
    }
    catch (ClassNotFoundException nfe) {}
  }

  public void handleEvent(EventObject e) {
    try {
      if (e instanceof ChessMoveEvent) {
        ChessMoveEvent cm = (ChessMoveEvent)e;
        ChessMove m = cm.getMove();
        switch (cm.getType()) {
          case ChessMoveEvent.SUBMIT:
            if (player.acceptMove(m)) {
              ChessMoveEvent conf = new ChessMoveEvent(m, player);
              conf.setConfirm();
              sendEvent(conf);

              ChessMove next = player.nextMove();
              if (next != null) {
                ChessMoveEvent submit = new ChessMoveEvent(next, player);
                sendEvent(submit);
              }
              else {
                sendEvent(new ChessConcedeEvent(player));
              }
            }
            else {
              ChessMoveEvent reject = new ChessMoveEvent(m, player);
              reject.setReject();
              sendEvent(reject);
            }
          break;

          case ChessMoveEvent.REJECT:
```

Example 6-15. An Event-Based Chess Server (continued)

```
            ChessMove next = player.nextMove();
            if (next != null) {
              sendEvent(new ChessMoveEvent(next, player));
            }
            else {
              sendEvent(new ChessConcedeEvent(player));
            }
          break;

            case ChessMoveEvent.CONFIRM:
              player.moveAccepted(m);
            break;
          }
        }
        // If we get a concede message, the other player has
        // given up and we win...
        else if (e instanceof ChessConcedeEvent) {
          player.conceded();
        }
      }
    catch (IOException ioe) {
        System.out.println("IO error while handling event.");
        ioe.printStackTrace();
      }
    }
  }
}
```

Both of these `EventObject` subclasses are shown in Example 6-16. Everything else is done in the `ChessEventServer.handleEvent()` method. When it receives a `ChessMoveEvent` from the remote agent, it checks the type of move event (SUBMIT, CONFIRM, or REJECT), and calls the appropriate method on the local player. If necessary, it takes output from the local player and sends it off to the remote player as a `ChessMoveEvent` or `ChessConcedeEvent`, calling its `sendEvent()` method to transmit the event to the remote agent. If a `Chess-ConcedeEvent` comes in, then it tells the local player that it won the game by calling its `conceded()` method.

Example 6-16. Chess-Specific EventObjects

```
package dcj.examples.message;

import java.util.EventObject;

public class ChessMoveEvent extends EventObject {
  ChessMove move;
  int type;
```

Example 6-16. Chess-Specific EventObjects (continued)

```java
    public final static int SUBMIT = 0;
    public final static int CONFIRM = 1;
    public final static int REJECT = 2;

    public ChessMoveEvent(ChessMove subject, ChessPlayer src) {
      super(src);
      move = subject;
      type = SUBMIT;
    }

    public int getType() { return type; }

    // Set the type of the move event
    public void setConfirm() { type = CONFIRM; }
    public void setReject() { type = REJECT; }
    public void setSubmit() { type = SUBMIT; }

    // Get and set the move
    public ChessMove getMove() { return move; }
    public void setMove(ChessMove m) { move = m; }
}

public class ChessConcedeEvent extends EventObject {
  // Just a placeholder class, no data or methods needed
  public ChessConcedeEvent(ChessPlayer src) {
    super(src);
  }
}
```

Pros and Cons

In terms of the overall utility of the system, this event-based message-passing system is about equivalent to the framework we developed earlier in the chapter. What it offers, however, is the possibility of integrating our distributed event-handling system with AWT-based applications to create distributed user interfaces of a sort. Since our EventTransceiver is written to handle events in the form of Java EventObject, there's no reason it can't send and receive AWT events from user interfaces between agents on the network, as long as they are Serializable. Figure 6-2, for example, demonstrates an AWT button with a listener (the SurrogateActionListener) attached that sends action events from the button through the EventTransceiver to a remote agent, where the action is processed. The listener would need to implement the java.awt.ActionListener interface, as well as our EventHandler interface, as shown in Example 6-17.

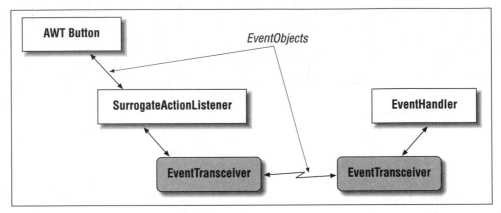

Figure 6-2. Distributing AWT events to remote handlers

Example 6-17. A Surrogate AWT ActionListener

```
import java.awt.event.*;
import dcj.util.message;

public class SurrogateActionListener implements ActionListener,
                                                EventHandler {

  private EventTransceiver xceiver;

  public SurrogateActionListener(EventTransceiver t) {
    xceiver = t;
    // Register as handler for global events
    xceiver.addHandler(this);
  }

  public void actionPerformed(ActionEvent e) {
    // A local action event has been generated - send it
    // to the remote agent
    xceiver.sendEvent(e);
  }

  public void handleEvent(EventObject) {
    // Do something with events from the transceiver...
  }
}
```

We could attach this listener to a local AWT interface element like a Button, and when the Button generates an action event, it will be passed to the sendEvent() method on the EventTransceiver to a remote agent. The remote agent may then do something in reaction to the button event, and perhaps generate an event in response. The event will be received by the local Event-

`Transceiver` and, since the `SurrogateActionListener` registers itself with its `EventTransceiver` as a handler for any events, the transceiver will call the `SurrogateActionListener`'s `handleEvent()` method, which can act on the event from the remote agent (change the button's color, put some text on the screen, etc.).

Using the `SurrogateActionListener`, we would only need to create an `EventTransceiver` as we did before, then construct a `SurrogateAction-Listener`, passing the `EventTransceiver` into its constructor. We would then register the listener as an `ActionListener` on the AWT Button by calling the Button's `addActionListener()` method. This would establish the event-passing link from the button, through the surrogate listener to the transceiver, and finally to the remote event handler.

Although this approach is interesting and potentially useful, you have to be careful what kinds of events you're trying to route over the network. The `Event-Object` is going to be serialized by the `EventTransceiver` and sent over the network to the remote transceiver. If the `EventObject` subclass keeps a non-transient reference to other local objects, like one of the AWT components, then these objects and any objects they reference, etc., down the whole reference tree, will be serialized and transmitted, too. This would result in an `IOException` if any of the objects in the tree aren't `Serializable`. If serialization succeeds, you might end up sending an unexpectedly large amount of data over the wire.

Be aware that the only state information that the remote event handler has to interpret the event is contained in the `EventObject` itself. Since the remote handler doesn't have direct access to the actual interface components (unless they were serialized within the `EventObject`), it can't directly query them for their state. So a little more care has to be taken in ensuring that each `Event-Object` contains all of the information the handler needs to deal with the event.

Using Remote Objects

Earlier in the chapter we mentioned some of the situations that might lead you to use message passing rather than remote objects to handle the agent-to-agent communication in your distributed system. To get a more concrete feeling for the differences between a message-passing system and one based on remote objects, this section describes an RMI implementation of our chess game.

The RMI implementation of the chess game uses two remote objects: a remote chess player and a remote chess move. The interface for the `RMIChessMove` object is shown in Example 6-18. It has essentially the same interface as the `ChessMove` class in our earlier examples.

Example 6-18. A Remote Chess Move Interface

```
package dcj.examples.message;

import java.rmi.RemoteException;

// Interface for an RMI-based chess move

public interface RMIChessMove {
  public String from() throws RemoteException;
  public void setFrom(String f) throws RemoteException;
  public String to() throws RemoteException;
  public void setTo(String t) throws RemoteException;
  public int checkFlag() throws RemoteException;
  public void setCheckFlag (String f) throws RemoteException;
}
```

Example 6-19 shows the `RMIChessMoveImpl` class, which is the server implementation of the chess move object.

Example 6-19. Chess Move Implementation

```
package dcj.examples.message;

import java.rmi.*;

public class RMIChessMoveImpl implements RMIChessMove extends Remote {
  String fromPos;
  String toPos;
  int checkFlag;

  public RMIChessMoveImpl(String from, String to, int ckFlag) {
    fromPos = from;
    toPos = to;
    checkFlag = ckFlag;
  }

  public String from() throws RemoteException {
    return fromPos;
  }

  public void setFrom(String f) throws RemoteException {
    fromPos = f;
  }

  public String to() throws RemoteException {
    return toPos;
  }

  public void setTo(String t) throws RemoteException {
```

Example 6-19. Chess Move Implementation (continued)

```
    toPos = t;
  }

  public int checkFlag() throws RemoteException {
    return checkFlag;
  }

  public void setCheckFlag(String f) throws RemoteException {
    checkFlag = f;
  }
}
```

Example 6-20 shows the interface for the `RMIChessPlayer`. It has essentially the same interface as the earlier `ChessPlayer`, except that we've changed the `next-Move()` method to return the player's move as an `RMIChessMove` object, rather than returning a boolean flag and filling in method arguments to indicate the move. We've also added a `gameOver()` method, which reveals whether the player has finished the game it was playing (win or lose).

Example 6-20. Remote Chess Player Interface

```
package dcj.examples.message;

import java.rmi.RemoteException;

// Interface for an RMI-based chess player

public interface RMIChessPlayer {
  public boolean acceptMove(RMIChessMove m) throws RemoteException;
  public RMIChessMove nextMove() throws RemoteException;
  public void moveAccepted(RMIChessMove m) throws RemoteException;
  public void conceded() throws RemoteException;
}
```

The server implementation of the `RMIChessPlayer` is shown in Example 6-21 as the `RMIChessPlayerImpl`. Again, it's very similar to the `ChessPlayer` implementation, with the addition of the `boolean gameOver` data member, the exceedingly simple `gameOver()` method, and a `main()` method. The `main()` method on the `RMIChessPlayerImpl` takes the place of the `ChessServer` in our message-passing chess game. If we call it with a single command line argument, then that argument is treated as the name used to register a local `RMIChessPlayerImpl` object with the RMI Naming service. Once the local player is registered with the RMI registry, the method loops waiting for a remote player to start a game, checking the local player to see when its game is over before quitting. If we invoke the class with a local player name plus a remote host name and remote player name on the command line, then the `main()` method

tries to look up a remote `RMIChessPlayer` on that host under that name. If it
finds one, it mediates a game between the remote and local players, iteratively
calling each player's `nextMove()` and `acceptMove()` methods.

Example 6-21. Chess Player Implementation

```
package dcj.examples.message;

// Server implementation of our RMI-based chess player

public class RMIChessPlayerImpl
   implements RMIChessPlayer extends Remote {

  // Our opponent
  protected RMIChessPlayer opponent = null;

  // Game-over indicator
  protected boolean gameOver = false;

  // Data structures for maintaining chess board state
  // ...

  public static final int CHECK = 0;
  public static final int CHECKMATE = 1;
  public static final int NO_CHECK = 2;

  public RMIChessPlayerImpl() {
    // Initialize chess board
  }

  public boolean acceptMove(RMIChessMove m) throws RemoteException {
    // Check validity of requested move.
    // If valid, apply to chess board and return true.
    // If invalid, return false.
    // ...
    return true;
  }

  public boolean nextMove(RMIChessMove m) throws RemoteException {
    // Generate our next move based on the current
    // state of the game board, and put it into the
    // ChessMove passed in.  If no move in this round,
    // return false.
    // ...
    return true;
  }

  public void moveAccepted(RMIChessMove m) throws RemoteException {
```

Example 6-21. Chess Player Implementation (continued)

```
    // Our move was accepted as valid, apply it to the
    // game board...
    // ...
  }

  public void conceded() throws RemoteException {
    // We've won!
    gameOver = true;
  }

  public static void main(String argv[]) {
    String playerName = argv[0];
    // Create the chess player for our side of the game
    RMIChessPlayerImpl me = new RMIChessPlayerImpl();

    // If we've been given an opponent, try to start
    // a game with them...
    if (argv.size > 2) {
      String oppName = argv[1];
      String oppHost = argv[2];
      RMIChessPlayer opponent =
        (RMIChessPlayer)Naming.lookup("rmi://" + oppHost
                                        + "/" + oppName);

      RMIChessMoveImpl myMove = new RMIChessMoveImpl();
      RMIChessMoveImpl theirMove = new RMIChessMoveImpl();

      while (!gameOver) {
        if (opponent.nextMove(theirMove)) {
          while (!me.acceptMove(theirMove) &&
                 opponent.nextMove(theirMove)) {
            // Don't have to do anything, the while
            // loop conditions do all the work.
          }
        }

        if (me.nextMove(myMove)) {
          while (!opponent.acceptMove(myMove) &&
                 me.nextMove(myMove)) {}
        }
      }
    }
    else {
      // No arguments telling us where our opponent is, so
      // we register the local player and wait for them to come
      // to us.

      // Bind the player to their name in the registry
```

Example 6-21. Chess Player Implementation (continued)

```
    Naming.rebind(playerName, player);
    // Now wait for another player to engage us in a game.
    while(1) {
      wait();
    }
  }
 }
}
```

In this version of our chess game, the `MessageHandler` and the various
`Message` subclasses have been replaced by the remote method-calling services
provided by RMI. The RMI-based chess game is also easier to extend with new
features—we just need to add new methods to our `RMIChessPlayer` interface.
In the worst case, we'll need to define some new remote objects to support new
features. In the message-passing version, we would need to extend the `Chess-`
`Player` interface, create new subclasses of `Message` to support the new
functions, and update the `ChessServer` class to support the new message types.
What we've lost in the RMI version is some flexibility in terms of the low-level
communication protocol. Since RMI is encapsulating all of the network-level
details of the remote method calls, we can't control the data protocol directly, as
we do with message passing. If RMI's network protocol imposes too much overhead on our distributed system, there's little we can do about it except minimize
the data members and method arguments on our remote objects. And if we're
faced with a firewall that blocks the RMI protocol (perhaps for reasons that are
known only to the network operator), then our distributed system is stopped dead
in its tracks. With a simple (some would say barebones) message-passing system,
we can directly control the format of both the serialized data and the communication protocol to suit our needs, and we can get our messages through using
relatively "unadorned" IP packets.

7

Databases

This chapter is a brief introduction to the topic of integrating databases into networked Java applications. As with many of the topics in this book, the development of database applications is a subject that can fill a book of its own. And it has, many times over. For the purposes of this book, rather than trying to cover the gamut of database design and development in depth, we will restrict this chapter to a discussion of the following topics:

- An overview of the primary database access API available in the Java environment, JDBC

- A discussion of the basic issues that arise in developing networked database applications

- The special issues that come into play when multiple distributed databases are accessed from a single application

We assume that the reader has a basic understanding of general relational database topics, such as SQL and the layout of data into tables and records. For more in-depth coverage of the JDBC package than we will be able to provide here, refer to George Reese's book, *Database Programming with JDBC and Java* (O'Reilly & Associates).

An Overview of JDBC

JDBC is the database connectivity package included in the core Java API.* JDBC gives you a database-independent interface for opening a connection to a relational database, issuing SQL calls to the database, and receiving a set of data as

---

* JDBC became a formal part of the JDK in version 1.1.

the result. In more technical terms, JDBC acts as a Java implementation of the standard SQL call-level interface (CLI) defined by X/Open and supported by most major relational database vendors. In order to perform transactions with a specific type of database, you need to have a JDBC driver that acts as a bridge between the JDBC method calls and the native database interface.

Data Retrieval Example

Perhaps the easiest way to get started with JDBC is to see a simple example of the API in action. Example 7-1 shows a Java code segment that opens a database connection, executes a query, and iterates through the results.

Example 7-1. A Simple JDBC Database Query

```
// Construct the database address
String dbaseURL = "jdbc:mysubprotocol://dbasehost/dbasename";
// Make the database connection
Connection dbConnection =
  DriverManager.getConnection(dbaseURL, "dbaseuser", "dbasepasswd");
// Create a statement and execute the SQL query
Statement query = dbConnection.getStatement();
ResultSet results =
  query.executeQuery("SELECT first_name, last_name from user_table");

// Iterate through the results and print them to standard output
while (results.next()) {
  String fname = results.getString("first_name");
  String lname = results.getString("last_name");
  System.out.println("Found user \"" + fname + " " + lname + "\"");
}
```

In the example, we refer to the database using a URL:

```
    String dbaseURL = "jdbc:mysubprotocol://dbasehost/dbasename";
```

This URL is passed to the JDBC DriverManager's getConnection() method, along with an account name and password, to open a connection to the database:

```
    Connection dbConnection =
      DriverManager.getConnection(dbaseURL, "dbaseuser", "dbasepasswd");
```

Once the connection is created, we construct a Statement object, which is used to issue an SQL query. In this case, we're retrieving all of the first and last names (user_fname and user_lname) from a table of user information (user_table). The results of the query are returned by JDBC as a ResultSet object:

```
    Statement query = dbConnection.createStatement();
    ResultSet results =
      query.executeQuery("SELECT first_name, last_name from user_table");
```

Finally, we can iterate over the results of the query and present them to the user:

```
while (results.next()) {
    String fname = results.getString("first_name");
    String lname = results.getString("last_name");
    System.out.println("Found user \"" + fname + " " + lname + "\"");
}
```

In the following sections, we'll examine JDBC in more detail to see how this and other database interactions are supported.

The API at a Glance

The JDBC API offers you interfaces that mirror the basic concepts surrounding relational databases. These interfaces, all part of the `java.sql` package, include interfaces for a `DriverManager`, a `Connection`, a `Statement`, and a `ResultSet`.

DriverManager

The `DriverManager` class provides the means to load database drivers into a Java application or applet; it is the primary way in JDBC to establish a connection to a database. A Java application first creates a `DriverManager` instance, then connects to a database by calling the `DriverManager`'s static `getConnection()` method, passing a URL-like reference to the database as a method argument. The `DriverManager` searches the set of available drivers for one that can support a connection to the referenced database. If it finds one, it passes the database address to the driver and asks it to create a connection. The connection to the database is returned in the form of a `Connection` object (described later).

All JDBC drivers provide an implementation of the `java.sql.Driver` interface. When a `DriverManager` is created, it attempts to load a set of drivers specified by the `sql.Driver`'s Java property, which can be set to a list of colon-delimited `Driver` class names. Additional drivers can also be loaded explicitly in the Java application as needed. When a `Driver` class is loaded into the Java runtime, it's responsible for creating an instance of itself and registering this instance with the resident `DriverManager`. So any additional drivers needed by an application can be loaded explicitly by using the `Class.forName()` method:

```
Driver myDriver = (Driver)Class.forName("specialdb.Driver");
```

Since the `Driver` class automatically registers itself with the `DriverManager`, there really isn't any reason to keep the reference to the `Driver`. You'll often see drivers loaded by just calling the `forName()` method and later referencing the driver by name when a database connection is made.

Connection

Once the necessary drivers have been loaded by the `DriverManager`, a connection to a database can be made through the `getConnection()` method of the `DriverManager` class. The desired database is specified with a `String` argument that acts as a URL-like address to the database. There is no standard format for this database address string; the `DriverManager` simply passes it to each loaded JDBC driver in turn and asks if it understands and supports the type of database being addressed. Typically, the database address will include explicit information about the type of driver to be used to make the connection. For example, JDBC drivers using ODBC protocol to establish database connections usually use addresses of the form:

```
jdbc:odbc:financedata,
```

where `financedata` is a local data source. Access to a remote database from a local client may involve an address of a slightly different form:

```
jdbc:drvr://dataserver.foobar.com:500/financedata.
```

The JDBC API specification recommends that database URLs take the form:

```
jdbc:<sub-protocol>:<sub-name>,
```

where `<sub-protocol>` specifies a database connection service and `<sub-name>` provides all of the information that the underlying service will need to find the database and connect to it. So in the remote database URL shown above, `drvr` is the sub-protocol, specifying a specific driver to use to connect to our database. The `dataserver.foobar.com:500/financedata` portion of the URL acts as the sub-name, and gives the information the driver needs to find our database. Other drivers may require you to specify sub-protocols and sub-names differently. You should consult the documentation for the JDBC drivers you're using to find out what form your database URLs should take.

The `getConnection()` method on `DriverManager` either returns a `Connection` object that represents the connection to the named database, or throws an exception if the connection couldn't be established.

Statement

The `Connection` interface allows the user to create query statements to the database. Query statements are represented as `Statement` objects or subclasses. The `Connection` interface provides three methods for creating database query statements: `createStatement()`, `prepareStatement()`, and `prepareCall()`. The `createStatement()` method is used for simple SQL statements that don't involve any parameters. This returns a `Statement` object that can be used to issue SQL queries to the database, normally using its `executeQuery()` method.

This method accepts an SQL statement as a string argument, and the results of the statement are returned in the form of a `ResultSet` object (described later). Other methods available in the `Statement` interface for issuing SQL statements to the database are `execute()`, which is used for SQL queries that can return multiple result sets, and `executeUpdate()`, which can be used to issue INSERT, UPDATE, or DELETE statements.

In addition to the basic `Statement` interface, a `Connection` object can be used to create precompiled `PreparedStatements`, and `CallableStatements` that represent stored procedures in the database. An SQL statement involving input parameters, or a statement that you want to execute multiple times, can be created using the `prepareStatement()` method on a `Connection` object, which returns a `PreparedStatement` object. The SQL statement passed into the `prepareStatement()` method is precompiled so that multiple executions of the statement will be more efficient. This subclass of `Statement` supports setting the values of precompiled input parameters through a series of `setXXX()` methods. The `PreparedStatement` object has an `executeQuery()` method that requires no arguments, and instead executes the precompiled SQL statement on the database. Note that not all database vendors or JBC drivers support precompiled statements, so check your DBMS documentation and JDBC driver specifications to see if you can use `PreparedStatements`.

A stored SQL procedure can be accessed through an SQL statement created through the `prepareCall()` method on a `Connection` object. This method returns a `CallableStatement` object, which lets you set input parameters and get output parameters from the statement.

By default, the JDBC package is configured to commit each `Statement` issued through a `Connection`. If you need to do rollbacks of transactions, or you want to commit multiple statements as a single transaction, or both, you can disable the autocommit feature by calling `Connection.setAutoCommit(false)`. Then a sequence of `Statements` can be created from a `Connection` object, executed against the database, and the entire transaction can be committed as one transaction by calling the `Connection`'s `commit()` method. If you want to abort the transaction, you can call the `Connection`'s `rollback()` method.

ResultSet

Rows of data returned from the execution of a statement against a database are represented as `ResultSet` objects in JDBC. For example, the `executeQuery()` method of the `Statement` interface returns a `ResultSet` object. A `ResultSet` object provides ways to iterate through the rows of data returned as the result of an SQL query, through its `next()` method; data fields within each row can be retrieved by name or by column index number using its `getXXX()` methods. The user needs to know the type of data to expect in each column of returned data, since each data item is retrieved through type-specific `getXXX()` methods.

Depending on how your JDBC driver is implemented, iterating through the rows of data in a `ResultSet` may cause individual data fetches from the database, or it may simply pull each row of data from a local cache. If the performance of your data transactions is an issue in your application, you should determine how returned data is handled by your vendor's drivers.

Remote Database Applications

As we alluded to earlier in the book, client-server applications are often broken down into different levels, or *tiers*, to use the current vernacular. A typical application breakdown involves three tiers: user-interface functions, application objects, and data access. Up until now, we've mostly been discussing ways of distributing the application logic across the network, using distributed objects or some form of message passing to allow elements of the core application to lie on remote hosts. In this chapter, we'll discuss the options available for implementing the data access level of a distributed application.

The data access tier of a multitiered distributed application can be divided into two subtiers, as shown in Figure 7-1. First, an interface must be established between JDBC and the actual DBMS holding the data. A set of data objects representing the concepts in the database can then be defined; these objects serve as an interface from the application-level objects to the data in the database. These data objects interact with the DBMS through the JDBC interface to perform operations on the low-level data that they represent. The application-layer objects interact with the data objects to query and update the data.

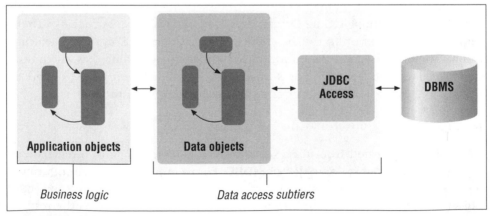

Figure 7-1. Breakdown of the data access tier

JDBC Driver Configurations

Before you can use the JDBC API to engage in transactions with your database, a JDBC driver that is connected to your database has to be available. The JDBC driver accepts the JDBC transaction protocol and converts it to the appropriate native commands for the type of RDBMS you are using.

Figure 7-2 shows the various ways that a JDBC driver can be configured to interact with an RDBMS. The first configuration involves a JDBC driver running on the database host machine and interacting directly with the relational database. The JDBC client, consisting of JDBC API code plus the JDBC driver, resides either on a remote machine or on the database host itself. The JDBC driver accepts connections from clients using the JDBC API to issue statements to the database. The driver converts the JDBC commands directly into the RDBMS native access protocol (typically SQL with the addition of some proprietary commands) and issues the native statements to the RDBMS. The results from the database are received by the JDBC driver, converted to the appropriate transmission format, and sent to the JDBC client, where they are returned in the form of a `ResultSet` object to the caller.

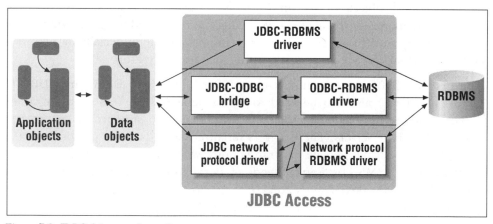

Figure 7-2. JDBC driver configurations

The second configuration is similar to the first, except that an ODBC driver sits between the JDBC driver and the relational database. ODBC is a standard relational database driver API that has become popular because it insulates applications from the specifics of particular relational databases. ODBC drivers are offered for nearly all major RDBMS vendors on the market today. In this configuration, the JDBC driver acts as before with respect to the client, accepting and responding to JDBC transaction requests. Now, however, these transactions are converted to ODBC statements and issued to the ODBC driver, which in turn converts the statements to the RDBMS native format. This configuration uses a JDBC-ODBC bridge, which is essentially a JDBC driver that speaks ODBC, rather than a specific database vendor's access protocol. The advantage to using ODBC to communicate with the database is the ability to migrate your data and its structure to another database, or to apply the same application to another database with an ODBC driver. ODBC is also an important option to consider when a native JDBC driver is not available for the database in question. However, adding an additional conversion step in the query process can be inefficient, and sometimes unacceptable in high-throughput applications.

The third configuration is one where a JDBC driver on the client converts JDBC statements directly into a networked protocol. This protocol is then transmitted to a remote database server fitted with a module capable of receiving this protocol and responding to it. The database client now contains only the JDBC API and the JDBC driver for this networked protocol. The advantage of this configuration is that the client element of the JDBC driver can be relatively simple, since it only needs to convert JDBC commands into the networked protocol. All of the logic for converting data types to native database types and back again, issuing statements to the native database through its access protocol, and mapping the results into either Java objects or the appropriate `Exception`, resides with the more complex agent on the database server. This option of reducing the amount of code residing on the data client can be an important one, especially in an applet context in which the client agent is running on a user's desktop.

The first two JDBC driver configurations (JDBC directly to DBMS and JDBC to ODBC to DBMS) also can be used to access databases on remote hosts. Many native DBMS drivers as well as ODBC drivers include support for networked access of database servers. These drivers serialize native database protocols or the ODBC protocol and engage in transactions with a remote DBMS over the network. The DBMS host server needs to be augmented with drivers that can accept these networked connections. In this case, the DBMS or ODBC drivers need to reside on the client host, in addition to the network transaction drivers.

Defining the Data Objects

With these database driver configurations, we can examine our options for implementing the data objects of our multitiered distributed application.

One of the design principles we've been advocating is encapsulation—hiding the low-level implementation details of a system or subsystem and providing a clean, well-defined interface to it. This principle is also applicable in the design of the data access layer of distributed applications. The "low-level details" we want to hide through encapsulation are things like the type of DBMS being used (e.g., relational or object-oriented, vendor name, DBMS version), the specific location (e.g., host, database name, etc.) of the data on the network, and even the structural layout of the data in the database (e.g., field, table, and view names in a relational database).

Data layer encapsulation is achieved in the Java environment by defining classes that represent the *conceptual* data stored in your database. Think about storing and retrieving personal information (e.g., name, address, phone number). Ignoring the data layout issues for the moment, we would normally want to encapsulate this data as a Java class that represents a person:

```
class DBPerson {
    Connection c;     // The connection to the database
    String name;      // Name of the desired person
    // Any other data we want to cache within the object
        ...

    public DBPerson(String name, Connection c, boolean preload) {
        dbConn = c;
        if (preload) {
            initFromDB();
        }
    }

    public String getAddress() {
        // Perform database transactions to retrieve
        // address information
            ...
    }
}
```

The data objects that we use to represent concepts stored in our database tables can be either local or remote with respect to the application logic of our system. If they are local, the data objects could be Java objects that access the database using JDBC directly. If our system will involve remote data objects, perhaps due to issues regarding direct access to the database, then the data objects would need to be accessible from the local client as a data server. This access could be provided through distributed objects implemented in RMI or CORBA, or it could be through simpler message-passing techniques such as those described in Chapter 6. In the following sections we'll examine an example database application, and the different ways the data objects could be implemented in both a local and remote context.

A Scheduling Example

To demonstrate these ideas, let's turn to a distributed application involving databases. Our example will revolve around a generic scheduling system, where the data to be stored in a DBMS will include information on resources, tasks to be accomplished with these resources, temporal constraints between tasks, and assignments of resources to tasks. Let's assume for now that the data is stored in a relational database of some sort, and is arranged into tables as shown in Figure 7-3. A RESOURCE record identifies an available resource, along with its name, coded type, and a size value that is interpreted based on its type (e.g., the size of a storage bin may be some volume measurement, while the size of a drill press may be the largest job it can process). A TASK record represents a task that needs to be accomplished using the available resources. It includes a coded type field and a size that is also interpreted based on its type. A TIME_CONSTRAINT record represents a constraint on the completion times of two tasks. A coded type field indicates what kind of temporal constraint is being placed on the two tasks (e.g., "before," "after," "during"). A RES_ASSIGNMENT record represents the assignment of a task to a resource at a given time. The complete set of RES_ ASSIGNMENT records represents a schedule for this set of resources and tasks. The RESOURCE and TASK tables have primary keys (rid and tid, respectively), which are unique identifiers for the records in these tables. The records in the TIME_CONSTRAINT table are keyed off of the TASK records that they reference in their task1 and task2 fields. The RES_ASSIGNMENT records are also indirectly keyed off of the resource and task IDs that they associate in time.

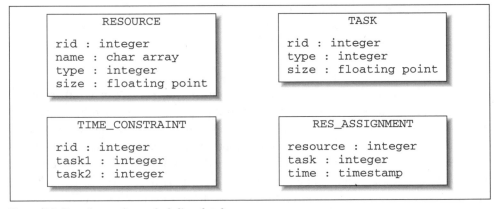

Figure 7-3. Data layout for a scheduling database

In designing the data objects that will be used to access this data, we have to consider several factors, including:

- What is a sensible way to represent this information in an application?

  In this case, it seems obvious that we will need object representations of resources and tasks. But what about temporal constraints and resource assignments? If the goal is to develop a scheduling application with update capabilities, then it will probably be worthwhile having an explicit object representation of both constraints and resource assignments, so that they can be created and manipulated directly by the scheduling algorithm. If we are developing a simple schedule viewing tool, then these objects may not be necessary, and it would be sufficient to be able to ask a resource object for a list of tasks assigned to it, and to ask a task for a list of the other tasks which constrain it temporally.

- How will the objects access the database—through a centralized access connection, or through individual database connections?

Generally, the best data throughput is achieved by creating a single database connection and accessing all data associated with various objects through it, rather than creating a new connection and executing a database transaction for each data element of each object. This is due to the overhead typically involved in setting up the connection to the database: if each new object has to create its own connection, setting up the connection will delay the availability of the data that object represents. There are situations, however, where it makes sense for a data object to manage its own database connection. A multi-database query interface, for example, may want to display a set of data hits using some metadata collected during the search, connected to a data object that is triggered to retrieve the actual data when the user selects it. If the set of remote databases included in the search is large or variable, it may be more sensible to have each data object manage its own connection to the source of its data.

- How dynamic will these objects be with respect to the database; i.e., how and when will an update to the database be reflected in corresponding Java data objects?

This also depends on the nature of the application being developed on top of this data. It's safest to have no data cached within the data objects themselves, and have every request generate a new transaction with the database to get the newest data. This guarantees that the data presented to the user or the requesting agent is always current. If, however, we know that the update frequency of the data on the database server is fairly low, if we are accessing remote data sources over a low-bandwidth or unreliable network, or if we suspect that the data server will be unable to handle the extra requests, then we may want to cache data in the data objects to improve the overall performance of the application.

- What kinds of privileges will these objects be expected to have over the data they represent (e.g., will they be able to update the database data, or only represent a read-only view of the data)?

Again, the answer to this depends on the nature of the application. If we are developing a schedule generation engine, then the data objects need update privileges on the database tables so that new time constraints and resource assignments can be added. If a schedule viewing tool is being developed, then the data object will simply need select privileges on the database tables.

For the scheduling example we are discussing, we can assume that the data objects will need to create new time constraint and resource assignment entries in the database. We should also provide a means to create new resources and tasks, unless we know that this data will always be created by another agent.

JDBC-Enabled Data Objects

For the first version of our scheduling data objects, we'll implement the Java classes using JDBC directly to access the scheduling database. We'll be depending on the JDBC driver configuration to provide networked access to remote databases. Later we'll look at how to access remote databases in other ways.

The Java classes for our JDBC example will be designed along the lines of Figure 7-4. A `DatabaseItem` class serves as the base class for all of our data objects. It maintains a global database `Connection` for all of the data objects in the application, and provides two abstract methods for reading and writing the objects in the database pointed at by the global `Connection`. The data objects that we'll derive from this base class will have a one-to-one mapping with the tables in our database.

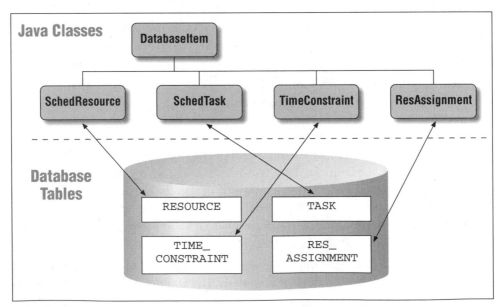

Figure 7-4. Data objects for the scheduling example

Example 7-2 shows the Java code for the `DatabaseItem` interface. This base class provides slots for a global `java.sql.Connection` object and for a validity flag. The global `Connection` is used for all transactions made by the data objects with the database to retrieve or update their data. The `DatabaseItem` interface also includes two abstract methods: `updateToDbase()` and `updateFrom-Dbase()`. These have to be implemented in subclasses to perform the necessary database transactions to store the object's data to the database, and to retrieve the object's current data from the database, respectively. Anytime during the lifetime of a `DatabaseItem`, its `updateFromDbase()` method can be called to refresh the local data from the database, or its `updateToDbase()` method can be called to update the database with the local data.

Example 7-2. Base Class for Database Items

```
package dcj.examples.dbase;

import java.sql.*;

abstract class DatabaseItem {
  static Connection dbConn;
  boolean valid;

  public boolean isValid() { return valid; }

  public abstract boolean updateToDbase();
  public abstract boolean updateFromDbase();
}
```

The classes representing the data objects for our scheduling examples are shown in Examples 7-3 through 7-6. The `SchedResource` and `SchedTask` classes in Examples 7-3 and 7-4 represent resources and tasks in the database, while the `TimeConstraint` and `ResAssignment` classes in Examples 7-5 and 7-6 represent constraints between tasks and assignments of resources to tasks.

Example 7-3. Schedule Resource Object

```
package dcj.examples.dbase;

import java.sql.*;
import java.util.Vector;

class SchedResource extends DatabaseItem {
  int rid;
  String name;
  int type;
  float size;

  public SchedResource(int id) {
```

Example 7-3. Schedule Resource Object (continued)

```
  rid = id;
  valid = updateFromDbase();
}

public SchedResource(String n, int t, float s) {

  try {
    Statement st = DatabaseItem.dbConn.createStatement();
    int rcnt = st.executeUpdate("INSERT INTO resource "
                      + "(rid, name, type, size) VALUES "
                      + "(ridseq.nextval, " + n + ", "
                      + t + ", " + s + ")");
    if (rcnt == 1)
      valid = true;
    else
      valid = false;
  }
  catch (SQLException e) {
    valid = false;
  }
}

public int    getId()              { return rid; }

public String getName()        { return name; }
public void   setName(String n) { name = n; updateToDbase(); }

public int    getType()         { return type; }
public void   setType(int t)    { type = t; updateToDbase(); }

public float  getSize()         { return size; }
public void   setSize(float s)  { size = s; updateToDbase(); }

public boolean updateFromDbase() {
  boolean success = true;

  try {
    Statement s = DatabaseItem.dbConn.createStatement();
    ResultSet r =
      s.executeQuery("SELECT name, type, size FROM resource WHERE rid = "
                      + rid);
    if (r.next()) {
      name = r.getString("name");
      type = r.getInt("type");
      size = r.getFloat("size");
    }
    else {
      success = false;
```

Example 7-3. Schedule Resource Object (continued)

```
    }

    s.close();
  }
  catch (SQLException e) {
    success = false;
  }

  return success;
}

public boolean updateToDbase() {
  boolean success = true;

  try {
    Statement s = DatabaseItem.dbConn.createStatement();
    int numr = s.executeUpdate("UPDATE resource SET name = " + name
                        + ", type = " + type + ", size = " + size
                        + " WHERE rid = " + rid);
    if (numr < 1) {
      success = false;
    }
  }
  catch (SQLException s) {
    success = false;
  }

  return success;
}

static public Vector getAllResources() {
  Vector resList = new Vector();
  try {
    Statement s = DatabaseItem.dbConn.createStatement();
    ResultSet r = s.executeQuery("SELECT distinct(rid) FROM resource");
    while (r.next()) {
      int id = r.getInt("rid");
      SchedResource res = new SchedResource(id);
      if (res.isValid()) {
        resList.addElement(res);
      }
    }
  }
  catch (Exception e) {};

  return resList;
}
}
```

An individual `SchedResource` or `SchedTask` object can be constructed in two ways: using an integer identifier for the desired database record, or using data items representing a new database record that is to be created. In the first case, the `SchedResource` and `SchedTask` constructors set their identifiers to the one given as an argument, then try to update themselves from the database by calling their `updateFromDbase()` methods. Their `updateFromDbase()` methods create a JDBC statement from the database connection and execute a `SELECT` query to the database to retrieve the data for the record. If the indicated record isn't found, then the `valid` flag on the object is set to `false`. In the second case, the constructor attempts to create a new record in the database with the given data by creating a JDBC statement and executing an INSERT query to the database. If the data insertion fails, then the `valid` flag on the object is set to `false`. The `SchedResource` and `SchedTask` classes also provide static methods for retrieving all of the resources or tasks from the schedule database. `SchedResource.getAllResources()` returns a vector of `SchedResources` representing all of the resource records found in the database, and the `Sched-Task.getAllTasks()` method does the same for `SchedTask` objects.

Example 7-4. Schedule Task Object

```
package dcj.examples.dbase;

import java.sql.*;
import java.util.Vector;

class SchedTask extends DatabaseItem {
  int tid;
  int type;
  float size;

  SchedTask(int id) {
    tid = id;
    valid = updateFromDbase();
  }

  SchedTask(int t, float sz) {
    type = t;
    size = sz;
    try {
      Statement s = DatabaseItem.dbConn.createStatement();
      int cnt = s.executeUpdate("INSERT INTO task (tid, type, size) "
                                + "VALUES (tidseq.nextval, " + type + ", "
                                + size + ")");
      if (cnt < 1) {
        valid = false;
      }
      else {
```

Example 7-4. Schedule Task Object (continued)

```
        valid = true;
      }
    }
    catch (SQLException e) {
      valid = false;
    }
  }

  public int     getId()            { return tid; }

  public int     getType()          { return type; }
  public void    setType(int t)     { type = t; }

  public float   getSize()          { return size; }
  public void    setSize(float s)   { size = s; }

  public boolean updateFromDbase() {
    boolean success = true;

    try {
      Statement s = DatabaseItem.dbConn.createStatement();
      ResultSet r =
        s.executeQuery("SELECT type, size FROM task WHERE tid = "
                       + tid);
      if (r.next()) {
        type = r.getInt("type");
        size = r.getFloat("size");
      }
      else {
        success = false;
      }

      s.close();
    }
    catch (SQLException e) {
      success = false;
    }

    return success;
  }

  public boolean updateToDbase() {
    boolean success = true;

    try {
      Statement s = DatabaseItem.dbConn.createStatement();
      int numr = s.executeUpdate("UPDATE task SET type = "
                              + type + ", size = " + size
```

Example 7-4. Schedule Task Object (continued)

```
                                   + " WHERE tid = " + tid);
      if (numr < 1) {
        success = false;
      }
    }
    catch (SQLException s) {
      success = false;
    }

    return success;
  }

  static public Vector getAllTasks() {
    Vector taskList = new Vector();

    try {
      Statement s = DatabaseItem.dbConn.createStatement();
      ResultSet r = s.executeQuery("SELECT distinct(tid) FROM task");
      while (r.next()) {
        int id = r.getInt("tid");
        SchedTask task = new SchedTask(id);
        if (task.isValid()) {
          taskList.addElement(task);
        }
      }
    }
    catch (Exception e) {}

    return taskList;
  }
}
```

TimeConstraints and ResAssignments are created using their constructors
with the relevant resource or task identifiers as arguments. The TimeConstraint constructor takes arguments that indicate its type, the IDs of two tasks
that are to be constrained, and an insert flag that indicates whether the new
constraint should be stored as a new record in the database. This flag is useful in
situations where a local-only object is desired (e.g., a possible schedule for the
existing tasks and resources is being evaluated locally before being committed to
the database). The ResAssignment constructor has arguments for the ID of the
resource being assigned, the ID of the task it is being assigned to, the time that
the assignment is to occur, and an insert flag similar to the one for the Time-
Constraint constructor. The TimeConstraint class also provides a static
method, constraintsFor(), which takes a task identifier and returns all of the
constraints from the database involving that task, as a list of TimeConstraint
objects. ResAssignment has a similar method, assignmentsFor(), which

takes a resource identifier and returns all assignments to tasks for that resource, in the form of a list of `ResAssignment` objects.

Example 7-5. Time Constraint Object

```
package dcj.examples.dbase;

import java.sql.*;
import java.util.Vector;

class TimeConstraint extends DatabaseItem {
  int ctype;
  int task1;
  int task2;

  // This constructor is used to create a representation
  // of a constraint in the database.
  public TimeConstraint(int type, int tid1, int tid2,
                        boolean insert) {
    ctype = type;
    task1 = tid1;
    task2 = tid2;

    if (insert) {
      // Create a new record in the database.
      try {
        Statement s = DatabaseItem.dbConn.createStatement();
        int numr = s.executeUpdate("INSERT INTO time_constraint "
                        + "(type, task1, task2) VALUES ("
                        + type + ", " + task1 + ", " + task2 + ")");
        if (numr != 1)
          valid = false;
        else
          valid = true;
      }
      catch (SQLException e) {
        valid = false;
      }
    }
  }

  public int getTask1Id() { return task1; }
  public int getTask2Id() { return task2; }
  public int getType() { return ctype; }

  static public Vector constraintsFor(int tid) {
    Vector constraints = new Vector();

    try {
```

Example 7-5. Time Constraint Object (continued)

```
      Statement s = DatabaseItem.dbConn.createStatement();
      ResultSet r = s.executeQuery("SELECT task1, task2, type FROM "
                              + "time_constraint where task1 = "
                              + tid + " or task2 = " + tid);
    while (r.next()) {
       int tid1 = r.getInt("task1");
       int tid2 = r.getInt("task2");
       int type = r.getInt("type");
       TimeConstraint c = new TimeConstraint(type, tid1, tid2,
                                         false);
       constraints.addElement(c);
    }
  }
  catch (Exception e) {}

  return constraints;
}


// This class represents non-indexed table data, so we can't
// load or update one uniquely from the database
public boolean updateFromDbase() { return false; }
public boolean updateToDbase() { return false; }
}
```

Example 7-6. Resource Assignment Object

```
package dcj.examples.dbase;

import java.sql.*;
import java.util.Vector;
import java.util.Date;

class ResAssignment extends DatabaseItem {
  int rid;
  int tid;
  Date timestamp;

  ResAssignment(int res, int task, Date time, boolean insert) {
    rid = res;
    tid = task;
    timestamp = time;

    if (insert) {
      // Create a new record in the database.
      try {
        Statement s = DatabaseItem.dbConn.createStatement();
        int numr = s.executeUpdate("INSERT INTO res_assignment "
                   + " (resource, task, time) VALUES ("
```

Example 7-6. Resource Assignment Object (continued)

```
                         + rid + ", " + tid + ", " + time + ")");
        if (numr != 1)
          valid = false;
        else
          valid = true;
      }
      catch (SQLException e) {
        valid = false;
      }
    }
  }

  public int  getResourceId() { return rid; }
  public int  getTaskId() { return tid; }
  public Date getTimeStamp() { return timestamp; }

  static public Vector assignmentsFor(int rid) {
    Vector ras = new Vector();

    try {
      Statement s = DatabaseItem.dbConn.createStatement();
      ResultSet r = s.executeQuery("SELECT task, time FROM "
                                   + "res_assignment where resource = "
                                   + rid);
      while (r.next()) {
        int tid = r.getInt("task");
        Date time = r.getDate("time");
        ResAssignment ra = new ResAssignment(rid, tid, time, false);
        ras.addElement(ra);
      }
    }
    catch (Exception e) {}

    return ras;
  }

  // This class represents non-indexed table data, so we can't
  // load or update one uniquely from the database
  public boolean updateFromDbase() { return false; }
  public boolean updateToDbase() { return false; }
}
```

With these data objects defined, we can now use them in several distributed application contexts to access local and remote schedule databases. If the schedule database is local, then we simply need to have the JDBC drivers for the DBMS on our class path when we run an application built against these objects. The application will create a `java.sql.Connection` object with the name of the local database and use it to initialize all schedule-related objects. If we want to put the database on a remote server, then we have two ways to connect these data objects to the database. If the native DBMS interface provides a network interface and if the JDBC drivers we are using support this vendor-specific network interface, then we can install the DBMS network interface and modify the URL used to create the JDBC connection to the database to reflect the remote location. If this is not an option, either because the DBMS has no network interface, or because we cannot use the DBMS network interface on the client machine for some reason, then we have the option of using JDBC drivers with their own network protocol (as we discussed in an earlier section). The database host machine would need to have the corresponding server drivers installed, including the drivers that speak the native DBMS interface protocol.

Data Caching Issues

The JDBC data objects previously shown cache all of their data locally, i.e., within the data object representation itself. When each data object is created, all of the data associated with that object is read from the database and stored in local data variables; these local data variables are returned in response to method calls on the data objects. This caching scheme is appropriate when the data being accessed is fairly stable, or is only updated from one client at any given time. If our scheduling database is being accessed from multiple clients, and each client updates objects in the database at will, we may want to think about a shorter-duration caching scheme.

At the opposite end of the caching spectrum are data objects that have no cached data. Each request for data from the object is serviced by generating an SQL query to the database that gets the current data from the source. If we reimplemented our `SchedResource` class to eliminate data caching, its data access methods would look something like this `getName()` method:

```
public String getName()
{
    String name;
    Statement s = null;
    try {
        s = dbConn.getStatement();
        ResultSet r =
          s.executeQuery("SELECT name FROM resource where rid = "
                            + rid);
        name = r.getString("name");
    }
    catch (Exception e) { name = null; }
    finally {
```

```
            if (s != null) {
                s.close();
            }
        }
        return name;
    }
```

Complete elimination of data caching is not generally useful for remote database applications, since the additional overhead involved in having all data read dynamically is usually unacceptable. Intermediate caching schemes involve data updates of varying frequency, and only a subset of the data served from the database is cached—the data that is least likely to be updated during the lifetime of the client agent. The data update frequency can be controlled using timers; for example, if we wanted the "name" field on our resource object to be cached, but have the cache refreshed from the database every hour in case of an update, then our getName() method on our SchedResource class might look something like this:

```
public String getName()
{
    String currName;
    Calendar now = Calendar.getInstance();
    Calendar lastUpdate = Calendar.getInstance();
    lastUpdate.setTime(nameTimestamp);
    // Add the cache expiration time (in minutes) to the time
    // of last update
    lastUpdate.add(cacheExpirationTime, Calendar.MINUTE);
    // If the name cache has expired, then go to the database
    if (lastUpdate.before(now)) {
        try {
            Statement s = dbConn.getStatement();
            ResultSet r =
             s.executeQuery("SELECT name FROM resource where rid = "
                            + rid);
            name = r.getString("name");
            // Reset the cache timer
            nameTimestamp = new Date();
        }
        catch {Exception e) { currName = name; }
    }
    // Otherwise, use the previous value cached in the class
    // data member
    currName = name;

    return currName;
}
```

In this example, the resource data object has a `nameTimestamp` variable that is used to expire the cache for the `name` data member. When `getName()` is called, the timestamp on the cache for that variable is checked. If the time since the cache was refreshed has gone beyond the limit we set (represented in minutes by the `cacheExpirationTime` data member), then a call to the database is made to refresh the cache. If not, then the local data member is used as the name of the resource.

Remote Data Servers

Now it may become necessary to isolate the direct data access portion of our data tier on a remote data server, and provide indirect data access to the application layer. One reason for this may be that the data representations required for a given application have many interdependencies and data constraints. If we want to keep the client-side data access lean and free from this complex data logic (e.g., if we are using these data objects in an applet), then we would prefer to put the data objects on a data server and provide a simplified data access layer to the client. An example of this is the potential complexity of the `SchedTask` data object. Updating this object in the database could involve some complex logic for verifying the validity of existing time constraints on the task, as well as resources currently assigned to completing the task. We could avoid inflicting this complexity on the client by providing a way for the client to transmit its update request to the data server, have the data server run the request through the data dependencies, update the database, and return the result to the client. Other reasons for separating data logic from the application tier may involve security issues (e.g., the potential for reverse-engineering the bytecodes of a data object to determine the proprietary structure of a database, physical access to the database server, etc.).

If the data objects also reside on a host that is remote from the client host, then we can interface the application tier to the data tier using either the message-passing techniques discussed in Chapter 6, or using distributed objects implemented in CORBA, Java RMI, or the equivalent. In the following sections, we'll examine both of these possibilities.

Message passing with the data server

To provide access to remote data using message passing, we first need to establish a data server that can respond to messages from clients and access the data referenced in the messages. This is easily accomplished using existing data objects such as those we saw earlier, by simply developing a set of messages that can talk to these data objects on the data server. We could have a `GetResourceMsg` class, for example, which is a message passed from a client to the data server asking for the data associated with a given resource. If we model this message-passing system after the `Message` and `MessageHandler` classes described in Chapter 6, then the `Do()` method on `GetResourceMsg` might look something like this:

```
public boolean Do() {
    boolean success = true;
    // Get the resource ID from the message arguments
    Integer rid = (Integer)argList.elementAt(0);
    // Connect to the database.
    Connection c = DriverManager.getConnection(...);
    // Create the referenced data object from the database
    SchedResource res = new SchedResource(rid.intValue(), c);

    GetResourceResp grr = new GetResourceResp();
    // If we were able to find the resource in the database,
    // return a success flag, along with the resource data.
    if (res.isValid()) {
        grr.addArg("success");
        grr.addArg(res.getName());
        grr.addArg(new Integer(res.getType()));
        grr.addArg(new Float(res.getSize()));
    }
    // If the database query failed, return a failure flag
    else {
        grr.addArg("failed");
        success = false;
    }

    handler.sendMsg(grr);
    return success;
}
```

A `GetResourceMsg` object would be created by the `MessageHandler` on the data server when a message of this type was received from a data client. This `Do()` method would then be invoked. A `SchedResource` object is created, which pulls the relevant data from the database using JDBC, and the resource data is formatted into a return message to the client. On the client, we could provide message-passing versions of our data objects. These could be modeled closely after the JDBC-enabled data objects, with the implementation altered to use messages for data transactions rather than the JDBC API. For example, the constructor for a message-passing version of our `SchedResource` object could be implemented as shown in Example 7-7. The constructor calls an `updateFrom-Dbase()` method, just as the JDBC data object does, but this method generates a `GetResourceMsg` message, sends it to the data server, then parses the response to extract the data.

Example 7-7. A Message-Passing Remote Data Object

```
class MPSchedResource {

      . . .

 MPSchedResource(int id, ScheduleMsgHandler h) {
    super(h);
    rid = id;
    valid = updateFromDbase();
  }

  public boolean updateFromDbase() {
    boolean success = true;

    try {
      GetResourceMsg gm = new GetResourceMsg(rid);
      handler.sendMsg(gm);
      Message gr = handler.readMsg();
      name = (String)r.getArg(0);
      Integer tmp = (Integer)r.getArg(1);
      type = tmp.intValue();
      Float ftmp = (Float)r.getArg(2);
      size = ftmp.floatValue();
    }
    catch (Exception e) {
      success = false;
    }

    return success;
  }


      . . .

}
```

With the data tier split in this way—message-passing objects on the client talking to JDBC-enabled data objects on the data server—the issue of data caching becomes more complicated. Data can now be cached in both the client agent and in the objects on the data server, if we so desire. Some of the same issues are involved in determining the proper level of caching on both levels of the data tier:

- How frequently is each data item updated on the next data level (data server or DBMS) by agents other than our own?

- What is the caching scheme used in the next data level?

- What is the nature of our connection to the next data level in terms of bandwidth and reliability, and what effect does this have on the effective data throughput from the database itself to the end user?

- How frequently can we update the local cache without imposing unreasonable overhead on data access times?

Other issues are specific to each level of the data tier. On the data server:

- Is the data server the single entry point for data clients (e.g., a multithreaded data server), or are multiple data servers servicing data transactions?

And on the data client:

- Are we the only client accessing this data server? Can we use network bandwidth issues alone to decide our caching scheme, or do we have to consider updates from external entities as well?

Distributed objects from the data server

Another option for splitting the data tier between the client and the data server is to use distributed objects. In this situation, data object stubs on the client use distributed object protocols to interact with data objects on the server. The server-side data objects then access the database directly, using JDBC or some other RDBMS interface library. In this section we'll develop an RMI interface to our scheduling data objects.

With the JDBC-enabled data objects for our scheduling application in hand, we need to perform the following steps to enable RMI access to them:

- Create stub interfaces to the data objects.

- Update the existing data objects so that they implement the stub interfaces and the appropriate RMI interfaces.

- Provide a registered server object that can act as a schedule object server. A stub to this object will be accessed by the client through the registry, and then remote objects will be generated through its interface.

Let's define the client stub interfaces to our data objects first. Each data object that we defined in the previous section will need a remote stub; the interfaces to the remote objects are shown in Example 7-8. The `RMIDatabaseItem` interface mirrors the `DatabaseItem` class, and exports the `updateToDbase()` and `updateFromDbase()` methods. Derived from this we have stub interfaces for each of our data objects: `RMISchedResource`, `RMISchedTask`, `RMITimeConstraint`, and `RMIResAssignment`. Each of these interfaces exports the `getXXX()` and `setXXX()` methods from the schedule data classes.

Example 7-8. Schedule Data Object Stub Interfaces

```
package dcj.examples.dbase;

import java.util.Date;
```

Example 7-8. Schedule Data Object Stub Interfaces (continued)

```java
import java.util.Vector;
import java.sql.*;
import java.rmi.*;

interface RMISchedDbaseItem extends Remote {
  public boolean updateFromDbase() throws RemoteException;
  public boolean updateToDbase() throws RemoteException;
}

interface RMISchedResource extends RMISchedDbaseItem {
  public boolean isValid() throws RemoteException;

  public int    getId() throws RemoteException;
  public String getName() throws RemoteException;
  public void   setName(String n) throws RemoteException;
  public int    getType() throws RemoteException;
  public void   setType(int t) throws RemoteException;
  public float  getSize() throws RemoteException;
  public void   setSize(float s) throws RemoteException;
}

interface RMISchedTask extends RMISchedDbaseItem {
  public boolean isValid() throws RemoteException;

  public int    getId() throws RemoteException;
  public int    getType() throws RemoteException;
  public void   setType(int t) throws RemoteException;
  public float  getSize() throws RemoteException;
  public void   setSize(float s) throws RemoteException;
}

interface RMITimeConstraint extends RMISchedDbaseItem {
  public boolean isValid() throws RemoteException;

  public int getTask1Id() throws RemoteException;
  public int getTask2Id() throws RemoteException;
  public int getType() throws RemoteException;
}

interface RMIResAssignment extends RMISchedDbaseItem {
  public boolean isValid() throws RemoteException;

  public int  getResourceId() throws RemoteException;
  public int  getTaskId() throws RemoteException;
  public Date getTimeStamp() throws RemoteException;
}
```

Now we need to provide the client with the ability to create new data objects. The only remote objects that the client can request directly from the remote server are objects that have been explicitly registered with the RMI registry running on the server. So we need to provide an object broker, similar to the object activation facilities provided in CORBA by the server's ORB. The RMISchedDbase interface shown in Example 7-9 serves this function by providing methods for creating new resources, tasks, constraints, and resource assignments in the database, and for retrieving existing data records from the database. The results are provided in terms of the remote stubs in Example 7-8. These methods replace the constructors and static utility methods in Example 7-7.

Example 7-9. A Schedule Data Object Server

```
package dcj.examples.dbase;

import java.rmi.*;
import java.util.Vector;
import java.util.Date;

public abstract interface RMISchedDbase extends Remote {
  // Methods for creating/retrieving resources
  public RMISchedResource getResource(int rid) throws RemoteException;
  public RMISchedResource newResource(String n, int t, float s)
                         throws RemoteException;
  public Vector getAllResources() throws RemoteException;

  // Methods for creating/retrieving tasks
  public RMISchedTask getTask(int id) throws RemoteException;
  public RMISchedTask newTask(int t, float sz) throws RemoteException;
  public Vector getAllTasks() throws RemoteException;

  // Methods for creating/retrieving constraints
  public RMITimeConstraint newConstraint(int type, int t1, int t2)
                         throws RemoteException;
  public Vector constraintsFor(int tid) throws RemoteException;

  // Methods for creating/retrieving resource assignments
  public RMIResAssignment newResAssignment(int rid, int tid, Date time)
                         throws RemoteException;
  public Vector assignmentsFor(int rid) throws RemoteException;
}
```

Now we need to turn to the server implementations of these interfaces. The server implementations of our RMI data objects are nearly identical to the first versions we discussed earlier, except that now they derive from the RMI UnicastRemote-Object class, and implement the corresponding RMI stub interface. For example, the RMI-enabled version of the SchedResource class is shown in

Example 7-10, and is called `SchedResourceImpl`. The implementation is nearly identical to that of the `SchedResource` class shown in Example 7-3, except that each RMI-exported method throws `RemoteException`, and the class implements its RMI stub counterpart as well as the `DatabaseItemImpl` base class. Also, the `DatabaseItemImpl` class, which isn't shown here, extends the `UnicastRemoteObject` class, so all of its subclasses become `UnicastRemote-Objects` as well.

Example 7-10. RMI-Enabled Resource Object

```
package dcj.examples.dbase;

import java.util.Vector;
import java.util.Date;
import java.sql.*;
import java.rmi.*;
import java.rmi.server.*;
import java.rmi.registry.*;

class SchedResourceImpl extends DatabaseItem implements RMISchedResource {
  int rid;
  String name;
  int type;
  float size;

  SchedResourceImpl(int id) throws RemoteException {
    rid = id;
    valid = updateFromDbase();
  }

  SchedResourceImpl(String n, int t, float s)
    throws RemoteException {

    try {
      Statement st = DatabaseItem.dbConn.createStatement();
      int rcnt = st.executeUpdate("INSERT INTO resource "
                  "(rid, name, type, size) VALUES (ridSeq.nextVal, "
                  + n + ", " + t + ", " + s + ")");
      if (rcnt == 1)
        valid = true;
      else
        valid = false;
    }
    catch (Exception e) {
      valid = false;
    }
  }
```

Example 7-10. RMI-Enabled Resource Object (continued)

```
public int     getId() throws RemoteException
                    { return rid; }
public String getName() throws RemoteException
                    { return name; }
public void    setName(String n) throws RemoteException
                    { name = n; updateToDbase(); }
public int     getType() throws RemoteException
                    { return type; }
public void    setType(int t) throws RemoteException
                    { type = t; updateToDbase(); }
public float  getSize() throws RemoteException
                    { return size; }
public void    setSize(float s) throws RemoteException
                    { size = s; updateToDbase(); }

public boolean updateFromDbase() throws RemoteException {
  boolean success = true;

  try {
    Statement s = DatabaseItem.dbConn.createStatement();
    ResultSet r =
      s.executeQuery("SELECT name, type, size FROM resource WHERE rid = "
                     + rid);
    if (r.next()) {
      name = r.getString("name");
      type = r.getInt("type");
      size = r.getFloat("size");
    }
    else {
      success = false;
    }

    s.close();
  }
  catch (SQLException e) {
    success = false;
  }

  return success;
}

public boolean updateToDbase() throws RemoteException {
  boolean success = true;

  try {
    Statement s = DatabaseItem.dbConn.createStatement();
    int numr = s.executeUpdate("UPDATE resource SET name = " + name
```

Example 7-10. RMI-Enabled Resource Object (continued)

```
                                    + " type = " + type + " size = " + size
                                    + " WHERE rid = " + rid);

      if (numr < 1) {
        success = false;
      }
    }
    catch (SQLException s) {
      success = false;
    }

    return success;
  }
}
```

The implementation of the `RMISchedDbase` is the `SchedDbaseImpl` class shown in Example 7-11. In addition to implementing the utility methods that create and retrieve schedule objects from the database, the `SchedDbaseImpl` class also has a `main()` method that registers an instance of the class with the local RMI registry under a name passed in as a command-line argument. This allows clients to obtain an RMI stub to the object by looking up the object by name through their local registries.

Example 7-11. RMI-Based Data Server Object

```
package dcj.examples.dbase;

import java.util.Vector;
import java.util.Date;
import java.sql.*;
import java.rmi.*;
import java.rmi.server.*;
import java.rmi.registry.*;

class SchedDbaseImpl extends UnicastRemoteObject
                     implements RMISchedDbase {

  public SchedDbaseImpl() throws RemoteException { super(); }

  // main() method registers a SchedDbaseImpl object with the
  // local RMI naming service, using the first command-line
  // argument as the name of the service, and the second as
  // the URL for the JDBC connection.
  public static void main(String argv[]) {
    System.setSecurityManager(new RMISecurityManager());

    try {
      String name = argv[0];
      String dbURL = argv[1];
```

Example 7-11. RMI-Based Data Server Object (continued)

```
      System.out.println("Registering SchedDbaseImpl with "
                          + "naming service as " + name);
      SchedDbaseImpl server = new SchedDbaseImpl();
      Class.forName("weblogic.jdbc.oci.Driver");
      SchedDbaseItem.dbConn =
        DriverManager.getConnection("jdbc:weblogic:oracle:hb1",
                                    "user", "passwd");
      Registry r = LocateRegistry.getRegistry(1234);
      r.rebind(name, server);
      System.out.println(name + " ready.");
    }
    catch (Exception e) {
      System.out.println("Exception while registering "
                          + "SchedDbaseImpl: \n");
      e.printStackTrace();
      System.exit(2);
    }
  }


    // Methods for creating/retrieving resources
  public RMISchedResource getResource(int rid)
                          throws RemoteException {
    SchedResourceImpl res = new SchedResourceImpl(rid);
    return res;
  }


  public RMISchedResource newResource(String n, int t, float s)
                          throws RemoteException {
    SchedResourceImpl res = new SchedResourceImpl(n, t, s);
    return res;
  }


  public Vector getAllResources() throws RemoteException {
    Vector resList = new Vector();
    try {
      Statement s = SchedDbaseItem.dbConn.createStatement();
      ResultSet r = s.executeQuery("SELECT distinct(rid) FROM resource");
      while (r.next()) {
        int id = r.getInt("rid");
        SchedResourceImpl res = new SchedResourceImpl(id);
        if (res.isValid()) {
          resList.addElement(res);
        }
      }
    }
    catch (Exception e) {}
```

Example 7-11. RMI-Based Data Server Object (continued)

```
    return resList;
  }

  // Methods for creating/retrieving tasks
  public RMISchedTask getTask(int id) throws RemoteException {
    SchedTaskImpl task = new SchedTaskImpl(id);
    return task;
  }

  public RMISchedTask newTask(int t, float sz) throws RemoteException {
    SchedTaskImpl task = new SchedTaskImpl(t, sz);
    return task;
  }

  public Vector getAllTasks() throws RemoteException {
    Vector taskList = new Vector();
    try {
      Statement s = SchedDbaseItem.dbConn.createStatement();
      ResultSet r = s.executeQuery("SELECT distinct(tid) FROM task");
      while (r.next()) {
        int id = r.getInt("tid");
        SchedTaskImpl task = new SchedTaskImpl(id);
        if (task.isValid()) {
          taskList.addElement(task);
        }
      }
    }
    catch (Exception e) {}

    return taskList;
  }

  // Methods for creating/retrieving constraints
  public RMITimeConstraint newConstraint(int type, int t1, int t2)
                          throws RemoteException {
    TimeConstraintImpl c = new TimeConstraintImpl(type, t1, t2);

    // Create a new record in the database.
    try {
      Statement s = SchedDbaseItem.dbConn.createStatement();
      int numr = s.executeUpdate("INSERT time_constraint SET type = "
                                + type + " task1 = " + t1
                                + " task2 = " + t2);
      if (numr != 1)
        c.valid = false;
      else
        c.valid = true;
    }
    catch (SQLException e) {
```

Example 7-11. RMI-Based Data Server Object (continued)

```
      c.valid = false;
    }

    return c;
}

public Vector constraintsFor(int tid) throws RemoteException {
  Vector constraints = new Vector();

  try {
    Statement s = SchedDbaseItem.dbConn.createStatement();
    ResultSet r = s.executeQuery("SELECT task1, task2, type FROM "
                            + "time_constraint where task1 = "
                            + tid + " or task2 = " + tid);
    while (r.next()) {
      int tid1 = r.getInt("task1");
      int tid2 = r.getInt("task2");
      int type = r.getInt("type");
      TimeConstraintImpl c = new TimeConstraintImpl(type, tid1, tid2);
      constraints.addElement(c);
    }
  }
  catch (Exception e) {}

  return constraints;
}

// Methods for creating/retrieving resource assignments
public RMIResAssignment newResAssignment(int rid, int tid, Date time)
                    throws RemoteException {
  ResAssignmentImpl r = new ResAssignmentImpl(rid, tid, time);

  // Create a new record in the database.
  try {
    Statement s = SchedDbaseItem.dbConn.createStatement();
    int numr = s.executeUpdate("INSERT res_assignment SET resource = "
                          + rid + " task = " + tid
                          + " time = " + time);
    if (numr != 1)
      r.valid = false;
    else
      r.valid = true;
  }
  catch (SQLException e) {
    r.valid = false;
  }
```

Example 7-11. RMI-Based Data Server Object (continued)

```
      return r;
  }

  public Vector assignmentsFor(int rid) throws RemoteException {
    Vector ras = new Vector();

    try {
      Statement s = SchedDbaseItem.dbConn.createStatement();
      ResultSet r = s.executeQuery("SELECT task, time FROM "
                                   + "res_assignment where resource = "
                                   + rid);
      while (r.next()) {
        int tid = r.getInt("task");
        Date time = r.getDate("time");
        ResAssignmentImpl ra = new ResAssignmentImpl(rid, tid, time);
        ras.addElement(ra);
      }
    }
    catch (Exception e) {}

    return ras;
  }
}
```

A client that uses RMI to look up objects in the database is shown in
Example 7-12. This particular client is requesting an RMISchedDbase object
registered under the name "ScheduleDataServer" on a remote host:

```
    RMISchedDbase dbase =
    (RMISchedDbase)Naming.lookup("//my.server/ScheduleDataServer");
```

Example 7-12. Client for the RMI-Based Schedule Data Server

```
package dcj.examples.dbase;

import java.rmi.*;
import java.util.Vector;

public class RMIScheduler {
  public static void main(String argv[]) {
    System.setSecurityManager(new RMISecurityManager());
    try {
      RMISchedDbase dbase =
        (RMISchedDbase)Naming.lookup("rmi://my.server/ScheduleDataServer");
      Vector resources = dbase.getAllResources();
      System.out.println("Got " + resources.size() + " resources.");
    }
    catch (Exception e) {
      System.out.println("Exception: " + e);
```

Example 7-12. Client for the RMI-Based Schedule Data Server (continued)

```
        e.printStackTrace();
    }
  }
}
```

Before this client can access the object, we have to register an instance of the `SchedDbaseImpl` class on the remote data server by invoking its `main()` method. This can be done by executing the following `rmiregistry` command (the commands shown are for a Unix server):

```
my.server% rmiregistry &
my.server% java dcj.examples.dbase.SchedDbaseImpl ScheduleDataServer
Registering SchedDbaseImpl with naming service as ScheduleDataServer
ScheduleDataServer ready.
my.server%
```

Then the client scheduler can be run (the commands are shown for a Windows-based client):

```
C:\SCHED> java dcj.examples.dbase.RMIScheduler
Got 17 resources.
C:\SCHED>
```

Multi-Database Applications

So far we've discussed simple local database access from Java using JDBC, and various approaches for connecting Java agents to remote databases. Some simple extensions to these approaches allow you to connect a Java agent to multiple remote databases, and create some interesting possibilities for applications in data analysis and management.

A feature of JDBC that should be obvious from earlier sections is that it insulates the application from the proprietary details of the database. So assuming that we've encapsulated the data-access tier of our application well, and that we have local JDBC drivers that can access each database server, we can easily distribute our data across multiple database servers and still pull the data together into a single set of data objects simply by using multiple `Connection` objects.

As an example, suppose that the tables shown in Figure 7-3 are stored in two separate databases: all tasks and time constraints on tasks are stored in a database named "sequence" on server "data1," while resource and resource assignment data is stored in a database named "schedule" on server "data2." Our JDBC-enabled data objects now simply need access to `Connections` to each of these databases, assuming that the tables in the separate databases are defined the same way they were in the single database. We can modify our `DatabaseItem` class to contain two `Connection` objects, as shown in Example 7-13.

Example 7-13. Multi-Database Schedule Data Item

```
abstract class DatabaseItem {
  static Connection seqConn;
  static Connection schedConn;

  boolean valid;

  public boolean isValid() { return valid; }

  protected abstract boolean updateToDbase();
  protected abstract boolean updateFromDbase();
}
```

Our application or applet would then initialize these database connections to access the correct DBMS servers:

```
Class.forName("my.custom.dbase.Driver");
SchedDbaseItem.seqConn =
    DriverManager.getConnection("jdbc:mydriver:data1:sequence",
                                "myuser", "mypassword");
SchedDbaseItem.schedConn =
    DriverManager.getConnection("jdbc:mydriver:data2:schedule",
                                "myuser", "mypassword");
```

Finally, each of our data objects would invoke the necessary `Connection` object to access its data. With these two database connections available to all `DatabaseItems` in the system, the `SchedResource.updateToDbase()` method would access the "schedule" database for its data,

```
Statement s = DatabaseItem.schedConn.createStatement();
int numr = s.executeUpdate("UPDATE resource SET name = " + name
                    + ", type = " + type + ", size = " + size
                    + " WHERE rid = " + rid);
```

while the `SchedTask.updateToDbase()` method would access the "sequence" database:

```
Statement s = SchedDbaseItem.dbConn.createStatement();
int numr = s.executeUpdate("UPDATE task SET type = "
                        + type + ", size = " + size
                        + " WHERE tid = " + tid);
```

The ease with which data in multiple databases is accessible using JDBC can be a bit deceiving, however. Many other issues come to bear on a system that is accessing or updating data from multiple remote data servers—one is the issue of maintaining data integrity between the databases. In our example, we've put ourselves in a tricky spot by requiring that the task and resource identifiers must be synchronized between the two sets of data tables. If we can guarantee that our Java data objects are the only agents that update data in these tables, it's simply a matter of building the right logic into our classes to ensure that identifiers are kept synchronized between the data servers. If not, then we should really look into other options, such as using our own secondary tables to maintain cross-references between the data servers, linking the two databases at the relational level (if the network connectivity between them allows us to do this), or even merging the two databases back into a single data server.

8

Bandwidth-Limited
Systems

Up until now, our discussions about network applications have asssumed that the reliability and capacity of the underlying network is sufficient for the task at hand. With the continued growth of wireless communications devices, as well as the ever-increasing use of multimedia content in networked applications, it's important to consider situations where this assumption is not valid—in other words, in situations where the distributed system is *bandwidth-limited*.

After a brief discussion of the overall topic of limited bandwidth, we'll show a framework for doing some crude bandwidth monitoring, built within the I/O stream classes in `java.io`. Then we'll show a general content consumer/ producer model that could be used in conjunction with the bandwidth monitoring utilities to implement adaptive buffering for data being streamed over the network.

Flavors of Limited Bandwidth

An application can be considered bandwidth-limited in two ways. First, the application can have relatively high bandwidth requirements (compared to average applications) that the communications scheme can't fully support. An application falls into this category when the required rate of data flow is very close to the capacity of the network connection. Streaming high-quality video for real-time playback is one such application—a constant, high-throughput, reliable network connection is necessary to support distributed video.

Bandwidth is also limited when the network connection has relatively low or unreliable capacity (compared to average network connections), and is insufficient for many data transactions. Current telephone modem throughput rates, for example, are insufficient to support downloading high-quality multimedia in real time. Many wireless communications schemes can be unreliable to the point that their effective throughput is much lower than their peak throughput, and a bandwidth-limited situation occurs.

In either case, the data requirements of the application exceed the available bandwidth, so measures must be taken to handle this situation without degrading our application's behavior unacceptably.

Coping with Limited Bandwidth

If our distributed application is bandwidth-limited in one of these ways, then our system needs to have a way to *monitor* our data feeds, and *manage* the bandwidth usage of the system. Monitoring data throughput is a way to detect changes in the runtime environment of the system, and managing bandwidth is a way to react to these changes. It's not sufficient to say "what you get is what you get"; we need to find out what bandwidth is available and optimize the way we use it.

Monitoring Bandwidth

You typically need to monitor the data flowing in and out of a local agent in terms of both raw and real data throughput. Raw data is fed into and out of the system at the socket or stream level. Below this level, the data is handled on the network, using the appropriate protocol. Raw data transmitted over the network may be compressed or otherwise encoded, and may require decoding before being usable as "real" data. A bandwidth-limited system needs to be capable of monitoring raw data throughput in order to respond to network variability (bandwidth fluctuations, loss of service, etc.). It must also monitor real data throughput in order to pick up on major fluctuations in its net bandwidth usage and local resources like CPU availability, while maintaining a certain performance level. How to measure performance depends on the application, but will typically be a function of responsiveness, relative rate of data delivery to the user, etc.

Managing Bandwidth

With bandwidth monitoring in place, a system can start managing its network resources in order to satisfy the application's requirements. A multimedia presentation with an audio track typically wants to ensure that the real input rate of audio samples into the local audio device is always greater than or equal to the playback rate, in order to avoid interruptions. An interactive chat client may want to balance input and output rates so that a user typing a response can see another chat user's response if they are sending a response at the same time.

In addition to managing bandwidth and local resources to support the type of data being processed, it is also possible to manage the nature of the data itself in order to match the bandwidth and local resource profile. When designing the distributed system, for example, the encoding format of the transmitted data should be chosen carefully to match both the expected bandwidth and local resource capabilities. Choosing data encoding schemes for limited bandwidth applications often involves a trade-off between these two resource types. If we strictly optimize for bandwidth, then we will use the encoding scheme that offers the best compression ratio (for low-bandwidth situations), or the most robustness in terms of lost data (for lossy network situations), or an effective combination when the network is both low in bandwidth and lossy. However, highly compressed data typically requires more CPU resources to encode and decode, especially if these operations have to occur in real time. If the application needs to run on hosts with limited CPU speed, you must also take the processing requirements into account when choosing an encoding scheme.

Levels of Monitoring and Management

Several network-level protocols that support monitoring and managing real-time data transmission have been proposed and are in use in various capacities. Perhaps the most widely accepted protocol suite is the Real-Time Protocol (RTP) and the Real-Time Control Protocol (RTCP), which is currently an IETF draft standard. RTP provides a protocol layered on top of a baseline network transport layer like TCP, with header information capable of providing data timing and ordering statistics. RTCP is meant to provide basic bandwidth management functions for RTP applications. Major vendors like Microsoft and Netscape have announced support for RTP and RTCP in various umbrella protocols, but an interface to RTP and RTCP has not yet been offered for the Java environment.*

At the application level, distributed systems can monitor the arrival and departure times of data transmitted over `InputStreams` and `OutputStreams`, and use these measurements to estimate the raw throughput rate they are achieving. Real data throughput rates can also be estimated by putting timestamps on data before encoding or after decoding. These measurements can then be used to make runtime decisions about resource allocation.

Scope of This Chapter

In this chapter, we will explore approaches to monitoring and managing bandwidth resources at the application level in the Java environment. We will not delve

---

* Support for RTP is promised in the Java Media Framework, currently in beta test.

into the ins and outs of real-time network protocols, nor will we touch on the use of native code modules in bandwidth-limited systems (e.g., native data decoders to improve CPU utilization). We will also avoid going into detail on data compression schemes and their trade-offs, other than to reinforce the notion that trade-offs do exist, and to point out where compression schemes play a role in the design of a bandwidth-limited system.

Monitoring Bandwidth

The ability to monitor the effective bandwidth previously seen by an application directly supports the ability to adapt to variable runtime environments. Some bandwidth measures that may be valuable to an adaptive distributed system are:

- Average data throughput rate over a given time period

- Total data throughput over a given time period

- Estimate of time until a given amount of data will be available

- Other first- and second-order statistics on data rate and throughput over time (variances, median rate, data "acceleration," or change in throughput rate, etc.).

Ideally, we would like to capture these bandwidth measures in real time, or as close to real time as we can get, and we would like to have these measures in terms of both raw (unprocessed) data throughput and real (application) data throughput.

The `DataMonitor` class shown in Example 8-1 provides a container for holding byte counts of data (either inbound or outbound), along with corresponding start and stop times. The start and stop times log the time interval for the data transaction. The `DataMonitor` provides an `addSample()` method for adding bandwidth measurement samples. Each of these samples is interpreted as being the number of bytes processed since the last sample, and the time interval during which the data was processed. Once a number of samples have been collected by the `DataMonitor`, it can be queried for statistics about the historical data rate. In this example we only show three methods offering basic measurements of data throughput: one provides the average data rate for all samples stored in the monitor (`getAverageRate()`), another provides the data rate for any given sample stored in the monitor (`getRateFor()`), and the third returns the data rate for the last sample stored (`getLastRate()`).

Example 8-1. A Data Monitoring Class

```
package dcj.util.Bandwidth;

import java.util.Vector;
```

Example 8-1. A Data Monitoring Class (continued)

```java
import java.util.Date;
import java.util.Enumeration;

class DataSample {
  long byteCount;
  Date start;
  Date end;

  DataSample(long bc, Date ts, Date tf) {
    byteCount = bc;
    start = ts;
    end = tf;
  }
}

public class DataMonitor {
  protected Vector samples;
  protected Date epoch;

  public DataMonitor() {
    samples = new Vector();
    epoch = new Date();
  }

  // Add a sample with a start and finish time.
  public void addSample(long bcount, Date ts, Date tf) {
    samples.addElement(new DataSample(bcount, ts, tf));
  }

  // Get the data rate of a given sample.
  public float getRateFor(int sidx) {
    float rate = 0.0;
    int scnt = samples.size();
    if (scnt > sidx && sidx >= 0) {
      DataSample s = samples.elementAt(sidx);
      Date start = s.start;
      Date end = s.end;
      if (start == null && sidx >= 1) {
        DataSample prev = samples.elementAt(sidx - 1);
        start = prev.end;
      }

      if (start != null && end != null) {
        long msec = end.getTime() - start.getTime();
        rate = 1000 * (float)s.byteCount / (float)msec;
      }
    }
```

Example 8-1. A Data Monitoring Class (continued)

```
    return rate;
  }

  // Get the rate of the last sample
  public float getLastRate() {
    int scnt = samples.size();
    return getRateFor(scnt - 1);
  }

  // Get the average rate over all samples.
  public float getAverageRate() {
    long msCount = 0;
    long byteCount = 0;
    Date start;
    Date finish;
    int scnt = samples.size();
    for (int i = 0; i < scnt; i++) {
      DataSample ds = (DataSample)samples.elementAt(i);

      if (ds.start != null)
        start = ds.start;
      else if (i > 0) {
        DataSample prev = (DataSample)samples.elementAt(i-1);
        start = ds.end;
      }
      else
        start = epoch;

      if (ds.end != null)
        finish = ds.end;
      else if (i < scnt - 1) {
        DataSample next = (DataSample)samples.elementAt(i+1);
        finish = ds.start;
      }
      else
        finish = new Date();

      // Only include this sample if we could figure out a start
      // and finish time for it.
      if (start != null && finish != null) {
        byteCount += ds.byteCount;
        msCount += finish.getTime() - start.getTime();
      }
    }

    float rate = -1;
    if (msCount > 0) {
```

Example 8-1. A Data Monitoring Class (continued)

```
      rate = 1000 * (float)byteCount / (float)msCount;
  }

  return rate;
 }
}
```

Raw Data Monitoring

Logically, in order to monitor the raw data throughput of our local agent, we need to put a "bytemeter" on the input and output streams used to transmit data. The RTInputStream and RTOutputStream classes shown in Examples 8-2 and 8-3 are extensions of FilterInputStream and FilterOutputStream that monitor their own data rates using the DataMonitor class. After each read() and write() operation, a data point is stored in the stream's DataMonitor. During the course of a transaction, the agent can query the stream for statistics on its throughput over time.

Example 8-2. A Self-Monitoring Input Stream

```
package dcj.util.Bandwidth;

import java.io.InputStream;
import java.io.FilterInputStream;
import java.util.Date;
import java.io.IOException;

public class RTInputStream extends FilterInputStream {
  DataMonitor monitor;

  RTInputStream(InputStream in) {
    super(in);
    monitor = new DataMonitor();
  }

  public int read() throws IOException {
    Date start = new Date();
    int b = super.read();
    monitor.addSample(1, start, new Date());
    return b;
  }

  public int read(byte data[]) throws IOException {
    Date start = new Date();
    int cnt = super.read(data);
    monitor.addSample(cnt, start, new Date());
    return cnt;
```

Example 8-2. A Self-Monitoring Input Stream (continued)

```
  }

  public int read(byte data[], int off, int len)
    throws IOException {
    Date start = new Date();
    int cnt = super.read(data, off, len);
    monitor.addSample(cnt, start, new Date());
    return cnt;
  }

  public float averageRate() {
    return monitor.getAverageRate();
  }

  public float lastRate() {
    return monitor.getLastRate();
  }
}
```

Example 8-3. A Self-Monitoring Output Stream

```
package dcj.util.Bandwidth;

import java.io.OutputStream;
import java.io.FilterOutputStream;
import java.util.Date;
import java.io.IOException;

public class RTOutputStream extends FilterOutputStream {
  DataMonitor monitor;

  RTOutputStream(OutputStream out) {
    super(out);
    monitor = new DataMonitor();
  }

  public void write(int b) throws IOException {
    Date start = new Date();
    super.write(b);
    monitor.addSample(1, start, new Date());
  }

  public void write(byte data[]) throws IOException {
    Date start = new Date();
    super.write(data);
    monitor.addSample(data.length, start, new Date());
  }
```

Example 8-3. A Self-Monitoring Output Stream (continued)

```
public void write(byte data[], int off, int len)
  throws IOException {
  Date start = new Date();
  super.write(data, off, len);
  monitor.addSample(data.length, start, new Date());
}

public float averageRate() {
  return monitor.getAverageRate();
}

public float lastRate() {
  return monitor.getLastRate();
}
}
```

One problem with monitoring resource usage is that measuring resources affects the measurements themselves (along the lines of the Hiesenberg Uncertainty Principle). In our case, adding more operations for gathering measurements of data rates can affect the rate that we send and receive data. In our `RTInputStream`, for example, we've added three operations to the `read()` method from `FilterInputStream`:

```
public int read() throws IOException {
    Date start = new Date();
    int b = super.read();
    monitor.addSample(1, start, new Date());
    return b;
}
```

Suppose we are streaming an audio file from a server for local, real-time playback. If we assume that data I/O, decoding, and writing to the local audio device are all done from a single thread, then the flow of control over time is fairly simple: some data is read in, which takes a finite amount of time. This data is decoded and converted to a format suitable for our audio device. Then the audio data is written to the audio device, and more data is read in to start the cycle over again. In this case, the effective raw data input rate for the system over one read/decode/write cycle is the total amount of data read (d_T), divided by the sum of the times for the reading (t_r), decoding (t_d) and writing (t_w) of the data:

$$R_T = \frac{d_T}{t_r + t_d + t_w}$$

Now suppose we use the `RTInputStream` to monitor the raw data rate that we see from the server in order to react to overflow or underflow of our buffers. Each read() operation now carries the additional overhead of registering a data sample with the DataMonitor on the RTInputStream (t_c). So our net data rate is modified by the addition of this term:

$$R_T = \frac{d_T}{t_r + t_d + t_w + t_c}$$

Ideally, the time to register a measurement is negligible compared to the time allocated to reading, decoding, and writing data, so that the effect of measuring on the data rate is minimized. One way to accomplish this is to read and process large amounts of data in each cycle (take relatively few data rate measurements). This hinders our ability to track data rate variations over time, relying instead on rate averages over significant stretches of time. The opposite approach is to ignore the effect of data monitoring, and read very small packets of data in each cycle, resulting in many rate measurements over time. This will cause a larger negative impact on the data rate itself. The art of effective data throughput monitoring lies in achieving a good compromise between these two positions: gather enough information to make reasonable judgements about the state of our bandwidth resources, but limit the information collection process so that the impact on the data rate is bearable.

Real Data Monitoring

A measurement of the raw data throughput our local agent is seeing only tells us how well we are pushing or pulling data at the network level. It doesn't tell us anything about whether our local data processing is keeping up with the network requirements of the system. For example, we may be pulling encoded audio data from the network fast enough, but if decoding that data takes longer than expected, then the playback quality may suffer from skips and silent gaps as our local buffers for holding raw data overflow, or our buffers for holding decoded data underflow. To detect and react to these situations, we need to be able to monitor real data throughput: the rate at which we are processing data from its format on the network to a format suitable for the local application, and vice versa.

With a basic data monitoring facility in place, such as our DataMonitor class, we can construct an infrastructure for monitoring the production and consumption of real application data. Data flowing into an agent from the network is generally filtered in some way before being displayed, saved, or otherwise used locally. Similarly, local data is typically filtered before being sent out on the network to another agent. These filters may compress, modify, or subdivide the data passed through them, for example. We can think of these filters as content producers, consumers, or both, depending on our perspective and their roles in the local agent. These producers and consumers are data processors that are wrapped around data input and output streams.

One way to construct this infrastructure is to develop basic interfaces for these content consumers and producers, which include the ability to monitor the rate at which data is consumed or produced. Example 8-4 shows a `ContentCon-sumer` class and Example 8-5 shows a `ContentProducer` class that demonstrates this idea. A `ContentConsumer` accepts data and consumes it, which can mean various things depending on the circumstances. A consumer may display data on the screen, store data in a database or file, or it may feed some kind of analysis engine. A `ContentProducer` generates data (perhaps by asking a user for manual input) by pulling data from persistent storage, or as a product of some processing by another producer. Both classes contain a source that is a `ContentProducer`, and a destination that is a·`ContentConsumer`. This allows for chaining consumers and producers together to form data processing pipelines. The source of a `ContentConsumer` is the `ContentProducer` that is feeding it data, and its destination is the next consumer in the pipeline. The source of a `ContentProducer` is the previous producer in the pipeline, and its destination is a consumer to which it can feed data.

Example 8-4. A Content Consumer Class

```
package dcj.util.Bandwidth;

import java.io.InputStream;
import java.io.OutputStream;

public class ContentConsumer
{
  protected ContentProducer source = null;
  protected ContentConsumer dest = null;
  protected DataMonitor     monitor = new DataMonitor();

  public ContentConsumer(ContentProducer src) {
    source = src;
  }

  public ContentConsumer(ContentConsumer dst) {
    dest = dst;
  }

  public void setSource(ContentProducer p) {
    source = p;
  }

  public void setDest(ContentConsumer c) {
    dest = c;
  }
```

Example 8-4. A Content Consumer Class (continued)

```
// Consume data from our producer until it is exhausted.
public boolean consumeAll() {
  boolean success = false;
  if (source != null) {
    byte[] data = source.produce(0);
    while (data != null) {
      success = consume(data);
      data = source.produce(0);
    }
  }

  return success;
}

// Consume a chunk of data
public boolean consume(byte[] data) {
  // Log the start of the consumption cycle
  Date start = new Date();

  boolean success;
  success = preConsume(data);
  if (success)
    success = doConsume(data);
  if (success)
    success = postConsume(data);

  // Mark the end of our consumption cycle
  monitor.addSample(data.length, start, new Date());

  // Pass the data on to the next consumer in the chain,
  // if present.
  if (dest != null) {
    dest.consume(data);
  }

  return success;
}

protected boolean preConsume(byte[] data) {
  return true;
}

// Default consumption procedure.
protected boolean doConsume(byte[] data) {
  return true;
}

// Default post-consumption procedure: log the data consumption
```

Example 8-4. A Content Consumer Class (continued)

```
  // size and finish time with our monitor.
  protected boolean postConsume(byte[] data) {
    return true;
  }
}
```

Example 8-5. A Content Producer Class

```
package dcj.util.Bandwidth;

import java.io.InputStream;
import java.io.OutputStream;

public class ContentProducer
{
  protected ContentProducer source = null;
  protected ContentConsumer dest = null;
  protected DataMonitor     monitor = new DataMonitor();

  public ContentProducer(ContentProducer src) {
    source = src;
  }

  public ContentProducer(ContentConsumer dst) {
    dest = dst;
  }

  public void setSource(ContentProducer p) {
    source = p;
  }

  public void setDest(ContentConsumer c) {
    dest = c;
  }

  // Produce data and pass it to our destination, if present.
  public boolean produceAll() {
    boolean success = false;
    if (dest != null) {
      byte[] data = produce();
      while (data != null) {
        success = dest.consume(data);
        if (success)
          data = produce();
        else
          data = null;
      }
    }
```

Example 8-5. A Content Producer Class (continued)

```
    return success;
  }

  // Produce a chunk of data, within the given limit.
  public byte[] produce(long limit) {
    // Record the start time.
    Date start = new Date();

    boolean success;
    byte[] data = null;
    success = preProduction(limit);
    if (success)
      data = doProduction(limit);
    if (success && data != null)
      success = postProduction(data, limit);

    // Record the data sample in our monitor.
    monitor.addSample(data.length, start, new Date());

    // Pass the data on to our destination, if present
    if (data != null && dest != null)
      dest.consume(data);

    return data;
  }

  // Default preconsumption procedure.
  protected boolean preProduction(long limit) {
    return true;
  }

  // Default production procedure: ask for data from our source,
  // if present, and pass along unmodified (e.g., a no-op).
  protected byte[] doProduction(long limit) {
    byte[] data = null;
    if (source != null) {
      data = source.produce(limit);
    }

    return data;
  }

  // Default postconsumption procedure.
  protected boolean postProduction(byte[] data, long limit) {
    return true;
  }
}
```

The `ContentConsumer` has `consume()` and `consumeAll()` methods. The `consumeAll()` method accepts no arguments, and its default implementation consumes data from its producer until it is exhausted. The `consume()` method accepts a data buffer in the form of a byte array, and consumes the data by calling its `preConsume()`, `doConsume()`, and `postConsume()` methods. The default implementation of the `preConsume()` method does nothing, but can be overridden in subclasses to prepare for the consumption process (e.g., open the database connection, connect to the display device, etc.). The default `doConsume()` method simply writes the data to the next consumer in the chain, if present, but could be overridden to store data in a database, draw data to a display device, etc. The default `postConsume()` method also does nothing, but can be overridden to clean up after the data is consumed (e.g., close the database connection, disconnect from the display device, etc.). In addition to calling these methods, the `consume()` method also creates a data sample for the `DataMonitor` associated with the consumer. The start of the `consume()` method is noted, the consumption methods are called in order, the finish time is noted, and the sample is given to the `DataMonitor` for recording.

A `ContentProducer` has `produce()` and `produceAll()` methods that are analogous to the `consume()` and `consumeAll()` methods on `ContentConsumer`. The `produceAll()` method produces data and passes it to the destination consumer, if present, until the producer is exhausted. The `produce()` method generates a chunk of data by calling the `preProduction()`, `doProduction()`, and `postProduction()` methods. The default `preProduction()` and `postProduction()` methods do nothing, and the default `doProduction()` method simply requests a data chunk from the previous producer in the chain, if present.

Using these classes, we can construct both consumption pipelines and production pipelines that monitor their data throughput. For example, we can create a consumption pipeline that sends an input data stream to replicated databases on the network:

```
ContentProducer input = new MyProducer(host, port);
ContentConsumer dbase1 =
    new RDBMSConsumer("jdbc:odbc://dbhost/mydata");
input.setDest(dbase1);
ContentConsumer dbase2 = ...;
dbase1.setDest(dbase2);
    ...
input.produceAll();
```

Once the replication process is finished, we can ask each consumer for its estimated average bandwidth to get a feel for the quality of our connection to each database. We could also monitor the bandwidth levels during the replication process if we wanted to try to optimize the process, perhaps by dropping off databases with unreasonably slow connections.

We can also create production pipelines. For example, we could generate a graphics pipeline where image data from a file is sequentially modified with various effects to produce a finished image that is displayed on the screen:

```
ContentProducer source = new FileProducer("source.jpg");
ContentProducer effect1 = new BlurEffect();
effect1.setSource(source);
ContentProducer effect2 = new GrainEffect();
effect2.setSource(effect1);
ContentConsumer display = new ScreenConsumer();
display.setSource(effect2);

display.consumeAll();
```

We can also monitor both raw and real data rates if we want to compare the two. Suppose we feed our image processing pipeline with an image read from an `InputStream`; we can wrap the input stream with an `RTInputStream` to monitor the rate of the "raw" image data flowing into the pipeline:

```
InputStream imgStream = ...;
RTInputStream rtStream = new RTInputStream(imgStream);
ContentProducer source = new StreamProducer(rtStream);
    ...
```

During or after the image processing, we can monitor the estimated rate of raw image input, or the rate of processed data production at any point in the pipeline.

Creating explicit representations of content consumers and producers is necessary only because we are discussing environments in which bandwidth is the limiting factor. Applications that deal with data in any way (which all applications do) can be broken down logically into data consumers and producers, and many of the objects that are defined to implement a system can be thought of as producers or consumers of data, or both. For example, in our scheduling database system from Chapter 7 we could consider the `SchedResource` class as both a producer and consumer of data, since it both delivered data from the schedule database to the local agent and delivered data from the local agent to the database when the parameters of the resource object were updated. It is only our need to monitor the flow of data that makes it valuable for us to represent our data flow with producer and consumer classes.

Bandwidth Management

Armed with a basic ability to monitor our data throughput over time, we can now discuss how to use this information to effectively manage the available bandwidth.

The general principle behind bandwidth management is to optimize the use of the available bandwidth to satisfy certain requirements of the system. The nature of these requirements varies greatly from one application to the next, and so do the approaches used to manage bandwidth. The general approach is to assess the performance of the system in terms of data input and output rates, content conversion rates, and computation times. Based on this assessment, we can try to adjust resource allocations to improve the overall performance of the system.

In order to demonstrate some of the ways that bandwidth can be managed, we'll first look at how a streaming audio agent would be implemented. In many ways, streaming audio is a worst-case scenario for bandwidth-limited applications, since there are heavy real-time constraints as well as computation requirements. After this, we will look at implementing a component of a Java-based WWW browser, to see how bandwidth can be managed across multiple input streams to maximize perceived performance.

Streaming Multimedia

In this case, the primary purpose of the local agent is to receive multimedia data from the network, process it as needed to convert it to a format suitable for presentation, and present the multimedia data to the user. The driving factor is optimizing the presentation to the user. We want audio to play without skips, video to play as smoothly and consistently as possible, and graphics to display when they are supposed to in the overall presentation. Typically, we also need the audio, video, and graphics display to be synchronized with each other, and to maintain that synchronization even if some data is late arriving.

In order to focus on the basic issues at play here, let's look at the simplest case: a single stream of media data being received in a low-bandwidth environment for real-time playback. This is a particularly relevant example, since modem-rate audio streaming has become so popular on the Web. The audio samples are typically compressed before being transmitted, so the audio receiver must decode the compressed data into audio samples before playing them on the local audio device. Using our `ContentConsumer` and `ContentProducer` classes, we can define a `StreamProducer` extension of `ContentProducer` that simply provides a `ContentProducer` interface to an `InputStream`. In our application, this `StreamProducer` acts as a source of compressed audio data. The `AudioProducer` is a `ContentProducer` extension that generates audio samples from compressed audio data by decoding the compressed data. We set its source to be the `StreamProducer` that we just wrapped around our `RTInput-Stream`. Finally, we define an `AudioConsumer` extension of `Content-Consumer` that consumes audio samples by sending them to the local audio device. We won't bother implementing these subclasses yet; for now we only need to note that they extend the `ContentConsumer` and `ContentProducer` interfaces.

With these classes in hand, our streaming audio playback might be implemented along the following lines:

```
// Get the audio input stream, typically from a Socket connection with
// a server.
InputStream audioIn = ...
// Wrap it with a real-time stream so we can monitor data throughput
// off of the wire
RTInputStream rtAudioIn = new RTInputStream(audioIn);
// Make our audio pipeline:
//        compressed audio -> raw audio -> audio device
StreamProducer stProd = new StreamProducer(rtAudioIn);
AudioProducer audioProd = new AudioProducer();
audioProd.setSource(stProd);
String audioFileSpec = "/dev/audio";
AudioConsumer audioCons = new AudioConsumer(audioFileSpec);
audioCons.setSource(audioProd);
// Start playback
audioCons.consumeAll();
```

Here we simply take our source of raw data, in the form of an `InputStream`, wrap it with an `RTInputStream` to allow us to monitor the input data rate, then wrap it with a `StreamProducer` so that we can build up the rest of the pipeline. We create an `AudioProducer` and set the `StreamProducer` as its source, then create an `AudioConsumer` pointing to an appropriate local device driver and set the `AudioProducer` as its source. To begin the streaming playback, we simply call the `consumeAll()` method on the `AudioConsumer`, which causes it to call the `produce()` method on its source, and so on up the pipeline until the `StreamProducer` does a read on its `InputStream`. All along the pipeline, we are maintaining data throughput measurements using the facilities built into our `RTInputStream`, `ContentConsumer`, and `ContentProducer` classes.

The input stream is something that we have little control over, so we can do little at that stage of our pipeline besides monitoring the input data rate using the `RTInputStream`. There are some data buffering issues that we have to deal with in the other stages, however. Let's start with the tail end of the pipeline, the `AudioConsumer`. Most audio devices on computers have a small internal data buffer in which to hold audio samples. Since in most cases an application can feed audio data to the device much faster than it can play the samples back in real time, our `AudioConsumer` needs to provide some external data buffering. For example, assuming that our audio device accepts 16-bit audio samples from an audio stream that was sampled at CD rates (e.g., 44,000 samples per second), the audio device plays back data at 44,000 x 2 = 88kB/s. Assuming a ready supply of audio data, such as a local audio file, this data rate will be well exceeded by the application feeding the audio device. So our `AudioConsumer` class will have to buffer audio samples when the audio device has filled its internal data buffers. Its `doConsume()` implementation may look something like the following:

```
public boolean doConsume(byte data[]) {
    // If we already have data queued in our local buffer, then
    // put this new data into the end of the queue and pull the
    // first data out of the queue
    if (!buffer.isEmpty()) {
        buffer.append(data);
        data = buffer.remove();
    }

    // Try to write the data to the audio device
    int numBytes = device.write(data);
    if (numBytes < data.length) {
        // Add any remaining bytes to the beginning of our
        // local buffer
        byte newBuf = new byte[data.length - numBytes];
        System.arraycopy(data, numBytes, newBuf, 0, newBuf.length);
        buffer.prepend(newBuf);
    }

    if (numBytes > 0)
        return true;
    else
        return false;
}
```

We assume that `device` is a data member of the `AudioConsumer` class that represents an interface to the audio device driver, and that `buffer` is another data member that is some sort of storage class for holding data arrays.

The workhorse of our audio pipeline is the `AudioProducer` class, and it's here that our data throughput monitoring will be the most useful. The `AudioProducer` must take the compressed audio data stream, decompress the data, and pass the audio samples on to the `AudioConsumer`. It will also have to maintain its own data buffer for compressed audio data, for the same reasons that the `AudioConsumer` needs to maintain its own data buffer. A given amount of compressed audio data will take some amount of time to be transmitted over the network and be fed to the `AudioProducer`. It also takes some non-finite amount of time for the `AudioProducer` to decode a chunk of compressed audio data into audio samples, and some time for the audio device to consume this data (e.g., to play the audio samples). Ideally, we want the audio playback to be continuous and free from skips or blank spots, since these are very noticeable to even the casual listener. The `AudioProducer` needs a data buffer so that it can maintain a constant flow of audio samples to the `AudioConsumer` regardless of the rates at which compressed data is fed into the producer, or audio samples are pulled out of the producer by the consumer. Our streaming audio pipeline now looks like Figure 8-1, with a compressed audio data buffer on the `AudioProducer`.

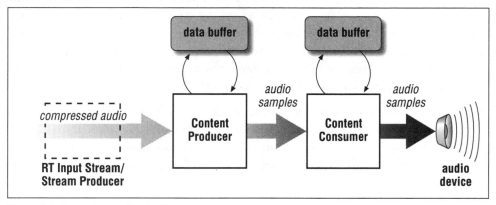

Figure 8-1. Streaming audio pipeline

Suppose the input stream of compressed audio starts, and we let the `AudioPro-ducer` begin decompressing data and immediately pass it on to the `AudioConsumer` before moving on to the next chunk of compressed audio data, with no data buffering. If the `AudioConsumer` finishes playing the first set of audio samples before the `AudioProducer` is ready with the next set, then we will hear a gap in the audio playback. This can happen if the compressed data stream slows down to the point that the time to download and decode a given amount of compressed audio is greater than the time for the resulting audio samples to be played. It can also happen if the local CPU resources become scarce (i.e., the user has started an intensive spreadsheet calculation while listening to the audio clip). In this case, the additional decode time makes the `AudioProducer`'s data production rate lag behind the `AudioConsumer`'s consumption rate, and we hear gaps in the audio again.

So now that we've justified the need for both the `AudioProducer` and the `AudioConsumer` to have data buffers, we need to decide how much data to buffer at each stage. We'll assume that the `AudioConsumer` will be the simpleton in the pipeline, and that it will simply buffer any data that the audio device can't buffer itself. This allows us to concentrate on the `AudioProducer` as the main data manager in the pipeline.

When the `AudioProducer` starts reading from the input stream, it doesn't know how fast to expect the compressed data to arrive, or how long it will take to decode the compressed data into audio samples. For this reason, the `AudioPro-`

ducer needs to read and decode some compressed data in order to gauge the effective bandwidth of the network connection and the rate at which the producer can output audio samples to the consumer; from this information `AudioProducer` estimates a safe data buffer size. During playback, it also needs to check the input rate of compressed data, and its own output data rate, to see if conditions warrant a change in the buffer size. A noticeable drop in the input rate may warrant a pause in the playback while the `AudioProducer` fills a larger buffer so that the remainder of the audio clip can be played without interruption. The same applies when local CPU resources have become scarce because other applications are starting or becoming more active, thus slowing the rate at which the `AudioProducer` can decode audio samples.

A partial implementation of our `AudioProducer` is shown in Example 8-6. We have not included the implementation of the audio decode algorithm, and we have also left out the implementation of the buffer manipulation routines, since their intended operation is obvious from their use in the rest of the class implementation.

Example 8-6. The AudioProducer Class

```
package dcj.examples.Bandwidth;

import dcj.util.Bandwidth.*;
import java.io.InputStream;
import java.io.OutputStream;

public class AudioProducer extends ContentProducer
{
  byte[] buffer = null;
  long maxBuffer = 0;
  long sampleRate;

  // Buffer operations...
  protected void appendToBuffer(byte[] data);
  protected byte[] removeFromBuffer(long size);

  // Method for computing new buffer size based on input
  // data rate, our production rate, and the audio sample rate
  protected void resizeBuffer(float inRate, float outRate,
                              long audioRate);

  // Method that decodes a given chunk of compressed data into
  // audio samples.
  protected byte[] decode(byte[] cData);

  public boolean produceAll() {
    if (buffer == null) {
```

Example 8-6. The AudioProducer Class (continued)

```
    int maxLoop = 10;
    long bytesPerLoop = 512;
    for (int loop = 0; loop < maxLoop; loop++) {
      byte[] data = produce(bytesPerLoop);
      appendToBuffer(data);
    }

    // Assuming we know the rate at which data is required by the
    // AudioConsumer (i.e., the sample rate of the audio), then
    // estimate the buffer size needed for continuous playback
    resizeBuffer(source.getAverageRate(), monitor.getAverageRate(),
                 sampleRate);
  }

  boolean success = false;
  if (dest != null) {
    byte[] data = produce();
    while (data != null) {
      success = dest.consume(data);

      // Re-estimate buffer size
      resizeBuffer(source.getLastRate(), monitor.getLastRate(),
                   sampleRate);
      if (success)
        data = produce();
      else
        data = null;
    }
  }

  return success;
}

protected byte[] doProduction(long limit) {
  byte[] sData = null;

  // Ask our source for compressed data, and decode it.
  if (source != null) {
    sData = source.produce(limit);
  }
  byte[] audioData = decode(sData);

  // If our buffer is not full, add the new data to it
  if (buffer.length < maxBuffer) {
    appendBuffer(audioData);
  }

  // If our buffer is now full, then return the requested
```

Example 8-6. The AudioProducer Class (continued)

```
  // amount of data, else return nothing.
  if (buffer.length > maxBuffer) {
    audioData = removeFromBuffer(limit);
  }
  else
    audioData = null;

  return audioData;
  }
}
```

Our `AudioProducer` class extends the `ContentProducer` class by reimplementing the `produceAll()` and `doProduction()` methods to deal with the data buffering requirements of our application. The `produceAll()` implementation has the same basic structure as the implementation in the `ContentProducer` class, but here the method is also responsible for initializing the data buffer to a size that matches the environment it encounters when first called. The first time `produceAll()` is called, the data buffer has not yet been initialized, so the `AudioProducer` must first process some data in order to gauge the expected input and output data rates. It does this by requesting a series of data chunks from the input stream and decoding them by calling its own `produce()` method. In this case, we use ten chunks of compressed data of 512 bytes each to gauge the throughput, but we could use a single larger chunk of data, or many small chunks of data. The important thing is to try to match the expected interaction with the input stream and decoder as much as possible. We chose a set of medium-size chunks of data because we will be running the producer this way in full operation—get some data from the input stream, decode it, and either buffer it or hand it off to the `AudioConsumer`. We typically won't be asking for the entire audio clip before decoding it, since the driving requirement is that we want to stream audio data and play it back in real time. We also don't want to fragment the clip into chunks that are too small because the setup time for the decoder will start to affect the throughput rate.

When we have an initial estimate for the buffer size, the `AudioProducer` starts requesting data from the input stream and producing audio samples by calling its `produce()` method. After each produce/consume cycle, the `produceAll()` method recalculates the required buffer size by calling the `resizeBuffer()` method again. We do this to track changes in the network bandwidth and the local environment. If the input rate from the network or the output rate from the decoder drops too low, we want to increase the data buffer. If the change is dramatic, this may mean pausing the playback while the buffer fills with data; if this prevents a series of interruptions later, then it is worth it in terms of playback quality.

The `doProduction()` method manages the data buffer. It first requests compressed data from the input stream, then sends the data through the decoder. If the buffer is not full, then the audio samples are appended to the buffer. If the buffer is full, then the requested amount of data is pulled from the buffer and returned.

On the server side, the bandwidth monitoring and management requirements are generally simpler, but can be made as complex as we would like. The primary requirement of the audio server is to send data over the network as quickly as possible, so that the client has a chance of playing the audio back in real time. If we are sending a pre-encoded data file, we may not even need a server agent; a simple file transfer is all that's required, assuming that the file system and the network I/O on the server is optimized to send data as quickly as possible. If we're streaming a live audio feed, the server will have to encode the audio stream as it is generated and send the compressed data over the network to the client. Again, assuming that the encoding scheme and the network connection are both fixed, there is not much the server agent can do to improve the situation if the network bandwidth to the client starts to degrade.

However, many client/server audio systems these days are designed to provide variable-bandwidth capabilities, so that the server can respond to the changing nature of the network connection. Typically, the server and the client engage in a bandwidth assessment period, much like the beginning of the `produceAll()` method in our `AudioProducer`. Once the expected bandwidth is known, then an encoding scheme with a given level of compression is chosen so that enough data will reach the client to allow constant playback. If the bandwidth changes significantly during the data streaming, then the client and server can renegotiate a new encoding scheme. The server alters its encoding process and begins sending compressed data in the new format; the client then alters its decoding process to handle the new format.

Web Browsing

One application that is often bandwidth-limited, but has very different constraints and goals from streaming audio, is viewing web pages. In this case, maintaining a constant stream of data to the final content consumer is not essential (unless the page has streaming audio incorporated). What is more important is allocating bandwidth to download page elements that are of most interest to the viewer, leaving the other elements to be downloaded later, or at a slower rate.

Let's suppose that we are asked to implement a web browser in Java. For discussion purposes, we'll ignore the initialization of the HTTP connection, and the download of the HTML code making up the requested page. We'll concentrate only on the next stage in loading a page, which is downloading all the media elements referenced in the page, such as images used for headers, icons, and figures. Our goal is to make it look like the page's images and other media elements are loading as fast as possible. In order to do that, we'll distinguish between elements of the page that the user is focusing on, and those that he isn't. If we take the whole HTML page and consider the segment that is inside the scrolling window of the user's web browser, as shown in Figure 8-2, then the focus elements are all of those media elements that lie inside of the scrolling browser window.

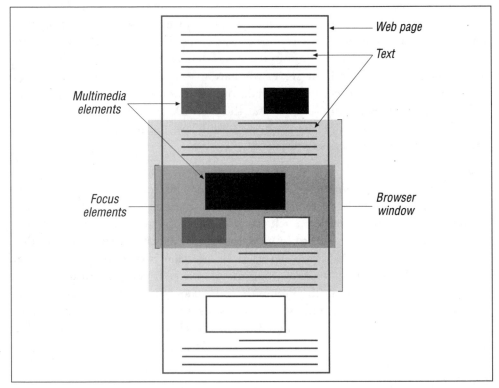

Figure 8-2. Focused and unfocused elements on a web page

Example 8-7 shows an `HTMLPageLoader` class that manages the loading of a set of HTML page elements. These page elements are given to the `HTMLPage-Loader` in the form of URL objects created by some outside agent, such as a web browser. The `HTMLPageLoader` maintains three lists of elements: one (`elements`) contains all elements the loader has been asked to load; another (`focusElements`) contains elements that are within the user's current focus on the screen; and the third (`loadedElements`) is a list of elements that have been completely downloaded from their URL address. An external agent can add elements to the `HTMLPageLoader` using the `addPageElements()` method,

and it can move elements on and off of the focus list using the focusElement()
and defocusElement() methods. The loadElements() method is the workhorse of the class, responsible for downloading the content of each element in
the page. The HTMLPageLoader class implements the Runnable interface so
that loading the page elements can be performed in a separate thread from the
agent that monitors and updates the focus list. The run() method simply calls
loadElements().

Example 8-7. An HTML Page Loader

```
package dcj.examples.Bandwidth;

import dcj.util.Bandwidth.*;
import java.io.InputStream;
import java.lang.Runnable;

public class HTMLPageLoader implements Runnable {
  Vector elements;
  Vector focusElements;
  Vector loadedElements;
  boolean focusUpdate;
  Hashtable elementConsumers = new Hashtable;

  public void run() {
    loadElements();
  }

  public HTMLPageLoader(Vector urlList) {
    elements = urlList.clone();
  }

  public void addPageElement(URL addr) {
    elements.addElement(addr);
  }

  public void focusElement(URL addr) {
    synchronized (elements) {
      if (!elements.contains(addr)) {
        addPageElement(addr);
      }
    }

    synchronized (focusElements) {
      if (!focusElements.contains(addr)) {
        focusElements.addElement(addr);
      }
      focusUpdate = true;
    }
  }
```

Example 8-7. An HTML Page Loader (continued)

```
public defocusElement(URL addr) {
  synchronized (focusElements) {
    if (focusElements.removeElement(addr)) {
      focusUpdate = true;
    }
  }
}

public void loadElements() {
  Vector localFocus = null;
  boolean done = false;
  boolean changedFocus = false;
  Vector consumers;

  synchronized (focusElements) {
    if (!focusElements.isEmpty()) {
      localFocus = (Vector)focusElements.clone();
    }
  }

  synchronized (elements) {
    if (localFocus == null) {
      localFocus = elements.clone();
    }
  }

  while (!done) {
    Enumeration e = localFocus.elements();
    while (e.hasMoreElements()) {
      URL element = (URL)e.nextElement();
      ContentConsumer c = getConsumer(element);
      long byteCount = elementSize(element);
      // Consume a maximum of 5 percent of the entire element
      // in each loop.
      if (byteCount > 20) {
        byteCount = byteCount / 20;
      }
      c.consume(byteCount);
      if (isComplete(element)) {
        doneElements.addElement(element);
        focusElements.removeElement(element);
        localFocus.removeElement(element);
      }
    }

    synchronized (focusElements) {
      if (focusUpdate) {
        localFocus = focusElements.clone();
```

Example 8-7. An HTML Page Loader (continued)

```
            focusUpdate = false;
            changedFocus = true;
          }
        }

        if (focusElements.isEmpty()) {
          // No focus elements left, so we're either done loading
          // the region the user is looking at, or we've finished
          // the entire page.
          if (doneElements.size() == elements.size()) {
            done = true;
          }
          else {
            localFocus = elements;
          }
        }
      }
    }

    protected Vector getConsumer(URL item) {
      ContentConsumer c;
      // If the element has a consumer already,
      // add it to the list.
      if (elementConsumers.contains(item)) {
        c = (ContentConsumer)elementConsumers.get(item);
      }
      else {
        try {
          InputStream in = item.openStream();
          StreamProducer sp = new StreamProducer(in);
          c = makeConsumerFor(item);
          c.setSource(sp);
          elementConsumers.put(item, c);
        }
        catch (Exception e) { }
      }

      return c;
    }
}
```

The first thing the HTMLPageLoader does in its loadElements() method is
check its focus list. If there are any elements on this list, these will be loaded first.
If there are no focus elements, the loader takes the entire element list and begins
loading them all. After initializing its hotlist, the loadElements() method
enters a loop, loading chunks of the page elements until they are completely

downloaded. Within the loop, the consumer for each element is obtained by calling the `getConsumer()` method. In the `getConsumer()` method, if a given element does not have a consumer already associated with it in the hashtable, one is generated and put into the hashtable. Each of the consumers associated with hotlist elements is then asked to consume a chunk of data for its element. If any of the elements are complete, the element is added to the "done" list. A check is made to see if the focus list has changed. If it has, the hotlist of elements is set to the current focus elements. If the list of focus elements is empty, we've either loaded all of the focus elements and can move on to the other page elements, or the page is completely loaded. If there are still unloaded elements, the hotlist is set to these elements. If not, the `done` flag is set to `true`, causing the `loadElements()` method to return.

The `HTMLPageLoader` class may be used in practice by a web browser as a separate I/O thread, running in parallel with a user interface thread that is redisplaying the page as the user scrolls up and down. The `HMTLPageLoader` thread is created once the URL elements of the page to be loaded have been determined:

```
Vector urls = ...
HTMLPageLoader loader = new HTMLPageLoader(urls);
Thread loaderThread = new Thread(loader);
loaderThread.start();
```

We could also initialize the list of focus elements before starting the loader thread. The page display component of the user interface can then have a `MouseMotionListener` attached to it, which listens for mouse motion events. This listener could implement its `mouseDragged()` method along these lines:

```
public void mouseDragged(MouseEvent e) {
    HTMLPageLoader loader = getLoader();
    Rectangle focusArea =
        getFocusArea(e.getX(), e.getY(), e.getComponent());
    Vector urlList = getFocusItems(focusArea);
    loader.defocusElements();
    Enumeration e = urlList.elements();
    while (e.hasMoreElements()) {
        loader.focusElement((URL)e.nextElement());
    }
}
```

This will cause the `HTMLPageLoader` to allocate the input bandwidth to the focus elements chosen by the user.

In this bandwidth-limited distributed application, we're not so much concerned with actual throughput rates, but rather with the relative amount of bandwidth allocated to different input streams in order to optimize the user's experience.

9

Collaborative Systems

In this chapter we'll examine the implementation of collaborative systems, a topic that will fuse most of the subjects we discussed earlier in the book. First we'll define what we mean by collaborative systems, and discuss what complications can arise while implementing these systems. Then we'll look at how these issues can be addressed in the Java environment by building a set of base classes that will act as a basic collaboration framework. In the next chapter, we'll present some complete collaborative systems.

What Is a Collaborative System?

A collaborative system is one where multiple users or agents engage in a shared activity, usually from remote locations. In the larger family of distributed applications, collaborative systems are distinguished by the fact that the agents in the system are working together towards a common goal and have a critical need to interact closely with each other: sharing information, exchanging requests with each other, and checking in with each other on their status. In this chapter, we'll consider a collaborative system as one that is also distinguished by a certain level of concurrency; i.e., the agents in the system are interacting with the system and with each other at roughly the same time. So a chat session is collaborative, because all of the agents involved need to coordinate with each other to be sure that the chatters don't miss anyone else's comments. An email system isn't collaborative, because each email client simply wants to be sure that its messages get to the right server, and eventually to the intended recipient. A particular email client doesn't care about the state of any other client, and doesn't need to coordinate with any of them in order to accomplish its goal.

Figure 9-1 depicts some of the elements that can go into a collaborative system:

- Autonomous or user-driven *agents*
- Operational and data *servers*
- Dynamic and persistent *data repositories*
- *Transactions* between agents, servers, and data

Agents, servers, data repositories, and transactions are all elements that make up distributed systems in general, but the nature of the transactions between agents and the shared goals of the agents make a system collaborative.

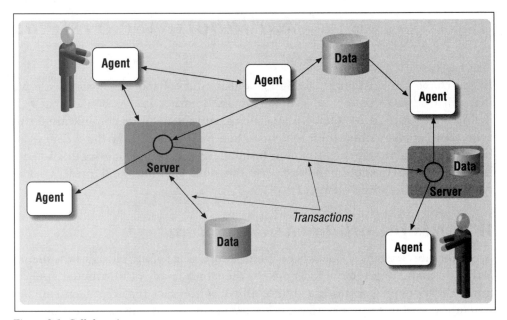

Figure 9-1. Collaborative systems structure

Here are some examples of what we refer to as collaborative systems:

- Shared whiteboards
- Interactive chat
- Distributed or parallel compute engines
- Coordinated data search agents (e.g., web "robots")

The first two involve collaborative agents under the direct control of human beings, while the last two involve agents that are programmed to act autonomously. So a collaborative system can involve concurrent transactions between people, between autonomous computing agents,* or some mixture of the two.

Issues with Collaboration

For the most part, the issues that come up with collaborative systems are similar to those that arise in other concurrent programming tasks. In the context of collaborative systems, some of these issues take on even more importance; and, of course, collaboration raises a few issues of it own. In this section, we'll look briefly at four of the most important issues: communication needs, identity management, shared state information, and performance.

Communication Needs

A collaborative system has multiple remote agents collaborating dynamically, so it must be flexible in its ability to route transactions. Depending on the application, the underlying communications might need to support point-to-point messages between agents, broadcast messages sent to the entire agent community, or "narrowcast" messages sent to specific groups of participating agents. An interactive chat server that supports chat rooms is a good example of this. Messages are normally broadcast to the entire group, but if an individual is in a single chat room, then her messages should only be sent to the other participants in that room. In some cases, you may need to support private, one-on-one messaging between agents or users in the system (e.g., for private discussions).

In addition to simple message-like communications, there may be a need for agents to have a richer interface to other agents. Agents may need to pass object data to each other, and remote agents may need to interact directly with each other through distributed object interfaces.

Maintaining Agent Identities

If multiple agents are engaged in a collaboration, there has to be some way to uniquely identify them so that messages can be addressed and delivered, tasks can be assigned, etc. Also, if access to the system or to certain resources associated with the system needs to be restricted, then participant identities will need to be authenticated as well. Depending on the application, there may also be data or other resources associated with individual agents. This information must be maintained along with agent identities, and in some cases access to these resources must be controlled based on identities.

---

* Here our use of the word "agent" is much closer to the academic term, e.g., an autonomous computing entity trying to achieve a goal of some kind.

A practical example of this issue is a shared whiteboard application. A shared whiteboard is a virtual drawing space that multiple remote users can view and "write" on in order to share information, ideas, etc.—the digital equivalent of a group of people working around a real whiteboard in a meeting room. In order for the individuals using the whiteboard to understand what is being contributed by whom, the whiteboard system has to keep some kind of identity information for each participant. Each participant's contributions to the whiteboard (e.g., written information, graphics, etc.) must be shown with a visual indication of who is responsible for it (e.g., color, shading, etc.). It may also be desirable to allow each individual the right to modify or delete only his contributions to the whiteboard, which means adding access control based on identities.

Shared State Information

In many collaborative systems some data and resources are shared among participants. Shared data is common to most distributed systems, but is particularly important in collaborative systems. A cooperative effort among computing agents is usually expressed in terms of a set of data that needs to be shared by all agents in the system. In our shared whiteboard example, the current contents of the whiteboard are shared among all agents. With multiple agents accessing and potentially modifying this shared state information, maintaining the integrity of the information will be an important issue. If two or more agents attempt to alter the same piece of shared state information, then there has to be a reasonable and consistent way to determine how to merge these requests, and how to make it known to the affected agents what's been done with their transactions.

Performance

Some collaborative systems have to make a trade-off between keeping shared state consistent across all the agents and maximizing the overall performance. There are situations, such as in shared whiteboard applications, where it's important that all of the agents in the system have their view of the shared state of the system kept up-to-date as closely as possible. The simplest way to do this is to have a central mediator acting as a clearinghouse for agent events. The mediator gets notified whenever an agent does something that changes the shared state of the system, and the mediator is responsible for sending these state updates to all of the agents in the system. This also makes it simple to ensure that updates are sequenced correctly across all agents, if that's important to the application.

The problem is that the central mediator can become a bottleneck as the size of the system scales up. If there are lots of agents to be notified or lots of changes that agents have to be notified about, then the mediator may have trouble keeping up with the traffic and the agents in the system will waste a lot of time waiting for updates. Another approach would be not to use a mediator at all, and instead have a peer-to-peer system where each agent broadcasts its updates to all the other agents. While this may improve the throughput of updates, it makes it difficult to maintain consistency across the system. With each update being broadcast independently and asynchronously, it can be quite a feat to make sure that each agent ends up with the same state after all the updates have been sent, especially if the order of the updates is important.

A Basic Collaborative Infrastructure

Before we explore some collaborative applications, let's take a look at a basic collaborative infrastructure implemented using some of the concepts presented earlier in this book. We'll build on this infrastructure to illustrate the development of various types of collaborative systems. The framework that we'll build involves a single *mediator* (the server) handling interactions among multiple *collaborators* (clients). Each collaborator has a unique identity, issued by the mediator, and each collaborator can either broadcast messages to all of the collaborators registered with the mediator, or it can send a message to a single collaborator.

One of the first steps in developing a collaborative system is deciding what kind of communications scheme is right for you. We've discussed several ways to connect remote agents, including basic socket communications, message passing, RMI remote objects, and CORBA remote objects. To illustrate our basic collaborative system, we'll show a version based on RMI and remote objects, and another version based on basic message passing. We'll start with the message-passing version, since this will let us look in detail at some of the dynamics of a distributed system involving many agents working together simultaneously. Then we'll look at ways to implement the same collaborative infrastructure using remote objects, where the object distribution system assumes responsibility for some of the issues we'll see in our message-passing version. For those readers only interested in the remote-object version, you can skip ahead to the section, "Collaborating with RMI."

Building the Infrastructure with Message Passing

To build a collaborative message-passing system, we'll start by expanding our message-passing classes from Chapter 6 to handle multiple agents passing messages through a single `MessageHandler`. In that chapter, the final version of our message-passing framework (see Example 6-10 and Example 6-11) used `MessageHandlers` passing `Messages` to each other. Each `Message` object has an identifier and a set of arguments. Each `MessageHandler` runs in a loop, reading messages from the network, constructing `Message` objects from the data received, and calling the `Message`'s `Do()` method to handle the message locally.

The `MessageHandler` reconstructs the `Message` from the incoming network data using a list of prototype `Message` objects. The identifier for the message is used to pick the right `Message` prototype, a copy of this `Message` is made, and the new copy is told to read its arguments from the input data stream. The set of `Message` prototypes serves to define the message protocol that the `Message-Handler` understands, and can be updated on the fly if needed.

If we look back at Figure 9-1 and assume that the general collaborative system depicted there is implemented using message passing, we'll see that a server or an agent in a collaborative environment may have to send or receive messages from multiple remote agents. Our `MessageHandler` class from Example 6-10 only supports point-to-point message passing, so if we wanted to use it for a collaborative system we would either need to create a `MessageHandler` object for each agent we want to talk to, or we could upgrade the `MessageHandler` to manage multiple network connections to agents. In some applications, we may have tens, hundreds, or even thousands of agents collaborating with each other, so creating an entire `MessageHandler` object for each (in addition to a socket connection and its input and output streams) may be too inefficient. Also, in many collaborative applications we need to use the same message protocol with every agent in the system, so forcing ourselves to replicate the same "flavor" of `Message-Handler` many times over doesn't seem to make sense.

Example 9-1 shows our updated `MessageHandler` class, with support for multiple agent connections. Two utility classes have been added to help manage agent connections. The `AgentConnection` class simply holds a pair of input and output streams connected to a remote agent. The `AgentHandler` class takes care of listening to a particular agent for asynchronous messages. We'll see exactly how the `AgentHandler` is used as we look at the rest of the updated `Message-Handler` class.

Example 9-1. Multi-Agent Message Handler Class

```
package dcj.util.Collaborative;

import java.util.Vector;
import java.util.Hashtable;
import java.util.Enumeration;
import java.net.SocketException;
import java.io.*;

class PeerConnection {
  public PeerConnection(InputStream i, OutputStream o) {
    in = i;
    out = o;
  }
  public InputStream in;
```

Example 9-1. Multi-Agent Message Handler Class (continued)

```
  public OutputStream out;
}

class PeerHandler implements Runnable {
  int peerId;
  MessageHandler handler;
  public PeerHandler(int id, MessageHandler h) {
    peerId = id;
    handler = h;
  }

  public void run() {
    System.out.println("ph: Starting peer handler for peer " + peerId);
    while (true) {
      try {
        Message m = handler.readMsg(peerId);
        System.out.println("ph: Got a message from peer " + peerId);
        m.Do(null, null);
      }
      catch (IOException e) {}
    }
  }
}

public class MessageHandler implements Runnable
{
  // A global MessageHandler, for applications where one central
  // handler is used.
  public static MessageHandler current = null;

  Hashtable connections = new Hashtable();
  Hashtable handlers = new Hashtable();
  Vector msgPrototypes = new Vector();

  public MessageHandler() {}
  public MessageHandler(InputStream in, OutputStream out) {
    addPeer(0, in, out);
  }

  synchronized public int nextPeerId() {
    return connections.size();
  }

  synchronized public Vector getPeerIds() {
    Vector ids = new Vector();
    Enumeration e = connections.keys();
    while (e.hasMoreElements()) {
      ids.addElement((Integer)e.nextElement());
```

Example 9-1. Multi-Agent Message Handler Class (continued)

```java
    }
    return ids;
}

synchronized public int addPeer(InputStream i, OutputStream o) {
  int nextId = nextPeerId();
  addPeer(nextId, i, o);
  return nextId;
}

synchronized public void addPeer(int id, InputStream i, OutputStream o) {
  connections.put(new Integer(id), new PeerConnection(i, o));
  PeerHandler ph = new PeerHandler(id, this);
  Thread phThread = new Thread(ph);
  phThread.start();
  handlers.put(new Integer(id), phThread);
}

synchronized public boolean removePeer(int id) {
  boolean success = false;
  Thread hthread = (Thread)handlers.remove(new Integer(id));
  if (hthread != null && connections.remove(new Integer(id)) != null) {
    hthread.stop();
    success = true;
  }

  return success;
}

synchronized protected PeerConnection getPeer(int id) {
  return (PeerConnection)connections.get(new Integer(id));
}

public void addMessageType(Message prototype) {
  msgPrototypes.addElement(prototype);
}

public Message readMsg(int id) throws IOException {
  Message msg = null;

  PeerConnection conn = getPeer(id);
  if (conn != null) {
    try {
      synchronized (conn.in) {
        DataInputStream din = new DataInputStream(conn.in);
        String msgId = din.readUTF();
        System.out.println("mh: Got message id " + msgId);
        msg = buildMessage(msgId);
```

Example 9-1. Multi-Agent Message Handler Class (continued)

```
            if (msg != null) {
              msg.readArgs(conn.in);
            }
            System.out.println("mh: Received complete message" + msg + ".");
          }
        }
      catch (SocketException s) {
        System.out.println("mm: Lost connection to peer " + id);
        removePeer(id);
        msg = null;
      }
      catch (Exception e) {
        msg = null;
      }
    }

    return msg;
  }


  // Send a message to a specific agent.
  public boolean sendMsg(Message msg, int id) throws IOException {
    boolean success = false;
    PeerConnection conn = getPeer(id);
    if (conn != null) {
      System.out.println("mh: Trying to lock on peer " + id);
      try {
        synchronized (conn.out) {
          System.out.println("mh: Got lock on peer " + id);
          DataOutputStream dout = new DataOutputStream(conn.out);
          System.out.println("mh: Printing message id...");
          dout.writeUTF(msg.messageID());
          System.out.println("mh: Printing message args...");
          msg.writeArgs(conn.out);
          success = true;
        }
      }
      catch (SocketException s) {
        System.out.println("mh: Lost connection to peer " + id);
        removePeer(id);
        success = false;
      }
      catch (Exception e) {
        success = false;
      }
    }
    return success;
  }
```

Example 9-1. Multi-Agent Message Handler Class (continued)

```java
  // Broadcast a message to all connected agents.
  public boolean sendMsg(Message msg) throws IOException {
    Enumeration ids = connections.keys();
    boolean success = true;
    while (ids.hasMoreElements()) {
      Integer id = (Integer)ids.nextElement();
      System.out.println("mh: Attempting send to peer " + id.intValue());
      if (!sendMsg(msg, id.intValue()))
        success = false;
      else
        System.out.println("mh: Sent message to peer " + id.intValue());
    }
    return success;
  }

  // Default run() method does nothing...
  public void run() {}

  protected Message buildMessage(String msgId) {
    Message msg = null;
    int numMTypes = msgPrototypes.size();
    for (int i = 0; i < numMTypes; i++) {
      Message m = null;
      synchronized (msgPrototypes) {
        m = (Message)msgPrototypes.elementAt(i);
      }
      if (m.handles(msgId)) {
        msg = m.newCopy();
        msg.setId(msgId);
        break;
      }
    }
    return msg;
  }
}
```

The updated `MessageHandler` maintains a table of agent connections, associating each connection with an ID number. A set of methods for adding, removing, and getting agent connections has been added to the `Message-Handler` interface. Two `addAgent()` methods are provided: the first takes the `InputStream` and `OutputStream` connections to the agent as arguments, and assigns the next available ID to the new agent connection; the second additionally accepts an ID number that the caller wants assigned to the agent. The `removeAgent()` method removes the agent with a given ID number. The `getAgent()` method is protected, and is used internally by the `Message-Handler` class to get the `AgentConnection` associated with a particular agent.

We've also updated the MessageHandler class by changing its readMsg() and sendMsg() methods so that we can specify which agent to talk to. The readMsg() method now accepts the ID number of the agent from which to read a message. There are now two versions of the sendMsg() method. One accepts an ID number, and sends the given message to that agent. The other version just takes a Message as an argument, and broadcasts the message to all agents the MessageHandler is connected to.

When a new agent is added to the MessageHandler using one of the addAgent() methods, an AgentConnection is made to hold the Input-Stream and OutputStream connected to the agent, and the connection is stored in a Hashtable using the agent's ID number as the key. Next, an AgentHandler is created and given the ID number of the new agent, along with a reference to the MessageHandler. Then a new thread is created for the AgentHandler, and the new thread is started. The AgentHandler implements the Runnable interface, and its run() method is a loop that continuously attempts to read messages from its agent, using the readMsg() method on the MessageHandler:

```
public void run() {
  System.out.println("ph: Starting peer handler for peer " + peerId);
  while (true) {
    try {
      Message m = handler.readMsg(peerId);
      m.Do();
    }
    catch (IOException e) {}
  }
}
```

So this new and improved MessageHandler manages multiple connections by creating a thread for each agent that can asynchronously read messages and act on them. New agents can be added to the handler at any time. To support these asynchronous operations, the MessageHandler implementation has been synchronized in a number of places. The readMsg() and sendMsg() methods synchronize on the input and output streams of each agent, for example. All of the methods for adding and removing agents from the MessageHandler are also synchronized to allow asynchronous agent handling.

Now that we have a MessageHandler that can support message passing in a collaborative environment, let's build our collaborative infrastructure on top of it. We can think of collaborative systems as being composed of *collaborators* and *mediators*. Collaborators are the agents that work together towards the common goal of the system, and mediators serve to facilitate the communications among the collaborators. Referring back to Figure 9-1, collaborators are the agents in the system, and mediators are the servers.

Before we delve into details, one of the primary needs of collaborative systems is the need to provide an identity for each agent in the system, so that transactions can be targeted and traced to individual agents. To support this, we have the Identity class shown in Example 9-2. This class consists of a Properties list, with methods for getting and setting a name property, which is a String, and an id property, which is an integer. These two properties will be used to identify each collaborator in the system. The name property is a descriptive name that can be used to specify each collaborator in a user interface, for example. The integer id is an internal identifier used to tag each collaborator uniquely.

Example 9-2. An Identity Class

```
package dcj.util.Collaborative;

import java.util.Hashtable;
import java.io.Serializable;

public class Identity implements Serializable {
  Hashtable props = new Hashtable();

  public Identity(int id) { props.put("idnum", new Integer(id)); }

  public boolean equals(Object o) {
    boolean same = false;
    if (o != null && o.getClass() == this.getClass()) {
      Identity oi = (Identity)o;
      if (oi == this ||
          (oi.getId() == this.getId() &&
            ((oi.getName() == null && this.getName() == null) ||
             (oi.getName() != null && this.getName() != null &&
              oi.getName().compareTo(this.getName()) == 0)))) {
        same = true;
      }
    }
    return same;
  }

  public int    getId() {
    Integer idNum = (Integer)props.get("idnum");
    return idNum.intValue();
  }

  public String getName() { return (String)props.get("name"); }
  public void    setName(String n) { props.put("name", n); }

  public Object getProperty(Object key) {
    return props.get(key);
  }
  public void    setProperty(Object key, Object val) {
```

Example 9-2. An Identity Class (continued)

```
    props.put(key, val);
  }
}
```

Additional properties can be added to the property lists of the collaborators to further define the identity of an agent in a system, or to hold state information related to the collaborative application. We've made the `Identity` class implement the `Serializable` interface, so that `Identity` objects can be passed back and forth between agents on the network to tag destination and source agents for transactions. This will come in handy whether your system uses message passing with `ObjectInputStreams` and `ObjectOutputStreams`, or RMI with `Identity` object arguments to remote methods. Since this class is meant to be serializable, however, any object added to the `Identity` as a property value or key, using the `setProperty()` method, also needs to be serializable; all objects that the `Identity` object references at the time that it is serialized and sent over the network will also be serialized and transmitted.

A collaborator has some pretty basic functional requirements. It needs to have a unique identifier in the system, so that messages can be routed to it. It needs to be able to connect to mediators, or to other collaborators, to engage in communication with them. Finally, it needs to be able to send messages and to be notified of incoming messages. Example 9-3 shows a `Collaborator` interface that includes these abilities.

Example 9-3. A Collaborator Interface

```
package dcj.util.Collaborative;

import java.util.Properties;
import java.io.IOException;
import java.rmi.RemoteException;

public interface Collaborator {
  public Identity getIdentity();

  // Connect to a mediator - subclasses dictate properties needed
  public boolean connect(Properties p);

  // Outgoing messages/data
  public boolean send(String tag, String msg, Identity dst)
               throws IOException;
  public boolean send(String tag, Object data, Identity dst)
               throws IOException;
  public boolean broadcast(String tag, String msg)
               throws IOException;
  public boolean broadcast(String tag, Object data)
```

Example 9-3. A Collaborator Interface (continued)

```
                throws IOException;

    // Incoming messages/data
    public boolean notify(String tag, String msg, Identity src)
                throws IOException;
    public boolean notify(String tag, Object data, Identity src)
                throws IOException;
}
```

The getIdentity() method returns an Identity for the Collaborator. This Identity may be given to the Collaborator when it connects to a mediator. The connect() method opens a connection to a remote collaborator or mediator. The values in the Properties argument to connect() specify how to locate the agent on the network. Some collaborators may only require a hostname and port number, others may need more information, like a registered name for the agent on an RMI server.

The Collaborator interface supports sending messages with its send() and broadcast() methods. These methods accept a message in the form of a tag or label string, which says what kind of message it is for the receiver, and the message itself, which is either a String or a generic Object. The send() methods also accept an Identity object, which specifies whom to send the message to. So a Collaborator sends a message to individual agents on the network using the send() methods, and it broadcasts messages to all of the agents using the broadcast() methods.

A Collaborator receives messages through its notify() methods. There are versions of notify() that accept a String or an Object as the body of the message. The notify() methods also have an Identity argument that specifies who sent the message. If the sender is unknown, the Identity argument will be null. When it is notified of the message, the Collaborator can react as needed, by adding the data in the message to a database, updating its display, or responding to the sender of the message.

A mediator has an equally simple set of tasks. It needs to be able to register new collaborators by providing them with unique identifiers, send messages to individual collaborators, and broadcast messages to all collaborators that it has registered. Example 9-4 shows a Mediator interface that supports these things. The newMember() method generates a unique identifier for a new collaborator. The removeMember() method removes the given collaborator from the Mediator's registry. The send() and broadcast() methods are analogous to the same methods on the Collaborator interface. Messages can be sent to individual agents using the send() methods, and they can be broadcast to all agents using the broadcast() methods.

Example 9-4. A Mediator Interface

```
package dcj.util.Collaborative;

import java.util.Vector;
import java.io.IOException;

public interface Mediator {
  public Identity newMember();
  public boolean  removeMember(Identity i);
  public Vector   getMembers();

  public boolean send(Identity to, Identity from, String mtag, String msg)
              throws IOException;
  public boolean broadcast(Identity from, String mtag, String msg)
              throws IOException;
  public boolean send(Identity to, Identity from, String mtag, Object data)
              throws IOException;
  public boolean broadcast(Identity from, String mtag, Object data)
              throws IOException;
}
```

We've been careful in designing the `Collaborator` and `Mediator` interfaces to allow for implementing these interfaces using whatever communications scheme the application developer chooses. Although the methods on the interfaces seem to suggest a message-passing scheme, the data in these "messages" could be passed using remote methods on RMI objects, or on CORBA implementations of the `Collaborator` and `Mediator` classes.

With our updated, multi-agent `MessageHandler` class in hand, implementing message-passing versions of the `Collaborator` and `Mediator` interfaces is a pretty simple matter. The `MessageMediator` class shown in Example 9-5 is an implementation of the `Mediator` interface that uses a `MessageHandler` to route messages back and forth between remote agents. The `MessageMediator` has a `MessageHandler` to route messages, a `ServerSocket` to accept socket connections from remote agents, and a port number that it listens to for connections. It also implements the `Runnable` interface so that it can sit in its own thread, listening for asynchronous connections from agents. This is the primary function of its `run()` method, where it creates the `ServerSocket` listening to its designated port, then loops continuously trying to accept connections over the socket. When a new connection is made, a new agent is added to the handler by calling its `addAgent()` method with the input and output streams from the `Socket` that is created to the agent. The `Mediator` creates a unique `Identity` for the agent by calling the `newMember()` method, which creates a new `Identity` and sets its ID number to the next available integer. Then a message is sent to the agent containing its `Identity`, so that it can identify itself in future messages.

Example 9-5. A Mediator Based on Message Passing

```
package dcj.util.Collaborative;

import java.lang.Runnable;
import java.util.Vector;
import java.util.Enumeration;
import java.net.ServerSocket;
import java.net.Socket;
import java.io.IOException;

public class MessageMediator implements Mediator, Runnable {
  MessageHandler mhandler = new MessageHandler();
  ServerSocket socket = null;
  int port = 5009;

  public MessageMediator(int p) {
    initHandler();
    port = p;
  }

  public MessageMediator() {
    initHandler();
  }

  protected void initHandler() {
    // Add the mediator message "prototype" to the handler
    Message m = new MediatorMessage(this);
    mhandler.addMessageType(m);
  }

  public void run() {
    // Make the server socket
    try {
      socket = new ServerSocket(port);
    }
    catch (IOException e) {
      System.out.println("Failed to bind to port " + port);
      return;
    }

    System.out.println("Mediator running on port " + port);

    // Listen for new clients...
    while (true) {
      try {
        Socket clientConn = socket.accept();
        Identity i = newMember();
        mhandler.addAgent(i.getId(), clientConn.getInputStream(),
                      clientConn.getOutputStream());
```

Example 9-5. A Mediator Based on Message Passing (continued)

```
      System.out.println("Got new connection...");
      Message imsg = new Message("identity");
      imsg.addArg(i);
      mhandler.sendMsg(imsg, i.getId());
    }
    catch (Exception e) {}
  }
}

public Identity newMember() {
  int id = mhandler.nextAgentId();
  Identity i = new Identity(id);
  return i;
}

public boolean remove(Identity i) {
  int id = i.getId();
  boolean success = mhandler.removeAgent(id);
  return success;
}

public Vector getMembers() {
  Vector members = new Vector();
  Vector ids = mhandler.getAgentIds();
  Enumeration e = ids.elements();
  while (e.hasMoreElements()) {
    Integer id = (Integer)e.nextElement();
    Identity i = new Identity(id.intValue());
    members.addElement(i);
  }
  return members;
}

public boolean send(Identity to, Identity from, String mtag, String s)
               throws IOException {
  boolean success = false;
  Message msg = new Message(mtag);
  msg.addArg(from);
  msg.addArg(s);
  return mhandler.sendMsg(msg, to.getId());
}

public boolean broadcast(Identity from, String mtag, String s)
               throws IOException {
  System.out.println("mm: Broadcasting message \"" + mtag + s + "\"");
  Message msg = new Message(mtag);
  msg.addArg(from);
  msg.addArg(s);
```

Example 9-5. A Mediator Based on Message Passing (continued)

```
    return mhandler.sendMsg(msg);
  }

  public boolean send(Identity to, Identity from, String mtag, Object o)
                 throws IOException {
    Message msg = new Message(mtag);
    msg.addArg(from);
    msg.addArg(o);
    return mhandler.sendMsg(msg, to.getId());
  }

  public boolean broadcast(Identity from, String mtag, Object o)
                 throws IOException {
    Message msg = new Message(mtag);
    msg.addArg(from);
    msg.addArg(o);
    return mhandler.sendMsg(msg);
  }
}
```

The `MessageMediator` initializes its `MessageHandler` in each of its constructors by calling the protected `initHandler()` method. This method adds a `MediatorMessage` to the handler's list of "prototype" messages. The `MediatorMessage`, shown in Example 9-6, keeps a reference to a `Mediator`, and its `Do()` method handles messages by checking the type of message and calling the appropriate method on its `Mediator`. This is the only message prototype added to the `MessageHandler`, and its `handles()` method always returns `true`, so all messages received by the `MessageHandler` will be handled by this message. If the message has a type of "send," then the next four arguments are assumed to be: an `Identity` object specifying the source of the message, another for the destination of the message, a `String` message tag, and a `String` or `Object` message body. These four arguments are passed into a call to the `Mediator`'s `send()` method. If a message with a type of "broadcast" is received, then only three arguments are expected: the `Identity` of the sender, a `String` message tag, and a `String` or `Object` message body. These three arguments are passed into the `Mediator`'s `broadcast()` method.

Example 9-6. A Mediator Message

```
package dcj.util.Collaborative;

import java.io.*;
import java.util.Vector;

public class MediatorMessage extends Message
```

Example 9-6. A Mediator Message (continued)

```java
{
  protected Mediator mediator = null;

  public MediatorMessage(Mediator m) {
    mediator = m;
  }

  public MediatorMessage(String mid) {
    super(mid);
  }

  public boolean Do()
  {
    boolean success = false;

    try {
      String mtype = messageID();
      if (mtype.compareTo("send") == 0) {
        Identity from = (Identity)getArg(0);
        Identity to = (Identity)getArg(1);
        String tag = (String)getArg(2);
        try {
          String s = (String)getArg(3);
          mediator.send(to, from, tag, s);
          success = true;
        }
        catch (ClassCastException cce) {
          // Argument wasn't a String, so send it as an Object
          Object oarg = getArg(3);
          mediator.send(to, from, tag, oarg);
          success = true;
        }
      }
      else if (mtype.compareTo("broadcast") == 0) {
        System.out.println("mm: Got broadcast message.");
        Identity from = (Identity)getArg(0);
        String tag = (String)getArg(1);
        System.out.println("mm: tag = \"" + tag + "\"");
        try {
          String s = (String)getArg(2);
          mediator.broadcast(from, tag, s);
          success = true;
        }
        catch (ClassCastException cce) {
          Object oarg = getArg(2);
          mediator.broadcast(from, tag, oarg);
        }
      }
```

Example 9-6. A Mediator Message (continued)

```
    }
    catch (Exception e) {
      success = false;
      System.out.println("mm: Error parsing message.");
      e.printStackTrace();
    }
    return success;
  }

  // We want to handle all messages.
  public boolean handles(String msgId) { return true; }

  public Message newCopy() {
    MediatorMessage copy;
    if (mediator != null) {
      // Make a new MediatorMessage with the same Mediator
      copy = new MediatorMessage(mediator);
      copy.setId(messageID());
    }
    else {
      copy = new MediatorMessage(messageID());
    }
    return copy;
  }
}
```

The remainder of the `MessageMediator` implementation consists of the `send()` and `broadcast()` methods. These methods simply take the arguments passed to them, bundle them into `Messages`, and instruct the `MessageHandler` to send them to the appropriate recipients. The `send()` methods call the `MessageHandler.sendMsg()` method with the ID number of the destination agent, while the `broadcast()` methods call the `MessageHandler.sendMsg()` method with no ID number; this causes the `MessageHandler` to send the message to all of the agents in its list.

The last piece of our message-passing collaborative system is a `Collaborator` implemented using message passing. The `MessageCollaborator` shown in Example 9-7 implements the `Collaborator` interface using a `MessageHandler`. Two constructors are provided: one with just a name for the collaborator, and the other with a name along with the host and port number of a mediator to which to connect. Both constructors initialize the `MessageHandler`, and the second version goes on to put the host and port number into a `Properties` list and call the `connect()` method to connect to the mediator at that network address. The `initHandler()` method simply adds a `CollaboratorMessage` to the message prototype list on the `MessageHandler`. This

Message subclass, shown in Example 9-8, is even simpler than the Media-
torMessage in Example 9-6. The Do() method takes the message ID, assumes
that the first argument is the Identity of the sender and that the second argument is the body of the message, and calls the collaborator's notify() method
with these arguments. The CollaboratorMessage also handles all messages by
returning a default of true from its handles() method.

Example 9-7. A Message-Passing Collaborator

```java
package dcj.util.Collaborative;

import java.io.IOException;
import java.net.Socket;
import java.util.Properties;

public class MessageCollaborator implements Collaborator
{
  MessageHandler handler = new MessageHandler();
  Identity id = null;
  String name;

  public MessageCollaborator(String n) {
    name = n;
    initHandler();
  }

  public MessageCollaborator(String host, int port, String n) {
    initHandler();
    name = n;
    Properties p = new Properties();
    p.put("host", host);
    p.put("port", String.valueOf(port));
    connect(p);
  }

  protected void initHandler() {
    handler.addMessageType(new CollaboratorMessage(this));
  }

  public Identity getIdentity() { return id; }

  public boolean connect(Properties p) {
    boolean success = false;

    String host = p.getProperty("host");
    String itmp = p.getProperty("port");
    if (host != null && itmp != null) {
      try {
        int port = Integer.parseInt(itmp);
```

Example 9-7. A Message-Passing Collaborator (continued)

```
        // Make a socket connection to the mediator.
        Socket mConn = new Socket(host, port);
        int pid = handler.addAgent(mConn.getInputStream(),
                                   mConn.getOutputStream());
        System.out.println("Got socket to Mediator, id = " + id + "...");
        // The mediator should send us an identity in a message...
        Message imsg = handler.readMsg(pid);
        System.out.println("Got message with id = " + imsg.messageID());
        if (imsg.messageID().compareTo("identity") == 0) {
          id = (Identity)imsg.getArg(0);
          id.setName(name);
          System.out.println("Got identity from mediator, id = "
                             + id.getId() + "...");
          success = true;
        }
        else {
          handler.removeAgent(pid);
          success = false;
        }
      }
      catch (Exception e) {
        success = false;
      }
    }
    else {
      success = false;
    }
    return success;
  }

  public boolean send(String tag, String msg, Identity dst)
                  throws IOException {
    boolean success = false;
    Message m = new Message("send");
    m.addArg(getIdentity());
    m.addArg(dst);
    m.addArg(tag);
    m.addArg(msg);
    success = handler.sendMsg(m);
    return success;
  }

  public boolean send(String tag, Object data, Identity dst)
                  throws IOException {
    boolean success = false;
    Message m = new Message("send");
    m.addArg(getIdentity());
    m.addArg(dst);
```

Example 9-7. A Message-Passing Collaborator (continued)

```
    m.addArg(tag);
    m.addArg("#OBJ");
    m.addArg(data);
    success = handler.sendMsg(m);
    return success;
  }

  public boolean broadcast(String tag, String msg)
                throws IOException {
    boolean success = false;
    Message m = new Message("broadcast");
    m.addArg(getIdentity());
    m.addArg(tag);
    m.addArg(msg);
    System.out.println("mc: Sending broadcast message \"" + tag + "\"");
    success = handler.sendMsg(m);
    System.out.println("mc: success = " + success);
    return success;
  }

  public boolean broadcast(String tag, Object data)
                throws IOException {
    boolean success = true;
    Message m = new Message("broadcast");
    m.addArg(getIdentity());
    m.addArg(tag);
    m.addArg("#OBJ");
    m.addArg(data);
    success = handler.sendMsg(m);
    return success;
  }

  public boolean notify(String tag, String msg, Identity src)
                throws IOException {
    System.out.println("Received \"" + tag + "\" message \""
                        + msg + "\" from " + src.getName());
    return true;
  }

  public boolean notify(String tag, Object data, Identity src)
                throws IOException {
    System.out.println("Received \"" + tag + "\" object \""
                        + data + "\" from " + src.getName());
    return true;
  }
}
```

The `connect()` method on the `MessageCollaborator` assumes that a host and port number will be in the `Properties` list passed to it. These are used to make a socket connection to that address. Once the connection is made, the input and output streams from the socket are passed to the `addAgent()` method on the `MessageHandler`. This adds the mediator at the other end of the socket to the list of agents in our `MessageHandler`. Since the first thing the `Message-Mediator` does is send the collaborator a message with its new `Identity` with the mediator, the next step in the `connect()` method is to read the message from the mediator and get our `Identity`. If we fail to get an `Identity` from the mediator, then we remove the mediator from the `MessageHandler` agent list by calling its `removeAgent()` method.

The rest of the `MessageCollaborator` is the implementation of the `send()`, `broadcast()`, and `notify()` methods. These are implemented much the same as on the `MessageMediator`. The `send()` methods bundle the source (the local `Identity`), destination, message type, and message body into a `Message` with an ID of "send," and send it to the mediator using the `sendMsg()` method on the `MessageHandler`. The `broadcast()` methods bundle the source `Identity`, the message type, and the message body into a `Message` with an ID of "broadcast," and send it with the `MessageHandler.sendMsg()` method. The `notify()` methods implemented here simply print out an indication that a message has been received. Subclasses would override these methods to check the message type or body, and react accordingly.

Example 9-8. A Collaborator Message

```
package dcj.util.Collaborative;

import java.io.*;
import java.util.Vector;

public class CollaboratorMessage extends Message
{
  protected Collaborator collaborator = null;

  public CollaboratorMessage(Collaborator c) {
    collaborator = c;
  }

  public CollaboratorMessage(String mid) {
    super(mid);
  }

  public boolean Do()
  {
    boolean success = false;

    try {
```

Example 9-8. A Collaborator Message (continued)

```
      String mtype = messageID();
      Identity from = (Identity)getArg(0);
      try {
        String s = (String)getArg(1);
        collaborator.notify(mtype, s, from);
        success = true;
      }
      catch (ClassCastException cce) {
        // Argument isn't a string, so send it as an object
        Object oarg = getArg(1);
        collaborator.notify(mtype, oarg, from);
        success = true;
      }
    }
    catch (Exception e) {
      success = false;
    }
    return success;
  }

  // We want to handle all messages to the collaborator
  public boolean handles(String msgId) { return true; }

  public Message newCopy() {
    CollaboratorMessage copy;
    if (collaborator != null) {
      // Make a new CollaboratorMessage with the same Collaborator
      copy = new CollaboratorMessage(collaborator);
      copy.setId(messageID());
    }
    else {
      copy = new CollaboratorMessage(messageID());
    }
    return copy;
  }
}
```

Our complete message-passing infrastructure allows us to create a `MessageMediator` on a given port number on a host. Then any client can connect to the mediator by creating a `MessageCollaborator` using the mediator's host and port number, and engage in a collaborative exercise with any other agent connected to it using the collaborator's `send()` and `broadcast()` methods. Each connection the `MessageMediator` accepts is serviced in a separate thread by an `AgentHandler`, which listens for messages from that agent and tells the `MessageMediator` to route them to the right `Collaborators`.

If we wanted to support the complete collaborative environment depicted in Figure 9-1, in addition to each `Mediator` serving multiple `Collaborators`, we would also want each `Collaborator` to be able to connect to more than one `Mediator`. We may want to have clusters of `Mediators` serving different portions of the overall community. This is a simple extension to the `Collaborator` and `MessageCollaborator` interfaces. First, the `Message-Collaborator` would need to maintain a table of mediators that it was connected to, along with their identities. The identity of a mediator could be as simple as an ID number that the `MessageCollaborator` generates on its own as a unique local identifier for the `Mediator`. A `Hashtable` could be used to store the table of `Collaborators` and their `Identitys`. The `send()` and `broadcast()` methods would need to include a new `Identity` argument, to specify which `Mediator` to route the message through. We may also want to add methods to broadcast a message through all available `Mediators` (e.g., a `broadcastAll()` method).

Collaborating with RMI

We implemented our message-passing version of a collaborative infrastructure to demonstrate the communication issues that the system needs to handle; now let's see what a version implemented in RMI would look like, and what pieces of the puzzle RMI handles for us. We'll construct our RMI collaboration system so that a `Mediator` is registered as an RMI server object to which remote `Collaborators` connect. The `Collaborators` can then register themselves with the `Mediator` by passing stub references to themselves through a remote method call to the `Mediator`. Once the `Mediator` has a stub for the `Collaborator` objects, and each `Collaborator` has a stub for the `Mediator`, the `Collaborators` can exchange messages by calling the appropriate method on the `Mediator` stub, which in turn passes the message to the appropriate `Collaborator` by calling the `notify()` method on its stub.

First, remember that a remote RMI object must have a stub interface that implements the `java.rmi.Remote` interface, and each method on the interface must throw a `java.rmi.RemoteException`. Also, the `Remote` object has to implement the `Remote` interface from the top of its inheritance tree (i.e., a remote object cannot implement a non-`Remote` interface). For these reasons, we need new versions of our `Collaborator` and `Mediator` interfaces for the RMI version of our system. The `RMICollaborator` interface in Example 9-9 has essentially the same interface as the `Collaborator` from Example 9-3, except that it implements `java.rmi.Remote`, and all methods throw the `java.rmi.RemoteException` in addition to any `Exceptions` that the original `Collaborator` interface throws.

Example 9-9. An RMI Collaborator Interface

```
package dcj.util.Collaborative;

import java.rmi.RemoteException;
import java.io.IOException;
import java.rmi.Remote;
import java.util.Properties;

public interface RMICollaborator extends Remote
{
  public Identity getIdentity() throws RemoteException;

  // Connect to a mediator - subclasses dictate properties needed
  public boolean connect(Properties p) throws RemoteException;

  // Outgoing messages/data
  public boolean send(String tag, String msg, Identity dst)
                throws IOException, RemoteException;
  public boolean send(String tag, Object data, Identity dst)
                throws IOException, RemoteException;
  public boolean broadcast(String tag, String msg)
                throws IOException, RemoteException;
  public boolean broadcast(String tag, Object data)
                throws IOException, RemoteException;

  // Incoming messages/data
  public boolean notify(String tag, String msg, Identity src)
                throws IOException, RemoteException;
  public boolean notify(String tag, Object data, Identity src)
                throws IOException, RemoteException;
}
```

The `RMIMediator` interface in Example 9-10 is adapted in the same way from the `Mediator` interface in Example 9-4, except that a new `register()` method has been added to allow each `RMICollaborator` to register itself with the `RMIMediator` once it has a stub.

Example 9-10. An RMI Mediator Interface

```
package dcj.util.Collaborative;

import java.rmi.RemoteException;
import java.io.IOException;
import java.rmi.Remote;
import java.util.Vector;

public interface RMIMediator extends Remote
{
  public boolean register(Identity i, RMICollaborator c)
```

Example 9-10. An RMI Mediator Interface (continued)

```
                throws RemoteException;
  public Identity newMember() throws RemoteException;
  public boolean  remove(Identity i) throws RemoteException;
  public Vector   getMembers() throws RemoteException;

  public boolean send(Identity to, Identity from, String mtag, String msg)
                throws IOException, RemoteException;
  public boolean broadcast(Identity from, String mtag, String msg)
                throws IOException, RemoteException;
  public boolean send(Identity to, Identity from, String mtag, Object data)
                throws IOException, RemoteException;
  public boolean broadcast(Identity from, String mtag, Object data)
                throws IOException, RemoteException;
}
```

The implementations of our RMI-based collaborator and mediator are surprisingly similar to our message-passing versions. The RMICollaboratorImpl in Example 9-11 has two constructors: one with just a name for the collaborator, the other taking a name, a host name, and the name of the remote RMIMediator object to lookup. The first constructor saves the name within an Identity object for the collaborator. The second does the same, then adds the host name and remote object name to a property list and calls the connect() method. The connect() method expects a host name saved as the host property in the Properties argument, and the name of a remote RMIMediator object as the mediatorName in the property list. Once it has these, the connect() method attempts to retrieve a stub to the remote mediator using the Naming.lookup() method with a URL constructed from the host name and the object name. Once the stub is received, the collaborator asks the RMIMediator for a new unique Identity by calling its newMember() method, then registers itself with the mediator by calling its register() method with a reference to itself and the new Identity.

Example 9-11. Implementation of an RMI Collaborator

```
package dcj.util.Collaborative;

import java.io.IOException;
import java.util.Properties;
import java.rmi.Naming;
import java.rmi.RemoteException;
import java.rmi.server.UnicastRemoteObject;
import java.rmi.RMISecurityManager;

public class RMICollaboratorImpl extends UnicastRemoteObject
                            implements RMICollaborator
{
```

Example 9-11. Implementation of an RMI Collaborator (continued)

```
protected Identity id = null;
protected RMIMediator mediator = null;

public RMICollaboratorImpl(String name, String host, String mname)
        throws RemoteException {
  id = new Identity(0);
  id.setName(name);
  Properties p = new Properties();
  p.put("host", host);
  p.put("mediatorName", mname);
  connect(p);
}

public RMICollaboratorImpl(String name) throws RemoteException {
  id = new Identity(0);
  id.setName(name);
}

public Identity getIdentity() throws RemoteException { return id; }

public boolean connect(Properties p) throws RemoteException {
  boolean success = false;
  String host = p.getProperty("host");
  String mName = p.getProperty("mediatorName");
  if (host != null && mName != null) {
    try {
      String url = "rmi://" + host + "/" + mName;
      System.out.println("looking up " + url);
      mediator = (RMIMediator)Naming.lookup(url);
      System.out.println("Got mediator " + mediator);
      Identity newId = mediator.newMember();
      mediator.register(newId, this);
      newId.setName(id.getName());
      id = newId;
      success = true;
    }
    catch (Exception e) {
      e.printStackTrace();
      success = false;
    }
  }

  return success;
}

public boolean send(String tag, String msg, Identity dst)
            throws IOException, RemoteException {
  boolean success = false;
```

Example 9-11. Implementation of an RMI Collaborator (continued)

```java
    if (mediator != null) {
      success = mediator.send(dst, getIdentity(), tag, msg);
    }
    return success;
  }

  public boolean send(String tag, Object data, Identity dst)
                throws IOException, RemoteException {
    boolean success = false;
    if (mediator != null) {
      success = mediator.send(dst, getIdentity(), tag, data);
    }
    return success;
  }

  public boolean broadcast(String tag, String msg)
                throws IOException, RemoteException {
    boolean success = false;
    if (mediator != null) {
      success = mediator.broadcast(getIdentity(), tag, msg);
    }
    return success;
  }

  public boolean broadcast(String tag, Object data)
                throws IOException, RemoteException {
    boolean success = false;
    if (mediator != null) {
      success = mediator.broadcast(getIdentity(), tag, data);
    }
    return success;
  }

  public boolean notify(String tag, String msg, Identity src)
                throws IOException, RemoteException {
    System.out.println("Got message: \"" + tag + " " + msg + "\""
                       + " from " + src.getName());
    return true;
  }

  public boolean notify(String tag, Object data, Identity src)
                throws IOException, RemoteException {
    System.out.println("Got message: \"" + tag + " " + data + "\""
                       + " from " + src.getName());
    return true;
  }

  public static void main(String argv[]) {
```

Example 9-11. Implementation of an RMI Collaborator (continued)

```
    // Install a security manager
    System.setSecurityManager(new RMISecurityManager());
    try {
      String name = argv[0];
      String host = argv[1];
      String mname = argv[2];
      Properties props = new Properties();
      props.put("host", host);
      props.put("mediatorName", mname);
      RMICollaboratorImpl c = new RMICollaboratorImpl(name);
      if (c.connect(props)) {
        System.out.println("Got mediator...");
        c.broadcast("msg", "hello world");
      }
    }
    catch (Exception e) {
      System.out.println("Caught exception:");
      e.printStackTrace();
    }
  }
}
```

Once the stub to the `RMIMediator` has been received, the `RMICollaboratorImpl` simply calls methods on the remote object to implement its `send()` and `broadcast()` methods. The `send()` methods call the mediator's `send()` methods with the appropriate arguments; the same goes for the `broadcast()` methods. Since the calls to `send()` and `broadcast()` are remote method calls, any `Objects` passed as the body of a message to the `RMIMediator` must implement the `Serializable` interface, or an exception will result when the remote methods are called. Again, the implementation of the `notify()` methods simply print out some text indicating that a message has been received.

The `RMICollaboratorImpl` interface also includes a `main()` method that demonstrates the use of the class with a mediator. The method takes command-line arguments that specify the name of the collaborator, the host for the mediator, and the name under which the mediator is registered. It creates an `RMICollaboratorImpl` object with the given name, then tells it to connect to the mediator registered as an RMI object under the given mediator name on the remote host. If it connects successfully, then we broadcast a friendly message to the other collaborators connected to the mediator.

The `RMIMediatorImpl` in Example 9-12 implements our `RMIMediator` interface. Its `newMember()` method generates a unique `Identity` for a collaborator, while its `register()` method adds its `Identity` and `RMICollaborator` arguments to a table of collaborators currently connected to the mediator. The

remove() method removes the identified collaborator from the table of
connected clients. The send() methods on RMIMediatorImpl retrieve the
referenced RMICollaborator from its internal table, and call the notify()
method on the collaborator with the appropriate arguments. The broadcast()
methods iterate through all of the RMICollaborators in the table, calling each
one's notify() method with the message from the remote RMICollaborator.

Example 9-12. Implementation of an RMI Mediator

```
package dcj.util.Collaborative;

import java.util.Vector;
import java.util.Hashtable;
import java.util.Enumeration;
import java.io.IOException;
import java.rmi.Remote;
import java.rmi.RemoteException;
import java.rmi.server.UnicastRemoteObject;
import java.rmi.RMISecurityManager;

public class RMIMediatorImpl extends UnicastRemoteObject
                             implements RMIMediator
{
  Hashtable clients = new Hashtable();
  Vector idList = new Vector();

  public RMIMediatorImpl() throws RemoteException {
    super();
  }

  public boolean register(Identity i, RMICollaborator c)
              throws RemoteException {
    System.out.println("Registering member " + i.getId()
                       + " as " + c.getIdentity().getName());
    clients.put(i, c);
    return true;
  }

  public Identity newMember() throws RemoteException {
    int max = -1;
    boolean found = true;
    Enumerator enum;
    synchronized (idList) {
       enum = idList.elements();
    }
    while (enum.hasMoreElements()) {
      Integer i = enum.nextElement();
      if (i.intValue() > max) {
        max = i.intValue();
```

Example 9-12. Implementation of an RMI Mediator (continued)

```
    }
  }

  Identity newId = new Identity(max + 1);
  synchronized (idList) {
    idList.addElement(newId);
  }
  return newId;
}

public boolean remove(Identity i) throws RemoteException {
  boolean success = true;
  synchronized (idList, clients) {
    if (idList.removeElement(i) && clients.remove(i) != null) {
      success = true;
    }
    else {
      success = false;
    }
  }
  return success;
}

public Vector getMembers() throws RemoteException {
  synchronized (idList) {
    return (Vector)idList.clone();
  }
}

public boolean send(Identity to, Identity from, String mtag, String msg)
                throws IOException, RemoteException {
  boolean success = false;
  RMICollaborator c = getMember(to);
  synchronized (c) {
    if (c != null) {
      success = c.notify(mtag, msg, from);
    }
  }

  return success;
}

public boolean send(Identity to, Identity from, String mtag, Object data)
                throws IOException, RemoteException {
  boolean success = false;
  RMICollaborator c = getMember(to);
  synchronized (c) {
    if (c != null) {
      success = c.notify(mtag, data, from);
```

Example 9-12. Implementation of an RMI Mediator (continued)

```
      }
    }
    return success;
  }

  public boolean broadcast(Identity from, String mtag, String msg)
                throws IOException, RemoteException {
    System.out.println("Broadcasting...");
    boolean success = true;
    Enumeration ids;
    synchronized (clients) {
      ids = clients.keys();
    }
    RMICollaborator target = null;
    while (ids.hasMoreElements()) {
      Identity i = (Identity)ids.nextElement();
      synchronized (clients) {
        target = (RMICollaborator)clients.get(i);
      }
      synchronized (target) {
        if (target == null ||
            !target.notify(mtag, msg, from)) {
          success = false;
        }
      }
    }
    return success;
  }

  public boolean broadcast(Identity from, String mtag, Object data)
                throws IOException, RemoteException {
    boolean success = true;
    Enumeration ids;
    synchronized (ids) {
      ids = clients.keys();
    }
    RMICollaborator target = null;
    while (ids.hasMoreElements()) {
      Identity i = (Identity)ids.nextElement();
      synchronized (clients) {
        target = (RMICollaborator)clients.get(i);
      }
      synchronized (target) {
        if (target == null ||
            !target.notify(mtag, data, from)) {
          success = false;
        }
      }
```

Example 9-12. Implementation of an RMI Mediator (continued)

```
    }
    return success;
  }

  protected RMICollaborator getMember(Identity i) {
    Enumeration ids;
    synchronized (clients) {
      ids = clients.keys();
    }
    RMICollaborator c = null;
    Identity tmp;
    while (c == null && ids.hasMoreElements()) {
      tmp = (Identity)ids.nextElement();
      if (tmp.equals(i)) {
        synchronized (clients) {
          c = (RMICollaborator)clients.get(tmp);
        }
      }
    }
    return c;
  }

  public static void main(String argv[]) {
    // Install a security manager
    System.setSecurityManager(new RMISecurityManager());

    try {
      String name = "TheMediator";
      System.out.println("Registering RMIMediatorImpl as \""
                          + name + "\"");
      RMIMediatorImpl mediator = new RMIMediatorImpl();
      System.out.println("Created mediator, binding...");
      Naming.rebind(name, mediator);
      System.out.println("Remote mediator ready...");
    }
    catch (Exception e) {
      System.out.println("Caught exception while registering: " + e);
    }
  }
}
```

At the end of the `RMIMediatorImpl` interface is a `main()` method that can be used to register a mediator with a local RMI registry. It just creates an `RMIMedia-torImpl` object and binds it with the RMI Naming service under the name *TheMediator*.

If you compare our RMI implementation of a collaborative system to our message-passing one, you'll notice that they are fairly similar in structure, with the exception that there is no equivalent to the `MessageHandler` in our RMI-based system. We don't need one; RMI handles the functionality provided by the `MessageHandler` internally when it marshals, transmits, and then unmarshals a remote method call's arguments between the `RMICollaborator` and the `RMIMediator`, and vice versa. It's also important to notice that, while the RMI connection between the two objects allows for asynchronous remote method calls between the two, we need to ensure that the `RMIMediatorImpl` implementation is multithread-safe, so that multiple connected `RMICollaborators` can asynchronously route messages by remotely calling its `send()` and `broadcast()` methods. We do this by synchronizing any code segments that directly access the `RMIMediatorImpl`'s data members, including the `RMICollaborator` stub references. By doing this, and by including the collaborators among the objects on which we synchronize, we ensure that asynchronous methods calls by remote agents do not interfere with each other, and we indirectly protect the remote `RMICollaboratorImpl` from asynchronous method calls by synchronizing locally on our stub reference. If we wanted the collaborator to have access to multiple mediators, then this measure wouldn't help, since each mediator could call methods on the collaborator asynchronously with respect to the other `Mediators`. If this was the case, we would have to ensure that the `RMICollaboratorImpl` methods were also multithread-safe.

Summary

The basic collaborative utility that we've built, in both message-passing and RMI flavors, can deal with asynchronous handling of multiple remote agents by a single mediator. The mediators are capable of issuing unique identities to each collaborator that is registered with it. And while we've provided a simple interface for sending point-to-point or broadcast messages across the system, we could implement specialized mediator and collaborator subclasses that use a custom interface to communicate.

10

Building Collaborative Applications

In the previous chapter we built up a set of base classes for building collaborative applications, in both RMI and message-passing forms. In this chapter, we'll put those classes to work, using them to build some collaborative applications: a simple chat system and a shared whiteboard. We'll only be building applications based on the RMI version of our collaborative framework, but the mapping to message-passing versions is straightforward.

A Simple Chat System

It's a pretty simple matter to build a basic chat system on top of our base classes. All we need to do is write a subclass of our collaborator that acts as a chat client, receiving messages from remote chat clients and displaying them in a text window next to their name. We can pull each client's name from its `Identity`. Example 10-1 shows an `RMIChatClient` based on our RMI collaborative system. The `RMIChatClient` extends the `RMICollaboratorImpl` class, and also implements the `java.awt.event.ActionListener` interface, so that it can act as a listener for its own AWT elements. This AWT interface includes a `TextArea` for showing the chat session, a `TextField` for the user to type in chat messages, and a `Button` to submit the messages to the chat server, which in our case is simply one of our `RMIMediatorImpl` objects routing messages to other `RMIChatClients`. The constructor for the `RMIChatClient` simply connects to the specified mediator, then initializes its graphical elements by calling its `init-Graphics()` method. The `initGraphics()` method creates a `Frame`, inserts the `TextArea`, `TextField`, and `Button` in the correct locations, then registers itself as an `ActionListener` for the button. The `RMIChatClient`'s `action-Performed()` method, which is called whenever the "Send" button is pressed, simply gets the text in the `TextField` when the button is pressed, and broadcasts it to all the other chat clients by calling its broadcast() method with a message tag of "chat." It then clears the TextField to let the user type in the next message. The RMIChatClient also has a notify() implementation that accepts chat messages from the mediator, and writes them to the TextArea along with the name of the sender (from its Identity). Figure 10-1 shows the chat screen that a user would see.

Example 10-1. An RMI-Based Chat Client

```
package dcj.util.Collaborative;

import java.awt.Frame;
import java.awt.TextArea;
import java.awt.TextField;
import java.awt.Button;
import java.awt.Label;
import java.awt.event.*;
import java.rmi.RemoteException;
import java.util.Properties;
import java.io.IOException;

public class RMIChatClient extends RMICollaboratorImpl
                        implements java.awt.event.ActionListener {
  TextArea chatArea;
  TextField chatInput;

  public RMIChatClient(String name, String host, String mname)
        throws RemoteException {
    super(name);
    Properties p = new Properties();
    p.put("host", host);
    p.put("mediatorName", mname);
    connect(p);
    initGraphics();
  }

  public boolean notify(String tag, String msg, Identity src)
              throws IOException, RemoteException {
    // Print the message in the chat area.
    chatArea.append("\n" + src.getName() + ": " + msg);
    return true;
  }

  protected void initGraphics() throws RemoteException {
    Frame f = new Frame();
    f.setLayout(null);
    f.addNotify();
    f.setSize(f.getInsets().left + 405, f.getInsets().top + 324);
    chatArea = new java.awt.TextArea();
    chatArea.setBounds(f.getInsets().left, f.getInsets().top,405, 300);
```

Example 10-1. An RMI-Based Chat Client (continued)

```
      f.add(chatArea);
      chatInput = new java.awt.TextField();
      chatInput.setBounds(f.getInsets().left + 84,
                          f.getInsets().top + 300,264,24);
      f.add(chatInput);
      Button button = new java.awt.Button("Send");
      button.setBounds(f.getInsets().left + 348,
                       f.getInsets().top + 300,60,24);
      f.add(button);
      button.addActionListener(this);
      Label label = new java.awt.Label("Chat here:");
      label.setBounds(f.getInsets().left,f.getInsets().top + 300,84,24);
      label.setAlignment(label.RIGHT);
      f.add(label);
      f.setTitle("RMI Chat Client");
      f.show();
  }

  public void actionPerformed(ActionEvent e) {
    // See if there's something to say...
    String msg = chatInput.getText();
    if (msg.length() > 0) {
      try {
        // Broadcast our message to the rest of the chat clients
        boolean success = broadcast("chat", msg);
        if (success) {
          System.out.println("Sent message OK.");
        }
        else {
          System.out.println("Failed to send message.");
        }
        // Clear the chat input field
        chatInput.setText("");
      }
      catch (Exception exc) {
      }
    }
  }
}
```

Our RMIChatClient's notify() method doesn't include any synchronized code blocks. Since each chat client connects to a single mediator, and since the mediator synchronizes all of its message-routing functions at any given time, there's only one thread that could be making remote calls to the chat client's notify() method.

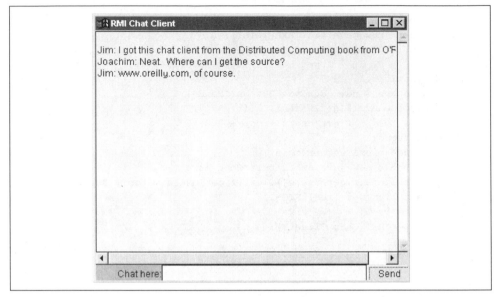

Figure 10-1. A chat client implemented using the RMICollaborator

This chat system was simple to implement because many of the really hard issues with collaborative systems are not a problem here. The data passed between the agents is small and simple (just text strings), so communication performance shouldn't be a problem. Every message is broadcast to every other chat client, so flexible communications aren't an issue either. And while there is a kind of shared "state" between the chatting agents (the list of chat messages that each displays), it isn't a problem keeping this shared state consistent. Each chat client sends its chat messages using the `broadcast()` method, but doesn't display the message locally until it's received back from the chat mediator. This way all messages displayed in each client's chat window are synchronized, because they all pass through the mediator and are sent in the same order to each chat client.

A Shared Whiteboard

Now we'll look at a collaborative application that's not so simple—a shared whiteboard. There are more things to worry about in this application because, while we still need to keep track of agent identities and communications, the data shared between agents is a bit more complicated and can lead to performance problems pretty quickly.

First let's build a simple shared whiteboard system based on our RMI collaborative classes. Like the chat example, our first version will use the standard mediator class, `RMIMediatorImpl`, because this version will only need the mediator to do the default routing of messages to the other agents. This initial whiteboard example will also need a new subclass of the RMICollaborator that acts as a whiteboard user. Actions that the user performs in the local whiteboard are broadcast to all other users so that their displays are updated properly.

Example 10-2 shows a WhiteboardUser class that subclasses RMICollaboratorImpl. It has a single constructor with four arguments: a name that the whiteboard user goes by, a color that is used when the user draws on the whiteboard, a host name for the mediator, and the mediator's name. The user name, host, and mediator name are passed to the RMICollaboratorImpl constructor to establish the connection to the mediator, and to initialize the collaborator's Identity. Once this is done, the color is added to the whiteboard user's Identity. We include the user's color in the Identity so other users of the shared whiteboard will know what color to use to draw our scribblings. When they receive the Identity in the remote call of their notify() methods, they can extract the Color object from the Identity and use it to draw the remote user's inputs. Since the java.awt.Color class implements the Serializable interface, we know that we can safely send the Color object through a remote method call via RMI.

Example 10-2. A Shared Whiteboard Client

```
package dcj.examples.Collaborative;

import dcj.util.Collaborative.*;
import java.awt.event.*;
import java.awt.*;
import java.util.Hashtable;
import java.util.Properties;
import java.io.IOException;
import java.rmi.RemoteException;

public class WhiteboardUser extends RMICollaboratorImpl
                           implements MouseListener, MouseMotionListener
{
  protected Hashtable lastPts = new Hashtable();
  protected Component whiteboard;
  protected Image buffer;

  public WhiteboardUser(String name, Color color, String host, String mname)
        throws RemoteException {
    super(name);
    Properties p = new Properties();
    p.put("host", host);
    p.put("mediatorName", mname);
    connect(p);
```

Example 10-2. A Shared Whiteboard Client (continued)

```java
    getIdentity().setProperty("color", color);
    System.out.println("color = " + color.getRed()
                          + " " + color.getGreen() + " "
                          + color.getBlue());
  buildUI();
}

protected void buildUI() {
  Frame f = new Frame();
  GridBagLayout gridbag = new GridBagLayout();
  GridBagConstraints c = new GridBagConstraints();
  f.setLayout(gridbag);
  f.addNotify();
  c.fill = GridBagConstraints.BOTH;
  c.gridwidth = GridBagConstraints.REMAINDER;
  Canvas canvas1 = new java.awt.Canvas();
  canvas1.setSize(240,180);
  canvas1.setBackground(Color.white);
  gridbag.setConstraints(canvas1, c);
  f.add(canvas1);
  String name = null;
  try {
    name = getIdentity().getName();
  }
  catch (Exception e) {
    name = "unknown";
  }
  Label label1 = new java.awt.Label("Your name: " + name);
  label1.setSize(100,30);
  gridbag.setConstraints(label1, c);
  f.add(label1);
  f.setSize(240,210);
  f.show();
  whiteboard = canvas1;
  whiteboard.addMouseListener(this);
  whiteboard.addMouseMotionListener(this);
  buffer = whiteboard.createImage(f.getSize().width,
                                    f.getSize().height);
}

public void mousePressed(MouseEvent ev) {
  Point evPt = ev.getPoint();
  try {
    broadcast("start", evPt);
  }
  catch (Exception e) {}
}
```

Example 10-2. A Shared Whiteboard Client (continued)

```java
  public void mouseReleased(MouseEvent ev) {
    Point evPt = ev.getPoint();
    try {
      broadcast("end", evPt);
    }
    catch (Exception e) {}
  }

  public void mouseDragged(MouseEvent ev) {
    Point evPt = ev.getPoint();
    try {
      broadcast("drag", evPt);
    }
    catch (Exception e) {
    }
  }

  public void mouseExited(MouseEvent ev) {}
  public void mouseMoved(MouseEvent ev) {}
  public void mouseClicked(MouseEvent ev) {}
  public void mouseEntered(MouseEvent ev) {}

  public boolean notify(String tag, Object data, Identity src)
                throws IOException, RemoteException {

    Color origColor = null;
    Color agentColor = null;
    Graphics gr = buffer.getGraphics();
    try {
      agentColor = (Color)src.getProperty("color");
      if (agentColor != null) {
        gr.setColor(agentColor);
      }
      else {
        System.out.println("No agent color available.");
      }
    }
    catch (Exception exc) {
      System.out.println("Exception while switching colors.");
      exc.printStackTrace();
    }

    if (tag.compareTo("start") == 0) {
      lastPts.put(src.getName(), data);
    }
    else if (tag.compareTo("drag") == 0) {
      Point lastPt = (Point)lastPts.get(src.getName());
      Point currPt = (Point)data;
```

Example 10-2. A Shared Whiteboard Client (continued)

```
      gr.drawLine(lastPt.x, lastPt.y, currPt.x, currPt.y);
      lastPts.put(src.getName(), data);
    }
    else if (tag.compareTo("end") == 0) {
      Point lastPt = (Point)lastPts.get(src.getName());
      Point currPt = (Point)data;
      gr.drawLine(lastPt.x, lastPt.y, currPt.x, currPt.y);
      lastPts.remove(src.getName());
    }

    whiteboard.getGraphics().drawImage(buffer, 0, 0, whiteboard);

    return true;
  }
}
```

The last thing that the `WhiteboardUser` constructor does is build the user interface by calling the `buildUI()` method. This method assembles the AWT elements that make up the whiteboard interface for the user. We won't delve into the
details of the interface, except to say that the main part of the whiteboard interface
is a simple `Canvas`, to which we attach the `WhiteboardUser` itself as a
`MouseListener` and a `MouseMotionListener` (notice that the `Whiteboard-
User` class implements both of these AWT interfaces). This is done near the end
of the `buildUI()` method.

All drawing operations are done using the `nextLine()` method. This method
draws a line from the last point on the user's drawing path, which is stored in a
`Hashtable`, to the next point; it's passed in as an argument. The color of the
line to be drawn is passed in as a `Color` argument. The line is drawn first on an
`Image` buffer, which was initialized in the `buildUI()` method, then the buffer
image is copied to the `Canvas`. We do this so that we can restore the whiteboard
display if the window becomes obscured by another window and becomes visible
again; all of the scribblings are stored in the `Image` buffer and can be recopied to
the `Canvas` when needed.

Since we've attached the `WhiteboardUser` to the `Canvas` as a `MouseLis-
tener` and a `MouseMotionListener`, it will get mouse click and motion events
from the `Canvas`, passed to it through calls to its `mouseXXX()` methods. When
the user presses a mouse button while the cursor is in the `Canvas`, the `White-
boardUser.mousePressed()` method is called. If the user drags the mouse
with the button pressed, the `WhiteboardUser.mouseDragged()` method is
called repeatedly, recording each new position of the cursor. When the user
releases the mouse, the `WhiteboardUser.mouseReleased()` method is
called. Each of these methods is passed a `MouseEvent` object as an argument,

which includes information about the event that triggered the method call. This information includes the position of the mouse within the Canvas.

To let the rest of the shared whiteboard users know what the local user has done (so they can update their displays), the mouse event-handling methods in White-boardUser broadcast a message to them all using the broadcast() method inherited from the RMICollaboratorImpl parent class. In mousePressed(), a "start" message is sent along with the coordinates of the mouse press (passed as the body of the message). This tells the other whiteboard users that this user has started drawing something at those coordinates. In mouseDragged(), a "drag" message is sent, with the coordinates of the mouse. mouseReleased() sends an "end" message with the coordinates of the mouse.

This gets the drawing actions of each whiteboard user to all of the other users; now we need to do something with this information. Remember that when the mediator calls the collaborator's notify() method, it passes in the message tag, the body of the message, and the Identity of the sender. The Whiteboard-User.notify() method first gets the drawing color of the remote agent from its Identity—remember that each agent adds its preferred color to its Iden-tity in its constructor. The notify() method sets the drawing color of the buffer image by getting its Graphics object and calling its setColor() method with the remote agent's color. Next, it checks the message tag. If this is a "start" message, then it just stores the mouse location in a Hashtable, so that it will know where to draw a line when the next mouse position comes as the user moves the mouse. When a "drag" message comes in, the last mouse position from this user is retrieved from the Hashtable, and a line is drawn from that point to the new point, using the agent's color. Then the last point is set to the current point, for the next drag message. If an "end" message is received, then a line is drawn from the last point to the new point, and the last point is removed from the Hashtable. Figure 10-2 shows the shared whiteboard in action, with two users sharing a whiteboard on remote machines.

Problems with the First Version

Although this first attempt works, it's not very useful. The event-handling methods on the WhiteboardUser don't do any drawing on the Canvas; all of the drawing is done in the notify() method. So even the local user's scribbles on the whiteboard are not shown in the local display until a message has been broadcast through the mediator, and received back through notify(). Even with a pretty fast network connection, users will see a noticeable (and annoying) delay between their mouse movements and the update of the Canvas.

This problem is simple to remedy. We need to draw the user's scribblings on the local whiteboard immediately, broadcast the event through the mediator, and

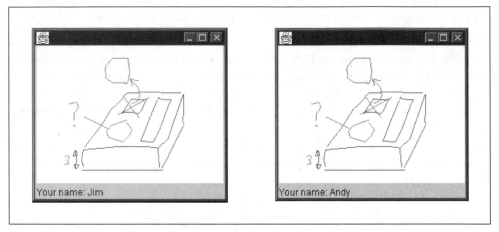

Figure 10-2. Our shared whiteboard in use

ignore any incoming notifications from the mediator that have our `Identity` on them (to avoid drawing the local stuff twice). We can do this by calling `next-Line()` right in the `mouseDragged()` and `mouseReleased()` methods, before we broadcast the event to the other users:

```
public void mouseReleased(MouseEvent ev) {
    Point evPt = ev.getPoint();
    try {
      nextLine(getIdentity().getName(), evPt,
              (Color)getIdentity().getProperty("color"));
      lastPts.remove(getIdentity().getName());
      broadcast("end", evPt);
    }
    catch (Exception e) {}
}
public void mouseDragged(MouseEvent ev) {
    Point evPt = ev.getPoint();
    try {
      nextLine(getIdentity().getName(), evPt,
              (Color)getIdentity().getProperty("color"));
      lastPts.put(getIdentity().getName(), evPt);
      broadcast("drag", evPt);
    }
    catch (Exception e) {}
}
```

Then we modify our `notify()` method to compare the identity of the source to our local identity. If they are the same, we just ignore the message, since we've already drawn our own scribblings locally:

```
public boolean notify(String tag, Object data, Identity src)
    throws IOException, RemoteException {
```

```
if (src.getName().compareTo(getIdentity().getName()) == 0) {
    return true;
}
    ...
```

A more subtle problem with this whiteboard client is the choppy drawing that results as the user drags the mouse across the `Canvas`. Instead of a smooth, curved line being drawn exactly where the mouse goes, I get a choppy line connecting points along the path I take. This happens because of the way we're handling mouse events in the `WhiteboardUser` class. Each event is passed into a call to one of the `mouseXXX()` methods. These methods broadcast the event to the other whiteboard users by calling the `broadcast()` method from `RMICollaboratorImpl`, which in turn remotely calls the mediator's `broadcast()` method. While the `WhiteboardUser` waits for the remote method call to complete, the user continues to move the mouse. In most AWT implementations, the event is passed into the event handler in the same thread that is polling for user events. This is done to ensure that events are handled in the order that they are received. If the AWT internals simply spawned off an independent thread to handle each incoming event, there would be no guarantee of the order in which the threads will run—it's up to the thread-scheduling process of the local virtual machine. In our case, if we blindly start a new thread to handle each draw event from the user, then some drag events may be handled out of sequence if their threads happen to get some CPU time before the earlier events. We'll end up drawing lines between disconnected points along the path of the mouse, which will result in a confusing mess. But with each event being handled in the same thread as the event poller, a lengthy or blocked event-handling thread can cause lost user events, which seems to be our problem here. Some of the mouse drag events are being lost while the event handling thread waits on the remote `broadcast()` call.

Fixing this problem is a bit more involved. We need to split the event handling part of our agent and the collaborative broadcasting part into separate threads, but we still need to be sure that the events are processed in the order in which they come in from the user. The easiest part for us to isolate into a new thread is the remote method calls, so that's what we'll do. The new thread simply broadcasts local events to the other users by calling the `WhiteboardUser`'s `broadcast()` method. The mouse-handling methods pass the events on to this thread as they come in. To ensure that the events get broadcast through the mediator in the right order, we'll put the data for each event onto an event queue, and the event broadcasting thread will poll this event queue and send out events in the order in which they appear in the queue (first-in, first-out).

Our event broadcasting thread is implemented using the `Msg` and `CommHelper` classes shown in Example 10-3. The `Msg` class is simply a container that holds the

data for each event. This data is just the tag that will be sent in the remote broad-
cast() method call, and the Object that is the body of the message (in our
case, a Point object). The CommHelper class extends Thread, and has a reference to the collaborator that it's helping, and a Vector of Msgs. The run()
method just polls the message list, sending them out as they come by calling the
collaborator's broadcast() method.

Example 10-3. A Thread for Broadcasting Whiteboard Events

```
class Msg {
  public Object data;
  public String tag;
  public Msg(String t, Object o) {
    data = o;
    tag = t;
  }
}

class CommHelper extends Thread {
  RMICollaborator collaborator;
  Vector msgs = new Vector();
  public CommHelper(RMICollaborator c) {
    collaborator = c;
  }

  public static void addMsg(String t, Object o) {
    synchronized (msgs) {
      msgs.addElement(new Msg(t, o));
    }
  }

  public void run() {
    while (true) {
      try {
        Msg m = null;
        synchronized (msgs) {
          m = (Msg)msgs.elementAt(0);
          msgs.removeElementAt(0);
        }
        collaborator.broadcast(m.tag, m.data);
      }
      catch (Exception e) {}
    }
  }
}
```

We just need to update our WhiteboardUser class to use this new thread to
broadcast user events rather than calling broadcast() directly from the event-
handling methods. The updated WhiteboardUser class is shown in

Example 10-4 as the `ThreadedWhiteboardUser`. This updated class also includes the changes described previously to avoid the local drawing delay. The changes are pretty minor: the `ThreadedWhiteboardUser` has a `CommHelper` reference, which it initializes in its constructor, passing a reference to itself as the collaborator; the `mouseDragged()` and `mouseReleased()` methods have also been updated to send the message tag and event location to the `CommHelper`, where the event will be queued for broadcast through the mediator.

Example 10-4. A Multithreaded Whiteboard Client

```
package dcj.examples.Collaborative;

import dcj.util.Collaborative.*;
import java.awt.event.*;
import java.awt.*;
import java.util.Hashtable;
import java.util.Properties;
import java.io.IOException;
import java.rmi.RemoteException;
import java.util.Vector;

public class ThreadedWhiteboardUser
    extends RMICollaboratorImpl
    implements java.awt.event.MouseListener,
               java.awt.event.MouseMotionListener
{
  protected Hashtable lastPts = new Hashtable();
  protected Component whiteboard;
  protected Image buffer;
  protected CommHelper helper;

  public ThreadedWhiteboardUser(String name, Color color,
                                String host, String mname)
      throws RemoteException {
    super(name, host, mname);
    getIdentity().setProperty("color", color);
    buildUI();
    helper = new CommHelper(this);
    helper.start();
  }

  protected void buildUI() {
    Frame f = new Frame();
    GridBagLayout gridbag = new GridBagLayout();
    GridBagConstraints c = new GridBagConstraints();
    f.setLayout(gridbag);
    f.addNotify();
    c.fill = GridBagConstraints.BOTH;
    c.gridwidth = GridBagConstraints.REMAINDER;
```

Example 10-4. A Multithreaded Whiteboard Client (continued)

```java
    Canvas canvas1 = new java.awt.Canvas();
    canvas1.setSize(240,180);
    canvas1.setBackground(Color.white);
    gridbag.setConstraints(canvas1, c);
    f.add(canvas1);
    String name = null;
    try {
      name = getIdentity().getName();
    }
    catch (Exception e) {
      name = "unknown";
    }
    Label label1 = new java.awt.Label("Your name: " + name);
    label1.setSize(100,30);
    gridbag.setConstraints(label1, c);
    f.add(label1);
    f.setSize(240,210);
    f.show();
    whiteboard = canvas1;
    whiteboard.addMouseListener(this);
    whiteboard.addMouseMotionListener(this);
    buffer = whiteboard.createImage(f.getSize().width,
                                    f.getSize().height);
  }

  protected void nextLine(String agent, Point pt, Color c) {
    Graphics g = buffer.getGraphics();
    g.setColor(c);
    Point lastPt = (Point)lastPts.get(agent);
    g.drawLine(lastPt.x, lastPt.y, pt.x, pt.y);
    whiteboard.getGraphics().drawImage(buffer, 0, 0, whiteboard);
  }

  public void mousePressed(MouseEvent ev) {
    Point evPt = ev.getPoint();
    try {
      lastPts.put(getIdentity().getName(), evPt);
      CommHelper.addMsg("start", evPt);
    }
    catch (Exception e) {}
  }

  public void mouseReleased(MouseEvent ev) {
    Point evPt = ev.getPoint();
    try {
      nextLine(getIdentity().getName(), evPt,
               (Color)getIdentity().getProperty("color"));
      lastPts.remove(getIdentity().getName());
```

Example 10-4. A Multithreaded Whiteboard Client (continued)

```
      helper.addMsg("end", evPt);
    }
    catch (Exception e) {}
  }

  public void mouseDragged(MouseEvent ev) {
    Point evPt = ev.getPoint();
    try {
      nextLine(getIdentity().getName(), evPt,
             (Color)getIdentity().getProperty("color"));
      lastPts.put(getIdentity().getName(), evPt);
      helper.addMsg("drag", evPt);
    }
    catch (Exception e) {}
  }

  public void mouseExited(MouseEvent ev) {}
  public void mouseMoved(MouseEvent ev) {}
  public void mouseClicked(MouseEvent ev) {}
  public void mouseEntered(MouseEvent ev) {}

  public boolean notify(String tag, Object data, Identity src)
                   throws IOException, RemoteException {

    // If this is our own event, ignore it since it's already been handled.
    if (src.getName().compareTo(getIdentity().getName()) == 0) {
      return true;
    }

    Color agentColor = null;
    try {
      agentColor = (Color)src.getProperty("color");
    }
    catch (Exception exc) {
      System.out.println("Exception while getting color.");
      exc.printStackTrace();
    }

    if (tag.compareTo("start") == 0) {
      // First point along a path, save it and continue
      lastPts.put(src.getName(), data);
    }
    else if (tag.compareTo("drag") == 0) {
      // Next point in a path, draw a line from the last
      // point to here, and save this point as the last point.
      nextLine(src.getName(), (Point)data, agentColor);
      lastPts.put(src.getName(), data);
    }
```

Example 10-4. A Multithreaded Whiteboard Client (continued)

```
  else if (tag.compareTo("end") == 0) {
    // Last point in a path, so draw the line and remove
    // the last point.
    nextLine(src.getName(), (Point)data, agentColor);
    lastPts.remove(src.getName());
  }

  return true;
  }
}
```

Some Further Improvements

This updated shared whiteboard system is still pretty simple, but useful. Each user can have her own color to distinguish herself from the other users, local drawing is done right away so there's no annoying delay as we drag the mouse over the whiteboard, and we've isolated the remote method calls from the event-handling thread so that none (or few) of the user's mouse events are lost while we block on the remote `broadcast()` call. But there are a few additional improvements that we could make so that this distributed application is more pleasant to use.

List of current users

When a user joins a shared whiteboard session, it would be nice to see who is currently using the whiteboard, what color they are using, etc. We could add this to our distributed application by defining a specialized mediator—a `WhiteboardMediator`—that sends a notification to each new agent with a list of all of the identities of the current users. The `WhiteboardMediator` would also send a notification to every existing user when a new user joins. The `WhiteboardUsers` could then update their local displays of remote users, using the name and color properties from the `Identity` list. To do this, we would just have to write a new implementation of the `register()` method on our `WhiteboardMediator`:

```
  public boolean register(Identity i, RMICollaborator c)
              throws RemoteException {
      super.register(i, c);
      send(i, getIdentity(), "userlist", getMembers());
  }
```

We'd also have to update the `notify()` method on the `WhiteboardUser` so that it could store the list of users and update its local display.

Maintain whiteboard state at the server

The most glaring flaw in our whiteboard is that we don't store the board's state on the mediator. This means that any new agents joining an existing whiteboard session won't be able to see what's already been drawn, just what's drawn from the time they join forward. It's easy to fix this problem with a specialized White-boardMediator. The mediator would just keep a history of all the scribbles that each user has made. New users joining the whiteboard receive a notification that includes all of the current scribbles that are on the whiteboard, so that they can draw them on their local display. The mediator could save the whiteboard state either as a table of point sets indexed by user Identity, or as an Image buffer. The table of point sets is more complicated to maintain, but opens up the possibility of removing individual user's actions (an "undo" feature), letting users change their personal color, etc. The Image buffer is easy to maintain and to send to new users, but doesn't allow us to pick out scribblings from particular users, since their actions have all been jumbled together into a single Image.

Performance improvements

We should be able to speed up the broadcasting and processing of drawing events by the other users. With the current whiteboard system, each mouse event from each whiteboard user is broadcast individually to the group through the mediator. The result is a delay from the time that one whiteboard user moves the mouse to the time that the line is drawn on another user's whiteboard. One way to speed things up is to batch the broadcasting of user events across the system, so that instead of broadcasting each event individually, we're broadcasting sets of events in a single remote broadcast() call. We can either batch the events at the WhiteboardUser, or on the WhiteboardMediator. If we batch them on the mediator, then we're still causing a remote method call for every mouse event the user makes; so it seems we would get the best improvement by doing the batching on the WhiteboardUser itself. We could do this by adding some code to the run() method of the CommHelper, so that local user events are sent a group at a time. We would also have to update the notify() method on the Whiteboard-User, so that it would recognize batch notifications and handle them appropriately.

A

Using the Examples in Applets

You may have noticed that most of the examples in this book are provided in a form suitable for use as Java applications, not as applets. Rather than interspersing applet examples with applications throughout the book, we decided to concentrate on distributed system development issues without the additional complications of applet programming. In this appendix, we'll see how some of the examples could be modified for use in applets.

Whiteboard Applet

One of the examples that seems like an obvious candidate for use as an applet is our whiteboard example from Chapter 10. Currently, support for RMI within web browsers is scarce, so let's concentrate on a message-passing version of the whiteboard, instead of the RMI-based version shown in Example 10-3. The message-passing version is very similar, but is based on the `MessageCollaborator` and `MessageMediator` classes from that chapter. This version, which we called the `MsgWhiteboardUser`, is shown in Example A-1. Since the differences between this and the RMI-based `WhiteboardUser` are minor, we won't go into details about the code here.

Example A-1. Message-Passing Whiteboard

```
package dcj.examples.Collaborative;

import dcj.util.Collaborative.*;
import java.awt.event.*;
import java.awt.*;
import java.util.Hashtable;
import java.util.Properties;
import java.io.IOException;
```

Example A-1. Message-Passing Whiteboard (continued)

```java
import java.util.Vector;

class Msg {
  public Object data;
  public String tag;

  public Msg(Object o, String t) {
    data = o;
    tag = t;
  }
}

class CommHelper extends Thread {
  Collaborator collaborator;
  static Vector msgs = new Vector();

  public CommHelper(Collaborator c) {
    collaborator = c;
  }

  public static void addMsg(Object o, String t) {
    synchronized (msgs) {
      msgs.addElement(new Msg(o, t));
    }
  }

  public void run() {
    while (true) {
      try {
        Msg m = null;
        synchronized (msgs) {
          m = (Msg)msgs.elementAt(0);
          msgs.removeElementAt(0);
        }
        collaborator.broadcast(m.tag, m.data);
      }
      catch (Exception e) {}
    }
  }
}

public class MsgWhiteboardUser
    extends MessageCollaborator
    implements java.awt.event.MouseListener,
               java.awt.event.MouseMotionListener
{
  protected Hashtable lastPts = new Hashtable();
  protected Component whiteboard;
```

Example A-1. Message-Passing Whiteboard (continued)

```
protected Image buffer;

public MsgWhiteboardUser(String name, Color color,
                        String host, int port) {
  super(host, port, name);
  getIdentity().setProperty("color", color);
  System.out.println("color = " + color.getRed()
                     + " " + color.getGreen() + " "
                     + color.getBlue());
  buildUI();
  CommHelper helper = new CommHelper(this);
  helper.start();
}


protected void buildUI() {
  Frame f = new Frame();
  GridBagLayout gridbag = new GridBagLayout();
  GridBagConstraints c = new GridBagConstraints();
  f.setLayout(gridbag);
  f.addNotify();
  c.fill = GridBagConstraints.BOTH;
  c.gridwidth = GridBagConstraints.REMAINDER;
  Canvas canvas1 = new java.awt.Canvas();
  canvas1.setSize(240,180);
  canvas1.setBackground(Color.white);
  gridbag.setConstraints(canvas1, c);
  f.add(canvas1);
  String name = null;
  try {
    name = getIdentity().getName();
  }
  catch (Exception e) {
    name = "unknown";
  }
  Label label1 = new java.awt.Label("Your name: " + name);
  label1.setSize(100,30);
  gridbag.setConstraints(label1, c);
  f.add(label1);
  f.setSize(240,210);
  f.show();
  whiteboard = canvas1;
  whiteboard.addMouseListener(this);
  whiteboard.addMouseMotionListener(this);
  buffer = whiteboard.createImage(f.getSize().width,
                                  f.getSize().height);
}


protected void nextLine(String agent, Point pt, Color c) {
```

Example A-1. Message-Passing Whiteboard (continued)

```java
    Graphics g = buffer.getGraphics();
    g.setColor(c);
    Point lastPt = (Point)lastPts.get(agent);
    g.drawLine(lastPt.x, lastPt.y, pt.x, pt.y);
    whiteboard.getGraphics().drawImage(buffer, 0, 0, whiteboard);
  }

  public void mousePressed(MouseEvent ev) {
    Point evPt = ev.getPoint();
    try {
      lastPts.put(getIdentity().getName(), evPt);
      CommHelper.addMsg(evPt, "start");
    }
    catch (Exception e) {}
  }

  public void mouseReleased(MouseEvent ev) {
    Point evPt = ev.getPoint();
    try {
      nextLine(getIdentity().getName(), evPt,
               (Color)getIdentity().getProperty("color"));
      lastPts.remove(getIdentity().getName());

      CommHelper.addMsg(evPt, "end");
    }
    catch (Exception e) {}
  }

  public void mouseDragged(MouseEvent ev) {
    Point evPt = ev.getPoint();
    try {
      nextLine(getIdentity().getName(), evPt,
               (Color)getIdentity().getProperty("color"));
      lastPts.put(getIdentity().getName(), evPt);

      CommHelper.addMsg(evPt, "drag");
    }
    catch (Exception e) {
    }
  }

  public void mouseExited(MouseEvent ev) {}
  public void mouseMoved(MouseEvent ev) {}
  public void mouseClicked(MouseEvent ev) {}
  public void mouseEntered(MouseEvent ev) {}

  public boolean notify(String tag, Object data, Identity src)
                 throws IOException {
```

Example A-1. Message-Passing Whiteboard (continued)

```
      if (src.getName().compareTo(getIdentity().getName()) == 0) {
        return true;
      }
      Color origColor = null;
      Color agentColor = null;
      Graphics gr = buffer.getGraphics();
      try {
        agentColor = (Color)src.getProperty("color");
        if (agentColor != null) {
          gr.setColor(agentColor);
        }
        else {
          System.out.println("No agent color available.");
        }
      }
      catch (Exception exc) {
        System.out.println("Exception while switching colors.");
        exc.printStackTrace();
      }

      if (tag.compareTo("start") == 0) {
        lastPts.put(src.getName(), data);
      }
      else if (tag.compareTo("drag") == 0) {
        Point lastPt = (Point)lastPts.get(src.getName());
        Point currPt = (Point)data;
        gr.drawLine(lastPt.x, lastPt.y, currPt.x, currPt.y);
        lastPts.put(src.getName(), data);
      }
      else if (tag.compareTo("end") == 0) {
        Point lastPt = (Point)lastPts.get(src.getName());
        Point currPt = (Point)data;
        gr.drawLine(lastPt.x, lastPt.y, currPt.x, currPt.y);
        lastPts.remove(src.getName());
      }

      whiteboard.getGraphics().drawImage(buffer, 0, 0, whiteboard);

      return true;
    }
  }
```

A quick and dirty way to use our message-passing whiteboard in an applet context is to just create a `MsgWhiteboardUser` from inside the `init()` method of an `Applet`:

```
    public class WhiteboardApplet extends Applet {
      private MsgWhiteboardUser wbUser;
```

```
    public WhiteboardApplet() {}
    public void init() {
      wbUser = new MsgWhiteboardUser("Fred", new Color(255, 0, 0),
                                     "medhost", 5009);
    }
  }
```

When the `MsgWhiteboardUser` initializes itself, one of the things it does is try to connect to a `MessageMediator` at the host and port number given to the constructor. This will work just fine, assuming that the applet security policy for your browser allows you to make network connections to the host on which the mediator is running. Typically a browser will only allow an applet to open connections to the host it came from, so you may be forced to have the mediator running on the same host serving the HTML page with your applet.

Since the whiteboard constructs its own top-level `Frame` inside the `buildUI()` method, using the `WhiteboardApplet` in a web page will cause a separate window to pop up on the user's machine. It would be nice to have the whiteboard GUI appear embedded in the web page itself. To do this, we'll need a way to pass the `Applet`'s top-level `Container` into the constructor for the `MsgWhiteboardUser`, so that it adds all of its user interface elements to the `Container` instead of a separate window. We just need to add an additional argument to the `MsgWhiteboardUser` constructor:

```
    public MsgWhiteboardUser(String name, Color color,
                             String host, int port, Container c) {
        . . .
```

Then we pass the external `Container` into the `buildUI()` method, which then uses it instead of a new `Frame` as the container for all of its AWT elements:

```
    protected void buildUI(Container cont) {
        if (cont == null)
          cont = new Frame();
        GridBagLayout gridbag = new GridBagLayout();
        GridBagConstraints c = new GridBagConstraints();
        cont.setLayout(gridbag);
        cont.addNotify();
        c.fill = GridBagConstraints.BOTH;
        c.gridwidth = GridBagConstraints.REMAINDER;
        Canvas canvas1 = new java.awt.Canvas();
        canvas1.setSize(240,180);
        canvas1.setBackground(Color.white);
        gridbag.setConstraints(canvas1, c);
        cont.add(canvas1);
        String name = null;
        try {
          name = getIdentity().getName();
        }
```

```
      catch (Exception e) {
        name = "unknown";
      }
      Label label1 = new java.awt.Label("Your name: " + name);
      label1.setSize(100,30);
      gridbag.setConstraints(label1, c);
      cont.add(label1);
      cont.setSize(240,210);
      cont.setVisible(true);
      whiteboard = canvas1;
      whiteboard.addMouseListener(this);
      whiteboard.addMouseMotionListener(this);
      buffer = whiteboard.createImage(cont.getSize().width,
                                 cont.getSize().height);
  }
```

Now our whiteboard will appear within the web page itself.

Many of the other examples in the book are even easier to apply in an applet context. They can be used within an applet you have developed, assuming that the browsers support the libraries used (e.g., RMI, CORBA, etc.). Of course, you must take applet security restrictions into account when you're deciding how to distribute your agents and how they'll talk to each other. (For example, if you put a server agent on machine X, will any browser running one of your client agents allow the agent to connect to the server machine?)

Class Downloads

Another issue when using applets is the number and size of the support classes that a client needs to run the applet. In the case of the `WhiteboardApplet` described earlier, in addition to its own class file, the applet needs to download the following support classes:

- `MsgWhiteboardUser`
- `Collaborator`
- `MessageCollaborator`
- `MessageHandler`
- `Message`

In the version of the JDK we used to compile these classes into Java bytecodes, the total size of the class files, including the `WhiteboardApplet`, is a little less than 20Kb. This is downloadable in around 7 seconds on a 28.8 Kbit/s modem—not bad at all. If the support classes for our applet are extensive, we have the option of providing them on the web server compressed in a *.jar* file or a *.zip* file, whichever one we think most of the client browsers will support.

B

CORBA Services

The CORBA standard is really a collection of standards and definitions. In addition to the core specifications for the Object Request Broker (ORB) and inter-ORB communication protocols such as IIOP, CORBA also includes specifications for services that distributed objects may require, such as naming services, security measures, etc. Taken as a whole, these specifications, backed up by solid implementations, provide a very powerful environment for the distributed application developer.

This appendix provides a brief overview of some of the key services currently included in the CORBA Services specification. Some of these services are similar in nature to features provided inherently by Java. In these cases, we discuss the contrasts between the Java-native service and the CORBA service.

Naming Service

The Naming Service is arguably the most commonly used service in the CORBA family. We used the Naming Service in our CORBA example in Chapter 3 to look up our CORBA-based `Solver` object. The Naming Service provides a means for objects to be referenced by name within a given naming context. A naming context is a scoping mechanism for names, similar in philosophy to class packages in Java. Within a particular context, names must be unique, and contexts can be nested to form compound contexts and names. Figure B-1 shows two naming contexts in the form of Venne diagrams: one, whose topmost context is named "BankServices," defines names for objects in a banking application; the other, named "LANResources," defines names for network resources such as printers, compute servers, data servers, etc. The "BankServices" naming context contains a single object named "AuthorizationAgent," and a subcontext named "Corporate-

Account." The "LANServices" context contains a "DataServer" context and a "Printer" context, and each of these contains two named objects.

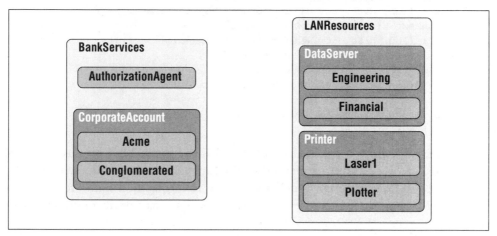

Figure B-1. Sample naming contexts

Agents in a distributed system can add named objects to the Naming Service by *binding* objects to a particular name within a context. Other agents can then look up these objects by *resolving* their names into object references. The name of an object is made up of a sequence of name components that specify the subcontexts that the object falls within. So, for example, the "Laser1" object in the "LANResources" context would be fully specified with a name made up of the ordered components "LANResources," "Printer," and "Laser1."

All of the interfaces making up the Naming Service are contained in the `CosNaming` module. The interface to the central Naming Service functions is the `NamingContext` interface, which provides methods for binding, rebinding, and unbinding objects to names, as well resolving object references from names. Using a Java implementation of the CORBA Naming Service, the "LANResources" context and all of its object "contents" might be built up as follows:

```
// Get handle on base naming context from the ORB
NamingContext base = ...
// Get references to the objects to be registered in Naming Service
omg.CORBA.Object engDataBaseRef = ...
omg.CORBA.Object finDataBaseRef = ...
omg.CORBA.Object laserPrinterRef = ...
omg.CORBA.Object plotterRef = ...
// Build up subcontexts for LAN resources
NameComponent lan = new NameComponent("LANResources", "");
NameComponent data = new NameComponent("DataServer", "");
NameComponent print = new NameComponent("Printer", "");
// Create context for LAN resources
```

```
NameComponent path[] = {lan};
NamingContext lanContext = base.bind_new_context(path);
// Bind all of the data servers to their names within the new context
path = {lan, data, new NameComponent("Engineering", "")};
lanContext.bind(path, engDataBaseRef);
path = {lan, data, new NameComponent("Financial", "")};
lanContext.bind(path, finDataBaseRef);
// Bind the printers to their names
path = {lan, print, new NameComponent("Laser1", "")};
lanContext.bind(path, laserPrinterRef);
path = {lan, print, new NameComponent("Plotter", "")};
lanContext.bind(path, plotterRef);
```

In this example, a new context is established first for the LAN resource objects. The `bind_new_context()` method of the `NamingContext` interface takes an array of `NameComponents`, which specify the fully qualified name for the new context. In this case, we simply need a single `NameComponent` to give the new context the name "LANResources."

Next, the object references are bound to their names within this new context. In each case, we create an array of `NameComponents` specifying the compound name for the object, then bind the object to its name by calling the `bind()` method on the `NamingContext`.

Agents that want to use these named objects can look them up by getting a reference to the `NamingContext` and resolving the object references from their full names:

```
NamingContext base = ...
NameComponent printerName ={new NameComponent("LANResources", ""),
                           new NameComponent("Printer", ""),
                           new NameComponent("Laser1", "")};
omg.CORBA.Object printerRef = base.resolve(printerName);
```

Comparison to the RMI Registry

There are many similarities between the RMI registry facilities, represented by the `java.rmi.Naming` interface, and the CORBA Naming Services, represented by the `NamingContext` interface in the `CosNaming` module. Each provides methods for binding and rebinding objects to names, removing these bindings, and looking up objects by name. They also both provide methods for listing the contents of a registry or `NamingContext`, respectively.

Where CORBA and RMI differ the most with regards to naming services is hierarchical naming contexts. RMI does not support them at all, while CORBA supports them extensively with the ability to both create hierarchical naming contexts and represent compound object names. In the RMI examples in this book, we got around this limitation of the RMI registry by registering a single factory object with the registry, which was then used to create references to other remote objects. So the client of the remote object would use a single, simple name to look up the remote factory object, and the factory object would be responsible for supporting the "lookup" of other objects within this "context."

In situations where hierarchical naming is critical, such as distributed directory services, this becomes a major deficiency in the RMI package, and a good reason to turn to the more comprehensive services provided by CORBA.

Event Service

The Event Service provides asynchronous communications between cooperating, remote objects. It's most similar in nature to the message-passing and event-based messaging we saw in Chapter 6.

The CORBA Event Service is based on a model involving *suppliers* and *consumers* of events, connected by *event channels* that carry events back and forth between the two. An event channel can support multiple event suppliers and multiple event consumers. The Event Service also supports two event propagation styles for both consumers and suppliers of events: *push* style and *pull* style. A push-style consumer has events pushed to it by its event suppliers, while a pull-style consumer explicitly pulls events from its suppliers. On the other end of the event channel, a push-style supplier pushes events to its consumers, while a pull-style supplier waits for its consumers to pull events from it. Figure B-2 shows the relationship between event suppliers, consumers, and channels. In the figure, arrows indicate flow of events, and the location of the head of the arrow indicates which entity drives the event transfer.

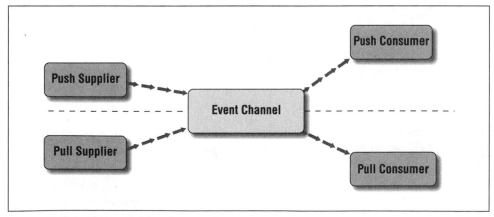

Figure B-2. Propagation model in the Event Services

Although the event channel provides a physical connection between consumers and suppliers in the Event Service model, logically each consumer attaches itself to one or more suppliers, and each supplier attaches itself to one or more consumers. Each consumer and supplier attaches itself to an event channel by attaching itself to a proxy supplier or consumer that the event channel exports. An event channel can be thought of as supporting both the supplier and consumer interfaces, simultaneously.

So here's the typical execution plan that an agent follows when using the CORBA Event Service:

- A reference to an event channel object is obtained, either using the Naming Service to look up a remote event channel object reference, or by invoking an operation on an existing remote object reference that dynamically opens an event channel.

- If the agent has any event suppliers, they register themselves with the event channel by attaching themselves to proxy consumers obtained from the channel. Pull-style suppliers attach themselves to proxy pull consumers created from the channel, and push-style suppliers attach themselves to proxy push consumers created from the channel.

- If the agent has any event consumers, they register themselves with the event channel in a similar way. Pull-style consumers attach themselves to proxy pull suppliers and push-style consumers attach themselves to proxy push suppliers.

- When suppliers on the agent's side of the channel generate events, the events are carried through the event channel to any consumers attached remotely to the channel. Push suppliers push their events through the channel by calling push() methods on the proxy consumers obtained from the channel. Pull suppliers wait for their proxy consumers to pull events from them through the channel.

- Consumers on the agent's side of the channel receive events from remote suppliers attached to the channel. Pull-style consumers pull events through the channel from their proxy suppliers by calling pull() methods on them. Push-style consumers wait for their proxy suppliers to give them events received through the channel.

The consumers and suppliers attached to a channel don't know or care about the type or implementation details of their counterparts on the other end of the event channel. A push consumer might attach itself to a channel with only a pull supplier on the other end; the event channel is responsible for ensuring that events are pulled from the supplier and pushed to the consumer, so that the flow of events is maintained. The same is the case when a pull consumer is attached to a push supplier—the event channel accepts the events pushed to it by the supplier, and buffers them until the consumer pulls them. Regardless of the types of suppliers and consumers attached to an event channel at any given time, you should assume that event delivery by the channel is asynchronous.

The Event Service specification provides both generic and typed event communication. In the generic case, the type of the event data is not specified in the interfaces for the suppliers, consumers, or channels. Event data is represented using the CORBA any data type, and suppliers and consumers call generic push() and pull() methods on each other to propagate events through the distributed system. In typed event communication, the interfaces for the suppliers, consumers, and channels can include type-specific event propagation methods and type-specific event representations. In this appendix we'll only discuss the generic event communication aspects of the Event Service.

Quality of Service for Channels

Any given implementation of the event channel interface can support a particular quality of service. Some implementations may guarantee delivery of every event to every consumer attached to the channel, while others may just guarantee to make a best effort to deliver the events generated by its suppliers. The Event Service specification leaves the implementation open to these different levels of service to allow for different application requirements. The trade-offs here are similar to those found at a lower level, in choosing between TCP and UDP packet delivery over IP network connections. Guaranteed event delivery typically means reduced net throughput. Best-effort event delivery can potentially provide higher event throughput, but at the cost of potentially undelivered events, or events delivered to only some of the consumers attached to the channel.

Interface Specifics

The Event Service includes several modules that provide IDL interfaces for suppliers, consumers, and event channels. In this appendix we'll briefly review the highlights of the interfaces for generic event communication. If you're interested, see the CORBA Services specification document.[*]

The CosEventComm module contains interface definitions for push and pull consumers and suppliers of events:

PushSupplier

    The PushSupplier interface has only one method, disconnect_push_ supplier(), which releases the supplier from its event communication link.

---

[*] CORBA Services Specification, OMG Technical Document formal/97-07-04, July 1997.

There's no exported method for getting events from the supplier, since it's responsible for pushing events to its attached consumer(s).

PushConsumer

The PushConsumer has a push() method, which accepts a single input argument of type any that represents the event data. The any type is an IDL language feature used to mark data that can be of any type. The receiver of the event is responsible for determining the actual data type. The PushConsumer also has a disconnect_push_consumer() method for releasing it from the event communication channel.

PullSupplier

This interface has two methods for pulling event data from the supplier: pull() and try_pull(). A consumer can choose to do a blocking event pull by calling pull(), or it can do a nonblocking polling of the event supplier by calling try_pull(). There is also a disconnect_pull_supplier() method.

PullConsumer

The PullConsumer just has a disconnect_pull_consumer() method, since it's responsible for internally pulling events from its suppliers.

The CosEventChannelAdmin module contains interfaces for event channels and their proxy consumers and suppliers:

EventChannel

This interface has three methods: for_consumers(), for_suppliers(), and destroy(). The for_consumers() method returns a reference to a ConsumerAdmin object, which can be used by consumers to get references to proxy suppliers. Likewise, the for_suppliers() method returns a SupplierAdmin object, which can be used by suppliers to get references to proxy consumers. The destroy() method destroys the channel and any communication resources it had been using.

ConsumerAdmin

This interface allows consumers to get references to proxy suppliers from an event channel. The obtain_push_supplier() method returns a reference to a ProxyPushSupplier object, and the obtain_pull_supplier() method returns a reference to a ProxyPullSupplier object.

SupplierAdmin

The SupplierAdmin interface allows suppliers to get references to proxy consumers from the channel. The obtain_push_consumer() method returns a ProxyPushConsumer reference, and obtain_pull_consumer() returns a ProxyPullConsumer reference.

`ProxyPushSupplier`

This interface derives from the `PushSupplier` interface in the `CosEvent-Comm` module. It adds a method, `connect_push_consumer()`, which allows a local `PushConsumer` to attach itself to the supplier. The method takes a single argument: a reference to a `PushConsumer`. Attaching a consumer to the proxy supplier sets up a path for events to flow from the remote suppliers attached to the channel, through the channel, to the local proxy supplier, and finally to the local consumer.

`ProxyPullSupplier`

This derives from `PullSupplier` and adds a `connect_pull_consumer()` method, which accepts a `PullConsumer` reference.

`ProxyPushConsumer`

This derives from `PushConsumer` and adds a `connect_push_supplier()` method, which accepts a `PushSupplier` reference. Attaching a supplier to a proxy consumer sets up a path for events to flow from the local suppliers attached to the channel to the local proxy consumer, through the channel, and finally to remote consumers attached to the channel.

`ProxyPullConsumer`

This derives from `PullConsumer` and adds a `connect_pull_supplier()` method, which accepts a `PullSupplier` reference.

Comparison to the Java Event Model

As we discussed in Chapter 6, the core Java API provides a basic framework for event-based communication between agents, remote or otherwise. The only full implementation of this framework present in the Java API is found in the AWT package, which uses the event delegation model to define the flow of user events from user interface elements to application objects that process the events, update the system state, and provide visual feedback to the user through changes to the user interface.

We showed in Chapter 6 how the delegation event model in Java could be used to build a remote messaging system. But the Java API didn't provide us much "out-of-the-box." There is no generic event-handling interface provided as an extension of the placeholder `EventListener` interface. We had to fill this gap ourselves by creating the `EventHandler` interface with its generic `handleEvent()` abtract method. And there is no interface supplied at all for event sources. This significantly limits the usefulness of the Java API as a broad framework for distributed event-passing systems, especially when it comes to interfacing with other event-based systems.

Security Service

The CORBA Security Service specification is one of the more complicated and detailed of the CORBA services. This is in large part due to the inherent complexity of security, and also to the fact that the Security Services specification includes security models and interfaces for application development, security administration, and the implementation of security services themselves.

In this section we'll only provide a brief overview of the security model and interfaces provided within the CORBA Security Services for application development. Later, we'll contrast the Security Services with the Java Security API.

Service Types

The CORBA Security Services provide interfaces for the following:

- Authenticating and generating credentials for principals, including the delegation of credentials to intermediary principals

- Performing secure transactions (e.g., method invocations, data transfers, etc.) between objects

- Auditing secure transactions for later review

- Non-repudiation facilities that generate evidence of transactions, to prevent principals involved in a secure transaction from denying that the action ever took place (e.g., the sender of a message denies ever sending it, or the receiver denies receipt)

All of these services and their interfaces are specified in an implementation-neutral manner. So the authentication service interface does not depend on the use of symmetric or asymmetric keys, and the interface to a principal's credentials is not dependent on the use of a particular certificate protocol like X.509.

Security Model

The model used by the CORBA Security Services specification involves principals that are authenticated using a `PrincipalAuthenticator` object. Once authenticated, a principal is associated with a `Credential` object, which contains information about its authenticated identity and the access rights that it has under this identity. These credentials are then used in secure transactions, to verify the access privileges of the parties involved, and to register identities for actions that are audited or carried out in a non-repudiation mode. A CORBA remote object request run under the security services is outlined in Figure B-3. The client requests a remote object through a local reference. The client's `Credentials` (generated earlier by authenticating the user using the `Princi-`

palAuthenticator interface) are attached to the request by the Security Services present in the ORB, and sent along with the request over the transport mechanism in use. The remote object receives the request through its ORB, along with the client's Credentials. The target object can decide whether to honor the request or not, based on the access rights of the client's identity.

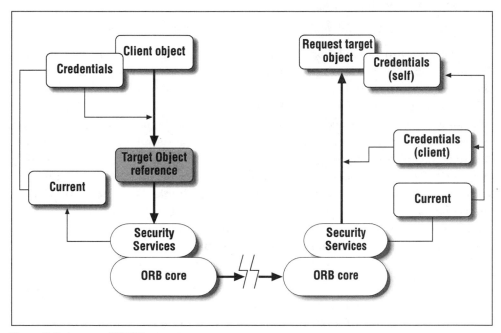

Figure B-3. A secure CORBA request

When a request is received from a remote agent, its right to access the resources requested can be checked through an AccessDecision object, which can be used to compare the remote principal's credentials against access control settings, like an ACL. There typically isn't a default access-control policy that the Security Services will enforce for requests, since checking access rights is usually very application-specific (e.g., "Is the client principal in the 'Credit Admin' group?", or "Has this principal tried and failed to access this resource more than *x* times?"). The target of a request can also explicitly audit the transaction using the Audit-Channel interface, or just check to see if auditing is required by the current security policy by calling the audit_needed() method on the AuditDecision interface. If non-repudiation services are available, then evidence of the action can be generated using the NRCredentials interface.

Comparison to the Java Security API

The CORBA Security Services specification defines a more comprehensive security API than the Java Security API, in the following ways:

- Direct support for security auditing and (through an optional set of interfaces) nonrepudiation services

- Direct support for delegation of requests to intermediary objects

However, the two specifications or APIs are also aimed at different goals. The Java Security API is primarily an interface to low-level security measures and utilities, like key generation and management, direct generation of message digests and digital signatures, etc. The CORBA Security Services are at a much higher level, defining a generic interface between applications and high-order security services, such as principal credentials, audit trails, and intermediaries. The Security Services specification never gets down to the level of defining interfaces based on families of security algorithms, like public key encryption. Even the interfaces provided for service implementors only provide hooks into the ORB request-handling and message-transfer functions. Likewise, the Java Security API never rises above the level of algorithm-independent interfaces to key generation, digital signatures, etc. There's no attempt to build a generic interface to credentials and access decisions, just specific interfaces to access-control lists, for example.

In fact, the two can be seen as complementary in many ways; the Java Security API could be considered a toolkit for building a Java implementation of the services defined at a higher level by the CORBA Security Services specification.

Other Key CORBA Services

In addition to the Naming, Event, and Security services that we discussed here, the CORBA Services Specification defines several other services, including:

Persistent object services
> Services for generating, retrieving, and maintaining persistent object states. This service is intended to be an interface between CORBA applications and object databases or other persistent object technologies.

Transaction service
> A service that supports issuing transactions across a distributed system. A transaction can be as simple or complex as needed, from a single remote-object request to a collection of multiple requests among many distributed objects. The side effects of all the requests comprising a transaction are not realized until the transaction is completed and committed. This service is similar in nature and scope to the JavaSpaces API, discussed in Appendix C.

Query service

This service has similar goals to JDBC. It provides an interface for querying and modifying collections of objects, including selecting, updating, inserting, or deleting objects from these collections. The most obvious implementation for this service would be an interface between CORBA applications and SQL-based relational databases or object databases.

C

JavaSpaces

JavaSpaces is a new distributed object system being proposed by Sun as a package at a higher level than the existing RMI and object serialization facilities built into Java. JavaSpaces provides a distributed, persistent object system that is roughly modeled after earlier shared memory systems, such as LINDA. While it has some analogies with parallel shared memory systems such as the Posix shm_xxx library and shared memory facilities in parallel languages like Python, it also has some important differences.

This appendix provides an overview of the general JavaSpace architecture as currently described in the draft JavaSpace specification. It doesn't go into detail about how to use the JavaSpace API, since the API isn't fully available yet. This appendix only includes the core elements of the specification, without discussing any proposed features that may or may not be in the final API.

Overview of JavaSpaces

The distributed application paradigm supported by JavaSpaces is one in which remote agents interact with each other indirectly through shared data object spaces. Objects are stored in a JavaSpace in the form of entries. Clients write entries into the space, read entries from the space, or take entries from the space, as shown in Figure C-1.

Access to the entries in JavaSpaces is through a small set of basic operations:

read
> Read an entry from the space that matches a template.

write
> Add an entry to the space.

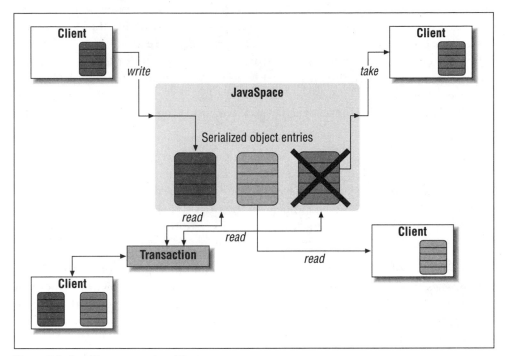

Figure C-1. JavaSpaces general architecture

take

> Read and remove an entry from the space.

notify

> Send a notification through a given event handler if entries that match a template are added to the space. A notification request has a time-out period associated with it: if a matching entry isn't added within the time-out period, the notify request fails and is dropped from the JavaSpace.

Multiple basic operations can be assembled into *transactions* that group basic operations into a single, atomic aggregate operation.

There can be many clients and many JavaSpaces in a given distributed application. One client, and even one transaction from one client, can access multiple JavaSpaces. So instead of one agent sending a message to another, or invoking a remote method directly on another object within an agent, agents interact by writing and reading objects in JavaSpaces. An important feature of the JavaSpaces specification is that all operations on a given JavaSpace are considered unordered. If you have multiple threads or multiple remote agents issuing operations on a JavaSpace, and for some reason you want to impose some order on the operations, then it's up to you to synchronize your threads or agents as needed.

Each JavaSpace holds data in the form of *entries*, which can either be *read*, *written*, or *taken* from a JavaSpace. Each entry has one or more fields that are used to match incoming requests from clients. Each request to read, take, or be notified about an entry includes a template for the entry to match. In order for an entry in the JavaSpace to match, the entry must be of the same type as the template object. Each field in the template can either have a non-null value, which must match the fields in a matching entry in the JavaSpace, or a null value, which matches any value in that field.

All operations on JavaSpaces are "transactionally secure," which means that each operation or transaction is either entirely committed or entirely noncommitted to a JavaSpace. So if a write to a JavaSpace succeeds, then you can be assured that the Entry was written and will appear in the next client read or take operation on the space. An operation on JavaSpaces can be either in the form of a simple operation, or a group of operations within a single Transaction.

The authors of the JavaSpace specification make a point of distinguishing JavaSpaces from a distributed database system. A JavaSpace knows the type of its entries, and can compare field values, but it doesn't understand anything about the structure of the data in its entries. It also isn't meant to provide opaque read/write access to persistent data. An entry in a JavaSpace is a serialized copy of the object written to the space, and entries returned to clients as a result of read or take operations are separate copies of the objects in the space.

Entry and EntryRep

Every JavaSpace consists solely of entries, which are represented by instances of the Entry class. An entry is a group of object references, which represent the fields in the Entry. When an entry is added to a JavaSpace, the entry is stored in serialized form by independently serializing each field in the Entry. Because of this, every field in an entry has to be public, has to be Serializable, and has to be an Object (not a primitive type).

EntryReps act as the conduit for Entrys into and out of JavaSpaces. They serialize Entrys before going into a JavaSpace during a write operation, and deserialize Entrys returned as the result of read, take, or notify operations. A given EntryRep can be written multiple times to the same JavaSpace, which would result in multiple identical entries in the space.

EntryReps are used to specify JavaSpace entries in read or take operations. A client creates an Entry with the values and wildcards that it wants to match in a JavaSpace. Then it wraps it in an EntryRep, which generates the serialized form of the template Entry and passes it to the JavaSpace as an argument of the operation. The JavaSpace compares the serialized bytes of the template Entry to its own `Entrys`, and matches on the first one whose serialized bytes are the same as those of the non-null fields in the template `Entry`.

Another benefit of serializing each field of an `Entry` independently is that it allows for fault-tolerant retrieval of entries from the space. If a `read`, `take`, or `notify` operation finds a match and an error occurs while deserializing it, an `UnusableEntryException` is thrown. The exception object contains a list of the fields from the entry that were successfully deserialized from the JavaSpace, along with a list of the unusable fields and a list of nested exceptions that explain why each unusable field failed to be deserialized. Some reasons for failed deserialization are missing class files on the client, or a `RemoteException` caused by a remote reference on the `Entry` that isn't valid any more. Your client can react in different ways to an `UnusableEntryException`: it can try to use the partial entry that it received, it can ignore the partial entry and try to read or take another entry, or it can give up altogether.

The authors of the JavaSpaces specification make a point of mentioning that, since at this time the Java API doesn't support persistent server objects, it's dangerous to put remote references into a JavaSpace as part of an `Entry`. If the server object behind the remote reference is destroyed for some reason (e.g., server restart, server crash, etc.), then the remote reference becomes invalid; however, this won't be discovered until a client tries to get the entry from the JavaSpace. The authors suggest that you use metadata about the remote object, namely its remote host and registry name, in the `Entry`, and let the client establish its own remote reference to the server object.

Transactions

A `Transaction` is a group of basic operations that act as an atomic operation on one or more JavaSpaces. A `Transaction` is atomic in the sense that all or none of the operations in the `Transaction` will be carried out. If any of the operations within the `Transaction` fail (e.g., a read fails to match an entry, or a notify times out before it is triggered), then the entire `Transaction` fails and any sub-operations that had succeeded are "rolled back," and the JavaSpace is left in the same state it would have been in if the `Transaction` had never been attempted.

The JavaSpace Interface

The JavaSpace specification also defines a `JavaSpace` class that provides an interface to a remote JavaSpace. The `JavaSpace` interface provides `read()`, `write()`, `take()`, and `notify()` methods, which allow clients to perform the basic operations on the JavaSpace. Each of these methods takes an `EntryRep` (used as either an entry to put into the space, or a template to use for matching an entry already in the space), an optional `Transaction` within which the operation should be carried out, and an optional `Identity`, which can be used to verify the client's access to the JavaSpace entries against an access-control list. The `Identity` can be used to verify the caller's right to execute the given operation on the `JavaSpace`, perhaps by checking an access-control list. The current specification is not clear about whether this `Identity` argument will use the `Identity` class from the Java Security API, but it seems likely that it would.

The rest of this section describes the methods available on the `JavaSpace` interface for executing operations and transactions against the space.

write()

```
void write(EntryRep r, Transaction t, Identity i)
    throws RemoteException, TransactionException, SecurityException
```

A `write()` call adds an `EntryRep` to the `JavaSpace`. Each field in the enclosed `Entry` is serialized independently, and the serialized bytes making up the entire `Entry` are sent to the `JavaSpace` for storage and later lookup. If a `Transaction` is included in the `write()` call, then the new entry isn't visible to other clients of the `JavaSpace` until the entire `Transaction` executes. If the entry is taken during the course of the rest of the `Transaction`, then the `Transaction`, including the write operation, will succeed, but the new entry will never be seen by other clients of the `JavaSpace`.

read()

```
EntryRep read(EntryRep template, Transaction t, Identity i)
    throws RemoteException, TransactionException, SecurityException
```

If an entry in the `JavaSpace` matches the `EntryRep` template, it is returned from the method call as an `EntryRep` object. If a non-null `Transaction` is included in the `read()` call, then a matching `EntryRep` will only be returned if the entire `Transaction` succeeds. Any entries that are read during the course of the enclosing `Transaction` are put on a pending list, and can't be taken by other operations or transactions until the read and its `Transaction` are finished (successfully executed or aborted). If all entries matching the `read()`'s template entry are pending in unfinished transactions, then a `TransactionConflict-Exception` is thrown.

take()

```
EntryRep take(EntryRep template, Transaction t, Identity i)
    throws RemoteException, TransactionException, SecurityException
```

The `take()` operation on the `JavaSpace` interface behaves much like the `read()` operation, except that a matching entry is also removed from the space. If the `Transaction` argument is non-null, then a matching entry won't be returned until the `Transaction` completes. If a `RemoteException` is raised by the `take()` call, then it's possible that the entry was removed from the space but not returned in its entirety.

notify()

```
EventRegID notify(EntryRep template, EventCatcher c, Transaction t,
                  Identity i, int timeout)
     throws RemoteException, TransactionException, SecurityException
```

A call to `notify()` serves to register interest in matching entries for a specific period of time. If a matching entry is written to the space before the notification request expires, then the `notify()` method on the given `EventCatcher` will be called. The `EventRegID` object returned to the client contains a set of long values, including an event ID that will come with the notification, a cookie value that can be used to renew or cancel the notification, and the actual timeout period assigned to the notification request by the `JavaSpace`. If a non-null `Transaction` is passed into the method call, then the event catcher will be notified of matching entries for the duration of the enclosing `Transaction`. At the end of the transaction, the notification request will be dropped from the space.

The `JavaSpace` interface also includes the following two methods for controlling notification requests that have been previously issued to the space.

renew()

```
long renew(long cookie, long extension)
     throws RemoteException, NotRegisteredException
```

This method allows a client to request an extension to a notification request. The `cookie` argument is the value returned in the `EventRegID` from the original `notify()` call and the extension is the desired extension to the registered notification. The method returns the actual time extension granted by the `JavaSpace`, if any. The units of these time values have not yet been detailed in the JavaSpaces specification.

cancel()

```
void cancel(long cookie) throws RemoteException, NotRegisteredException
```

The notification request associated with the `cookie` is cancelled.

D

RMI Quick Reference

This appendix is a quick reference guide to RMI, the remote object package included in JDK 1.1. Since there are many examples in the book that use RMI, we felt it would be useful for you to have this reference right here at your fingertips.

The RMI API is contained in the `java.rmi` package, which includes three major sub-packages: `java.rmi.dgc`, `java.rmi.registry`, and `java.rmi.server`. We include all but the `java.rmi.dgc` package in this reference; that package is really internal to the RMI implementation, having to do with distributed garbage collection, and the average reader won't have any reason to use the package directly.

This reference is broken down into sections by packages. First we look at the classes in the base `java.rmi` package, then `java.rmi.registry`, and, finally, `java.rmi.server`. Within each package, the classes are listed alphabetically.

The java.rmi Package

The core package in RMI contains the `Remote` interface as well as the `Naming` class and the `RMISecurityManager` class. These interfaces are used by both RMI clients and servers to define remote interfaces, look them up over the network and use them securely. In addition, this core package contains a number of basic RMI exception types used during remote object lookups and remote method calls.

java.rmi.AccessException

A `RemoteException` caused by an attempt to perform an improper operation on the `Naming` or `Registry` interface. A registry only allows local requests to bind, rebind or unbind objects, so an attempt to call these methods on a remote registry results in an AccessException.

```
public class AccessException extends java.rmi.RemoteException {
// Public constructors
    public AccessException(String descr);
    public AccessException(String descr, Exception detail);
}
```

java.rmi.AlreadyBoundException

An exception that is thrown when an attempt is made to bind an object to a name that is already bound.

```
public class AlreadyBoundException extends java.lang.Exception {
// Public constructors
    public AlreadyBoundException();
    public AlreadyBoundException(String descr);
}
```

java.rmi.ConnectException

A RemoteException that's thrown when a remote host refuses to connect during a remote method call.

```
public class ConnectException extends RemoteException {
// Public constructors
    public ConnectException(String descr);
    public ConnectException(String descr, Exception nestedExc);
}
```

java.rmi.ConnectIOException

A RemoteException thrown if there is an I/O error while attempting to make a remote method call.

```
public class ConnectIOException extends RemoteException {
    public ConnectIOException(String descr);
    public ConnectIOException(String descr, Exception ex);
}
```

java.rmi.MarshalException

A RemoteException thrown if an I/O error occurs while attempting to marshal any part of a remote method call (header data or method arguments).

```
public class MarshalException extends RemoteException {
// Public constructors
```

```
        public MarshalException(String s);
        public MarshalException(String s, Exception ex);
    }
```

java.rmi.Naming

This is the primary application interface to the naming service within the RMI registry. References to remote objects are obtained with the lookup() method. Local object implementations can be bound to names within the local registry using the bind() and rebind() methods. Locally bound objects can be removed from the name registry using unbind(). All of the names for objects currently stored in the registry can be obtained using the list() method.

Each name argument to the methods on the Naming interface takes the form of a URL (e.g., *rmi://remoteHost:port/objName)*. If a local object is being referenced, and the object is exported to the default registry port, then the URL can simply take the form of the object's name in the local registry (e.g., objName). This is possible because the rmi: protocol is assumed if it isn't present in the URL, and the default host is the local host.

While the lookup() method can reference any remote RMI registry, the bind(), rebind(), and unbind() methods can only be called on the local registry. Attempting to call these methods against a remote registry will result in an Access-Exception being thrown.

```
    public final class Naming {
    // Class Methods
        public static void bind(String name, Remote obj) // Register
            throws AlreadyBoundException, java.net.MalformedURLException,
            UnknownHostException, RemoteException;
        public static String[] list(String name) // List bound object names
            throws RemoteException, java.net.MalformedURLException,
            UnknownHostException
        public static Remote lookup(String name) // Gets remote object
            throws NotBoundException, java.net.MalformedURLException,
            UnknownHostException, RemoteException;
        public static void rebind(String name, Remote obj)
            throws RemoteException, java.net.MalformedURLException,
            UnknownHostException;
        public static void unbind(String name) // Remove an object
            throws RemoteException, NotBoundException,
            java.net.MalformedURLException, UnknownHostException;
    }
```

java.rmi.NoSuchObjectException

A `RemoteException` thrown when you attempt to invoke a method on a remote object that is no longer available.

```
public class NoSuchObjectException extends java.rmi.RemoteException {
// Public constructors
    public NoSuchObjectException(String descr);
}
```

java.rmi.NotBoundException

An exception that is thrown when a lookup is attempted using a name with no object bound to it.

```
public class NotBoundException extends java.lang.Exception {
// Public constructors
    public NotBoundException();
    public NotBoundException(String descr);
}
```

java.rmi.Remote

Every remote object has to implement this interface, and any methods intended to be remotely callable have to be defined within a `Remote` interface. This is a placeholder interface that identifies all remote objects, but doesn't define any methods of its own.

```
public interface Remote {}
```

java.rmi.RemoteException

An `IOException` that is thrown when an error occurs during any remote object operation. The `RemoteException` includes a `Throwable` data member that represents the nested exception that caused the `RemoteException` to be thrown. For example, if an exception occurs on the server while executing a remote method, then the client receives a `RemoteException` (in the form of a `Server-Exception`, one of its subclasses) with its `Throwable` data member initialized to the server-side exception that caused the client-side `RemoteException`.

```
public class RemoteException extends java.io.IOException {
// Public Constructors
    public RemoteException();
    public RemoteException(String descr);
    public RemoteException(String descr, Throwable nestedExc);
// Public Instance Methods
```

```
    public String getMessage();
// Public Instance Variables
    public Throwable detail;
}
```

java.rmi.RMISecurityException

A `SecurityException` thrown by the `RMISecurityManager` when a security violation is detected during a remote operation.

```
public class RMISecurityException extends java.lang.SecurityException {
// Public Constructors
    public RMISecurityException(String name);
    public RMISecurityException(String name, String arg);
}
```

java.rmi.RMISecurityManager

The `RMISecurityManager` enforces the security policy for classes that are loaded as stubs for remote objects, by overriding all of the relevant access-check methods from the `SecurityManager`. By default, stub objects are only allowed to perform class definition and class access operations. If the local security manager is not an `RMISecurityManager` (using the `System.setSecurityManager()` method), then stub classes will only be loadable from the local file system.

You normally won't need to interact with the `RMISecurityManager` directly within your application code, except to set it as the system security manager before entering your RMI code.

```
public class RMISecurityManager extends SecurityManager {
// Public Constructors
    public RMISecurityManager();
// Public Instance Methods
    public synchronized void checkAccept(String host, int port);
    public synchronized void checkAccess(Thread t);
    public synchronized void checkAccess(ThreadGroup g);
    public void checkAwtEventQueueAccess();
    public synchronized void checkConnect(String host, int port);
    public void checkConnect(String host, int port, Object context);
    public synchronized void checkCreateClassLoader();
    public void checkDelete(String file);
    public synchronized void checkExec(String cmd);
    public synchronized void checkExit(int status);
    public synchronized void checkLink(String lib);
    public synchronized void checkListen(int port);
    public void checkMemberAccess(Class clazz, int which);
    public void checkMulticast(InetAddress maddr);
    public void checkMulticast(InetAddress maddr, byte ttl);
```

```
    public synchronized void checkPackageAccess(String pkg);
    public synchronized void checkPackageDefinition(String pkg);
    public void checkPrintJobAccess();
    public synchronized void checkPropertiesAccess();
    public synchronized void checkPropertyAccess(String key);
    public synchronized void checkRead(FileDescriptor fd);
    public synchronized void checkRead(String file);
    public void checkRead(String file, Object context);
    public void checkSecurityAccess(String provider);
    public synchronized void checkSetFactory();
    public void checkSystemClipboardAccess();
    public synchronized boolean checkTopLevelWindow(Object window);
    public synchronized void checkWrite(FileDescriptor fd);
    public synchronized void checkWrite(String file);
    public Object getSecurityContext();
}
```

java.rmi.ServerError

An error that occurs while a server is executing a remote method. The nested
Throwable data member (inherited from RemoteException) contains the
server-side exception that generated the error.

```
public class ServerError extends RemoteException {
// Public Constructors
    public ServerError(String descr, Error err);
}
```

java.rmi.ServerException

An exception that occurs while a server is executing a remote method. The nested
Throwable data member (inherited from RemoteException) contains the
server-side exception that generated the exception.

```
public class ServerException extends RemoteException {
// Public Constructors
    public ServerException(String descr);
    public ServerException(String descr, Exception nestedExc);
}
```

java.rmi.ServerRuntimeException

A RemoteException that occurs while the server is executing a remote method.

```
public class ServerRuntimeException extends RemoteException {
// Public Constructors
    public ServerRuntimeException(String descr, Exception nestedExc);
}
```

java.rmi.StubNotFoundException

This exception can occur either when an object is being exported to participate in remote RMI calls, or during a remote method call. During export on the server, this exception is thrown if the stub class for the object can't be found or used for some reason (e.g., the stub class isn't in the CLASSPATH of the server process, or the stub class can't be instantiated). During a remote method call, the client can receive this exception if the remote object hasn't been exported completely or correctly.

```
public class StubNotFoundException extends RemoteException {
// Public Constructors
    public StubNotFoundException(String s);
    public StubNotFoundException(String s, Exception ex);
}
```

java.rmi.UnexpectedException

All exceptions are unexpected, right? An UnexpectedException is thrown if an exception that isn't specified on a remote method's signature is encountered during the return from a remote method call. The unexpected exception can occur on the server or on the client. The nested Throwable object inherited from RemoteException contains the actual exception that occurred.

```
public class UnexpectedException extends RemoteException {
// Public Constructors
    public UnexpectedException(String descr);
    public UnexpectedException(String descr, Exception NestedExc);
}
```

java.rmi.UnknownHostException

This RemoteException is thrown if the host specified during a Naming lookup can't be found.

```
public class UnknownHostException extends RemoteException {
// Public Constructors
    public UnknownHostException(String descr);
    public UnknownHostException(String descr, Exception nestedEx);
}
```

java.rmi.UnmarshalException

This RemoteException is thrown if an error occurs while unmarshaling the return value from a remote method call. The source of the error could be an I/O error while sending the header or the value of the return from the server to the client, or the fact that the class of the return object is not found.

```
public class UnmarshalException extends RemoteException {
// Public Constructors
    public UnmarshalException(String s);
    public UnmarshalException(String s, Exception ex);
}
```

The java.rmi.registry Package

This package contains classes that provide an interface and implementation for the various elements of the RMI object registry.

java.rmi.registry.LocateRegistry

This is a low-level interface to the RMI registry service, either on the local host or on remote servers. On lookups, the Naming service parses the host and port from the remote object URL and uses the LocateRegistry to connect to the remote registry. The various getRegistry() methods provide the means to get a reference to the local registry, or a stub to a remote registry running on a given host and port. The createRegistry() method creates a registry running on the local host on the given port number.

```
public final class LocateRegistry {
// Class Methods
    public static Registry createRegistry(int port) throws
RemoteException;
    public static Registry getRegistry() throws RemoteException;
    public static Registry getRegistry(int port) throws
RemoteException;
    public static Registry getRegistry(String host)
        throws RemoteException, UnknownHostException;
    public static Registry getRegistry(String host, int port)
        throws RemoteException, UnknownHostException;
}
```

java.rmi.registry.Registry

The Registry is an interface to the RMI object registry that runs on every node in a distributed RMI system. While the Naming interface can be used to look up objects stored in any registry on the network, a Registry operates on a single registry on a single host. URL object names are passed into methods on the Naming service, which finds the right Registry stub using the LocateRegistry interface, and then calls the lookup() method on the remote (or local) Registry to get a stub for the remote object. A similar sequence of calls takes place with the local Registry when bind(), rebind(), or unbind() are called on the Naming interface.

The Registry stores objects under unique names. An object is assigned to a name in the Registry using its bind() method. The object assigned to a particular name can be changed using the rebind() method. Objects are removed from the Registry using the unbind() method. The lookup() method is used to find objects by name in the Registry, and the list() method is used to get a list of the names of all of the objects currently in the Registry.

```
public interface Registry extends Remote {
// Class Constants
    public static final int REGISTRY_PORT = 1099;
// Public Instance Methods
    public void bind(String name, Remote obj) throws RemoteException,
        AlreadyBoundException, AccessException;
    public String[] list() throws RemoteException, AccessException;
    public Remote lookup(String name)
        throws RemoteException, NotBoundException, AccessException;
    public void rebind(String name, Remote obj)
        throws RemoteException, AccessException;
    public void unbind(String name) throws RemoteException,
        NotBoundException, AccessException;
}
```

java.rmi.registry.RegistryHandler

This interface is mainly of interest to implementors of RMI registry services. It defines the interface to the internal registry-handling implementation.

```
public interface RegistryHandler {
// Public Instance Methods
    public Registry registryImpl(int port) throws RemoteException;
    public Registry registryStub(String host, int port)
                throws RemoteException, UnknownHostException;
}
```

The java.rmi.server Package

This package contains the classes used in server implementations of remote objects. The RemoteServer class acts as the base class for all RMI server objects. UnicastRemoteObject, the single subclass of RemoteServer provided in this package, implements a non-persistent, point-to-point object communication scheme. Other subclasses of `RemoteServer` could be written to implement multi-cast object communication, replicated objects, etc. The `java.rmi.server` package also contains several `Exception` subclasses relevant to the server implementation of a remote object.

java.rmi.server.ExportException

This `RemoteException` is thrown if an attempt is made to export a remote object on a port that is already in use.

```
public class ExportException extends java.rmi.RemoteException {
// Public Constructors
    public ExportException(String descr);
    public ExportException(String descr, Exception nestedExc);
}
```

java.rmi.server.LoaderHandler

This defines the interface to the internal handler used by the `RMIClassLoader` to load classes over the network.

```
public interface LoaderHandler {
// Class Constants
    public final static String packagePrefix;
// Public Instance Methods
    public Object getSecurityContext(ClassLoader loader);
    public Class loadClass(String name);
    public Class loadClass(URL codebase, String name)
                throws MalformedURLException, ClassNotFoundException;
}
```

java.rmi.server.LogStream

This class provides the server with an output stream to an error log. `LogStreams` can't be created directly by the application. Instead, a handle on a `LogStream` is obtained by calling the static `log()` method with the name of the desired log. If the named log doesn't exist, the default log is returned. The default `PrintStream` used to create new `LogStreams` can be gotten through the `getDefaultStream()` method, and set using the `setDefaultStream()` method.

```
public class LogStream extends PrintStream {
// Class Constants
    public static final int SILENT;
    public static final int BRIEF;
    public static final int VERBOSE;
```

```
// Class Methods
    public static synchronized PrintStream getDefaultStream();
    public static LogStream log(String name);
    public static int parseLevel(String s);
    public static synchronized void setDefaultStream(
        PrintStream newDefault);
// Public Instance Methods
    public synchronized OutputStream getOutputStream();
    public synchronized void setOutputStream(OutputStream out);
    public String toString();
    public void write(byte b[], int off, int len);
    public void write(int b);
}
```

java.rmi.server.ObjID

An ObjID is used on an object server to uniquely identify exported remote objects. It's used primarily in an RMI server during distributed garbage collection.

The equals() method is overridden from Object to return true only if the objects identified by the two ObjIDs are equal. The ObjID class also has read() and write() methods that serve to marshal and unmarshal an ObjID from I/O streams.

```
public final class ObjID implements java.io.Serializable {
// Public Constructors
    public ObjID();
    public ObjID(int num);
// Class Constants
    public static final int REGISTRY_ID;
    public static final int DGC_ID;
// Class Methods
    public static ObjID read(ObjectInput in)
                        throws java.io.IOException;
// Public Instance Methods
    public boolean equals(Object obj);
    public int hashCode();
    public String toString();
    public void write(ObjectOutput out) throws java.io.IOException;
}
```

java.rmi.server.Operation

An Operation contains a description of a method on a remote object.

```
public class Operation {
// Public Constructors
    public Operation(String op);
```

```
// Public Instance Methods
    public String getOperation();
    public String toString();
}
```

java.rmi.server.RemoteCall

A RemoteCall is the interface used by stubs and skeletons to perform remote method calls. The getInputStream() and getOutputStream() methods return streams that can be used to marshal arguments or return values, and unmarshal them on the other end of the method call.

```
public interface RemoteCall {
    public void done() throws IOException;
    public void executeCall() throws Exception;
    public ObjectInput getInputStream()  throws IOException;
    public ObjectOutput getOutputStream()  throws IOException;
    public ObjectOutput getResultStream(boolean success)
                        throws IOException, StreamCorruptedException;
    public void releaseInputStream() throws IOException;
    public void releaseOutputStream()  throws IOException;
}
```

java.rmi.server.RemoteObject

The RemoteObject class reimplements key Object methods for remote objects, and maintains a RemoteRef object that is a handle to the actual remote object. The equals() implementation returns true only if the two referenced remote objects are equal. The hashCode() method is implemented so that every remote stub that refers to the same remote object will have the same hash code.

```
public abstract class RemoteObject
    implements Remote, java.io.Serializable {
// Protected Constructors
    protected RemoteObject();
    protected RemoteObject(RemoteRef newref);
// Protected Instance Variables
    transient protected RemoteRef ref;
// Public Instance Methods
    public boolean equals(Object obj);
    public int hashCode();
    public String toString();
}
```

java.rmi.server.RemoteRef

A handle on the object implementing a remote object reference. Each `RemoteObject` contains a `RemoteRef`, which acts as its interface to the actual remote object it represents. Normally, you won't need to interact directly with `RemoteRefs` from your application code. Rather, application code will interact with `RemoteObjects`, which use their internal `RemoteRefs` to perform remote method invocations.

The `newCall()` method is used to create a call object for invoking a remote method on the referenced object. The `invoke()` method actually executes a remote method invocation. If a remote method returns successfully, then the `done()` method is called to clean up the connection to the remote object.

The `remoteEquals()`, `remoteHashCode()`, and `remoteToString()` methods on `RemoteRef` are used by `RemoteObjects` to implement the remote versions of the `equals()`, `hashCode()`, and `toString()` methods.

```java
public interface RemoteRef extends java.io.Externalizable {
// Class Constants
    public final static String packagePrefix;
// Public Instance Methods
    public void done(RemoteCall call) throws RemoteException;
    public String getRefClass(java.io.ObjectOutput out);
    public void invoke(RemoteCall call) throws Exception;
    public RemoteCall newCall(RemoteObject obj, Operation[] op,
                          int opnum, long hash)
                throws RemoteException;
    public boolean remoteEquals(RemoteRef obj);
    public int remoteHashCode();
    public String remoteToString();
}
```

java.rmi.server.RemoteServer

This class acts as an abstract base class for all remote object server implementations. The intent is for subclasses to implement the semantics of the remote object (e.g., multicast remote objects, replicated objects). In the current version of RMI, the only concrete subclass provided is `UnicastRemoteServer`, which implements a nonreplicated remote object.

The `getClientHost()` method returns the name of the host for the client being served in the current thread. The `getLog()` and `setLog()` methods access the call log for this `RemoteServer`.

```java
public abstract class RemoteServer extends RemoteObject {
// Protected Constructors
```

```
    protected RemoteServer();
    protected RemoteServer(RemoteRef ref);
// Class Methods
    public static String getClientHost()
                            throws ServerNotActiveException;
    public static java.io.PrintStream getLog();
    public static void setLog(java.io.OutputStream out);
}
```

java.rmi.server.RemoteStub

All client stub classes generated by the *rmic* compiler are derived from this abstract class. A client receives a RemoteStub when it successfully looks up a remote object through the RMI registry. A client stub serves as a client interface to the remote object it references, converting method calls on its interface into remote method invocations on the remote object implementation.

```
    public abstract class RemoteStub extends RemoteObject {
    // Protected Constructors
        protected RemoteStub();
        protected RemoteStub(RemoteRef ref);
    // Protected Class Methods
        protected static void setRef(RemoteStub stub, RemoteRef ref);
    }
```

java.rmi.server.RMIClassLoader

This class loads classes over the network using URLs. The class has two load-Class() methods: one for loading a class from a given (absolute) URL, and another for loading a class from a given (relative) URL, which starts at a particular codebase.

```
    public class RMIClassLoader {
    // Class Methods
        public static Object getSecurityContext(ClassLoader loader);
        public static Class loadClass(String name)
            throws MalformedURLException, ClassNotFoundException;
        public static Class loadClass(URL codebase, String name)
            throws MalformedURLException, ClassNotFoundException;
    }
```

java.rmi.server.RMIFailureHandler

The failure() method on the current RMIFailureHandler is called when the RMI communications system fails to create a Socket or ServerSocket. The current handler is set using the setFailureHandler() method on RMISocket-

Factory. The `failure()` method returns a boolean value that indicates whether the RMI system should retry the socket connection.

```
public interface RMIFailureHandler {
// Public Instance Methods
    public boolean failure(Exception ex);
}
```

java.rmi.server.RMISocketFactory

This abstract class provides an interface for the RMI internals to use to create sockets. The factory can create either `Sockets` for clients, or `ServerSockets` for servers. The factory maintains an `RMIFailureHandler` that it uses to deal with failures encountered while attempting to create sockets. If an error is encountered while creating a socket, the `failure()` method on the current `RMIFailureHandler` is called. If the return value is `true`, then the `RMISocket-Factory` attempts the socket creation again, otherwise the factory gives up and throws an `IOException`.

Client sockets are created using the `createSocket()` method, while server sockets are created using the `createServerSocket()` method. The current `RMISocketFactory` is accessed using the static `getSocketFactory()` and `setSocketFactory()` methods. The `RMIFailureHandler` for the current factory is accessed using the `getFailureHandler()` and `setFailureHandler()` methods.

```
public abstract class RMISocketFactory {
// Public Instance Methods
    public abstract ServerSocket createServerSocket(int port)
                             throws IOException;
    public abstract Socket createSocket(String host, int port)
                         throws IOException;
// Class Methods
    public static RMIFailureHandler getFailureHandler();
    public static RMISocketFactory getSocketFactory();
    public static void setFailureHandler(RMIFailureHandler fh);
    public static void setSocketFactory(RMISocketFactory fac)
                         throws IOException;
}
```

java.rmi.server.ServerCloneException

This exception is thrown if an attempt to clone a `RemoteServer` object fails while the clone is being exported. The nested exception is the `RemoteException` that was thrown during the cloning operation.

```
public class ServerCloneException extends CloneNotSupportedException {
// Public Constructors
    public ServerCloneException(String desc)
    public ServerCloneException(String desc, Exception nestedExc);
// Public Instance Variables
    public Exception detail;
// Public Instance Methods
    public String getMessage();
}
```

java.rmi.server.ServerNotActiveException

This exception is thrown if the getClientHost() method is called on a Remote-Server when the server isn't handling a remote method call.

```
public class ServerNotActiveException extends java.lang.Exception {
// Public Constructors
    public ServerNotActiveException();
    public ServerNotActiveException(String desc);
}
```

java.rmi.server.ServerRef

This is an interface to the server-side implementation of a remote object. The getClientHost() method returns the name of the host whose remote method call is currently being serviced by the object implementation. If the server object is not servicing a remote method call when getClientHost() is called, then a ServerNotActiveException is thrown. The exportObject() method is meant to either create or find a client stub for the given object implementation, using the data provided.

```
public interface ServerRef extends RemoteRef {
    public RemoteStub exportObject(Remote obj, Object data)
                       throws RemoteException;
    public String getClientHost() throws ServerNotActiveException;
}
```

java.rmi.server.Skeleton

A Skeleton object lives with a server-side object implementation, dispatching method calls to the remote object implementation. Server implementations generated by the *rmic* compiler use skeletons.

The dispatch() method invokes the method specified by the operation number opnum on the object implementation obj. It unmarshals the method arguments from the input stream obtained from the RemoteCall argument, passes them to the appropriate method on the Remote object, marshals the results (if any), and returns them to the caller using the output stream on the RemoteCall. The getOperations() method returns an array of Operation objects, which represent the methods available on the remote object.

```
public interface Skeleton {
    public void dispatch(Remote obj, RemoteCall theCall,
                          int opnum, long hash)
            throws Exception;
    public Operation[] getOperations();
}
```

java.rmi.server.SkeletonMismatchException

This RemoteException is thrown during a remote method call if a mismatch is detected on the server between the hash code of the client stub and the hash code of the server implementation. It is usually received by the client wrapped in a ServerException.

```
public class SkeletonMismatchException extends RemoteException {
// Public Constructors
    public SkeletonMismatchException(String s);
}
```

java.rmi.server.SkeletonNotFoundException

This RemoteException is thrown during the export of a remote object, if the corresponding skeleton class for the object either can't be found or can't be loaded.

```
public class SkeletonNotFoundException extends RemoteException {
// Public Constructors
    public SkeletonNotFoundException(String desc);
    public SkeletonNotFoundException(String desc, Exception nestedEx);
}
```

java.rmi.server.SocketSecurityException

This exception is a subclass of ExportException that is thrown if a socket security violation is encountered while attempting to export a remote object. An example would be an attempt to export an object on an illegal port.

```
public class SocketSecurityException extends ExportException {
    public SocketSecurityException(String s);
    public SocketSecurityException(String s, Exception ex);
}
```

java.rmi.server.UID

A UID is an identifier that is unique with respect to a particular host. UIDs are used internally by RMIs distributed garbage collector, and are generally not dealt with directly in application code.

```
public final class UID implements java.io.Serializable {
// Public Constructors
    public UID();
    public UID(short num);
// Class Methods
    public static UID read(DataInput in) throws java.io.IOException;
// Public Instance Methods
    public boolean equals(Object obj);
    public int hashCode();
    public String toString();
    public void write(DataOutput out) throws java.io.IOException;
}
```

java.rmi.server.UnicastRemoteObject

This class represents a nonreplicated remote object: one that lives as a singular implementation on a server with point-to-point connections to each client. through reference stubs. This remote server class does not implement persistence, so client references to the object are only valid during the lifetime of the object. This is the only concrete subclass of RemoteServer offered in the standard JDK 1.1 distribution.

```
public class UnicastRemoteObject extends RemoteServer {
// Protected Constructors
    protected UnicastRemoteObject() throws RemoteException;
// Class Methods
    public static RemoteStub exportObject(Remote obj)
                                throws RemoteException;
// Public Instance Methods
    public Object clone() throws CloneNotSupportedException;
}
```

java.rmi.server.Unreferenced

Appropriately enough, the last interface in this reference is the Unreferenced interface. If a server object implements this interface, then the unreferenced() method is called by the RMI runtime when the last client reference to a remote object is dropped. A remote object shouldn't be garbage collected until all of its remote and local references are gone. So the unreferenced() method isn't a trigger for an object to be finalized, but rather a chance for the remote object to respond appropriately when its client reference count goes to zero. The unreferenced object could, for example, start a timer countdown to move the object to persistent storage after a given idle time.

```
public interface Unreferenced {
// Public Instance Methods
    public void unreferenced();
}
```

Index

About the Author

Jim Farley is a software engineer, computer scientist, and IT manager. His recent activities have included heading up the engineering group at the Harvard Business School and bringing good things to life at GE's Research and Development center. He's dealt with computing (distributed and otherwise) in lots of different ways, from automated image inspection to temporal reasoning systems. Jim has Bachelor's and Master's degrees in computer systems engineering from Rensselaer Polytechnic Institute.

Colophon

Our look is the result of reader comments, our own experimentation, and feedback from distribution channels. Distinctive covers complement our distinctive approach to technical topics, breathing personality and life into potentially dry subjects.

The image of the Gabriel® Original Tinkertoy® Construction Set on the cover of *Java Distributed Computing* was photographed by Edie Freedman and manipulated using Adobe Photoshop 3.0 and Adobe Gallery Effects filters. The cover layout was produced by Hanna Dyer using Quark XPress 3.3 and the Bodoni Black font from URW Software.

The inside layout was designed by Nancy Priest. Text was prepared by Mike Sierra in FrameMaker 5.0. The heading font is Bodoni BT; the text font is New Baskerville. The illustrations that appear in the book were created in Macromedia Freehand 7.0 by Robert Romano.

Whenever possible, our books use RepKover™, a durable and flexible lay-flat binding. If the page count exceeds Repkover's limit, perfect binding is used.

 # More Titles from O'Reilly

Java Programming

Java in a Nutshell, DELUXE EDITION

By David Flanagan, et al.
1st Edition June 1997
628 pages, includes CD-ROM and book
ISBN 1-56592-304-9

Java in a Nutshell, Deluxe Edition, is a Java programmer's dream come true in one small package. The heart of this Deluxe Edition is the Java Reference Library on CD-ROM, which brings together five volumes for Java developers and programmers, linking related info across books. It includes: *Exploring Java, 2nd Edition, Java Language Reference, 2nd Edition, Java Fundamental Classes Reference, Java AWT Reference*, and *Java in a Nutshell, 2nd Edition*, included both on the CD-ROM and in a companion desktop edition. *Java in a Nutshell, Deluxe Edition*, is an indispensable resource for anyone doing serious programming with Java 1.1.

The Java Reference Library alone is also available by subscription on the World Wide Web. Please see **http://www.oreilly.com/catalog/javarlw/** for details. The electronic text on the Web and on the CD is fully searchable and includes a complete index to all five volumes as well as the sample code found in the print volumes. A web browser that supports HTML 3.2, Java, and Javascript, such as Netscape 3.0 or Internet Explorer 3.0, is required. (The CD-ROM is readable on all UNIX and Windows platforms. However, current implementations of the Java Virtual Machine for the Mac do not support the Java search applet in the CD-ROM.)

Exploring Java, 2nd Edition, introduces the basics of Java. *Java Language Reference, 2nd Edition*, is a complete reference that describes all aspects of Java 1.1. Java Fundamental Classes Reference provides complete reference documentation on the core Java 1.1 classes that comprise the *java.lang, java.io, java.net, java.util, java.text, java.math, java.lang.reflect,* and *java.util.zip* packages. *Java AWT Reference* provides complete reference documentation on the Abstract Window Toolkit (AWT). And, *Java in a Nutshell, 2nd Edition*, covers all the classes in the Java 1.1 core API with the exception of the still-evolving Enterprise APIs.

Exploring Java, Second Edition

By Pat Niemeyer & Josh Peck
2nd Edition September 1997
614 pages, ISBN 1-56592-271-9

Whether you're just migrating to Java or working steadily in the forefront of Java development, this book, fully revised for Java 1.1, gives a clear, systematic overview of the language. It covers the essentials of hot topics like Beans and RMI, as well as writing applets and other applications, such as networking programs, content and protocol handlers, and security managers.

Java Language Reference, Second Edition

By Mark Grand
2nd Edition July 1997
492 pages, ISBN 1-56592-326-X

This book helps you understand the subtle nuances of Java—from the definition of data types to the syntax of expressions and control structures—so you can ensure your programs run exactly as expected. The second edition covers the new language features that have been added in Java 1.1, such as inner classes, class literals, and instance initializers.

Java Fundamental Classes Reference

By Mark Grand & Jonathan Knudsen
1st Edition May 1997
1114 pages, ISBN 1-56592-241-7

The *Java Fundamental Classes Reference* provides complete reference documentation on the core Java 1.1 classes that comprise the *java.lang, java.io, java.net, java.util, java.text, java.math, java.lang.reflect,* and *java.util.zip* packages. Part of O'Reilly's Java documentation series, this edition describes Version 1.1 of the Java Development Kit. It includes easy-to-use reference material and provides lots of sample code to help you learn by example.

O'REILLY™

TO ORDER: **800-998-9938** • **order@oreilly.com** • **http://www.oreilly.com/**

OUR PRODUCTS ARE AVAILABLE AT A BOOKSTORE OR SOFTWARE STORE NEAR YOU.

FOR INFORMATION: **800-998-9938** • **707-829-0515** • **info@oreilly.com**

Java Programming *(continued)*

Java Distributed Computing

By Jim Farley
1st Edition January 1998 (est.)
392 pages (est.)
ISBN 1-56592-206-9

Java Distributed Computing offers a general introduction to distributed computing, meaning programs that run on two or more systems. It focuses primarily on how to structure and write distributed applications and, therefore, discusses issues like designing protocols, security, working with databases, and dealing with low bandwidth situations.

Java Examples in a Nutshell

By David Flanagan
1st Edition September 1997
414 pages, ISBN 1-56592-371-5

Java Examples in a Nutshell is chock full of practical real-world Java programming examples that you can learn from and modify for your own use. From the author of the bestselling *Java in a Nutshell*, this companion book picks up where *Java in a Nutshell* leaves off, providing a suite of example programs for novice Java programmers and experts alike. It doesn't hold your hand or supply detailed explanations of Java syntax or method calls; it simply delivers well-commented, working examples that help you explore the wide range of what is possible with Java 1.1.

Java Examples in a Nutshell contains all of the example programs from the first edition of *Java in a Nutshell*, completely updated for Java 1.1, and expands on the examples from the second edition that demonstrate the new features in Java 1.1. It also provides never-before-published programming examples for remote method invocation, database connectivity, and security—important elements of the Java Enterprise APIs. Finally, the book offers a glimpse of the features of "Swing", the set of new components that are part of the forthcoming Java Foundation Classes (JFC).

Netscape IFC in a Nutshell

By Dean Petrich with David Flanagan
1st Edition August 1997
370 pages, ISBN 1-56592-343-X

This desktop quick reference and programmer's guide is all the documentation programmers need to start creating highly customizable graphical user interfaces with the Internet Foundation Classes (IFC), Version 1.1. The IFC is a Java class library freely available from Netscape. It is also bundled with Communicator, making it the preferred development environment for the Navigator 4.0 web browser. Master the IFC now for a head start on the forthcoming Java Foundation Classes (JFC).

Developing Java Beans

By Robert Englander
1st Edition June 1997
316 pages, ISBN 1-56592-289-1

Developing Java Beans is a complete introduction to Java's component architecture. It describes how to write Beans, which are software components that can be used in visual programming environments. This book discusses event adapters, serialization, introspection, property editors, and customizers, and shows how to use Beans within ActiveX controls.

Java Virtual Machine

By Jon Meyer & Troy Downing
1st Edition March 1997
452 pages, includes diskette
ISBN 1-56592-194-1

This book is a comprehensive programming guide for the Java Virtual Machine (JVM). It gives readers a strong overview and reference of the JVM so that they may create their own implementations of the JVM or write their own compilers that create Java object code. A Java assembler is provided with the book, so the examples can all be compiled and executed.

O'REILLY™

TO ORDER: **800-998-9938** • *order@oreilly.com* • *http://www.oreilly.com/*

OUR PRODUCTS ARE AVAILABLE AT A BOOKSTORE OR SOFTWARE STORE NEAR YOU.

FOR INFORMATION: **800-998-9938** • **707-829-0515** • *info@oreilly.com*

Java Programming *(continued)*

Java Network Programming

By Elliotte Rusty Harold
1st Edition February 1997
442 pages, ISBN 1-56592-227-1

The network is the soul of Java. Most of what is new and exciting about Java centers around the potential for new kinds of dynamic, networked applications. *Java Network Programming* teaches you to work with Sockets, write network clients and servers, and gives you an advanced look at the new areas like multicasting, using the server API, and RMI. Covers Java 1.1.

Java in a Nutshell, Second Edition

By David Flanagan
2nd Edition May 1997
628 pages, ISBN 1-56592-262-X

The bestselling Java book just got better. Java programmers migrating to 1.1 find this second edition of *Java in a Nutshell* contains everything they need to get up to speed. Newcomers find it still has all of the features that have made it the Java book most often recommended on the Internet. This complete quick reference covers all the classes in the Java 1.1 API, with the exception of the still-evolving Enterprise APIs, making it the only quick reference that a Java programmer needs.

The second edition of *Java in a Nutshell* includes all of the material from the first edition, as well as the following updated information for Java 1.1:

- A detailed overview of all of the new features in Java 1.1, both on a package-by-package basis and in terms of overall functionality
- A comprehensive tutorial on "inner classes" that explains how to use all of the new types of inner classes
- Practical, real-world example programs that demonstrate the new features in Java 1.1, including object serialization, the new AWT event handling model, internationalization, and a sample Java Bean
- A complete quick reference for all of the classes, methods, and variables in the core Java 1.1 API, with indicators that make it easy to find the new 1.1 material

Database Programming with JDBC and Java

By George Reese
1st Edition June 1997
240 pages, ISBN 1-56592-270-0

Database Programming with JDBC and Java describes the standard Java interfaces that make portable,object-oriented access to relational databases possible and offers a robust model for writing applications that are easy to maintain. It introduces the JDBC and RMI packages and includes a set of patterns that separate the functions of the Java application and facilitate the growth and maintenance of your application.

Java Threads

By Scott Oaks and Henry Wong
1st Edition January 1997
268 pages, ISBN 1-56592-216-6

With this book, you'll learn how to take full advantage of Java's thread facilities: where to use threads to increase efficiency, how to use them effectively, and how to avoid common mistakes like deadlock and race conditions. Covers Java 1.1.

Java AWT Reference

By John Zukowski
1st Edition April 1997
1074 pages, ISBN 1-56592-240-9

The *Java AWT Reference* provides complete reference documentation on the Abstract Window Toolkit (AWT), a large collection of classes for building graphical user interfaces in Java. Part of O'Reilly's Java documentation series, this edition describes both Version 1.0.2 and Version 1.1 of the Java Development Kit, includes easy-to-use reference material on every AWT class, and provides lots of sample code.

Developing Web Content

WebMaster in a Nutshell, Deluxe Edition

By O'Reilly & Associates, Inc.
1st Edition September 1997
374 pages, includes CD-ROM & book
ISBN 1-56592-305-7

The Deluxe Edition of *WebMaster in a Nutshell* is a complete library for web programmers. The main resource is the Web Developer's Library, a CD-ROM, containing the electronic text of five popular O'Reilly titles: *HTML: The Definitive Guide, 2nd Edition*; *JavaScript: The Definitive Guide, 2nd Edition*; *CGI Programming on the World Wide Web*; *Programming Perl, 2nd Edition*—the classic "camel book," written by Larry Wall (the inventor of Perl) with Tom Christiansen and Randal Schwartz; and *WebMaster in a Nutshell*. The Deluxe Edition also includes a printed copy of *WebMaster in a Nutshell*.

WebMaster in a Nutshell, Deluxe Edition, makes it easy to find the information you need with all of the convenience you'd expect from the Web. You'll have access to information webmasters and programmers use most for development—complete with global searching and a master index to all five volumes—all on a single CD-ROM. It's incredibly portable. Just slip it into your laptop case as you commute or take off on your next trip andyou'll find everything at your fingertips with no books to carry.

System requirements: A web browser that supports HTML 3.2, Java, and Javascript, such as Netscape 3.0 or Internet Explorer 3.0. (The CD-ROM is readable on all UNIX and Windows platforms. However, current implementations of the Java Virtual Machine for the Mac do not support the Java search applet in the CD-ROM. A Web version of the Library is also available. See www.oreilly.com for more information.)

WebMaster in a Nutshell

By Stephen Spainhour &
Valerie Quercia
1st Edition October 1996
374 pages, ISBN 1-56592-229-8

Web content providers and administrators have many sources for information, both in print and online. *WebMaster in a Nutshell* puts it all together in one slim volume for easy desktop access. This quick reference covers HTML, CGI, JavaScript, Perl, HTTP, and server configuration.

HTML: The Definitive Guide, 2nd Edition

By Chuck Musciano & Bill Kennedy
2nd Edition May 1997
552 pages, ISBN 1-56592-235-2

This complete guide is chock full of examples, sample code, and practical, hands-on advice to help you create truly effective web pages and master advanced features. Learn how to insert images and other multimedia elements, create useful links and searchable documents, use Netscape extensions, design great forms, and lots more. The second edition covers the most up-to-date version of the HTML standard (HTML version 3.2), Netscape 4.0 and Internet Explorer 3.0, plus all the common extensions.

JavaScript: The Definitive Guide, 2nd Edition

By David Flanagan
2nd Edition January 1997
664 pages, ISBN 1-56592-234-4

This second edition of the definitive reference guide to JavaScript, the HTML extension that gives web pages programming-language capabilities, covers JavaScript as it is used in Netscape 3.0 and 2.0 and in Microsoft Internet Explorer 3.0. Learn how JavaScript really works (and when it doesn't). Use JavaScript to control web browser behavior, add dynamically created text to web pages, interact with users through HTML forms, and even control and interact with Java applets and Navigator plugins. By the author of the bestselling *Java in a Nutshell*.

CGI Programming on the World Wide Web

By Shishir Gundavaram
1st Edition March 1996
450 pages, ISBN 1-56592-168-2

This book offers a comprehensive explanation of CGI and related techniques for people who hold on to the dream of providing their own information servers on the Web. It starts at the beginning, explaining the value of CGI and how it works, then moves swiftly into the subtle details of programming.

O'REILLY™

TO ORDER: **800-998-9938** • *order@oreilly.com* • *http://www.oreilly.com/*
OUR PRODUCTS ARE AVAILABLE AT A BOOKSTORE OR SOFTWARE STORE NEAR YOU.
FOR INFORMATION: **800-998-9938** • **707-829-0515** • *info@oreilly.com*

Developing Web Content *(continued)*

Information Architecture for the World Wide Web

By Louis Rosenfeld & Peter Morville
1st Edition January 1998 (est.)
200 pages (est.), ISBN 1-56592-282-4

Learn how to merge aesthetics and mechanics to design web sites that "work." This book shows how to apply principles of architecture and library science to design cohesive web sites and intranets that are easy to use, manage, and expand. Covers building complex sites, hierarchy design and organization, and techniques to make your site easier to search. For webmasters, designers, and administrators.

Learning VBScript

By Paul Lomax
1st Edition July 1997
616 pages, includes CD-ROM
ISBN 1-56592-247-6

This definitive guide shows web developers how to take full advantage of client-side scripting with the VBScript language. In addition to basic language features, it covers the Internet Explorer object model and discusses techniques for client-side scripting, like adding ActiveX controls to a web page or validating data before sending it to the server. Includes CD-ROM with over 170 code samples.

Web Client Programming with Perl

By Clinton Wong
1st Edition March 1997
228 pages, ISBN 1-56592-214-X

Web Client Programming with Perl shows you how to extend scripting skills to the Web. This book teaches you the basics of how browsers communicate with servers and how to write your own customized web clients to automate common tasks. It is intended for those who are motivated to develop software that offers a more flexible and dynamic response than a standard web browser.

Building Your Own WebSite

By Susan B. Peck & Stephen Arrants
1st Edition July 1996
514 pages, ISBN 1-56592-232-8

This is a hands-on reference for Windows® 95 and Windows NT™ users who want to host a site on the Web or on a corporate intranet. This step-by-step guide will have you creating live web pages in minutes. You'll also learn how to connect your web to information in other Windows applications, such as word processing documents and databases. The book is packed with examples and tutorials on every aspect of web management, and it includes the highly acclaimed WebSite™ 1.1 server software on CD-ROM.

Designing for the Web: Getting Started in a New Medium

By Jennifer Niederst
with Edie Freedman
1st Edition April 1996
180 pages, ISBN 1-56592-165-8

Designing for the Web gives you the basics you need to hit the ground running. Although geared toward designers, it covers information and techniques useful to anyone who wants to put graphics online. It explains how to work with HTML documents from a designer's point of view, outlines special problems with presenting information online, and walks through incorporating images into web pages, with emphasis on resolution and improving efficiency.

O'REILLY™

TO ORDER: **800-998-9938** • *order@oreilly.com* • *http://www.oreilly.com/*

OUR PRODUCTS ARE AVAILABLE AT A BOOKSTORE OR SOFTWARE STORE NEAR YOU.

FOR INFORMATION: **800-998-9938** • **707-829-0515** • *info@oreilly.com*

How to stay in touch with O'Reilly

1. Visit Our Award-Winning Web Site

http://www.oreilly.com/

★ "Top 100 Sites on the Web" —*PC Magazine*
★ "Top 5% Web sites" —*Point Communications*
★ "3-Star site" —*The McKinley Group*

Our web site contains a library of comprehensiveproduct information (including book excerpts and tables of contents), downloadable software, background articles, interviews with technology leaders, links to relevant sites, book cover art, and more. File us in your Bookmarks or Hotlist!

2. Join Our Email Mailing Lists

New Product Releases

To receive automatic email with brief descriptions of all new O'Reilly products as they are released, send email to:
listproc@online.oreilly.com
Put the following information in the first line of your message (*not* in the Subject field):
subscribe oreilly-news

O'Reilly Events

If you'd also like us to send information about trade show events, special promotions, and other O'Reilly events, send email to:
listproc@online.oreilly.com
Put the following information in the first line of your message (*not* in the Subject field):
subscribe oreilly-events

3. Get Examples from Our Books via FTP

There are two ways to access an archive of example files from our books:

Regular FTP

* ftp to:
  ftp.oreilly.com
  (login: anonymous
  password: your email address)
* Point your web browser to:
  ftp://ftp.oreilly.com/

FTPMAIL

* Send an email message to:
  ftpmail@online.oreilly.com
  (Write "help" in the message body)

4. Contact Us via Email

order@oreilly.com
To place a book or software order online. Good for North American and international customers.

subscriptions@oreilly.com
To place an order for any of our newsletters or periodicals.

books@oreilly.com
General questions about any of our books.

software@oreilly.com
For general questions and product information about our software. Check out O'Reilly Software Online at **http://software.oreilly.com/** for software and technical support information. Registered O'Reilly software users send your questions to: **website-support@oreilly.com**

cs@oreilly.com
For answers to problems regarding your order or our products.

booktech@oreilly.com
For book content technical questions or corrections.

proposals@oreilly.com
To submit new book or software proposals to our editors and product managers.

international@oreilly.com
For information about our international distributors or translation queries. For a list of our distributors outside of North America check out:
http://www.oreilly.com/www/order/country.html

O'Reilly & Associates, Inc.
101 Morris Street, Sebastopol, CA 95472 USA
TEL   707-829-0515 or 800-998-9938
          (6am to 5pm PST)
FAX   707-829-0104

Titles from O'Reilly

Please note that upcoming titles are displayed in italic.

WEB PROGRAMMING
Apache: The Definitive Guide
Building Your Own Web Conferences
Building Your Own Website
CGI Programming for the World Wide Web
Designing for the Web
HTML: The Definitive Guide, 2nd Ed.
JavaScript: The Definitive Guide, 2nd Ed.
Learning Perl
Programming Perl, 2nd Ed.
Mastering Regular Expressions
WebMaster in a Nutshell
Web Security & Commerce
Web Client Programming with Perl
World Wide Web Journal

USING THE INTERNET
Smileys
The Future Does Not Compute
The Whole Internet User's Guide & Catalog
The Whole Internet for Win 95
Using Email Effectively
Bandits on the Information Superhighway

JAVA SERIES
Exploring Java
Java AWT Reference
Java Fundamental Classes Reference
Java in a Nutshell
Java Language Reference, 2nd Edition
Java Network Programming
Java Threads
Java Virtual Machine

SOFTWARE
WebSite™ 1.1
WebSite Professional™
Building Your Own Web Conferences
WebBoard™
PolyForm™
Statisphere™

SONGLINE GUIDES
NetActivism   NetResearch
Net Law   NetSuccess
NetLearning   NetTravel
Net Lessons

SYSTEM ADMINISTRATION
Building Internet Firewalls
Computer Crime: A Crimefighter's Handbook
Computer Security Basics
DNS and BIND, 2nd Ed.
Essential System Administration, 2nd Ed.
Getting Connected: The Internet at 56K and Up
Linux Network Administrator's Guide
Managing Internet Information Services
Managing NFS and NIS
Networking Personal Computers with TCP/IP
Practical UNIX & Internet Security, 2nd Ed.
PGP: Pretty Good Privacy
sendmail, 2nd Ed.
sendmail Desktop Reference
System Performance Tuning
TCP/IP Network Administration
termcap & terminfo
Using & Managing UUCP
Volume 8: X Window System Administrator's Guide
Web Security & Commerce

UNIX
Exploring Expect
Learning VBScript
Learning GNU Emacs, 2nd Ed.
Learning the bash Shell
Learning the Korn Shell
Learning the UNIX Operating System
Learning the vi Editor
Linux in a Nutshell
Making TeX Work
Linux Multimedia Guide
Running Linux, 2nd Ed.
SCO UNIX in a Nutshell
sed & awk, 2nd Edition
Tcl/Tk Tools
UNIX in a Nutshell: System V Edition
UNIX Power Tools
Using csh & tsch
When You Can't Find Your UNIX System Administrator
Writing GNU Emacs Extensions

WEB REVIEW STUDIO SERIES
Gif Animation Studio
Shockwave Studio

WINDOWS
Dictionary of PC Hardware and Data Communications Terms
Inside the Windows 95 Registry
Inside the Windows 95 File System
Windows Annoyances
Windows NT File System Internals
Windows NT in a Nutshell

PROGRAMMING
Advanced Oracle PL/SQL Programming
Applying RCS and SCCS
C++: The Core Language
Checking C Programs with lint
DCE Security Programming
Distributing Applications Across DCE & Windows NT
Encyclopedia of Graphics File Formats, 2nd Ed.
Guide to Writing DCE Applications
lex & yacc
Managing Projects with make
Mastering Oracle Power Objects
Oracle Design: The Definitive Guide
Oracle Performance Tuning, 2nd Ed.
Oracle PL/SQL Programming
Porting UNIX Software
POSIX Programmer's Guide
POSIX.4: Programming for the Real World
Power Programming with RPC
Practical C Programming
Practical C++ Programming
Programming Python
Programming with curses
Programming with GNU Software
Pthreads Programming
Software Portability with imake, 2nd Ed.
Understanding DCE
Understanding Japanese Information Processing
UNIX Systems Programming for SVR4

BERKELEY 4.4 SOFTWARE DISTRIBUTION
4.4BSD System Manager's Manual
4.4BSD User's Reference Manual
4.4BSD User's Supplementary Documents
4.4BSD Programmer's Reference Manual
4.4BSD Programmer's Supplementary Documents
X Programming
Vol. 0: X Protocol Reference Manual
Vol. 1: Xlib Programming Manual
Vol. 2: Xlib Reference Manual
Vol. 3M: X Window System User's Guide, Motif Edition
Vol. 4M: X Toolkit Intrinsics Programming Manual, Motif Edition
Vol. 5: X Toolkit Intrinsics Reference Manual
Vol. 6A: Motif Programming Manual
Vol. 6B: Motif Reference Manual
Vol. 6C: Motif Tools
Vol. 8 : X Window System Administrator's Guide
Programmer's Supplement for Release 6
X User Tools
The X Window System in a Nutshell

CAREER & BUSINESS
Building a Successful Software Business
The Computer User's Survival Guide
Love Your Job!
Electronic Publishing on CD-ROM

TRAVEL
Travelers' Tales: Brazil
Travelers' Tales: Food
Travelers' Tales: France
Travelers' Tales: Gutsy Women
Travelers' Tales: India
Travelers' Tales: Mexico
Travelers' Tales: Paris
Travelers' Tales: San Francisco
Travelers' Tales: Spain
Travelers' Tales: Thailand
Travelers' Tales: A Woman's World

International Distributors

UK, EUROPE, MIDDLE EAST AND NORTHERN AFRICA (EXCEPT FRANCE, GERMANY, SWITZERLAND, & AUSTRIA)

INQUIRIES

International Thomson Publishing Europe
Berkshire House
168-173 High Holborn
London WC1V 7AA, UK
Telephone: 44-171-497-1422
Fax: 44-171-497-1426
Email: itpint@itps.co.uk

ORDERS

International Thomson Publishing Services, Ltd.
Cheriton House, North Way
Andover, Hampshire SP10 5BE,
United Kingdom
Telephone: 44-264-342-832 (UK)
Telephone: 44-264-342-806 (outside UK)
Fax: 44-264-364418 (UK)
Fax: 44-264-342761 (outside UK)
UK & Eire orders: itpuk@itps.co.uk
International orders: itpint@itps.co.uk

FRANCE

Editions Eyrolles
61 bd Saint-Germain
75240 Paris Cedex 05
France
Fax: 33-01-44-41-11-44

FRENCH LANGUAGE BOOKS

All countries except Canada
Telephone: 33-01-44-41-46-16
Email: geodif@eyrolles.com
english language books
Telephone: 33-01-44-41-11-87
Email: distribution@eyrolles.com

GERMANY, SWITZERLAND, AND AUSTRIA

INQUIRIES

O'Reilly Verlag
Balthasarstr. 81
D-50670 Köln
Germany
Telephone: 49-221-97-31-60-0
Fax: 49-221-97-31-60-8
Email: anfragen@oreilly.de

ORDERS

International Thomson Publishing
Königswinterer Straße 418
53227 Bonn, Germany
Telephone: 49-228-97024 0
Fax: 49-228-441342
Email: order@oreilly.de

JAPAN

O'Reilly Japan, Inc.
Kiyoshige Building 2F
12-Banchi, Sanei-cho
Shinjuku-ku
Tokyo 160 Japan
Tel: 81-3-3356-5227
Fax: 81-3-3356-5261
Email: kenji@oreilly.com

INDIA

Computer Bookshop (India) PVT. LTD.
190 Dr. D.N. Road, Fort
Bombay 400 001 India
Tel: 91-22-207-0989
Fax: 91-22-262-3551
Email: cbsbom@giasbm01.vsnl.net.in

HONG KONG

City Discount Subscription Service Ltd.
Unit D, 3rd Floor, Yan's Tower
27 Wong Chuk Hang Road
Aberdeen, Hong Kong
Telephone: 852-2580-3539
Fax: 852-2580-6463
Email: citydis@ppn.com.hk

KOREA

Hanbit Publishing, Inc.
Sonyoung Bldg. 202
Yeksam-dong 736-36
Kangnam-ku
Seoul, Korea
Telephone: 822-554-9610
Fax: 822-556-0363
Email: hant93@chollian.dacom.co.kr

TAIWAN

ImageArt Publishing, Inc.
4/fl. No. 65 Shinyi Road Sec. 4
Taipei, Taiwan, R.O.C.
Telephone: 886-2708-5770
Fax: 886-2705-6690
Email: marie@ms1.hinet.net

SINGAPORE, MALAYSIA, THAILAND

Longman Singapore
25 First Lok Yan Road
Singapore 2262
Telephone: 65-268-2666
Fax: 65-268-7023
Email: db@longman.com.sg

PHILIPPINES

Mutual Books, Inc.
429-D Shaw Boulevard
Mandaluyong City, Metro
Manila, Philippines
Telephone: 632-725-7538
Fax: 632-721-3056
Email: mbikikog@mnl.sequel.net

CHINA

Ron's DataCom Co., Ltd.
79 Dongwu Avenue
Dongxihu District
Wuhan 430040
China
Telephone: 86-27-3892568
Fax: 86-27-3222108
Email: hongfeng@public.wh.hb.cn

AUSTRALIA

WoodsLane Pty. Ltd.
7/5 Vuko Place, Warriewood NSW 2102
P.O. Box 935,
Mona Vale NSW 2103
Australia
Telephone: 61-2-9970-5111
Fax: 61-2-9970-5002
Email: info@woodslane.com.au

ALL OTHER ASIA COUNTRIES

O'Reilly & Associates, Inc.
101 Morris Street
Sebastopol, CA 95472 USA
Telephone: 707-829-0515
Fax: 707-829-0104
Email: order@oreilly.com

THE AMERICAS

McGraw-Hill Interamericana Editores, S.A. de C.V.
Cedro No. 512
Col. Atlampa 06450
Mexico, D.F.
Telephone: 52-5-541-3155
Fax: 52-5-541-4913
Email: mcgraw-hill@infosel.net.mx

SOUTHERN AFRICA

International Thomson Publishing
Southern Africa
Building 18, Constantia Park
138 Sixteenth Road
P.O. Box 2459
Halfway House, 1685 South Africa
Telephone: 27-11-805-4819
Fax: 27-11-805-3648